Los Ang
& San Diego

Brian Eads

Mitchell Beazley

THE AMERICAN EXPRESS ® TRAVEL GUIDES

Published by Mitchell Beazley International Ltd, Michelin House, 81 Fulham Road, London SW3 6RB

Edited, designed and produced by Castle House Press, Llantrisant, Mid Glamorgan CF7 8EU, Wales

First published 1990 as *The American Express Pocket Guide to Los Angeles & San Francisco*. This adapted and expanded edition published 1993.

A cataloguing-in-publication record for this book is available from the British Library.
ISBN 1 85732 919 8

The editors thank Molly Wachs and Carol Martinez of the Greater Los Angeles Visitor and Convention Bureau, Elizabeth Nesbitt of the J. Paul Getty Museum, and Anne Ryland for their kind assistance. Warm thanks are due to Neil Hanson of Lovell Johns, David Haslam, Sharon Charity, Sally Darlington, Melanie Gould, Anna Holmes and Andrea Thomas for their assistance during the preparation of this edition.

Some text in this edition was adapted from *The American Express Pocket Guide to California* by Bob Thompson (1983, second edition 1987).

FOR THE SERIES:
Series Editor:
   David Townsend Jones
Map Editor: David Haslam
Indexer: Hilary Bird
Gazetteer: Anne Evans
Cover design:
   Roger Walton Studio

FOR THIS EDITION:
Edited on desktop by:
   David Townsend Jones
Art editor: Eileen Townsend Jones
Illustrators: Karen Cochrane, Sylvia Hughes-Williams,
Cover photo: Michael J Howell/ Colorific

FOR MITCHELL BEAZLEY:
Art Director: Tim Foster
Managing Editor: Alison Starling
Production: Matthew Batchelor

PRODUCTION CREDITS:
Maps by Lovell Johns, Oxford, England
Typeset in Garamond and News Gothic
Desktop layout in Ventura Publisher
Linotronic output by Tradespools Limited, Frome, England
Printed and bound in Great Britain by HarperCollins Manufacturing, Glasgow

Contents

Los Angeles

San Diego

Maps

How to use this book

Few guidelines are needed to understand how this book works:

- For the general organization of the book, see CONTENTS on the pages preceding this one.
- Wherever appropriate, chapters and sections are arranged alphabetically, with headings appearing in **CAPITALS.**
- Often these headings are followed by location and practical information printed in *italics.*
- As you turn the pages, you will find subject headers, similar to those used in telephone directories, printed in CAPITALS in the top corner of each page.
- If you still cannot find what you need, check in the comprehensive and exhaustively cross-referenced INDEX at the back of the book.
- Following the index, a LIST OF STREET NAMES provides map references for all roads and streets mentioned in the book that are located within the areas covered by the main city maps.

CROSS-REFERENCES

These are printed in SMALL CAPITALS, referring you to other sections or alphabetical entries in the book. Care has been taken to ensure that such cross-references are self-explanatory. Often, page references are also given, although their excessive use would be intrusive and ugly.

FLOORS

We use the American convention in this book: "first floor" means the floor at ground level.

AUTHOR'S ACKNOWLEDGMENTS

The author wishes to thank Judy, his wife and fellow traveler, and all those in Southern California and Nevada who shared their knowledge and insights, especially Gary C. Sherwin and Connie Eldridge of the Los Angeles Convention & Visitors Bureau, Laurie Allison of the San Diego Convention & Visitors Bureau, Don Payne of the Las Vegas News Bureau, Henry Schielein of the Ritz Carlton Laguna Niguel, and David and Agnes Leah of Orange County.

He also wishes to thank American Airlines for their generosity in assisting with his travel arrangements. Details of American Airlines' telephone numbers in Los Angeles and Great Britain are given on pages 55 and 56.

KEY TO SYMBOLS

☎	Telephone	⬍	Elevator
Fx	Facsimile (fax)	⟐	Facilities for disabled
★	Recommended sight		people
☆	Worth a detour	▯	TV in each room
i	Tourist information	▱	Telephone in each room
⬅	Parking	🐾	Dogs not allowed
⛫	Building of architectural	≋	Swimming pool
	interest	✿	Garden
▣	Free entrance	≪	Good view
▨	Entrance fee payable	⚓	Good beach nearby
▪	Entrance expensive	♪	Tennis
⍓	Photography forbidden	⚕	Gym/fitness facilities
⌿	Guided tour	☲	Bar
▬	Cafeteria	▤	Mini-bar
✸	Special interest for children	☜	Sauna
⚘	Hotel	⚌	Conference facilities
♛	Luxury hotel	⇒	Restaurant
❁	Good value (in its class)	⚬	Simple restaurant
▭	Cheap	⌂	Luxury restaurant
▱	Inexpensive	▭	A la carte available
▰	Moderately priced	▬	Set (fixed-price) menu
▰	Expensive		available
▰	Very expensive	≡	Good wines
AE	American Express	⚘	Open-air dining
◉	Diners Club	●	Disco dancing
⬤	MasterCard	☾	Nightclub
VISA	Visa	♫	Live music
⬛	Secure garage	⚐	Dancing
⌂	Quiet hotel	☒	Adults only

HOTEL AND RESTAURANT PRICE CATEGORIES

These are denoted by the symbols ▭ (cheap), ▱ (inexpensive), ▰ (moderately priced), ▰ (expensive) and ▰ (very expensive). They correspond approximately to the following actual local prices, which give a guideline **at the time of printing**. Naturally, prices tend to rise, but, with a few exceptions, hotels and restaurants will remain in the same price category.

Price categories	Corresponding to approximate prices for **hotels** *double room with bathroom + breakfast; singles are not much cheaper*	for **restaurants** *meal for one with service, tax and house wine*
▰ very expensive	over $210	over $65
▰ expensive	$160-210	$45-65
▰ moderately priced	$100-160	$30-45
▱ inexpensive	$50-100	under $30

About the author

Brian Eads was born in Lincoln, England and educated at Cambridge University. For many years he was a foreign correspondent, writing variously for *The Observer, The Economist, The Washington Post* and *Newsweek,* from Paris, Bangkok, Hong Kong and Los Angeles. He currently works for Granada Television, making current affairs documentaries. They have included *The Last Blockade,* a film about the struggle of indigenous peoples in the Borneo rainforest, and *Danger on the Edge of Town,* a search for two American photo-journalists missing in action in Cambodia for 20 years. Home is now in the hills of Derbyshire in the northwest of England, but he spends part of each year in California. In this series he has also written *American Express San Francisco and the Wine Regions* (1992) and this book's immediate predecessor, *The American Express Pocket Guide to Los Angeles and San Francisco* (1990).

Bob Thompson, who contributed the WINES AND WINERIES chapter, has written numerous books, including *The Californian Wine Book* with Hugh Johnson, *The Pocket Guide to Californian Wines* and this book's ancestor, *The American Express Pocket Guide to California.*

A message from the series editor

In designing *American Express Los Angeles and San Diego* we aimed to make this brand-new edition simple and instinctive to use, like all its sister volumes in our new, larger paperback format.

The hallmarks of the relaunched series are clear, classic typography, confidence in fine travel writing for its own sake, and faith in our readers' innate intelligence to find their way around the books without heavy-handed signposting by editors.

Readers with anything less than 20:20 vision will doubtless also enjoy the larger, clearer type, and can now dispense with the mythical magnifying glasses we never issued free with the old pocket guide series.

Months of concentrated work by the author and our editors have been dedicated to ensuring that this edition is as accurate and up to date as possible as it goes to press. But time and change are forever the enemies, and in between editions we very much appreciate it when you, our readers, keep us informed of changes that you discover.

As ever, I am indebted to all the many readers who wrote during the preparation of this edition. Please remember that your feedback is extremely important to our efforts to tailor the series to the very distinctive tastes and requirements of our sophisticated international readership.

Send your comments to me at Mitchell Beazley International Ltd, Michelin House, 81 Fulham Road, London SW3 6RB; or, in the US, c/o American Express Travel Guides, Prentice Hall Travel, 15 Columbus Circle, New York, NY 10023.

David Townsend Jones

Los Angeles
& San Diego

California dreamin'

"My first impulse was to get out in the street at high noon and shout four-letter words." So said novelist Raymond Chandler on arriving in San Diego's fashionable seaside suburb of La Jolla in 1949. He lived there for ten years, while the hero of his imagination, private detective and knight errant Philip Marlowe, plumbed the depths of corruption beneath the gloss of Los Angeles to the north.

It is tempting to make something of this: LA as vivid, inspirational, extreme, rich, but ultimately rotten; San Diego as a congenial place, if maybe a tad dull. That was over 40 years ago. Does it still hold good?

Well, yes and no. After all, the two cities, California's largest, have much in common. For example, their history. Europeans, led by Portuguese-born sailor Juan Rodriguez Cabrillo acting on behalf of the Spanish Viceroy of recently conquered Mexico, made their first landfall in California at San Diego Bay on December 28, 1542. Later that same year Cabrillo sighted San Pedro and Santa Monica. Inland he saw wood smoke from the fires of Native Americans living on the site of what is now Downtown LA. The first settlements in each city were established during the progress of the Sacred Expedition that created 21 Catholic missions along the length of California in the late 18th century. San Diego de Alcalá was first, San Gabriel Arcángel fourth.

During the 20th century, both cities first hugged the Pacific Ocean and then spilled back across parched foothills toward the desert. And, following World War II, both cities rode a boom in science-based industries.

On the other hand, Los Angeles seems to have had more than its fair share of economic breaks, the biggest of them being Hollywood and the motion picture industry. This, and the tireless boosterism of developers, spread the myth, and sometimes benign realities, of LA far and wide. The city grew and grew. San Diego, meanwhile, developed at a gentler pace, less extreme in everything.

Nowadays, Los Angeles is indisputably a world city, poised to take the Western lead in the next, Pacific, century. The downside, of course, is the kind of problems that attend big cities everywhere — and then some. The California dream is alive and well in affluent LA. In not-so-affluent LA it is sliding into nightmare. For many, a contemporary mythology of universal well-being is unraveling. LA has already fragmented along class and ethnic lines. Of course, the city continues to thrill, charm and amuse. It will continue to be a financial and industrial powerhouse. It will continue to spin legends.

But it is as if the idyll has, for a while, gone south. And its new capital is probably San Diego. No longer a dull place, San Diego retains a unity and coherence that in Los Angeles seems only a fond memory. Where LA is in danger of becoming too exciting for its own good, San Diego is content to be charming.

There is a nice symmetry to all this. After all, San Diego is where Southern California began. LA, it's said, is where it is headed. They have distinctive but evolving roles as powerhouses of Southern California. Forewarned, the visitor can savor and relish the play between them.

Los Angeles

Only in LA

It could be the supposed eccentricity of the people; their laid-back, often anti-intellectual lifestyles and the readiness of at least some Angelenos to embrace the latest off-the-wall fad. It could be that out-siders succumb to an envy excited by visions of perpetual sunshine, designer bodies and conspicuous consumption. Perhaps it is the ex-cesses and extremes of the place. Maybe it is because Los Angeles is like nowhere they've ever been; more varied, more cosmopolitan, more gracious, more grotesque. In fact, more everything.

Whatever, for those seeking in-a-nutshell assessments of the place or memorable jibes that point up its unique character, there is plenty on offer. There's Woody Allen's famous put-down of LA: that the only cultural advantage of living there is being able to turn right on a red light. Gertrude Stein should have had the city in mind with the remark, "There's no there, there." In fact, she was referring to Oakland near San Francisco. But that's another, less interesting story. Certainly, only Los Angeles could have been accused of being "49 suburbs in search of a city." Or have been the butt of comedian Fred Allen's wisecrack that "It's a nice place to live . . . if you're an Orange."

Angelenos don't much mind. Rather they relish the attention. They know their city is special, without precedent, in the vanguard of modern urban life. (The *Los Angeles Times* runs a daily column entitled "Only in LA," where the peculiarities of the city and its people are gleefully recorded.) So, a useful maxim for visitors could be: don't knock it until you've tried it.

The chance to turn right on a red light: this could be about the most generous and sensible freedom granted to drivers anywhere. "49 suburbs . . .": well, 49 suburbs each with its own city center seems like a significant improvement on 49 suburbs with just one center. And if the choice is between nice weather for oranges or nice weather for ducks or polar bears, then surely there's no contest.

This is not to say that Los Angeles is a city without shortcomings. Which major city is? Its problems are well publicized: smog and freeway gridlock; homelessness and gang violence; careless hedonism and thoughtless greed. And, most striking to the visitor from a conventional city, the skeletal public transportation system is woefully inadequate.

The riots of April 1992, costly in human lives, property and the city's utopian image, focused unprecedented attention on the shortcomings.

They were sparked by the acquittal of LA police officers charged with beating a black motorist, an incident recorded on amateur video and broadcast countless times on TV. Underlying the mayhem of violence, arson and looting that followed was a mix of anger, frustration and opportunism. Tinseltown doesn't glitter for everyone, particularly in the trough of a recession. The riots brought promises of federal help. We'll see. But, as the *New York Times,* not noted for its uncritical affection for Los Angeles, asked, "If this is hell, why is it so popular?"

It could be that some of the more well-off will be rethinking their futures in the city. But, on the whole, the popularity seems undiminished. Newcomers continue to flock into Los Angeles and adjacent counties. California registers some 600,000 new arrivals every year, and most head for the Southlands. You are as likely to meet a first-generation migrant arrived from elsewhere as a native-born Angeleno.

THE GOLDEN STATE

The reason is that the City, and the "Golden State" it inhabits — El Dorado to the earliest Spanish explorers with their visions of gold and exotic spices — continue to excite both senses and imaginations. The excitement generated by the promise of California is central both to its myths and its realities.

Few have captured it better than the 19th-century author Robert Louis Stevenson in his book *The Amateur Immigrant.* Traversing the western slopes of the Sierra Nevada 120 years ago, he felt the weariness of an arduous journey from his native Scotland slip from his shoulders. "At every turn we looked further into the land of our happy future. At every turn the cocks were tossing their clear notes into the golden air and crowing for the new day and the new country. For this was indeed our destination — this was 'the good country' we have been going to for so long."

Much has changed since then. Much remains the same: enthusiasm for the future rather than the past; extraordinary energies and creativity unencumbered by the constraints of tradition; the chance to start anew in an almost perfect climate. No other city on earth seems to promise so much to so many.

Some succeed, others fail. But, by and large, Los Angeles still delivers. The 1980s were boom years of record growth in the economy, population, jobs, output and incomes. It is immigrant energy and the belief that tomorrow can be better than yesterday that makes this possible.

Los Angeles continues to have the feel of an unfinished place. And when the only certainty is change, it is possible, indeed almost irresistible, to believe in change for the better. The dreams can be as corny as a Hollywood movie script, or as hardheaded as a regular income and decent schooling for the children. Under cloudless blue skies in crystalline desert light, it is just about impossible to believe that they won't be attainable. The "can-do" mentality is alive and well.

It would be misleading to suggest that the entire population inhabits a sun-drenched, pastel-hued idyll of blissful affluence. The society offers fewer safety nets for under-achievers than many others, especially Western Europeans, now take for granted. Los Angeles is a libertarian but not a liberal society.

As the highly visible jobless and homeless testify, recession has taken its toll here too. Nowhere is the gulf between the haves and the have-nots wider or deeper. South Central Los Angeles, where the 1992 riots were worst, is a study in urban degeneration and deprivation that has more in common with a third-world city than with the manicured lawns and interior-designed dwellings of Westside communities. While Bel Air shops for fine art, Watts spray-paints graffiti.

At the same time, population growth has resulted in wholesale congestion and pressure on both infrastructure and resources. Houses, and land for houses of the sort that the space-hungry Angelenos have grown to expect, are in increasingly short supply. Already property prices in Los Angeles are among the highest in the United States. Probably, things will get worse before they get better. That is the price to be paid for a modern mythology of prosperity and well being that has been broadcast around the world.

THE DREAM MACHINE

Yet, for the majority, it would be difficult to conceive a more attractive playground. Los Angeles may be short on history and tradition. But the range of entertainments is hard to match. The choice and quality of foods, produce and cuisines rival any other city on earth. There is shopping to exhaust the most dedicated shopaholic. Mile after mile of Pacific Ocean-lapped public beaches are open to everyone. Dress codes are lax; a string bikini or shorts will do nicely. And it is almost impossible to overestimate the importance of this to the collective psyche. The beach offers a kind of liberation and equality that would baffle political scientists. Not much farther away are mountains for winter sports, and deserts of dramatic, pristine beauty — all under the same robin's-egg-blue sky in golden sunlight.

And, to match the pleasures of the great outdoors, there are entire other worlds indoors, with the latest movies fresh from the nearby studios. What is playing in Los Angeles today probably won't reach the rest of the world for several months. For many viewers it will set the cultural agenda.

Under the circumstances, it is scarcely surprising that some Angelenos have a tenuous grip on what the rest of us presume to call reality. Who has the time to squeeze into spandex shorts and slalom a skateboard through Venice Beach traffic cones on a Tuesday afternoon? Why does the checkout boy at Ralph's 24-hour supermarket jive his way through the day like some hyperactive Michael Jackson wannabe?

Then there are the storefront psychic advisers, the elderly man easing his Chevy down the freeway one-handed while playing a trumpet with the other, the man with dark glasses and white cane riding his bicycle down a rural highway, the heavily mustachioed man cruising into a nightclub in a sequined sheath dress and stiletto heels. Or the Julia Roberts lookalikes who recite daily menus the length of a short novel before serving up the guaranteed cholesterol-and-sodium-free salad.

When there is the freedom to establish your own norms of behavior, just about everything can be accepted as normal. In the movies, just about anything can happen, and in "Tinseltown" just about everyone is starring in their own personal movie. It may sound bizarre, but for many the entertainment industry serves as history, current affairs, literature, theology and philosophy. If you inhabit a dream machine, it can be tough to regain full consciousness. As the architect and author Reyner Banham wrote 20 years ago, "Hollywood brought Los Angeles an unprecedented population of genius, neurosis, skill, charlatanry, beauty, vice, talent and plain old eccentricity . . . ." And this spicy cocktail still has the power to intoxicate.

Inevitably, some of the excesses and deviations from the norm are neither inspiring, engaging nor amusing. There are areas of Los Angeles that it is probably unwise to visit in daylight and positively deranged to enter after dark, notably parts of East and South Central LA. Narcotics and youth gangs have made for a sometimes violent subculture that doesn't welcome sightseers. In Greater Los Angeles around 1,000 people a year die violent deaths. Still, this isn't to say that LA is the most violent or dangerous city in the United States, and prudent visitors have little to fear. Most areas of Greater LA are safe and civilized.

PACIFIC POWERHOUSE

Mostly, the people of Los Angeles and its neighboring counties are life-enhancing optimists, with impeccable manners and sunny dispositions. Their's is a Pacific culture, far from the leaden skies and inhibiting chills of the North Atlantic coasts. Through the centuries, the opportunities for work and play have drawn wave after wave of immigrants: Hispanics, Anglo-Saxons, Southern and Central Europeans, Jews, Blacks, Armenians, Arabs and Asians. They're still arriving, armed with a preparedness to work as hard, maybe harder, than they play.

Los Angeles and the adjacent counties are powerhouses of business, manufacturing, aerospace, agriculture and hi-tech industry. As an independent economic entity, California would rank sixth in the world. In US tables it leads all other states in manufacturing, agriculture and entertainment, and ranks fourth in oil and gas. The recession has bitten deep of late, but where hasn't it? And LA is best placed to ride the upturn.

> [Los Angeles is] a city that [will be] for the Pacific what New York had once been for the Atlantic: a great and majestic gateway and a great and dignified port, the natural eastern capital for the newest, loveliest, richest and most populous quarter of the 21st-century world.
> (Simon Winchester, author of *Pacific Rising*)

The key to a future a rosy as its relatively short yet extraordinary past will be Los Angeles' location. To the east are the natural barriers of deserts and mountains, and beyond them, for many, memories of altogether less sun-kissed lives. The physical, psychological and economic orientations are to the west — a reality that will be further reinforced by quickening immigration from Asia.

Los Angeles, like San Diego to the south and San Francisco to the north, is now more than ever a city of the Pacific Rim. Henceforth, what happens in Tokyo is likely to be of more importance than what happens in New York. As the economic pundits continually remind us, we are approaching the Pacific Century, with booming Asian economies accelerating a spiral of rising prosperity. The challenge for LA is to continue as a leading player in the future.

To be sure, there have been a few blows to Angelenos' seemingly boundless confidence. Not least when cash-rich Japanese big business began buying up not only real estate but major motion picture studios and record companies — far more precious and potent icons of the collective identity. Still, the deal-makers of Hollywood have eased the pain somewhat by revealing that the Japanese paid far too much.

Change, the opportunities it offers, and the likelihood that the sun will shine, remain about the only verities. Los Angeles has wide skies and distant horizons, promising a sort of infinity. Its notions of utopia have to do with space, growth, property and the kind of limitless personal mobility symbolized by the automobile, cheap gasoline and the urban freeway. As befits the dream factory of the Western World, it reserves the right to reinvent itself time and again. The sometimes flimsy architecture speaks of future possibilities. Where else would a leading modern art museum be housed in renovated warehouses and be christened the "Temporary Contemporary"? Temporary much of LA might be. Contemporary it certainly is. And its freeway-scored, sometimes tacky, often innovative, supremely functional, low-rise sprawl is the prototype of an urban giantism that could be our future.

The city that brought us Mickey Mouse, designer pizza and valet parking continues to be a vivid tableau of the American dream — like nowhere else in America, but still the quintessentially American city. As the writer and environmentalist Wallace Stegner observes, "America, only more so." It is a glossy, excessive, deluxe version, seldom dull, predictable only in its unpredictability. It is, says writer Shiva Naipaul, "thronged not only with seekers of fame and fortune but seekers of new selves."

It is perhaps appropriate that California's motto is "Eureka" . . . "I have found it."

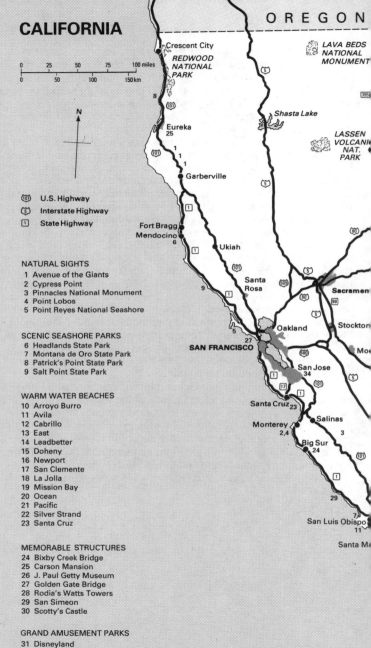

CALIFORNIA

OREGON

0 25 50 75 100 miles
0 50 100 150 km

N

(101) U.S. Highway
(5) Interstate Highway
[1] State Highway

NATURAL SIGHTS
1 Avenue of the Giants
2 Cypress Point
3 Pinnacles National Monument
4 Point Lobos
5 Point Reyes National Seashore

SCENIC SEASHORE PARKS
6 Headlands State Park
7 Montana de Oro State Park
8 Patrick's Point State Park
9 Salt Point State Park

WARM WATER BEACHES
10 Arroyo Burro
11 Avila
12 Cabrillo
13 East
14 Leadbetter
15 Doheny
16 Newport
17 San Clemente
18 La Jolla
19 Mission Bay
20 Ocean
21 Pacific
22 Silver Strand
23 Santa Cruz

MEMORABLE STRUCTURES
24 Bixby Creek Bridge
25 Carson Mansion
26 J. Paul Getty Museum
27 Golden Gate Bridge
28 Rodia's Watts Towers
29 San Simeon
30 Scotty's Castle

GRAND AMUSEMENT PARKS
31 Disneyland
32 Knott's Berry Farm
33 Marineland
34 Marriott's Great America
35 Sea World
36 Six Flags Magic Mountain
37 Universal Studios

Crescent City
REDWOOD NATIONAL PARK

LAVA BEDS NATIONAL MONUMENT

Shasta Lake

LASSEN VOLCANIC NAT. PARK

Eureka
25

Garberville

Fort Bragg
Mendocino
6

Ukiah

Santa Rosa

Sacramento

Oakland

Stockton

SAN FRANCISCO
27

San Jose
34

San Luis Obispo
11

Santa Ma

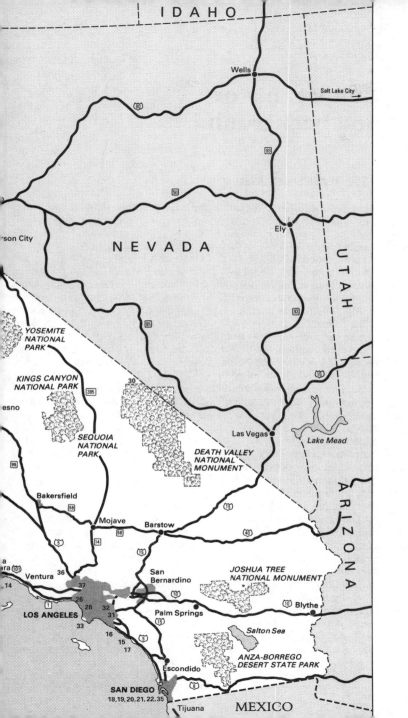

Culture, history and background

The urban setting

What first becomes clear about the city, descending by airplane into LAX, ideally at night, or driving across it, is that it is vast, bigger than any first-time visitor could ever imagine. Jean Baudrillard, French philosopher and Post-Modern theorist, succeeds in capturing the scale with his description of LA by night: "A sort of luminous, geometric, incandescent immensity, stretching as far as the eye can see . . . the muted fluorescence of all the diagonals: Wilshire, Lincoln, Sunset, Santa Monica . . . you come upon the horizontal infinite in every direction."

After this, the second thing is perhaps that it is not one city at all. Rather it is a collection of intermingling communities. For sure, the City of Los Angeles as such exists. Its population is around 3.4 million people in an area of 467 square miles. But only the eagle-eyed visitor, capable of spotting small City Limits signs along the freeways, will fathom where it begins and ends.

LA City joins seamlessly with the rest of LA County, an area of 4,083 square miles, with some 8.6 million people inhabiting a total of 88 incorporated cities. Not all are as populous as LA City; the City of Vernon's last population count totaled just 152 people. Not all the land is fully tamed and overbuilt. There are wild hillsides and relatively unspoiled canyons amid the jumble of freeways, shopping malls and residential streets. But to residents and visitors alike it all qualifies as Los Angeles. To visitors it can be daunting and bewildering, not least because most of it is unplanned in any conventional sense. No master builder ever sketched out a grand plan for Greater LA.

The residents, of course, have the advantage. They live in the place and, to a greater or lesser extent, understand its many identities, its complexities and its dynamics. Broadly speaking, they succeed in enjoying the best of a whole host of worlds, and they are able to do this because they are mobile. Things do divide people — money, interests, language, race sometimes, even fear — but geography is not one of them.

To be a fully functioning inhabitant of the LA Mega-City is to drive. Only the very poor and the eccentric take buses. And the automobile, wedded to cheap gasoline and an unrivaled network of urban freeways and broad boulevards, gives access to everywhere to just about everyone. Thus Angelenos will think little of driving an hour to a good restaurant or a tennis match, two to a beach or a ski slope, or more across the so-called "Five-County Area" of Los Angeles, Riverside, Ventura, Orange and San Bernadino. *They* will know when they cross Cities and Counties, although inevitably they will have preferences, prejudices and knowledge that is localized to some degree.

For the notion of an undifferentiated, indistinguishable sprawl is not only misleading, but plain wrong. Different parts of the Greater City have different characters and flavors. The shape, tone and grammar of the place can seem foreign and impenetrable at first. Just as with a new language, what is needed is a little effort, and plenty of patience. Many of the residents too have had to learn from scratch.

Nowadays, fluent Angelenos regard pretty much everything to the west and south of the Nevada border as a legitimate and accessible destination. (It's worth remembering that Disneyland, a major "Los Angeles" attraction, is actually in neighboring Orange County.) If they are to begin to taste the rich variety of LA and Southern California, visitors should be prepared to do the same. To be sure, parking can be difficult, expensive, or both. But validated and valet parking, and the acres of space beneath shopping malls, ease the pain. And it is, after all, central to the authentic LA experience.

Although it often seems so, these fully automated Angelenos, with their three-vehicle garages and personalized license plates, shouldn't be viewed as Flying Dutchmen of the freeways. Part of the attraction of LA and neighboring Counties is space, and the determination to explore it is almost a requirement for residence.

But the citizen of Greater LA is also likely to have a focus tighter than just the urban giant. What really distinguishes the City from anywhere else is that it lacks the single focus of conventional cities. Certainly, there is Downtown. It is the oldest part of the City, dating back to 1781 when a settlement was founded near Olvera Street. It is the center for civic and commercial activity, and by day up to 250,000 people work there. But it is not the only center, and traditional patterns of movement between home, work and recreation do not really apply.

Rush-hour movement isn't just in and out of Downtown. Rather it is in several dozen different directions that crisscross the Greater City, between scores of different focuses. Modern communications systems, including 1,500 miles of freeway, and the telephone, fax and computer modem, mean that it's every bit as easy and efficient to headquarter yourself in congenial surroundings in Beverly Hills, Century City, Pasadena, even Venice Beach, as it is to operate from a Downtown base. Thus the one-direction lemming commute is, in part at least, avoided.

The notional "49 suburbs in search of a city" long ago gave up the search. Most are now cities within their own right, with all the essentials, and inessentials, of municipal, economic and social life available within their distinctive communities in the valleys, the foothills, the canyons, at the beaches and in the basin. Some remain primarily residential communities. Compared with traditional cities, they are remarkably low-density, low-rise, low-key sorts of places. Yet they work. Critics say they lack the energy and intensity of the more familiar crowded, stacked-up metropolis; enthusiasts that they are a more civilized and sophisticated approach to city life than anything attempted before.

21

There is certainly a downside for Downtown. Its residential population is only around 20,000. And, though its reputation as a financial center and its daytime workforce have grown steadily in recent years, and its cultural and artistic scene often glitters, the nighttime streets can be deserted and rather forbidding. If Downtown vanished tomorrow most Angelenos probably wouldn't know or care.

The "suburbs," with their theaters, cinemas, schools, hospitals, sports facilities, shopping and nightlife, continue to multiply their choices and variety and to refine and solidify their identities. Nor have Angelenos entirely lost the use of their legs. Having parked the car in a mall or behind a major shopping and eating street in one of LA's constituent cities, they often can and will stroll on streets altogether more pedestrian-friendly than those of thickly congested conventional cities.

At the same time, a resident of, say, Santa Monica may well be proud to be a citizen of LA, and prouder still to be a citizen of Santa Monica. The identification with both, and loyalty to both, intensifies when face to face with anyone from outside the greater LA extended family. Thus Manhattan Beach and Glendale are not the same. But both are a world away from Manhattan, and to their inhabitants it is a *shared* world.

The Los Angelenos

The most recent official statistics list the inhabitants of the Los Angeles Five-County area as follows: White, non-Hispanic 49.7 percent; Hispanic 32.9 percent; Asian/Pacific Islander 8.4 percent; Black 8 percent; and American Indian/Other 1 percent. The demographic reality of Los Angeles is that the minorities are now the majority, and the broad categories of ethnic origin only hint at the racial, cultural, religious and linguistic variety and vitality of the City and its neighboring areas. That 85 languages are spoken in LA schools is just one measure of the extent to which it has become a global city.

In the modern era, the first to arrive were the Spanish, soon joined by the Yankees who rapidly outnumbered them and created a West Coast bastion of essentially "Anglo" culture that held sway for 150 years. There were important minority groups, most notably Jews, Blacks, Hispanics, Chinese, Koreans, Japanese and Armenians. Each tended to mark out areas of the city to call their own. And those cultural echoes live on along Fairfax Ave., in Watts, Downtown and in Glendale. But none was large enough to alter significantly the ethnic, cultural or political landscape.

Mostly this still holds true; much of LA, particularly prosperous LA, remains White Anglo-Saxon, albeit spiced with Jewish, Eastern European, Mediterranean and other success stories. But 20 years ago things began to change, and the pace of change has been quickening ever since. As usual, immigration has been the key to change. But, whereas previous generations of immigrants came from the geographic east (the cultural West), more recent arrivals have come mostly from the west (Asia) and the south (Mexico and Central America).

As almost always happens, newcomers have tended to cluster together — not as in the ghettos of old conventional "vertical" cities, but still in identifiable geographic areas. Chinese from Mainland China, Taiwan and Hong Kong, along with Vietnamese, Koreans, Japanese and Filipinos, have made large parts of Greater LA their own. In most respects, Monterey Park or San Gabriel could have been airlifted wok, stock and barrel from Asia. Hispanics have wrought a comparable transformation on East LA, now 90-percent Latino, and, to a lesser extent, the previously Black ghetto of Watts, now 50-percent Latino. Relatively high birth rates and continued immigration mean the Hispanic and Asian communities will grow larger still in the future, making a deeper impact on the whole.

The changing face of Greater LA has brought some inter-racial tensions. But optimists take the view that a new wave of ambitious people hungry for prosperity is only for the good, as LA re-invents itself yet again. And on the whole, LA's diverse citizenry co-exist happily enough, enjoying each other's culinary and cultural delicacies, crossing racial and class divides more easily than older, more hidebound societies.

It is not a melting-pot by any measure. But it is economic differences rather than racial ones that continue to divide. Angelenos tend to take themselves less seriously than the inhabitants of many other great cities, which helps them get along. And if they have a tendency to take things to extreme, that goes for their tolerance of others also.

Away from the East, it is said, restraint seems to fall away.
The gravitational force exerted by tradition weakens . . .
California is thronged not only with seekers of fame and fortune
but seekers of new selves.
(Shiva Naipaul)

The natural setting

From the earliest years of its history, the economic riches of California and its principal cities have been derived from the land: gold in the north, oil in the south, and an agriculturalist's Eden along the length of its Central Valley. This material wealth is matched by the esthetic richness of the setting.

Greater Los Angeles drapes itself across a wide basin, along the coast, and through the valleys and foothills of the five ranges of mountains that surround it. It is no accident that one of LA's best-known thoroughfares is named "Sunset Boulevard," or that the street runs from east to west, following the sun to the Pacific Ocean. Between Malibu and Balboa, LA's white sandy beaches run almost unbroken for 70 miles. Only the beaches of Rio de Janeiro come close, and they don't have the Pacific sunset — often so beautiful one suspects it's been manufactured by a major studio. (In fact, the smog helps by increasing the intensity of the sunsets.)

LA's subtropical climate lends itself to the cultivation of just about anything that can be irrigated, as best evidenced in the 200 acres of the Huntington Botanical Gardens, with its desert garden, roses, camellias and azaleas. The weather allows the private gardener to indulge in a botanical anarchism that would be doomed to failure elsewhere. It is harder to find nature untamed in the Greater LA area. Although some of the steeper hills within the 4,000-acre Griffith Park and parts of the wilder canyons are untouched by development or human manipulation, they offer little beyond curiosity value to the casual visitor, not least when compared with the rich profusion of colors and varieties in public and private gardens.

Beyond the metropolis are mountains, deserts, lakes, fertile valleys, cathedral-high coastlines and rugged offshore islands. From the northeast corner of the state, the **Sierra Nevada** mountain range runs south for some 400 miles, a solid granite barrier reaching a height of 14,495 feet at Mount Whitney. Lower down its slopes are forests of giant sequoia, pine, fir and cedar. From the northwest, the gentler **Coastal** ranges, with elevations of between 2,000 and 7,000 feet, extend almost to Los Angeles, with northern evergreens giving way to oaks and finally a chaparral of stunted shrubs. Between the two there is the fertile Central Valley, some 40-50 miles wide.

San Francisco's favorite nature playground is probably **Yosemite National Park**, 1,169 square miles of protected wilderness on the western slope of the Sierra Nevada to the southeast of the city. Extending from the mountains at the crest of the granite Sierra in the east to the dry foothills where the mountains run into the San Joaquin valley in the west, it is an area of startling beauty that quickly exhausts descriptive superlatives. All the hugeness of wild California is there. Its chain of mountains averages 10,000 feet; there are 429 lakes, canyons, glaciers, forests of oak, fir, maple and pine, and high mountain meadows. The **Upper Yosemite Falls** tumble 1,430 feet, or nine times as far as Niagara! The name "Yosemite" is thought to mean "grizzly bear" in the language of the original Miwok Indian inhabitants. Bears are still in residence, along with around a hundred varieties of mammal, 230 varieties of bird, and 1,200 types of flowering plants and ferns.

One third of California is desert. But it is seldom desert characterized by the monotony of sand dunes. The **High Desert** or **Mojave**, most of which falls within San Bernardino County, and the **Low Desert** or **Colorado** in the southeast of the state, can both be unforgiving. Joshua trees, cacti, scrub and man-made oases aside, their flora offers little excitement, and the visible fauna seems limited to an occasional coyote.

Nonetheless, the landscape serves up an artist's palette of colors and shapes that might have been formed by whimsical giants. **Death Valley** offers a tranquility that is hard to duplicate.

Most of the **lakes** are in the north, and Tahoe, the biggest, ranks as one of the world's great alpine lakes. Farther south, the high, man-made **Arrowhead** and **Big Bear Lakes** provide easily accessible playgrounds for LA. Along much of the coast, particularly south of Monterey and north of San Francisco, the Pacific Coast Highway hairpins above majestic cliffs.

The views, like the drive along Highway 1, can be literally breathtaking, especially if they include a sighting of migrating whales.

Sea bathing is another matter. North and south of San Francisco, as far as Santa Barbara, the waters of the Pacific Ocean are cold and more suited to well-kitted-out sailors or fishermen. Only south of Santa Barbara does the water become warm and the waves ruler-straight, making it a swimmer's and surfer's paradise.

Early sailors, less well equipped, believed California to be an island. We know better, but islands there are: the four **Catalinas**, the four **Santa Barbaras**, and a dozen smaller ones. Much of Santa Catalina, 27 miles southwest of LA's harbor at Wilmington, is preserved, largely unscathed, as "open land."

Californians in general, and San Franciscans in particular, are more passionate about, and caring of, their natural environment than most. The outdoors, and the beauty of the natural environment, are a large part of why people choose to live there. But it has to be said that LA and Southern California have been less diligent about protecting their environment than have San Francisco and the north of the State. The Sierra Club conservationists are headquartered in San Francisco.

Recently, after several years of drought, doubts about the wisdom of mankind's stewardship of natural California have grown. In the Central Valley, intensive agriculture, with its associated toxic residues, overgrazing by cattle, and a sinking water table, have raised the specter of a repeat of the Oklahoma dustbowl disaster. Likewise, the fire that swept through suburban Oakland in October 1991, destroying 1,800 homes, posed questions about the breakneck colonization of rural California. And the possibly dire consequences of wholesale mountain "cropping" — literally, slicing the peaks off hilltops to facilitate building — around LA have yet to become clear. The big earthquake yet to happen is lodged in everyone's subconscious.

Transforming California into the richest and most populous state in the United States has involved considerable violence to the natural environment. Still, "green" issues and initiatives are more to the fore than ever. The big, as yet unanswered question is the extent to which "green" solutions will require curbs on growth and rising prosperity. For now, however, much of the state remains generally unspoiled, having proved too big, uncompromising and remarkable even for late 20thC pioneers.

> You get the distinct feeling that the sun only touched
> Europe lightly on its way to rising properly here, above
> this plane geometry where its light is still that brand new light
> of the edge of the desert."
> (Jean Baudrillard, French sociologist, philosopher
> and Post-Modern theorist)

The historic background

The history of Los Angeles must be viewed in context, and the context is California as a whole. The earliest known inhabitants of the State were seminomadic Native Americans (to use today's "Politically Correct" term). They numbered perhaps 150,000 at their peak, with a score of distinct language groups and more than a hundred regional dialects. They fared badly after the arrival of European settlers. Their population was ravaged by alien diseases, land-grabbing by Europeans, and Indian "wars." By the early years of the 20thC, the total Indian population was put at 16,000.

The European explorations gathered pace in the **16thC**, with Spanish explorers seeking to expand their king's Mexican dominion ever farther to the north and west. They were seeking a land of legend called "California," described as being " . . .very near to the Terrestrial Paradise." In **1525** Hernán Cortés discovered a land he named California. But the first White man known to have seen the place was Juan Rodriguez Cabrillo, a Portuguese navigator in the service of Spain. Cabrillo National Monument in San Diego marks his landing there in **1542**. In the same year he sighted San Pedro harbor and named it "Bay of Smokes;" legend has it that he saw the campfire smoke of Indian villages within the present LA County.

Then Spanish interest flagged. It was almost 40 years before it revived with the news that the Englishman Sir Francis Drake had anchored his *Golden Hinde* near what is now San Francisco and claimed the new land for England. More thorough Spanish explorations of the coast followed, and in **1602** Sebastian Vizcaino reasserted his monarch's claim. But it was not until **1697** that Jesuits received royal warrants to enter the territory, and it was another 70 years before the first permanent colony was established at San Diego. In **1769** Padre Junipero Serra established Mission San Diego de Alcalá on Presidio Hill. It was the first stage of the "Sacred Expedition." Later, with Jesuits out of favor, it was left to Franciscan friars and the army to extend the northward penetration.

Between them, the Cross and the sword had by **1823** established a chain of 21 missions along 600 miles of the Camino Real or King's Highway. In **1776** a mission, Dolores, and a small military fortress had been founded at San Francisco. One of the first civilian settlements, in **1781**, was Los Angeles, established with 44 settlers. By 1800 the San Diego settlement's non-Indian population was still only 167.

Earnest development began in the **19thC**. First, in **1821**, Mexico won its independence from Spain and retained California as a colony. Relations between the Californios and their Mexican governors were strained, sometimes violent. But the watershed came in the early **1840s** with a quickening influx of American settlers. The Californios welcomed them; Mexico banned their further immigration. Finally, in **1846**, a small group of yanquis staged the "Bear Flag Revolt," declaring the California Republic. Then, 23 days later, Commodore John D. Sloat raised the American flag over Monterey and claimed California for the US.

The next surge of immigration followed almost immediately. News of

James Wilson Marshall's discovery of gold, near what is now Sacramento, in **January 1848**, prompted what has been described as the greatest mass movement of people since the Crusades. The previous year, the population had been put at 15,000. By **1850**, when California became the 31st state, it was nudging 100,000. A decade later it was close to 400,000. Many were "'49ers," as the Gold Rush arrivals were called, and much of the growth was in and around San Francisco, which fast emerged as the dominant city on the West Coast. Now it was a city confident enough to humor a man such as Joshua Abraham Norton, a failed English businessman and eccentric who, in **1859**, declared himself Emperor of the United States, and commanded his San Franciscan subjects to build bridges. In due course they did and, at the end of his 21-year "reign," 30,000 people attended his funeral.

By comparison, it took the completion of the transcontinental railroads — the South Pacific in **1876** and the Santa Fe in **1885** — to begin the transformation of Los Angeles from a sleepy pueblo. The people of the Mid-West began boarding trains and heading for Los Angeles and the newly irrigated farmlands around it. Just as important, moving labor and equipment in, moving produce out, was the newly constructed network of local railroads, to Wilmington and Santa Monica on the coast, to San Fernando in the north, to Anaheim in the south and to Pomona in the east. By the **1880s**, LA was the center of an hysterical property boom.

To the south, San Diego also boomed, after the arrival in **1885** of the Santa Fe Railroad, and its population grew to 40,000. An even more profound change in economic fortunes came around **1900** with the discovery and commercial exploitation of oil in the area of Los Angeles.

San Francisco, with its cable cars, enclaves of wealth and style and cosmopolitan sophistication, continued to overshadow the southern city until the turn of the century. Indeed, San Francisco was known as "The City." Then two things happened that altered the relationship. One was the quickening pace of LA's economic expansion and population growth. The other was the San Francisco earthquake on **April 18, 1906**. In the fire that followed, 500 died or went missing and 5 square miles of the San Francisco area were destroyed.

Reconstruction plans were being drawn even as the ruins smoked, and within three years 20,000 new buildings had been constructed. But meanwhile Los Angeles had been accelerating ahead. Oil, the movies (the first motion picture studio opened in **1906**), the increasingly busy port of San Pedro, and agriculture fed by the astounding hydrological engineering feats of William Mulholland, all accelerated LA's growth. By the end of the **1920s** the population stood at 1.2 million, and already the city sprawled. Motion pictures became a billion-dollar industry.

Post-quake San Francisco did its best to bounce back. The opening of the Panama Canal in **1914** boosted trade and manufacturing industries, and a year later the city celebrated its recovery with the Panama-Pacific International Exposition. San Diego too staged a Panama-California Exposition (in **1915-16**), in the newly landscaped Balboa Park. San Diego was finally on the map as a modern, noteworthy city, and began to profit from major Army and Navy bases set up in the city during World War I.

Immigrants continued to arrive — in the **1930s**, refugees from the Mid-West Dustbowl, many traveling down the famous Route 66; in the **1940s**, Europeans fleeing war and tyranny, and tens of thousands of servicemen demobilized on the West Coast after World War II; in the **1950s**, Blacks from the south and northeast; and, through the decades, a rainbow of races, people from the "rustbelt states," from Eastern Europe, Indochina, the Middle East, Central America, seeking the better life so temptingly portrayed by Hollywood. Every wave fed the cities' and the State's greatest resource — the ambitious, enthusiastic, innovative, enterprising minds of its people.

In the process came Henry Huntington's Pacific Electric Railway Company and its "Red Cars," giving LA the finest interurban railroad network in the world; the unprecedented irrigation scheme of the Central Valley Project (**1935**); the Golden Gate Bridge (**1937**); the Manhattanization of downtown San Francisco as it grew into the West Coast's Wall Street; Disneyland (**1955**); the aerospace industry embodied in Lockheed, Northrop and Douglas; Silicon Valley; and an array of new hi-tech industries.

In **1980** Ronald Reagan, former Hollywood movie star and Governor of California from **1967-73**, became US President and served for two terms. It seemed to set the political seal on what West Coast people already knew; Los Angeles and the other great cities of California had not only arrived, they were the vanguard of the nation's economic and cultural life, with their front door on the Pacific, the ocean of the future. Now they *must* be taken seriously.

Landmarks in California's history

Los Angeles did not evolve in a vacuum. It is part of the wider historical experience of the State of California. The following chronology reflects this.

1510: "California" received its first mention, in Montalvo's fiction *Las Sergas de Esplandian*. **1542:** Sailing from New Spain (Mexico), Juan Rodriguez Cabrillo discovered San Diego Bay and claimed it for Spain.

1579: Sir Francis Drake landed near San Francisco, named what he saw "New Albion" and claimed it for England.

1769: Father Junipero Serra established Spain's first California colony at San Diego. Gaspar de Portola's expedition reached San Francisco Bay.

1776: As the American colonies declared independence from Great Britain, a Spanish mission and *presidio* (fortress) were founded at San Francisco. **1777:** Felipe de Neve made Monterey capital of California.

1781: Pueblo (civilian settlement) founded at Los Angeles.

1796: First US ship, Ebenezer Dorr's *Otter,* anchored in a California port. **1812:** As the US fought the War of 1812, Russian fur traders established a colony at Fort Ross on the Sonoma coast.

1821: Mexico achieved independence from Spain, keeping California as a colony. **1828:** Jedediah Smith became the first White man to cross the Sierra Nevada. **1845:** Mexico ineffectually banned immigration of US settlers into California. Mary Peterson and James Williams became the first Americans to marry in California. **1846:** American settlers who overthrew the Mexican Government of General Mariano Vallejo in Bear Flag Revolt at Sonoma were put out of power within weeks as the US declared war on Mexico and seized California. Yerba Buena became San Francisco.

1848: John Marshall discovered gold in American River at Coloma, setting off the Gold Rush of **1849**. **1850:** California became the 31st American state. **1854:** Sacramento became the state's permanent capital.

1861: As the US was consumed by Civil War, California remained little more than a bystander, its sympathies divided between Union and Confederacy. The state's first vineyards were planted with 1,400 varieties of vines shipped in from Europe.

1868: The University of California was established at Berkeley. **1869:** The first transcontinental railroad was completed at Promontory Point, Utah, linking California with the E and ending the era of Pony Express and clipper ships around Cape Horn. "Emperor" Norton commanded bridges built across San Francisco Bay. **1872:** End of the Modoc War, the last major confrontation with the Indians of California.

1873: The first San Francisco cable car began operating. **1885:** The transcontinental Santa Fe Railroad reached San Diego, its Western terminus. **1900:** Major oil discoveries in Los Angeles produced an economic boom there. **1904:** A.P. Giannini created the Bank of Italy in San Francisco. Eventually it would become the Bank of America.

1906: The Great Earthquake and Fire leveled much of San Francisco. Rebuilding began almost immediately. Beverly Hills was founded, along with the first motion picture studio. **1908:** The first commercial motion picture was filmed in Los Angeles, beginning the phenomenon of Hollywood.

1913: The 250-mile Los Angeles Aqueduct, bringing water from the distant Owens Valley, was completed. It allowed LA to annex the entire San Fernando Valley. **1915:** Panama-Pacific International Exhibition held in San Francisco, and Panama-California Exposition in San Diego. First transcontinental telephone call.

1928: Daily San Francisco-LA passenger flights began. **1932:** San Francisco opened its Opera House, and Los Angeles staged the summer Olympic Games. **1935:** Donald Douglas' great airplane, the DC-3, ushered in the age of air travel and launched California as a center of aerospace technology. Construction of the Central Valley Project began.

1937: The Golden Gate Bridge was opened. **1945:** As World War II drew to a close, the United Nations founding assembly was held in San Francisco.

1955: Disneyland opened, the forerunner of a host of theme parks and symbol of California's playfulness. **1958:** Planar technique of producing transistors devised by Fairchild Semiconductor, an electronics company in Santa Clara Valley, to the SE of San Francisco. This paved the way for the silicon chip, cornerstone of the microelectronics revolution.

Major league baseball arrived with the San Francisco Giants and the Los Angeles Dodgers. **1960:** The Winter Olympics were held at Squaw Valley.

1964: California surpassed New York as the most populous US state. John Steinbeck won the Nobel Prize for Literature. **1967:** Ronald Reagan was elected State Governor, the *Queen Mary* was moored at Long Beach, and *Rolling Stone* magazine began publication in San Francisco. **1968:** The Summer of Love: hippies discovered sex and drugs and rock 'n' roll.

1971: Earthquake in the San Fernando Valley killed 64 people and caused more than $1 billion in damage. **1980:** Ronald Reagan elected US President. **1981:** The Mediterranean fruit fly (Medfly) infested Santa Clara County and neighboring areas, ushering in tight agricultural controls on the state's borders.

1984: LA staged the summer Olympic Games for a second time, matching the record of Athens, Paris and London. **1989:** Ronald and Nancy Reagan retired to Bel Air. The US's second-worst earthquake hit the Bay Area, making thousands homeless and causing more than $2 billion in damage.

1991: California imposed water rationing after five years of drought.

1992: Fire swept through Oakland at a cost of $1.5 billion. In the spring, violent rioting erupted in South Central Los Angeles after the acquittal of four white LA policemen accused of unlawfully beating a black motorist. The incident had been recorded on amateur video. National guardsmen were mobilized to quell the rioting, said to be the worst in US history. When the smoke cleared, 58 people had died and damage was estimated at around $1 billion. The City enlisted Peter Uberroth, credited with the success of the 1984 Los Angeles Olympics, as chairman of a "Rebuild LA" campaign.

The arts

Anyone interested in debunking the suggestion that the West Coast's premier city is a cultural wasteland need only spend an hour or three leafing through the newspapers' arts and entertainments supplements.

Los Angeles is home to the world's wealthiest cultural institution, the **J. Paul Getty Museum** at Malibu. The Getty is blessed with an endowment of $3.5 billion and an obligation to spend $150 million a year. Fitting perhaps for the world's most conspicuously wealthy society, the museum is housed in a replica of a Herculaneum villa, amid large and immaculately manicured gardens, in what is one of the most expensive and exclusive sections of Greater LA. And plans are in hand for the opening in 1996 of a new $360-million headquarters in the foothills of the Santa Monica Mountains. With that kind of money to spend, the Getty could have found a welcoming home almost anywhere.

Not so the **movies**. The motion picture industry is quintessential LA. The earliest movie-makers came to escape the monopolistic stranglehold of the east's Motion Pictures Patent Co. Among the bonuses were the wonderful quality of the light and a seemingly inexhaustible choice of locations. The talented, and the not so talented, followed. If the city sometimes seems to have a shaky hold on reality, then the movies are probably to blame.

The first commercial picture produced in LA was *The Count of Monte Cristo* (1908), fiction with a vengeance. The earliest passions for a good drama, thrill-packed action, and $10,000-a-week stars such as Charlie Chaplin and Mary Pickford, spilled off the movie sets and into everyday expectations. And such is the irrationality of the industry that, 90 years on, future stars are *still* discovered parking cars or serving hamburgers.

In recent years, parts of the industry have fled LA; costs are lower and trade unions less troublesome in places such as Canada and Florida. But the deals are still done in LA and, through film and, increasingly in a deregulating world industry, television, Hollywood continues to set a cultural agenda, not only for California, but for much of the world.

To hundreds of millions, the city and its locations are almost as familiar as their home town. The consequence for LA is paradoxical. Noël Coward's observation that "There is always something so delightfully real about what is phoney here. And something so phoney about what is real" still holds true. Indeed, even now, the full flavor of the real thing is seldom captured on celluloid or video.

Some would argue that the city's enduring legacy to 20thC culture was born of the ultimate masquerade: the Technicolor illusions of Walt Disney's animation. Just off the Santa Ana freeway, 30 miles south of downtown, is **Disneyland**, which with typical Southern California hyperbole bills itself the "Happiest Place on Earth." There are places where to call something "Mickey Mouse" is a considered insult, implying shoddy workmanship, shallowness and unreliability. But Mickey is a billion-dollar industry. Talk-show host and Mid-Westerner Johnny Carson says that the only culture in LA is yogurt; and as a "cultural" experience Disneyland is about as nutritional as junk food. But Disneyland is also about as popular as popular culture can be. "The Magic Kingdom," with its idealized "Main Street, USA," fast food, technical sophistication, thrilling rides into the past and the future, and wholesome fun for all the family, serves as mythology for modern America in general and for LA in particular.

None of which is to say that Tinsel Town is entirely without non-movie glitter. The **Los Angeles Philharmonic**, whose summer season is staged in the 18,000-seat Hollywood Bowl auditorium, is world-class. The galleries and museums, including the Getty, **Los Angeles County Museum of Art**, downtown's **Museum of Contemporary Art** (MOCA), the **Norton Simon Museum of Art** with its marvelous collection of Impressionists, and the **Huntington Art Gallery** with its *Blue Boy,* testify to an enthusiasm for the visual arts, and to patrons with the wherewithal to acquire the best.

LA is also the nation's **popular music** capital. It is home to more top-rated, and up-and-coming, musicians, producers and technicians than any other city, and it has the recording studios, record labels and venues where they perform. And in the field of live **stand-up comedy**, only New York comes close.

MOVIES

Any consideration of the true literature of California cannot ignore motion pictures. From D.W. Griffith's *The Birth of a Nation,* through Orson Welles' *Citizen Kane,* Mike Nichols' *The Graduate* and Roman Polanski's *Chinatown* to Robert Towne's *Tequila Sunrise,* they and scores of other movies tell a vivid story of each generation's distractions and preoccupations. Whether it be sexual mores, the violent struggle for control of water, cocaine trafficking, or the latest trends in designer pasta, nowhere has had its social and cultural history more closely, creatively and entertainingly documented on film.

A personal choice of movies that capture some quintessential element of California over the decades would include:

The Barbary Coast, 1935 — Edward G. Robinson costume drama of San Francisco's wildest days.

A Star is Born, 1937 and 1954 — vintage movie landmarks.

The Maltese Falcon, 1941 — Bogart stars as Hammett's hard-boiled private detective with an office on Van Ness Ave.

Snow White and the Seven Dwarfs, 1943 — Walt Disney's first feature-length animated cartoon.

The Big Sleep, 1946 — Bogart again, this time as Chandler's Philip Marlowe in LA.

Sunset Boulevard, 1950 — high drama of fading actress and young screenwriter.

Rebel Without a Cause, 1955 — James Dean works out his frustrations in Griffith Park.

Vertigo, 1958 — Hitchcock's psychological thriller, taking in some of San Francisco's best-loved locations.

Some Like It Hot, 1959 — Marilyn Monroe, among others, wiggling and giggling down San Diego's Coronado beachfront.

The Loved One, 1965 — Evelyn Waugh's biting satire on LA as entombed in the Forest Lawn Cemetery.

Bullitt, 1968 — Steve McQueen in classic car-chase cop movie.

Zabriskie Point, 1970 — Antonioni explores LA and Death Valley.

Dirty Harry, 1971 — Carmel's favorite son Clint Eastwood plays merciless detective prowling San Francisco.

What's up Doc? 1972 — classic comedy remake of *Bringing up Baby,* with Barbara Streisand being wacky in San Francisco.

The Long Goodbye, 1973 — Elliot Gould plays Chandler's Philip Marlowe in contemporary LA.

Chinatown, 1974 — jaded Jack Nicholson uncovers LA's corrupt battles for water in the atmospheric 1930s.

Shampoo, 1975 — Warren Beatty as a Beverly Hills hairdresser on the make.

Annie Hall, 1977 — I Love New Yorker Woody Allen hates LA.

Invasion of the Body Snatchers, 1978 — aliens target San Francisco.

Bladerunner, 1982 — futuristic story of lunatic LA circa 2019.

E.T., 1982 — Steven Spielberg's cuddly creature from outer space visits the San Fernando Valley.

Top Gun, 1986 — Air Force fighter pilot Tom Cruise excites the girls and San Diego.

The Two Jakes, 1990 — Jack Nicholson gumshoeing through LA history again, in a postwar drama as decadent and corrupt as Chinatown.

LA Story, 1991 — funnyman Steve Martin as a TV weatherman unhinged by LA's nonstop sunshine.

BACKGROUND READING

There is no shortage of significant literature preceding and paralleling the movies. Richard Henry Dana's *Two Years Before the Mast* contains excellent descriptions of Southern California in the years before it was settled. Mark Twain's *The Celebrated Jumping Frog of Calaveras County* is only one example of his brilliant reporting of the Gold Country and early San Francisco. Robert Louis Stevenson's essays, collected as *From Scotland to Silverado,* tell wonderfully evocative tales of life in 1879-80, from crossing the Atlantic in steerage to the beginnings of the Napa Valley wine country. Even more romantic is Helen Hunt Jackson's *Ramona,* a sentimental novel that in its day captivated millions of Americans.

CALIFORNIA WRITERS

Among the first California-born writers to command more than local attention was Jack London. His early works, *Tales of the Fish Patrol* and *John Barleycorn,* set in his native San Francisco Bay area, contradict Stevenson's idyllic descriptions. John Steinbeck goes even further in *The Grapes of Wrath,* and his story of the San Joaquin Valley establishment resisting an influx of impoverished farmers in *East of Eden* is one of the grimmest views of California on record. Steinbeck offers a more comic view of Monterey in two books, *Tortilla Flat* and *Cannery Row.* Nathanael West's *Day of the Locust* and Evelyn Waugh's *The*

Loved One each provides in its different way a sharp-eyed, sharp-tongued exploration of Southern California, in West's case through Hollywood, in Waugh's, inimitably, through the funeral industry.

However, the literature of LA and San Francisco probably reached its apogee in two writers who perfected a home-grown genre — that of the hard-boiled private eye. Dashiell Hammett's *The Maltese Falcon* and Raymond Chandler's *The Long Goodbye, Farewell My Lovely* and *The Big Sleep* are unequaled in their evocation of the moods, styles, geography and underlying realities of the cities. Inevitably perhaps, their works were turned into memorable movies.

More recently, Tom Wolfe's *Electric Kool-Aid Acid Test* and *The Pump House Gang* chronicle the Flower Power era in much the same kind of personal journalism that Mark Twain practiced on an earlier Californian society in upheaval. Ray Bradbury captures the essence of the sun-kissed society in one of his Martian tales *Dark They Were and Golden Eyed*. Gore Vidal's *Myra Breckinridge,* for all its rather heavy-handed symbolism, is an entertaining romp through multilayered Californian illusion.

Native Californian Joan Didion's fiction and nonfiction work, including *Slouching Towards Bethlehem, Play It As It Lays* and *The White Album,* are acerbic, reflective, humorous, unfailingly honest commentaries on the American Way of Life, California-style, from the 1960s onward; on the whole, she is revolted by it. (However, much of her early work is out of print, so check the public library.) And the works of thriller writers Robert Campbell and James Ellroy offer a chilling contemporary vision of LA's "mean streets."

Among many nonfiction works on the cities and their State, the British architect Reyner Banham's *Los Angeles: the Architecture of Four Ecologies* is probably the most intelligent and thought-provoking, along with California historian Carey McWilliams' politically conscious *Southern California: An Island on the Land.*

An altogether more radical critique is offered by Mike Davis in *City of Quartz,* a sort of "history noir" of greed, manipulation, power and prejudice in LA. For a Hollywood version of greed, manipulation etc., there's *You'll Never Eat Lunch in This Town Again,* Julia Phillips' best-selling expose of drugs, betrayals, backbiting, egos and excess among the movie elite. (Phillips was a major player herself; she produced, among other movies, *The Sting* and *Close Encounters of the Third Kind*).

For a crazed introduction to Las Vegas (see FARTHER AFIELD, page 182), read Dr. Hunter S. Thompson's *Fear and Loathing in Las Vegas,* a savage journey to the heart of the American Dream.

PICTURES AND PAINTERS

In California, photographs are to paintings what motion pictures are to plays. The photographs of Ansel Adams, from the 1930s onward, have given the world images of the Californian landscape (most notably of Yosemite National Park and Death Valley) that are as potent and memorable, if not more so, than those of Albert Bierstadt, the state's most celebrated landscape painter. Photography in California began with the Gold Rush and provides a wonderful historical record. Interest in photography as an art form here is such that outstanding prints can command prices that are comparable with those fetched by paintings and drawings.

Among contemporary artists, the British painter David Hockney, a longtime LA enthusiast and resident, has done something to redress the balance. He taught at the University of California from 1965 to 1967. His seemingly clichéd paintings of deep-blue swimming pools, flanked by palm trees, and cube-shaped buildings in desert colors, capture a unique reality that is at once both commonplace and central to the experience of Southern California.

Also prominent on the extremely fertile art scene are internationally acclaimed artists such as Robert Graham, Richard Diebenkorn, Ed Ruscha, Billy Al Bengston and Charles Arnolds.

It is Southern California light,
and it has no counterpart in the world.
(Carey McWilliams, author)

LA's architecture

Although frequently undervalued by critics, the architecture of Los Angeles is extraordinary. Its moderate critical standing might be explained in several ways. LA can hardly boast a long or deep architectural heritage. This is a libertarian city, inclined to experiment more freely than most, and therefore much of the architecture to be found here is relatively recent.

Even LA's fabled climate seems to count against it, for it encourages an open, expansive approach to architectural design. By comparison, other cities place such a premium on scarce building space that technical wizardry becomes an essential precondition for critical acclaim.

Finally, as this essay seeks to explain, across the vastness of the LA megalopolis it is not easy to categorize and interpret the city's architecture in the language, styles and trends that are familiar in smaller, older, more conventional cities.

There is certainly some distinguished work here, not least because in Los Angeles some distinctively American architectural styles have reached their apotheosis. It was here, after all, that Frank Lloyd Wright, regarded by many as the most influential American architect this century, came nearest to realizing his ideal. Wright's vision was fundamentally at odds with the orthodox European-style city. Instead of the cramped, vertical, quintessentially urban environment found in a Paris, New York or San Francisco, he envisaged a loose, low-density, horizontal spread, integrated with the natural environment, and made functional by a passionate commitment to the automobile. This, essentially, is the reality of Los Angeles.

For this is a horizontal city. The most significant exception is Downtown — and the main reason why skyscrapers were built there at all is that the city fathers decided that the rest of the world would not take Los Angeles seriously unless it conformed to big-city architectural norms, at very least at its administrative and financial heart.

St Vincent de Paul

But elsewhere, LA is astonishingly eclectic. Most of its buildings are low-rise. Much of it is a quirky mishmash of borrowings and idiosyncrasies. Yet these are seldom pointless, for the majority of the city's architecture responds faithfully to the demands and opportunities of its environment. Many of the buildings seem slight, almost temporary. (Indeed, one of the city's most popular art galleries rejoices in the name **The Temporary Contemporary**.) That is sensible enough, perhaps, given the benign climate, seemingly unlimited space, and the enduring Angeleno goal of breaking down the barriers between inside and out. Unlike, say, San Francisco to the north, Los Angeles could never be accused of being an East Coast city planted on the Pacific.

For all that, there are many buildings here that will stand the test of time, and plenty to interest, impress, amuse and intrigue: in the public realm, the 28-story **Los Angeles City Hall** (1928), variously characterized as Italian Classic, Romanesque, Byzantine and Hollywood Historical, or the **Los Angeles Museum of Contemporary Art** (1984), Arata Isozaki's excursion into Post-Modernist geometry; among churches, such gems as the ornately Spanish-styled **St Vincent de Paul** Roman Catholic church (1923); corporate extravagances like the splendid Art Deco **Bullock's Wilshire** department store (1928); the quirky domestic architecture of Wright, Richard Neutra, Rudolph Schindler and Frank Gehry; and much, much more besides.

Conversely, there is more than enough to appall even the unschooled observer. The **Beverly Center** shopping mall (1982), for example, has a wonderfully bright, well-articulated interior. But the blank, colorless, eight-story exterior is no more than a tragically wasted opportunity. What follows here ignores the worst, while seeking to make sense of the best of Los Angeles' architectural past and present.

HISPANIC THEMES

For the Southlands in general, and Los Angeles in particular, the most widespread, enduring and characteristic style is Spanish/Mexican. The Mission style, derived from the chain of missions established by Franciscan friars, involves thick, undecorated masonry walls with simple wooden detail. Ironically, the popularity of the style at the turn of the 20thC prompted the restoration of original missions fallen into disrepair after their lands were secularized in the 1820s. Of the LA missions, **San Gabriel Arcángel** is nearer to the original, unromanticized truth of Mission architecture and life than **San Fernando Rey de España**, which, critics say, has been restored beyond belief. The austere **Southwest Museum** (1912) is a secular example of the Mission style, in an idealized form.

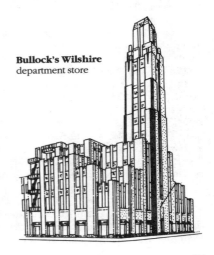

Bullock's Wilshire
department store

Subsequent variations on the Hispanic theme include Spanish Colonial Revival, with thick white walls and low-pitched, tiled roofs. Major concentrations of private homes in this style are found in **Santa Barbara**, **Pasadena** and **Palos Verdes**. Spanish Baroque, employed in the public areas of the **Biltmore Hotel** (1923), is characterized by more flamboyant Churrigueresque decoration, in the florid, late Baroque style that derived from a family of 17th-18thC Barcelona sculptors who specialized in piling up elaborate surface ornamentation and gained wide popularity in Spain and Mexico.

Hispanic Modern is a mix of earlier influences informed by contemporary European ideas of line and integration with natural surroundings. Downtown's **Union Station** (1934) is a fine example of Colonial Revival style inspired by Streamline Moderne touches. The Hispanic/Mediterranean tradition is still alive today; in the Southern California climate, with ample space for horizontal growth, it makes good sense. The original idea was that thick adobe kept interiors cool during the heat of the day, then released accumulated warmth in the chill of the night. Even with the universal introduction of air conditioning, the principle still holds good. But equally important, framed by palm trees, cacti and the wide, blue desert sky, the style looks perfectly at home.

THE CONVENTIONAL . . .

The same could hardly be said of the host of relatively high-rise Neoclassical, Beaux-Arts designs to be found Downtown. Similar buildings can be found throughout the United States. Originally, LA's city fathers decided that the center of a major metropolis needed monumental structures. That thinking was best typified in the 1920s-built **City Hall**, a 28-story stepped tower (pictured on page 81) that mixed Greek, Roman and Renaissance influences. Until 1957, when height restrictions in the city were lifted, this was LA's tallest building, and to this day Angelenos regard it with affection.

Efforts since, notably from the late 1960s onward, to invest LA's financial district with a degree of corporate grandeur have brought a succession of tall buildings Downtown and, to a lesser extent, in Century City. Much of what has gone up has been bland and unremarkable. As an attempt to dramatize LA's seriousness and importance as a commercial and financial center, the skyscrapers work best viewed from a distance; for example, by night from the Griffith Observatory.

But the city has scored some real architectural successes. Albert C. Martin's **Los Angeles Department of Water and Power Building** (1963), opposite the Music Center, is a delightfully simple glass and steel stack that at night seems to hover like an extra-terrestrial space ship. Also by Martin, **ARCO Plaza** (1972) comprises two dignified, polished stone-clad 52-story towers. John Porter's **Westin Bonaventure Hotel** (1976), with its five glass-sided tubes, sets a futuristic tone. The **Crocker Center** (1982, Skidmore, Owings & Merrill), two knife-edged 760-foot towers of polished granite and tinted glass, seeks to humanize itself with the "Garden Court," a glass atrium filled with plants and sculptures.

Taller still will be I. M. Pei's 73-story cylindrical tower, a trade-off for the developers in return for their restoration of the fire-damaged **Los Angeles Central Library** (1922). By way of contrast, the library (by Bertram Goodhue and Carleton Winslow) was a marvelous pastiche of

Beaux-Arts, Roman, Egyptian and Byzantine borrowings, with a dash of Art Deco for good measure.

... AND THE UNCONVENTIONAL

Such flights of fancy are not untypical of LA. Across the city, there are enough to be found to redress high-rise corporate conservatism:

- Egyptian Revival, sparked by the discovery of the tomb of Tutankhamun in 1922. The **Samson Tyre and Rubber Company Building** (1928) and J.M. Close's **Karnak** and **Ahmed apartment blocks** (1925) in Hollywood are good examples.
- Pre-Columbian, exploring notions of Native American architecture before the arrival of Christopher Columbus. It is seen at its craziest in the **Mayan Theater** (1926) and at its best in some of Frank Lloyd Wright's private homes.
- Hollywood Norman Gothic: **Château Marmont** (1927), *the* Sunset Strip hotel.
- Italianate, styled after an Italian country villa. The **Perry House** (1876) in Heritage Sq. is the leading example.
- Art Deco, a passion initially fired by the Paris Exposition Internationale des Arts Décoratifs in 1925. In the late 1920s, Art Deco's hard-edged elegance, energy and completeness reflected the city's upbeat mood. Prime examples are **Bullock's Wilshire** (1929) and the **Griffith Observatory** (1934: illustrated on page 89).
- Zigzag Moderne, a streamlined refinement of Art Deco. Two fine examples on Wilshire Blvd. are the **Pellisher Building** (1931) and **Wilshire Tower** (1929).
- "Less is more" Modernism: mirrored glass boxes etc. for corporate customers in the 1960s and early '70s, particularly in **Century City**.
- High Tech: self-conscious celebrations of the machine and computer age that aspire to be art objects. Examples: Downtown's **Well's Fargo Building** (1979); the **Santa Monica Transportation Center** (1983).

Pacific Design Center:
the Blue Whale

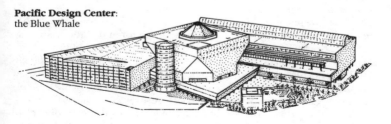

One distinctive LA style can be termed "Industrial," and West Hollywood's **Pacific Design Center** (1975-90) is its outstanding proponent: three aircraft-hangar-sized hulks wrapped in cobalt blue, green and red glass. Dean of Architecture at Yale, Cesar Pelli's work is described by one critic as a "metaphor for a place long known as a city of illusion." Locals have nicknamed them the Blue, Red and Green Whales.

The most recent enthusiasm, here as elsewhere, is Post-Modernism, typically on display at Gehry's **Loyola Law School** (1981), the **Ma Maison-Sofitel Hotel** (1987, Starkmen, Vidal & Christiensen) and Isozaki's **Museum of Contemporary Arts (MOCA)** (1986). Indeed, Post-Modernism could well prove to be the perfect vehicle for Los Angeles' architects. It is, above all, a self-conscious style: late-Modern buildings embellished with as many decorative borrowings as take the designer's fancy. It is self-regarding, demonstrative, colorful, up to the minute, entertaining and slightly disquieting. In short, very LA.

THE AUTOMOBILE

Styles come and go, but in LA one factor is constant. The city's buildings have more often than not been designed with the automobile, as much as people, in mind. For a city that lives by the car it is imperative. Since 1929, when **Bullock's Wilshire**, the delightful Art Deco department store, was the nation's pioneer in providing car-parking for shoppers, catering to the automobile has become as important and inevitable in architectural design as adding the roof. Parking lots can be over, under, beside, in front or in back, and their importance soon becomes apparent.

However, LA's parking lots tend to be very matter of fact. For a really spectacular experience, connoisseurs need to travel to Las Vegas, where the **Mirage Hotel** (1989) promises unrivaled thrills while parking your automobile.

DOMESTIC STYLES

The architectural landscape of Los Angeles is at its most distinctive at the domestic level. This is where the city's mythological dimension, Arcadia made real, comes into its own. Primarily what this is all about is the individual family home, on its own plot of land, representing the apogee of the American dream. Much domestic architecture in LA, as elsewhere, is uninspired and uninspiring. For many, Arcadia is mile after mile of "tract" homes, standardized, low-cost, pre-fabricated wood-frame bungalows set on concrete bases.

Yet everywhere the philosophical subtext is faithfully observed. Most homes are open-plan, seeking to integrate interior and exterior spaces, and they afford a degree of privacy and territoriality quite unthinkable in the conventional city apartment block. And within its own context, much of the architecture does soon becomes recognizable as an authentic LA style in its own right. "California Ranch," for example (the name defines itself), predominates in post-World War II residential suburbs. Some of what is visible can seem almost like temporary structures of no historical or artistic consequence. Along the way, however, LA's size and exuberance have found space not only for the tackiest, the wackiest and the most self-indulgent in house designs, but also for the most sublime.

Arguably, the most fascinating structures have come after older influences have been shaken off. In the best of them, it is noticeable that in Southern California, more than anywhere else, the architecture of family residences candidly reveals the personal idiosyncrasies of the people who live within them.

AT HOME IN LA

In the cannon of domestic architecture, a number of influential architects warrant special attention. The legendary Frank Lloyd Wright (1867-59) set one direction. His earliest work in LA in the 1910s and '20s reinforced a sense of regional identity, using modern construction techniques but exploring pre-European designs. **Hollyhock House** (1917-21) in Barnsdall Park, the **Ennis House** (1923-4) in Pasadena, the **Storer House** (1923-4) and the **Freeman House** (1923-4), both in Hollywood, are classic examples of his Pre-Columbian borrowings. Wright aimed to emphasize the independence of the New World from the Old, with buildings that were natural and "organic." Landscaping was of critical importance. In the housing boom after 1945, his rectilinear, family home design became the norm.

The brothers Charles (1868-1957) and Henry Greene (1870-54) exemplified a different but compatible tradition sprung from the Arts and Crafts Movement and the influence of Japanese carpentry. Their timber **Gamble House** in Pasadena, again with an interpenetration of interior and exterior spaces, remains a classic.

Rudolph Schindler (1887-1953) and Richard Neutra (1892-1970) were natives of Vienna who moved to Los Angeles in the 1920s. Both made important contributions to the city's continually evolving style. Most notable of Schindler's designs are his own **Studio House** (1921-22) in West Hollywood, which mixes slab concrete, glass, craftsman, Hispanic and Japanese traditions with typical LA verve, and the **Lovell Beach House** (1922-26) at Newport Beach, regarded as a key work of 20thC architecture. Best known in Neutra's large body of work is the **Lovell House** (1927-29), a Modern masterpiece in the Hollywood Hills.

Irving Gill (1870-1936) is noteworthy for his pursuit of efficient, low-cost housing, which he sought with a whitewashed, concrete abstraction of Southwest Indian pueblo styles. His legacy might be described as "Mission meets Cubist." Alas, his LA masterpiece, the **Dodge House** (1914-16) in West Hollywood, has been demolished.

Among architects active in Los Angeles today, Canadian-born Frank O. Gehry is pre-eminent. Gehry began work in LA in 1963 and within a decade was being described as a "punk-style" architect. His early work was on single family houses, including his own in Santa Monica, which he transformed from unassuming Dutch Colonial to provocative artwork with corrugated metal, chain link fencing and exposed wooden frames. "If Jasper Johns and Donald Judd can make beauty with junk materials, then why can't that transfer into architecture?" says Gehry.

His major commissions have included the **Santa Monica Place** (1979-81) shopping mall, Midtown's **Loyola Law School** (1981-4), the **Aerospace Museum** in Exposition Park (1982-84), Downtown's **Temporary Contemporary Museum** (1982-83), the **Goldwyn Regional Branch Library** (1984) in Hollywood, the **Cabrillo Marine Museum** (1981) in San Pedro, and the **Disney Concert Hall**, an addition to the Downtown Los Angeles Music Center scheduled to open in 1995. Gehry's mischievous Deconstructivism will go down as the dominant voice among the current generation of LA architects.

Basic
information

Before you go

DOCUMENTS REQUIRED

British citizens except those from Northern Ireland, and citizens of New Zealand, Japan, and all Western European countries except Greece, no longer need a visa to visit the US, provided that their stay will last for 90 days or less and is for vacation or business purposes. If arriving by air or sea, the visitor must be traveling with an approved carrier (most are) and must have an **onward or return ticket**. (Open or standby tickets are acceptable.) If entering overland from Canada or Mexico, no visa is required. An unexpired **passport** is also essential.

British subjects will need to obtain a visa, as will any British citizen who wishes to stay more than 90 days for whatever reason, has a criminal record, has suffered from tuberculosis, is suffering from AIDS, is HIV-positive or has previously been refused a visa. The US embassy in London has a useful recorded message for all general visa inquiries (☎ (0898) 200290). If you need a visa, it is wise to allow plenty of time.

You must show a valid **driver's license** and, unless you are a US citizen, a passport, in order to rent a car. For visitors from most countries, an international driver's license is not required. Some firms ask to see your return ticket. Most rental companies will offer to sell you short-term insurance and it is wise to take it, unless your own policy gives adequate coverage. If you are arriving by private car from other states or countries, bring the **car registration document** and **certificate of insurance**.

TRAVEL AND MEDICAL INSURANCE

US medical care is good, but expensive, and medical insurance is strongly recommended for visitors from other countries. UK travel agents have the necessary forms, and tour operators frequently include medical coverage in their packages.

Baggage insurance is recommended in case of theft. American Express offers baggage insurance to card members, as do automobile clubs.

MONEY

The basic unit is, of course, the dollar ($). It is divided into 100 cents (¢). Coins are: the penny 1¢, nickel 5¢, dime 10¢, quarter 25¢ and half dollar 50¢. Bank notes (bills) in general circulation are in denominations of $1, $5, $10, $20, $50 and $100. A few $2 bills are in circulation.

Any amount of money may be imported or exported, but when the total exceeds $10,000 you must register with the US Customs Service.

It is wise to carry **cash** in small amounts only, keeping the remainder in dollar **travelers checks**. Those issued by American Express, Bank of America, Barclays, Citibank and Thomas Cook are widely recognized, and MasterCard and Visa have also introduced them. Make sure you read the instructions included with your travelers checks. **Note separately the serial numbers and the telephone number to call in case of loss.** Specialist travelers check companies such as American Express provide extensive local refund facilities through their own offices or agents. Many shops accept dollar travelers checks.

Charge/credit cards are welcomed by nearly all hotels, airlines and car rental agencies, and most restaurants, garages and shops. American Express, Diners Club, MasterCard and Visa are the major cards in common use. While personal checks drawing on out-of-town banks are seldom accepted, many hotels will cash small amounts in conjunction with a charge or credit card.

American Express also has a **Moneygram®** money transfer service that makes it possible to wire money worldwide in just minutes, from any American Express Travel Service Office. This service is available to all customers and is not limited to American Express Card members. Payment can be made in cash, or with an American Express Card with a Centurion Credit Line, an American Express Optima (SM) Card, Visa or MasterCard. See USEFUL ADDRESSES on page 55.

CUSTOMS

Returning US citizens present themselves and their luggage to a single officer for inspection. All others must first clear passport control, collect their baggage and then move on to a Customs official. Although the process has been streamlined, the combination of three Jumbo jets disgorging at once and government concern over smuggling can slow things down to a crawl. It may take no more than 30 minutes from plane to street, but an hour or more is not unusual.

Nonresidents can bring in any items clearly intended for personal use, duty-free, with the exceptions noted below.

Tobacco goods   200 cigarettes *or* 50 cigars *or* $4\frac{1}{2}$ lbs (2kg) tobacco. An additional 100 cigars may be brought in under your gift exemption (see OTHER GOODS below).

Alcoholic drinks   Adults over 18 are allowed up to 1 quart (1 liter) of liquor (spirits).

Other goods   Nonresidents may also import up to $100 in gifts without tax or duty if remaining in the US at least 72 hours. Returning residents are granted a duty-free allowance of $400 on goods brought back personally. Families traveling together can pool their allowances to cover joint purchases.

For more information on Customs regulations, a brochure entitled *US Customs Hints* can be obtained from US embassies and consulates, or directly from the Department of the Treasury, US Customs Service, Box 7407, Washington, DC 20044.

TOURIST OFFICE

American visitors should make contact with the **Los Angeles Convention and Visitors Bureau** (*515 S Figueroa St., 11th Floor, Los Angeles, CA 90071* ☎ *(213) 624-7300* Fx *(213) 624-9746*). Visitors from the UK can obtain much useful information from the **US Travel and Tourism Administration**, P.O. Box 1EN, London W1A 1EN (☎ *(071) 495-4466* Fx *(071) 495 4377*).

GETTING THERE

Almost all international and US domestic airlines serve **Los Angeles International Airport (LAX)**, the world's third busiest airport, receiving more than 45 million passengers in 1990. There are four E-W runways, and the central complex comprises eight separate terminals around a two-level loop. In addition, the nearby West Imperial Terminal to the S handles charter aircraft and nonscheduled flights.

Free **Airline Connection** buses, colored blue, green and white, run between the different terminals at both levels. Departures are at the upper level, arrivals at the lower. There are the usual restaurants, bars, gift stores and newsstands. At the arrival level are to be found baggage claim, greeting areas, foreign currency exchange counters, information desks and courtesy phones for transport and accommodation information. The new Tom Bradley International Terminal also offers the **Skytel** facility, where travelers can shower and sleep.

LAX has its own multilingual information service, and inside the airport yellow telephones link directly to **Airport Information Aides** from 7am-11.30pm daily. For telephone numbers of individual airlines see the Yellow Pages.

ALTERNATIVE AIRPORTS

Los Angeles International is the biggest but not the only airport in the LA area. There are smaller airports that could be a more convenient alternative for flights within the US:

Burbank-Glendale-Pasadena Airport   2627 N Hollywood Way, Burbank ☎(818) 840-8847, map **1B2**

John Wayne Airport   MacArthur Blvd., Orange County ☎(714) 252-5006, map **2E5**

Long Beach Airport   4100 Douglas Dr., Long Beach ☎(310) 421-8293, map **1D3**

Ontario International Airport   Mission Blvd., Ontario ☎(714) 988-2700, map **10I7**

BY CAR

For drivers, five major interstate freeways ("I" routes) connect California to points S, E and N. The all-year routes leading to Los Angeles are I-8 running E-W along the Mexican border, I-10 running E-W from Arizona, and the I-15 running NE-SW through Las Vegas and the intermountain basin. The I-5, running from San Diego in the S through the length of California and up to the Pacific Northwest, is kept open all year, but drivers can be subject to winter delays when snowstorms blanket the Siskiyou Mountains on the California-Oregon border. The more northerly I-80 crosses some of the higher parts of both the Sierra Nevada and the Rocky Mountains before ending at San Francisco. Although it too is kept open all year, there can be snowstorms between October and April.

For information on **highway conditions** ☎ (213) 626-7231.

BY TRAIN

Amtrak *(Union Passenger Station N of Downtown, at 800 N Alameda St.* ☎ *(800) USA-RAIL, map 6 D9),* the subsidized passenger rail service, runs daily trains on three interstate routes. One daily train connects both Los Angeles and San Francisco with the Pacific Northwest. The second connects San Francisco with Chicago via Reno and Denver. The third connects Los Angeles with points NE and SE including Las Vegas, Phoenix, Houston and New Orleans. Amtrak also runs a regular service down the coast to San Diego.

OTHER TRANSPORT

Los Angeles is also served by **Greyhound/Trailways** *(Downtown depot at 208 E 6th St.* ☎ *(800) 237-8211, map 6 D9.)*

CLIMATE

Summers in Los Angeles and along the S coast are hot and dry, but the Pacific Ocean and the mountains along the Los Angeles coastal basin act as a buffer against the heat of the desert. Winters are mild, with plenty of sunshine. You are most likely to encounter one of the city's famous smogs in the summer, worth remembering particularly if you have a respiratory complaint. However, contrary to the songs, it does rain occasionally, and coastal areas can experience chilly winter fog. (Average temperatures midday are 28°C (83°F) from June to October and 18°C (65°F) from November to May.)

Elsewhere in the state, inland areas have drier, hotter summers that are less oppressive on the hills than in the valleys. Winters are colder and drier than on the coast. Southern deserts are warm in winter but often intolerably hot in summer.

Mountain regions enjoy four distinct seasons: fine, cold winters; warm, sunny summers; and changeable springs and falls.

For **daily weather information** ☎ (213) 554-1212.

CLOTHES

Los Angeles and San Diego are intensely fashion-conscious cities, but generally dress is functional and casual. Some of the smarter clubs and restaurants insist on jackets, a few of the smartest insist on neckties, and many frown on "sneakers." Elsewhere, the not uncommon notice "No shoes, no shirt, no service" speaks for itself.

Travelers who intend venturing outside the city should be prepared for climatic surprises; in any case, temperature differences between night and day make a sweater and jacket wise inclusions on your packing list. Even if your visit is to Los Angeles alone, where pedestrianism is considered eccentric, be sure to take a pair of comfortable shoes. But keep your baggage light: baggage trolleys and porters can be hard to find.

MAIL

Visitors choosing not to receive mail in care of their hotels can use US Postal Service General Delivery (poste restante), addressed to the main post office in the city. Outgoing mail can be sent from these and smaller post offices, and stamps can frequently be bought in hotels and drugstores. Post office counter service often involves a long wait in line. However, stamps are also dispensed by vending machines, so a handful of small change can be useful.

The main **post office** in Los Angeles is located at 7001 S Central Ave. at Florence Ave. ☎(213) 586-1723.

At the airport

FROM THE AIRPORT TO THE CITY

Ground transport between the airport (off the San Diego Freeway 405 at Florence/Century exits) and other districts of Los Angeles is excellent. However, with so many buses and taxis circling the airport, the system can appear haphazard and confusing.

Shuttle services, like those listed below, will generally want to fill their vans before leaving the airport. So using them could involve a wait and dropping off other passengers en route to your destination. But they are cheaper than taxis and limousines unless there are three or more people traveling together. Vans and buses load from the center islands outside baggage claim areas, but baggage capacities can be limited. Car rental agencies with LAX operations run shuttle services to their depots.

For information on all buses, taxis, limousines and other transport ☎(310) 247-7678. Advance reservations are recommended for limousines and rentals.

Among the choices available are those listed below.

BUSES FROM THE AIRPORT

From all of the airports there are shuttle bus services that run to locations throughout the city and beyond. For these, it is necessary to purchase a ticket beforehand at a sales point in the airport. However, if yours is not one of the first destinations on the route, the shuttle buses can be slow and tiring after a long flight.

Airlink   To Downtown LA hotels ☎(800) 962-1976

Fun Bus Systems   Nonstop express service from LAX to Disneyland every $\frac{1}{2}$ hour ☎(800) 962-1976

Golden Star Airport Shuttle   Door-to-door transport between LAX and the Greater Los Angeles area and Orange County ☎(800) 660-6042, (310) 645-4566

Great American Stage Lines   To w San Fernando Valley and Ventura ☎(805) 499-1995

Prime Time Shuttle   Links all LA area airports ☎(310) 558-1606
RTD Airport Services   Regular buses to most parts of town, and regular 24-hour shuttle to its Airport Transfer Terminal ☎(213) 625-4455
Supershuttle Inc.   Door-to-door service throughout LA and Orange County ☎(800) 554-3146, (310) 338-1111, (818) 244-2700, (310) 417-8988

TAXIS

In general, taxis are rare and expensive, but a selection of operators, reliable at the time of writing, follows.
Airport Taxi Service   From and to LAX ☎(310) 837-7252
Checker Cab Company   From and to LAX ☎(310) 204-4833
Independent Cab Company   24-hour driver-owned cabs ☎(213) 385-8294
LA Taxi   Air-conditioned cabs with uniformed drivers ☎(213) 627-7000, (213) 627-7000
United Independent Taxi   Throughout LA County, major charge/credit cards accepted ☎(213) 653-5050

LIMOUSINES

Limousine services are available, although it is essential to reserve in advance.
Music Express Limousine   Sedans, Cadillac and "Presidential" stretch limos ☎(800) 255-4444, (213) 849-2244
On the Scene Limousine   Cadillacs and Lincolns with all the essentials and trimmings ☎(213) 938-4700 Fx(213) 930-1840

CAR RENTAL

All the major car rental agencies are sited near the airport and run complimentary minibus services to and from the airport for customers. It isn't necessary to reserve a ride; just flag the bus down as it passes.
Alamo Rental and Leasing   Competitive rates, 24-hour LAX pick-up ☎(310) 649-2245
Avis Rent-a-Car   75 locations in Southern California ☎(310) 646-5600, (800) 331-1212
Budget Rent-a-Car   American and prestige European cars, convertibles ☎(310) 649-7500, (800) 527-0700
Dollar Rent-a-Car   Late-model economy and luxury American and Japanese cars ☎(213) 776-8100, (800) 421-6868
Hertz Corporation   Ford cars, with special group and convention rates ☎(310) 646-4861, (800) 654-3131
Regency Exotic Car Rental   Sports and luxury cars including Rolls-Royce, Porsche, Jaguar, Corvette ☎(800) 545-1020
Rent-A-Wreck   No airport pick-up, but used cars, vans and trucks at rates up to 50 percent below competitors ☎(818) 762-3628, (818) 343-0047, (310) 478-0676
Thrifty Rent-a-Car   Convention rates ☎(310) 645-1880, (800) 367-2277

RECREATIONAL VEHICLES

Budget Rent-a-Car and Truck   Economy and luxury campers (motorhomes), airport pick-up ☎(800) 446-7368, (310) 670-1744
Cruise America-RV Rentals   Campers and custom vans, LAX pick-up ☎(800) 327-7778, (714) 772-9030
El Monte Rents/LA Motor Home Rental Center   Campers and trailers, multilingual service ☎(800) 367-3687, (818) 443-6158

Getting around LA

PUBLIC TRANSPORT

Attempting LA without a car, save for the briefest of visits, is to invite frustration and/or unnecessary expense. The **Automobile Club of Southern California** *(2601 S Figueroa St., map 6E8)* is a superb source of information for drivers — but alas only for members *(for membership details ☎(213) 741-4880)*.

However, there are local bus services. **Southern California Rapid Transit District** operates buses throughout the Los Angeles Basin and Orange County, with more than 1,900 buses covering 2,200 square miles *(☎(213) 625-4455 Mon-Fri 6am-midnight, Sat-Sun 6am-6pm, no information service on major holidays except Jan 1; impaired hearing ☎(800) 252-9040; information and rover ticket sales kiosk on Underground Level B, ARCO Plaza, 5th St. and Flower St., map 6D9, Mon-Fri 9am-5pm, closed Sat-Sun and major hols; RTD's free "Rider's Kit" gives information on fares and routes)*. Buses are equipped with automatic wheelchair lifts. Culver City, Santa Monica and several other independent cities within RTD's service area operate a supplementary local service.

City Bus Services (RTD) provides infrequent services and runs specials to major attractions such as **Disneyland** *(information on services and routes from RTD Information ☎(213) 625-4455; information for those with impaired hearing ☎(800) 252-9040)*.

Some relief of LA's unsatisfactory public transport situation is promised by the **Metro Rail Plan**, but the scheme won't make a major impact until the 21stC. To date, only the **Metro Blue Line**, running between Downtown and Long Beach, is operational.

TAXIS

Taxi stands operate at Los Angeles International airport, at rail and bus stations and at major hotels. Fares are $1.90 at flagdrop, plus $1.60 per mile. But, given LA's sprawl and the likelihood that the driver won't know LA, or how to read a map of it, any better than you, taxis are almost invariably an expensive and inefficient way to get around.

RENTING A CAR

The best way to travel . . . . Major car rental firms include Airway, Avis, Alamo, Budget, Dollar, Econocar, Hertz, National and Thrifty. All have a Downtown office, and a depot near Los Angeles International airport;

most have them at smaller airports too. Many have toll-free (**800**) numbers through which reservations can be made. It is wise to reserve in advance. If you are unhappy with a particular vehicle, it is usually a straightforward matter to swap for another.

It pays to shop around even among the major firms; rates can vary and managers are often open to negotiation. Fly-drive packages, available through airlines, may offer the most favorable rates for renting a car. Rent-it-here/leave-it-there arrangements are available but can be expensive. In addition, major cities have cut-price firms such as **Rent-a-wreck** offering old but basically sound vehicles at relatively low prices.

Most firms offer insurance packages additional to those required by law. Given the high costs of medical care and the possibly astronomical costs of litigation, these are well worth considering. The especially cautious should consult their insurance broker before leaving home. Limousine services are widely available as a relaxing alternative. See LIMOUSINES on page 47.

TOURS

Agentours Inc.   11321 Iowa St., LA 90025 ☎(310) 473-2456, map **3**E1. Scheduled sightseeing tours, multilingual services, hotel pick-up.

Judith Benjamin   2210 Wilshire Blvd., Suite 754, Santa Monica 90403 ☎(213) 826-8810. Luxury personal limousine tours.

Blue Line Tour and Charter Inc.   PO Box 25 "B" 17, LA 90025 ☎(310) 312-3326. Scheduled local tours including beaches and Getty Museum.

California Parlor Car Tours   515 S Olive St., LA 90017 ☎(800) 227-4250, (213) 742-9839, map **6**D9. 3-6 day tours including Hearst Castle, Monterey, Yosemite, San Diego.

Casablanca Tours   6362 Hollywood Blvd., Hollywood 90028 ☎(213) 461-0156, map **5**B6. 4-hour tours of stars' homes, Chinese Theater, Sunset Strip, Rodeo Drive, Farmers Market.

Grave Line Tours   PO Box 931694, Hollywood 90093 ☎(213) 469-4149. Macabre tour around sites of Hollywood's famous murders, suicides, scandals and crimes, in a renovated hearse.

Gray Line Tours Co.   1207 W 3rd St., LA 90017 ☎(800) 538-5050, (213) 481-2121, map **6**D9. Standard bus tours.

Hollywood Fantasy Tours   1721 N Highland Ave., Hollywood 90028 ☎(800) 782-7287, (213) 469-8184, map **5**B5. Stars' homes, movie studios and landmarks, in double-decker and open buses.

Insider Tours   1109 Pearl St., Santa Monica 90405 ☎(310) 392-4435. Maxi-van tours of Venice, Santa Monica, Rustic Canyons.

Piuma Aircraft   PO Box 1201, Malibu 90265 ☎(818) 591-0576. Hot-air balloon flights plus champagne lunch: reserve ahead.

Starline/Gray Line Tours   6845 Hollywood Blvd., Hollywood 90028 ☎(800) 451-3131, (213) 856-5900, map **5**B6. Stars' homes, Hollywood, Beverly Hills.

Tour Elegante   15446 Sherman Way, Suite 3-118, Van Nuys 91406 ☎(818) 786-8466. City tours, 6-hour beach tour, plus wine country and coastal tours as far as San Francisco.

The Wilderness Institute Inc.   23018 Ventura Blvd., Suite 202, Woodland Hills 91364 ☎(818) 991-7327. Naturalist-led tours of scenic spots.

DRIVING

Like it or not, you'll almost certainly need to. Taxis don't cruise the streets as in other cities. Public transport leaves much to be desired.

The freeway system can be unforgiving, but it is understandable. Interchanges and exit roads are signaled well in advance, and it is essential to heed the signs overhanging the freeway and to be in the correct lane at the correct time. A mistake can involve miles of needless driving before there's an opportunity to rectify it.

Lane discipline is of a different order from what some visitors might be used to. There isn't a slow, fast and faster lane. Rather, drivers choose lanes according to speed, intentions and the progress of other vehicles. Expect to be passed on the inside.

Freeways also change name and number; thus the 134 Ventura becomes the 210 Foothill; the 5 is variously the Golden State, Santa Ana and San Diego. The solution is to study the map and plan ahead, making a note of proposed routes. Mark both the name and number of the freeways you plan to use, and know your destination in terms of N, S, E or W. Disabled vehicles should be parked on the shoulder, along which there are yellow phone booths at frequent intervals. Wait for assistance with closed windows and locked doors. For updated traffic information listen to local radio stations or ☎(213) 626-7231.

Whatever their shortcomings, the freeways are usually the best way to travel any significant distance. When traveling the major boulevards and smaller roads, known locally as "surface streets," expect to move more slowly and have your progress interrupted by stop signs, traffic lights and turning vehicles. Don't rely only on a street name and number to find addresses; streets run for miles, numbers run into the ten-thousands, and different cities have different systems. Find out the nearest intersection and take it from there.

WALKING

Mostly people don't. Angelenos and their cars are like cowboys and their horses: almost inseparable. Except in the glossier recreational and shopping areas of Downtown, Beverly Hills, Hollywood and Santa Monica, walkers are regarded as mad or bad or possibly both.

However, where walking is relatively risk-free, for example along trendy Melrose Ave. between Fairfax Ave. and Doheny Dr., it can be a pleasure. The land is flat and the Mediterranean weather perfect. But remember that LA blocks are huge. What appears on a map to be a manageable six-block walk may be anything but easy.

It is best to cross only at pedestrian crossings — usually at traffic lights and intersections. When there are pedestrian signals, cross only when the light reads "Walk" or a small walking figure appears. At crossings without traffic lights, traffic is supposed to but doesn't always stop for pedestrians.

You are prohibited from walking along or across freeways. Walking alone at night should be avoided in some neighborhoods.

SPEED LIMITS
Maximum speed limits are indicated on most California roads. Freeway and highway maximums are normally 55mph; on some busy highways, speed limits may be 50 or 45mph. In city and town centers and in residential areas, the maximum speed is 25mph; on main urban thoroughfares, 30 or 35mph. On roads that pass schools, there is a speed limit of 25mph during school hours. All of these are maximums: you can be charged with reckless driving at lower speeds if driving conditions are poor.

On-the-spot information

PUBLIC HOLIDAYS
January 1; **Martin Luther King Day**, third Monday in January; **President's Day**, third Monday in February; **Memorial Day**, last Monday in May; **Independence Day**, July 4 (but businesses close on nearest Monday or Friday); **Labor Day**, first Monday in September; **Columbus Day**, second Monday in October; **Veterans Day**, November 11; **Thanksgiving**, last Thursday in November; **December 25**.

Banks and almost all businesses are closed on these days, although shops frequently stay open for sales. **Good Friday** is a half-day holiday; many offices close on **Easter Monday**.

TIME ZONES
All of California is within the **Pacific Time Zone**: 3 hours behind New York, 2 hours behind Chicago and 1 hour behind Denver. The Pacific Time Zone is 8 hours behind Greenwich Mean Time. California law establishes **Daylight Saving Time** from the first Sunday in April through the last Saturday in October.

BANKS AND FOREIGN EXCHANGE
Normal business hours for banks are Monday to Thursday 10am-3pm and Friday 10am-5pm. An increasing number of banks in Los Angeles keep later weekday hours; fewer open on Saturday. Travel service firms typically open Monday through Friday 9am-5pm and Saturday 10am-noon.

Banks vary in their policies on cashing travelers checks; most often they do not; some will provide the services only for regular customers; some charge commission; others provide the service free. American Express and Thomas Cook travel service offices are more consistent and reliable.

SHOPPING AND BUSINESS HOURS
Department stores and **clothes and sports equipment stores**

generally open between 9 and 10am and close at 5.30 or 6pm. **Late-night shopping**, particularly in the malls, is usually until 9pm on Thursday. The larger **supermarket chains** and **drugstores** are open 24 hours seven days a week.

Coffee shops and **fast-food restaurants** may open as early as 6am and close as late as midnight; some stay open around the clock. More **formal restaurants** open from about noon-3pm and 6-11pm, with last orders an hour earlier. **Bars** and **cocktail lounges** do not have to close until 2am.

In general, LA restaurants close earlier than those in European cities or those in the cities of the Eastern US. Budget travelers should watch out for "Early Bird Specials" — discounted dinners for early (i.e., late afternoon) diners.

RUSH HOURS

Morning freeway rush hours begin at 6am, reach a peak between 7 and 8am, then ebb by 9.30am; the evening rush begins by 4pm, peaks by 5pm, and ebbs at major intersections after 7pm.

COMMUNICATIONS

Public telephones are numerous and are usually in working order. Pay telephones accept 5¢, 10¢ and 25¢ coins. Local calls cost between 15¢ and 25¢. Long-distance charges are paid as the call progresses, so arm yourself with a heap of coins. Helpful operators will give guidance on how much you need. Long-distance rates reduce sharply between 6pm and 8am and are lowest on Saturday.

For further information on area codes and toll-free numbers, see below.

Hotels, and many motels, have **fax** as well as **IDD telephone** services. **Telex** is still around, but is less common than it once was. For anyone needing these facilities elsewhere, help is available from the nearest **Main Post Office**:

- Downtown at 900 N Alameda St.
- In Beverly Hills at 9300 Santa Monica Blvd.
- In Santa Monica at Main St. and Pacific Ave.
- Near LAX at 5800 W Century Blvd.
- In Van Nuys at 15701 Sherman Way.

Telegrams can be sent from these post offices, and **General Delivery (Post Restante)** services are also available.

TELEPHONE AREA CODES AND 800 NUMBERS

California is divided into a dozen telephone area codes — an especially important point to note in Los Angeles, where boundaries fall across populous areas in a seemingly arbitrary manner. To make things even more complicated, in 1991 a new **310** area code was added in the LA area. The boundaries for the new code are La Cienega Blvd. to the w, El Segundo Blvd. to the s, the Montebello city line to the E, and the 818 area code boundary to the N. Among cities affected are Beverly Hills, Santa Monica and Long Beach, as well as LAX. Downtown LA,

Hollywood, Huntington Park, Verron and Montebello retain the **213** area code.

Area codes are dialed before the local number **only** when calling from one area to another. Note that from some areas a preliminary **1** is required for any long-distance call; check the telephone directory or consult a local person before dialing.

In addition to their regular numbers, airlines, car rental firms and hotels often have **no-charge (toll-free) numbers** with an **800** prefix. Numerous hotel, tourist information and other listings in this book have toll-free 800 numbers. Often these are valid only for calls within California — and calls made from outside the state commonly require a different number after the 800 prefix. Before dialing national hotel chains or other nationwide service companies from out-of-state, check the local Yellow Pages to verify 800 numbers. Remember to prefix **800** with a **1**.

PUBLIC LAVATORIES/BATHROOMS

On interstate and US highways, California maintains excellent public lavatories in roadside miniparks called "rest areas." Many gas stations maintain facilities for their customers. In cities, lavatories are commonplace in shopping malls, department stores, restaurants, fast-food chains and hotels. Public lavatories are less common: try to avoid them.

ELECTRIC CURRENT

Electric current is 110-120V 60 cycles AC. Conventional household appliances generally have standard two-prong plugs or earthed plugs with an additional half-cylinder prong. Most wall outlets are designed to accept either type of plug. Anyone wanting to use non-US-style plugs should purchase an adaptor before leaving home, although major department stores may sell adaptors in their travel departments.

LAWS AND REGULATIONS

Smoking is prohibited in elevators and buses, theaters and movie theaters. Restaurants and public rooms allow it only in specified areas. Many hotels now have nonsmoking floors. Laws prohibit **jaywalking** and **littering** but are unevenly enforced. **Hitchhiking** is also illegal, and although seldom punished it is strongly discouraged on freeways. **Topless bathing** is against the law.

Parking violations are not taken lightly, so pay attention to color-coded curbing. **Red** means no stopping or parking, **Yellow** means a maximum half-hour loading time for vehicles with commercial plates, **Blue** is reserved for disabled people, **Green** allows 10 minutes' parking for all vehicles, and **White** gives a 5-minute limit during business hours. Do not park at bus stops or fire hydrants. Violation can incur a fine of up to $20, and charges rise dramatically if you park in a space reserved for disabled people or your vehicle is towed away.

In general, traffic rules, including SPEED LIMITS (see page 51), are rigorously enforced, and should be taken seriously at all times. **Drunk driving**, if detected, will result in arrest. State law demands the wearing of **seat belts** in private vehicles. Turning **right on red** (after stopping) is allowed, unless there is a sign to the contrary. **Pedestrians** have the right of way.

Persons must be 21 years or older to buy, serve or consume **alcoholic beverages** in California, and proof of age can be required. Liquor may not be purchased, served or consumed in public eating places and bars from 2-6am. The consumption of "controlled substances" (narcotic drugs) is prohibited by law; far more severe laws prohibit their sale.

CUSTOMS AND ETIQUETTE

Although they are almost unfailingly polite, as a rule Californians are not overtly formal. But there are certain conventions. It is customary to shake hands on meeting. Once people have been introduced, first names are used in all but the most formal circumstances.

Californians can be erratic about lining up; they form orderly lines outside movie theaters and intercity bus stations, but not for sporting events or for buses in the cities themselves. Courtesy is important: on buses men still give up seats for women; and everyone urges everyone else to "have a good day."

TIPPING

Waiters expect a tip of between 15 and 20 percent of the bill before tax, although you may feel inclined to tip more if service has been especially good, less if it has been poor. Barmen and hairdressers should also receive 15 percent. Doormen and staff who valet park your car expect $2, bellhops $1 per bag, and bathroom attendants (rarely encountered) $1. When there is no fixed charge for leaving coats and parcels, give $1 per item.

DISABLED TRAVELERS

California law requires new hotels, restaurants and other public buildings to be accessible to wheelchairs and to have wheelchair bathrooms. Older hotels and restaurants have converted rooms. Many cities reserve curbside parking for handicapped people, as do major banks, supermarkets and drugstores. Some companies operate buses with wheelchair lifts (see PUBLIC TRANSPORT, page 48).

A free brochure listing services for disabled people is published by the **Los Angeles County Commission on Disabilities** *(383 Hall of Administration, 500 W Temple St. ☎ (213) 974-1053, (213) 974-1707, map 6 D9).*

Around the Town with Ease is an 80-page guide, published by the Junior League of Los Angeles, to wheelchair facilities in 100 popular attractions. *(To obtain a copy,· write enclosing $2 for postage and handling to Los Angeles Junior League, Farmers Market, Third and Fairfax ☎ (213) 937-5566, map 4 C5).*

PUBLICATIONS

Los Angeles is rich in newspapers and magazines, as indeed is the entire State of California. In the *Los Angeles Times* it boasts one of the nation's most authoritative papers. Newspapers publish comprehensive entertainment sections, notably in Friday editions for the weekend and in Sunday editions for the week ahead.

In addition, monthly glossies such as *Los Angeles Magazine* and weekly freesheets such as *LA Weekly* offer up-to-date information on the hot spots from everything to eating out, shopping and the arts. Newsstands offer a wealth of local, national and international publications. Most hotels provide useful but advertisement-filled magazines.

The **LA Convention and Visitors Bureau** (☎ *(213) 624-7300)* publishes frequently updated booklets detailing what's on offer.

Guidebooks and maps from bookstores: *LA Access* (Access Press); *Gault Millau The Best of Los Angeles* (Prentice Hall); *Flashmaps Instant Guide to Los Angeles* (Random House); *Thomas Brothers Road Atlas and Driver's Guide to Los Angeles* (Thomas Bros Maps).

Useful addresses

TOURIST INFORMATION
American Express Travel Service offers a valuable source of information for any traveler in need of help, advice or emergency services, as well as a full range of travel services, currency handling, and tours:
- 8493 W 3rd St. ☎(310) 659-1682, map **4**C**4**
- 901 W 7th St. ☎(213) 627-4800, map **6**D**8**
- 327 N Beverly Dr., Beverly Hills ☎(310) 274-8277, map **3**C**3**
- 251 S Lake Ave., Pasadena ☎(818) 449-2281, map **1**B**3**

California State Park System PO Box 2390, Sacramento 95811; in Los Angeles ☎(800) 444-7275, for camping reservations forms and list of parks.

Department of Motor Vehicles ☎(213) 744-2000, for *California Driver's Handbook,* summarizing traffic regulations. Parking violations are dealt with by the local police department.

Department of Fish and Game 1416 9th St., 12th Floor, Sacramento 95814 ☎(916) 445-3531, for fishing and hunting license requirements, seasons, and game limits.

Hollywood Visitor Information Center The Janes House, 6541 Hollywood Blvd., Hollywood 90028 ☎(213) 689-8822.

US Forest Service 630 Sansome St., San Francisco 94111 ☎(415) 556-0122, for camping reservations forms and information on national forests.

Ticketron For a computerized reservations agency for all state and national park campgrounds ☎(800) 622-0904). For entertainment, see NIGHTLIFE, pages 141 and 144.

AIRLINES
The following list gives toll-free telephone numbers of the major airlines serving Los Angeles International Airport.
- **Air Canada** ☎(800) 422-6232
- **American Airlines** ☎(800) 433-7300

- **British Airways** ☎(800) 247-9297
- **Delta Airlines** ☎(800) 221-1212
- **Japan Airlines** ☎(800) 525-3663
- **Northwest Airlines** ☎(800) 225-2525
- **United Airlines** ☎(800) 241-6522
- **USAir** ☎(800) 428-4322

The following airlines offer flights to Los Angeles from the United Kingdom.

- **Air New Zealand:** in the UK ☎(081) 741-2299, in the US ☎(800) 262-1234; nonstop flights from Gatwick.
- **American Airlines:** in the UK ☎(0800) 010-151, in the US ☎(800) 433-7300; nonstop flights from Heathrow.
- **British Airways:** in the UK ☎(081) 897-4000, in the US ☎(800) 247-9727; nonstop flights from Heathrow.
- **United Airlines:** in the UK ☎(0800) 888-555, in the US ☎(800) 241-6522; nonstop flights from Heathrow.
- **Virgin Atlantic Airways:** in the UK ☎(0293) 562-000, in the US ☎(800) 862-8621; nonstop flights from Heathrow.

CONSULATES
Australia   611 N Larchmont Blvd. ☎(213) 469-4300
Canada   300 S Grand Ave. ☎(213) 687-7432, map **6**D9
Japan   250 E 1st St., Suite 608 ☎(213) 624-8305, map **6**D9
Mexico   125 Paseo de la Plaza ☎(213) 624-3261
South Africa   9107 Wilshire Blvd. ☎(310) 858-0380, map **3**D3
United Kingdom   3701 Wilshire Blvd. ☎(310) 477-3322, map **5**D7

POST OFFICES
See COMMUNICATIONS, page 52.

Emergency information

EMERGENCY SERVICES
Los Angeles Police Dept. (LAPD)   ☎911 in emergencies; otherwise ☎(213) 485-2121
California Highway Patrol   ☎911 in emergencies and ask for Highway Patrol; otherwise ☎(213) 736-3374

- **Fire** ☎911
- **Coast Guard**   ☎(310) 499-5380
- **Ambulance**   ☎911
- **Paramedics**   ☎911; for nonemergency ☎(213) 483-6721
- **Medical Society referrals**   ☎(213) 483-6122
- **Suicide Prevention**   ☎(213) 381-5111
- **Drug Hotline**   ☎(213) 463-6851

OTHER MEDICAL EMERGENCIES
To find a private doctor, consult the Yellow Pages of the telephone directory under *Physician*. Or, in Los Angeles, contact the **LA County Medical Association Physician Referral Service** *(☎(213) 484-6122)*. Dentists are listed under *Dentist*. If in a hotel, ask the reception desk for help.

LATE-NIGHT PHARMACIES
Difficult to find in cities, they seldom exist in smaller towns. Consult Yellow Pages under *Pharmacies*. For LA, see LATE-NIGHT, overleaf.

HELP LINES (CRISIS LINES)
Some crisis intervention organizations are quasi-official; many are private; all are local or narrowly regional. For help consult the Yellow Pages under: *Crisis Intervention Service; Drug Abuse Information and Treatment Centers;* or *Suicide Prevention Counselor*.

A useful contact point is **Traveler's Aid**: in Los Angeles ☎(213) 625-2501.

AUTOMOBILE ACCIDENTS
- Call the police immediately.
- **On city streets**, call municipal police at emergency number, which is universally **911**. Nonemergency numbers are in local telephone directories. **On all freeways** (even within city limits) and **all highways and roads** outside municipal boundaries, call California Highway Patrol (CHP). **On urban freeways**, roadside phone booths automatically connect to the nearest CHP office. **Elsewhere** ☎911 in emergency.
- If a car is rented, call the number in the rental agreement. (You should carry this, and your license, at all times when driving. Failure to do so can complicate matters.)
- Never admit liability or incriminate yourself.
- Ask eyewitnesses to stay, and take down their names, addresses and statements.

- Exchange names, addresses, car details, driver's license numbers, insurance companies' names and policy code numbers.
- Remain at the scene of the accident to give your statement to the police.

CAR BREAKDOWNS

Call one of the following from the nearest telephone.
- The number indicated in the car rental agreement.
- The local office of AAA if you are a member. The AAA is listed as California State Automobile Association (CSAA) in northern California, or Automobile Club of Southern California (ACSC) in Southern California.
- The nearest garage with towing service (listed under *Towing-Automotive* in Yellow Pages).

LOST TRAVELERS CHECKS

Notify the local police immediately, then follow the instructions provided with your travelers checks, or contact the issuing company's nearest office. Contact your consulate or American Express (see page 55) if you are stranded without money.

LATE-NIGHT

Pharmacies:
- **Thrifty Drugstore**   1533 N Vermont Ave., LA ☎(213) 666-5083, map **5**B7, open 24 hours
- **Horton & Converse Pharmacy**   6625 Van Nuys Blvd., Van Nuys ☎(818) 782-6251, open 24 hours
- **Bel-Air Pharmacy**   820 Moraga Dr., Bel-Air ☎(310) 472-9593, on call 24 hours
- **Robert Burns Pharmacy**   9049 Burton Way, LA ☎(310) 271-5126, map **3**C3, on call 24 hours
- **Family Pharmacy Service**   8314 Wilshire Blvd., LA ☎(213) 653-4070, map **4**D4, on call 24 hours

Locksmiths:
- **Wilshire Lock and Key**   ☎(213) 389-8433, 24-hour service

Baby-sitters:
- **Sitters Unlimited**   ☎(213) 595-8186

Planning
your visit

When to go

For many non-Californians the classic image of LA weather is New Year's Day on a sun-drenched beach. The notion of an all-year playground is indeed appropriate for the coastal areas s from Santa Barbara. Mild, sunny days come to this region in rows throughout January and February; summer is simply warmer and drier, and ocean breezes act as nature's air conditioning.

The hottest months are August through October, when scorching Santa Ana winds often blow in from the desert. The bonus is that, on the days they sweep into the LA basin, they drive away the smog (which is most severe in August and September). The coolest months are December through March.

That said, the variations are usually quite modest. Midday summer temperatures average 83°F (28°C); midday winter temperatures average 65°F (18°C). Nightime temperatures are some 20°F (5-6°C) cooler. Most of the annual rainfall, around 15 inches when it rains at all, arrives between November and March. However, temperature fluctuations can be unpredictable; temperatures as wide apart as 95°F and 30°F have been recorded in December. In short, October is probably the choicest month of all.

The San Fernando Valley is generally a few degrees warmer than areas s of the Hollywood Hills.

Inland, expectations, and wardrobe, must be a little more flexible. Palm Springs and other desert communities only a few score miles inland from the s coast are delightfully warm from Thanksgiving to Easter, but grow so hot in summer that many resorts close down from June to the end of September. Death Valley, which has one of the world's hottest summer climates, throttles back to half speed from May to October. Desert variations between day and night temperatures can be as wide as 40°F (22°C).

Weather is not the only factor to consider in scheduling an LA vacation: events crowd the calendar. These are summarized in the CALENDAR OF EVENTS, on the following pages.

Visitors are thickest on the ground in the summer months, when major attractions can be oversubscribed and crowded.

Calendar of events

See also OUTDOOR ACTIVITIES on page 159, PUBLIC HOLIDAYS on page 51, and SAN DIEGO CALENDAR OF EVENTS on page 207. Some dates vary from year to year, so check ahead.

JANUARY

Tournament of Roses Parade, Pasadena ☎(818) 449-4100.
• **Rose Bowl Collegiate Football game**, Pasadena ☎(818) 793-7191. • **World of Wheels**, LA ☎(213) 587-5100. • **Thoroughbred horse racing**, Santa Anita ☎(818) 574-7223. • **Japanese New Year Celebrations**, Little Tokyo ☎(213) 628-2725. • **Whale migration watching**, Southern California coast ☎(310) 548-7562. • **Basketball season** begins ☎(310) 412-5000. • **Ice hockey season** begins ☎(310) 412-5000. • **Annual dog-sled races**, Palm Springs (weather permitting) ☎(619) 327-8411.

FEBRUARY

Mardi Gras, Olvera St., LA ☎(213) 680-2525/(213) 744-4210.
• **Chinese New Year Celebrations and Golden Dragon Parade**, LA ☎(213) 628-1828. • **South California Boat Show**, LA Convention Center ☎(213) 741-1151. • **Laguna Beach Winter Festival**, with arts and crafts fair ☎(714) 494-1018.
• **Bob Hope Desert Golf Classic**, Palm Springs ☎(619) 325-1577.
• **Riverside County National Date Festival**, Indio ☎(619) 347-0676. • **Pismo Beach Clam Festival**, with jazz, parade and fair ☎(805) 773-4382.

MARCH

Long Beach Grand Prix, Long Beach (Formula 1) ☎(310) 436-7727.
• **Los Angeles Marathon**, LA ☎(213) 624-7300. • **Annual Academy Awards**, LA ☎(310) 278-8990. • **Kite Festivals**, Santa Monica and Redondo Beach ☎(310) 392-9631. • **Fiesta de las Golondrinas**, celebrating swallows' return, San Juan Capistrano ☎(714) 493-1111. • **International Film Festival**, Santa Barbara ☎(805) 963-0023.

APRIL

National Mime Week, LA ☎(213) 242-9163. • **International Folk Dance Festival**, LA ☎(310) 273-5539. • **Easter Sunrise Services**, Hollywood Bowl ☎(213) 850-2000. • **Filmex**, the LA film exposition ☎(213) 856-7707. • **Cherry Blossom Festival**, Little Tokyo ☎(213) 628-2725. • **International Orchid Show**, Santa Barbara ☎(805) 687-0766. • **Baseball season** begins ☎(213) 224-150. • **Toyota Grand Prix**, Long Beach ☎(310) 436-3645. • **Hollywood Park thoroughbred racing**, Inglewood ☎(310) 419-1500. • **Blessing of the Animals**, traditional Mexican parade, Olvera St., LA ☎(213) 624-7300.

MAY

Cinco de Mayo Celebrations marking Mexican Independence ☎(213) 688-7330. • **UCLA Mardi Gras**, Spaulding Field ☎(310) 825-4321. • **Pacific Southwest Tennis Championship**, LA Tennis Club ☎(213) 464-3195. • **Bullfight season** opens, Tijuana ☎(619) 565-9949.

JUNE

Grand Irish Fare and Music Festival, Burbank ☎(213) 624-7300. • **Highland Games**, Santa Monica Scottish festival ☎(310) 393-9825. • **Playboy Jazz Festival**, Hollywood Bowl ☎(213) 850-2000. • **Dragon Boat Festival**, Chinatown ☎(213) 624-7300. • **Gay Pride Week**, West Hollywood.

JULY

Hollywood Bowl Summer Festival/LA Philharmonic season opens, Hollywood Bowl ☎(213) 850-2000. • **4th July Celebrations/Fireworks**, Catalina and elsewhere. • **Watts Jazz Festival**, LA ☎(213) 624-7300. • **Grand Prix Bicycle Race**, Manhattan Beach ☎(310) 545-5313.

AUGUST

International Surf Festival, Hermosa, Manhattan and Redondo beaches ☎(310) 545-5042. • **Beach Volleyball Championship**, Laguna Beach ☎(714) 494-1018. • **Old Miners Day**, with races, parades and dances, Big Bear Lake ☎(714) 866-4601. • **Old Spanish Days**, rodeo, Santa Barbara ☎(815) 965-3021. • **Nisei Week**, celebration of Japanese-American culture, Little Tokyo ☎(213) 687-7193.

SEPTEMBER

LA City Birthday and Mexican Independence celebrations, Olvera St. ☎(213) 680-2525. • **LA County Fair**, the nation's largest, Pomona ☎(714) 623-3111. • **Pro Beach Volleyball Championships**, Redondo Beach ☎(213) 245-3778. • **National Football League season** begins ☎(213) 322-5901/(714) 277-4700. • **Hollywood Bowl season** ends, with fireworks finale ☎(213) 850-2000.

OCTOBER

Discovery of California/Cabrillo Landing Pageant, Cabrillo Marine Museum ☎(310) 548-7562. • **Festival of Masks**, Hancock County Park ☎(213) 937-5544. • **LA Philharmonic season** opens ☎(213) 972-7211. • **Oak Tree Meeting**, Santa Anita ☎(818) 574-7223. • **Grand National Irish Fair**, Northridge ☎(818) 885-2519. • **Sandcastle building contest**, Corona del Mar ☎(714) 644-8211.

NOVEMBER
Hollywood Christmas Parade, Hollywood ☎(213) 469-8311.
• **Dia de los Muertos**, Olvera St., LA. • **Death Valley Days**, Furnace Creek and Stovepipe Wells ☎(714) 786-2331. • **Annual "Doo Dah" parade**, Pasadena, local zanies romp through the streets in themeless, prizeless, judgeless, orderless march ☎(818) 795-3355.

DECEMBER
Annual 10k and Waiters/Waitresses 5K race, Beverly Hills ☎(213) 624-7300. • **Christmas Boat Parade**, Marina del Rey ☎(310) 822-0119. • **Las Posadas**, Mexican candlelit parade, Olvera St., LA.

Life in Los Angeles is by no means dull.
Its vitality comes from extraordinary contrasts.
It also has the energy . . . and the creative spirit . . .
of an unfinished city.
(Professor Frank McShane, Columbia University)

Sightseeing

LA: the districts and neighboring areas

Los Angeles fits no traditional notion of a city. To think of LA County as 82 towns, with 1,500 miles of freeway and 12,500 miles of paved streets, or of the city of LA as the country's second largest with a land area of 464 square miles, is almost inevitably to be overawed and overwhelmed. That is not the way Angelenos look at the place.

Rather they break it down, geographically and psychologically. Freeways replace conventional thoroughfares as the only manageable links between neighborhoods that were two days apart before cars replaced horses. Seemingly endless commercial strips run alongside or beneath the freeways, making it possible to spend what seems like two days crossing a city more than 52 miles across at one point, but barely half a mile wide on another axis.

These bizarre boundaries exist because Los Angeles flowed around what it could not flow over in its heyday of growth. Beverly Hills, Pasadena, Santa Monica and other incorporated cities were drawn in largely because to stay outside was to be denied water.

But few outsiders would claim to understand the complexity of today's local politics. It is probably best not to dwell too long on the detailed patchwork. The city can be understood more easily as six adjacent districts: **Downtown**, **Hollywood**, **Westside**, **Coastal**, **Valleys** and **Central**. Neighboring areas of interest are the **Mountains**, the **Desert**, the **Central Coast**, **Orange County** and **San Diego** (which is the subject of the second part of this book, starting on page 201).

That way, the potentially bewildering sprawl of LA and Southern California is broken down into more manageable areas — in much the same way that Angelenos themselves understand and inhabit the city and its neighboring areas.

DOWNTOWN *(map 6)*
12 miles E of the Pacific Ocean, within the area described by the wobbly trapezoid of the Harbor (SR-11), Hollywood (US-101) and Santa Monica (I-10) freeways, is the daytime center for business and civic activity. But it is not only that. As well as the **Civic Center** and the **commercial district**, it encompasses **Chinatown**, **Little Tokyo** and the historic Hispanic heart of the city, **El Pueblo de Los Angeles**. The heart of the heart is the **Plaza** (N Main St. and Paseo de la Plaza), the tree-shaded venue for annual Mexican festivities such as Cinco de

63

Mayo. Running into the Plaza is **Olvera St.**, re-created in 1930 as a Mexican marketplace/theme park. (See EL PUEBLO DE LOS ANGELES PARK.)

The surrounding area is rich in historically and architecturally significant buildings such as the Renaissance-style Masonic Temple, the Victorian Old Firehouse and Mission-style UNION PASSENGER STATION. The contemporary hub of Downtown Hispanic life is Broadway, which in its colorful, slightly seedy bustle is reminiscent of Tijuana, the Mexican border town to the S. Around N Broadway, CHINATOWN is an equally coherent ethnic minority enclave, with Chinese shops, restaurants and homes. Ethnic Chinese immigrants from Vietnam and Cambodia now contribute to the area's vitality. To the S, LITTLE TOKYO, around Central Ave. and 1st St., is a more orderly and contrived attraction, although no less culturally authentic.

The financial district lies to the S and W, centered around Flower St. It boasts some top-class hotels, several fine shopping arcades and restaurants, and is conveniently placed for the MUSIC CENTER OF LOS ANGELES, the MUSEUM OF CONTEMPORARY ART and the TEMPORARY CONTEMPORARY. The city is now engaged in its largest ever public works program: a $500-million doubling of the size of the Los Angeles Convention Center, making it the biggest on the West Coast. But after dark the district's streets are still somewhat desolate.

Farther S and W the terrain becomes more commercial, with the garment district, the wholesale flower market and manufacturing premises. Probably of most interest to visitors are a number of notable architectural landmarks, such as Robert Derrah's Coca Cola Building (at 1334 S Central Ave.), the Mayan Theater (at 1040 S Hill St.) and Julia Morgan's Spanish Mission Revival HERALD EXAMINER BUILDING (at 1111 S Broadway). Also of interest are EXPOSITION PARK with its great museums, and, as venues for sports and the arts, the MEMORIAL COLISEUM and the Shrine Auditorium.

HOLLYWOOD *(maps 4 & 5)*

As you would expect, Hollywood straddles the Hollywood Freeway, 101, taking in flatland in the S and foothills in the N. The HOLLYWOOD SIGN is still there on the S slopes of Mt. Lee, but Hollywood is no longer physically the movie capital of the world. Most of the big studios have moved to Burbank, the stars to Beverly Hills and Malibu, and the fabled intersection of Hollywood Blvd. and Vine St. ranges between tawdry and sleazy.

But a sustained effort to rehabilitate and revitalize **Hollywood Blvd.** is starting to work. In June 1991 the El Capitan Theater, where *Citizen Kane* had its world premiere, reopened after a $6-million remodeling. Also reopened in 1991 after renovation was the Silent Movie Theater near Fairfax. As another part of the Hollywood Redevelopment Plan, an 8-block stretch of the boulevard, including the El Capitan, has been named the "Cinema District." There are plans to remodel other historic theaters, recapture the glamor of the 1920s and '30s, and turn Hollywood Blvd. into a showcase for the entertainment industry.

But while there is some truth in the wisecrack that "Hollywood is the place where people from Iowa mistake each other for stars," the district is still rich in movie nostalgia. The heart of Hollywood Blvd., roughly between Vine and Sycamore, is designated a National Historic District, and much of its 1920s and '30s architecture is intact, along with MANN'S CHINESE THEATER and the WALK OF FAME. Movie studios, labs and agents are still in residence, as is the music industry, most visibly in the CAPITOL RECORDS TOWER.

The four parallel E-W boulevards, **Hollywood**, **Sunset**, **Santa Monica** and **Melrose**, apart from their daytime commercial activity, have become centers of vivid nightlife, with more than their fair share of fashionable hotels, restaurants, nightclubs, bookstores and galleries. Perhaps surprisingly, Hollywood is now the center of legitimate theater in LA, and the HOLLYWOOD BOWL remains one of the world's great natural amphitheaters.

The hills to the N, cut through by **Laurel** and **Nichols Canyons** and **Mulholland Dr.**, are much more prosperous but less interesting, save for their scenic beauty and the sometimes bizarre architectural taste of the literary and artistic inhabitants.

WESTSIDE *(map 1 B2)*

In a lop-sided rectangle W of Hollywood, S of Mulholland Dr., E of the San Diego Freeway 405, N of the Santa Monica Freeway 10 and bisected by Wilshire Blvd. running E-W, is the Westside, the area containing LA's ritziest, most affluent communities: **Beverly Hills**, **Bel Air**, **Westwood Village** and **Brentwood**. N of Wilshire they have the cleanest streets, the most perfectly manicured lawns, the lowest crime rate, the shiniest imported luxury cars, the best schools, the costliest stores, some of the finest restaurants, and hotels with a broad range of prices, beginning with expensive. But don't be daunted; there's no visa required or entry fee into this Monaco-like enclave of wealth and extravagance. In the southern part of Wilshire, things are more modest and restrained, becoming less polished to the S and E.

Among the residential communities, Beverly Hills, Bel Air and Brentwood lead in the mansion, swimming pool and exclusive country club stakes. The infrastructure reflects that; commercial activity is of the white-collar, nonpolluting kind, and everything is tightly regulated, even the dimensions of signboards. Consuming, and watching the sleek inhabitants consume, is the main leisure activity.

The stretch of Wilshire Blvd. running E-W into Beverly Hills from Downtown is an interesting and important example of the type of connective tissue that unifies LA. Toward the Downtown end, the focal points for visitors are the hotels; near Beverly Hills, it is the museums, such as the LOS ANGELES COUNTY MUSEUM OF ART and the recently opened $250-million ARMAND HAMMER MUSEUM OF ART, and the restaurants.

At the SW corner of Beverly Hills, **Century City** used to be 20th Century Fox's back lot. In the 1960s, developers threw up clusters of high-rise condominiums, making it a rather soulless place. More recent high-rise office buildings have done little to humanize it, though a new movie theater and restaurant complex, the ABC ENTERTAINMENT CENTER and Century Plaza Towers, has enlivened its nightlife. Other redeeming features are Century City Shopping Center, a pleasant enough shopping mall with some good restaurants, and a handful of theaters.

Westwood Village, near the UNIVERSITY OF CALIFORNIA, LOS ANGELES (UCLA), has fared equally poorly at the hands of developers. But it boasts the highest concentration of first-run movie theaters, and the nearby campus adds a frisson of youthful energy, useful restaurants with prices students can afford, and a good choice of stores selling sports equipment, books and collegiate fashions. Also of note is the Westwood Memorial Cemetery, where Marilyn Monroe and Natalie Wood are buried.

COASTAL *(map 10 I5-6, and map opposite)*

Between the exclusive Malibu colony in the NW and the major port city of Long Beach in the SE is "surfurbia," the coastal communities that make LA an extra-special city. Traveling from N to S, they are **Malibu**, **Pacific Palisades**, **Santa Monica**, **Venice**, **Marina del Rey**, **Manhattan Beach**, **Hermosa Beach**, **Redondo Beach** and **Palos Verdes**. Although they all nuzzle the Pacific, and most are accessible along the Pacific Coast Highway, all are evidently different.

Forget the bogus maps sold along Hollywood Blvd. Where the movie stars really live is in Malibu. However, there isn't much to interest the visitor at the so-called Malibu Colony; the beach is private, screened from the highway by often nondescript homes tightly packed together townhouse-style. You are no more likely to see a Hollywood idol than one of the luxury homes fall down a crumbling cliff. It happens occasionally but not very often.

Few of the restaurants are good enough to warrant a special journey, but there are other attractions. The drive down from **Woodland Hills** along winding **Topanga Canyon Blvd.**, a 1960s hippie haven, is delightful; the J. PAUL GETTY MUSEUM is at the S edge of the town; Will Rogers' old house is also now a museum, within the 187-acre WILL ROGERS STATE HISTORIC PARK; and the public beach is a good one with excellent surfing.

To the E and high above the highway is **Pacific Palisades**, the district with the highest average income in LA. Apart from its wealth, the most noteworthy fact about the area is that it was originally founded as a community by the Methodist Church, and many of the streets are named after its bishops.

To the S, **Santa Monica** is a different story. One of the most engaging places in LA, it is easily reached from the E via the Santa Monica Freeway 10 and the Wilshire and Santa Monica Blvds. Efforts by residents and the city council to keep down rents earned it the nickname "The People's Republic of Santa Monica." The people seem to be running Santa Monica pretty well.

Just a stone's throw from Santa Monica's original downtown is one of the finest beaches in all of Southern California. On a fine day, up to a million people will descend upon it. SANTA MONICA PIER is slightly worn at the edges but is everything a pier should be, with all the familiar diversions from popcorn to carousels. There are good hotels, with a welcome range of affordable prices, near and on the beach, excellent to extraordinary restaurants throughout town, and good shopping both

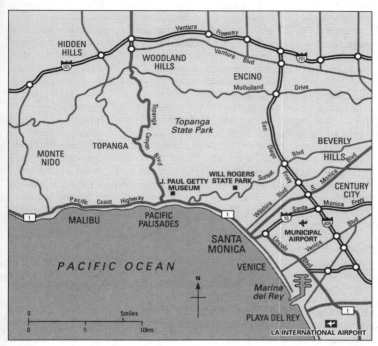

downtown and along gentrified **Main St.**, and along the new 3-block pedestrian thoroughfare **Third Street Promenade**. Clean sea breezes and an easy-going atmosphere continue to attract a population of wealthy families and upwardly mobile young professionals.

To the s is **Venice**, begun as a sincere attempt to imitate the best of the original. In the early years of the century, 16 miles of canals were built, but somewhere along the way VENICE took a wrong turn, or maybe a right turn, and decided that the counter-culture was probably more fun than medieval culture. Ever since, it has attracted the eccentric and the exhibitionist, most of whom seem to turn out for the amusement of visitors and each other along **Ocean Front Walk**. Apart from this street theater, Venice has some excellent restaurants, noteworthy buildings, pleasant narrow streets, countless artists and a few surviving canals.

Marina del Rey, s of Venice, is yet another part of LA where what ought to be fantasy functions as opulent reality. Sited around a man-made marina with moorings for 10,000 pleasure craft, the area has good hotels and motels, excellent beaches and water sports, and is supremely convenient for LAX to the s and Downtown to the E. The only drawback is that everything seems too good to be true.

Beyond LAX is **Manhattan Beach**, along with its two neighbors to the s, **Hermosa Beach** and **Redondo Beach**, the spiritual home of beach culture. There are beautiful homes, beautiful beaches and beautiful

67

people intent on enjoying themselves to the utmost, along with relaxing, reasonably priced hotels and a few notable restaurants.

Farther s is the **Palos Verdes Peninsula**, an exclusive dormitory community set precariously on terraced hills above steep coastal cliffs. The audacity of the civil engineering and the physical drama of the place warrant a visit. Additional attraction are Lloyd Wright's WAYFARER'S CHAPEL (a monument to Swedish theologian and mystic Emanuel Swedenborg) and some splendid whale-watching spots.

Around the peninsula, reached by either the Pacific Coast Highway or the Harbor Freeway 110, **San Pedro** is what one expects of a major international port. But amid the docks and cargo containers there are some interesting relics of the 19thC, an intriguing fishing pier and good fresh seafood right off the boats. Many of the fishermen are of Greek, Portuguese or Yugoslav origin, and their cultural input enlivens the town. San Pedro also has an embarkation pier for ferry cruises to **Catalina Island** (see page 165), directly beneath the Vincent Thomas Bridge to Terminal Island and Long Beach, reached by taking the Harbor Blvd. exit from the Harbor Freeway.

Finally, at the southern tip of LA County down Freeway 710, is **Long Beach** (see page 168), a major city in its own right which has much to recommend it to the visitor. At its southern end is **Naples**, a human-scale, Italianate community crisscrossed with canals. The downtown area is an unappetizing study in high-rise building, but there are good hotels, and elsewhere there are notable museums, such as the Long Beach Museum of Art, some historic landmarks, and the two biggest tourist attractions: the retired luxury liner *Queen Mary* and Howard Hughes' extraordinary airplane *Spruce Goose*. Equally unusual are the offshore oil wells cunningly disguised as tropical islands.

VALLEYS *(map 10 I6)*

North of the Santa Monica Mountains, running W-E between Ventura Freeway 101 and the Simi Valley 118 and Foothill 210 Freeways, is the **San Fernando Valley**, known locally as "the Valley." To the E, bounded by mountains to the N and hills to the S, and encircled by the Glendale 2, Foothill 210 and Santa Monica 10 freeways, is the **San Gabriel Valley**. These are the Valleys, with dozens of overlapping communities whose inhabitants have created Middle America with palm trees.

What characterizes the Valleys above all is that even by LA standards they are big; they make Hollywood seem almost dinky in comparison. The Valley covers 220 square miles. When LA annexed the San Fernando Valley in 1915 it more than doubled its size. Parts of the 4,000-acre GRIFFITH PARK overlook the Fernando Valley floor. Both valleys are predominantly white, middle-class and residential, with pockets of entertainment and hi-tech industries, and their main thoroughfares, such as Ventura and Colorado Blvds., serve as the axis for a giant grid sprawling for miles in all directions.

Residents would disagree, but there is little to help the visitor distinguish between the various merged-together towns. Strung out E-W along

Ventura Blvd., **Studio City**, **Sherman Oaks**, **Encino**, **Tarzana** (named after Edgar Rice Burroughs' jungle hero) and **Woodland Hills** have similar tracts of homes, similar shopping malls, and a similar choice of restaurants and motels. Much the same is true of other nearby districts such as **Van Nuys** and **North Hollywood**.

It is less true farther E. The characters of **Universal City** and **Burbank** are colored by the highly visible presence of major movie and TV studios, notably Burbank, Disney, NBC and Universal. The Studios Tour at UNIVERSAL STUDIOS, which includes a behind-the-scenes look at movie-making, is one of LA's must-do attractions.

Neighboring **Glendale**, meanwhile, has at least two claims to fame: the biggest community of Armenians outside Armenia, and the rolling acres of FOREST LAWN, the one-of-a-kind cemetery that at times seems like a theme park for the deceased. In addition, there are some goodish restaurants patronized by locals and the media folk, and a few outstanding hotels. But apart from the tours of the studios, the main attraction of this part of the Valley is that it is a less costly base than Westside and less nerve-wracking than Hollywood, yet, thanks to Highways 101, 134 and 405, it is within reach of just about anywhere.

East down Freeway 134/210 are the communities of the **San Gabriel Valley**, once famed for its groves of oranges, lemons and walnuts. **Pasadena** is the most well established and defined: old money, attractive homes and gardens, a sedate, cultured atmosphere, with some of LA's best museums and botanic gardens, the best theater company (the Pasadena Playhouse — see page 142), many interesting buildings and good restaurants, and pleasant walks through the well-preserved architecture of **Old Pasadena**. Last but not least, every year on New Year's Day Pasadena plays host to the stunning Tournament of Roses.

To the SE, and even wealthier, is **San Marino**, once the fiefdom of tycoon Henry E. Huntington whose enduring legacy is the magnificent HUNTINGTON LIBRARY, ART GALLERY AND BOTANICAL GARDENS. Almost due S is **Monterey Park**, increasingly know as "Little Taiwan." The area is the most favored destination for middle-class Chinese immigrants, and the restaurants and shops reflect this. Of interest elsewhere in the San Gabriel Valley is Santa Anita racetrack, E of Pasadena in **Arcadia**, and the LA State and County Arboretum, also in Arcadia.

CENTRAL LOS ANGELES *(map 1 C3)*

South of Santa Monica Freeway 10, E and N of San Diego Freeway 405, is Central Los Angeles, taking in **East LA** and **South Central LA**. The former, with **Whittier Blvd.** as its main artery, has a population that is 90-percent Hispanic in origin. The latter, running S from **Watts**, birthplace of Eldridge Cleaver, has LA's largest African-American community. Sadly both areas have crime rates well above the average and, while most citizens are as law-abiding as anyone in LA, visitors are often deterred by reports of drug-related killings and gang warfare. Although sometimes exaggerated, the reports are usually true. But it would be wrong to characterize Central LA as a war zone; as a rule the violence is localized and selective.

And there are good reasons to visit. Watts is home to the extraordinary WATTS TOWERS, and to the w is **Hollywood Park**, venue for horse-racing and site of the 17,000-seat GREAT WESTERN FORUM, where, in season, the LA Lakers and the LA Kings play basketball and ice hockey respectively. Hispanic East LA has good fresh-food markets, inexpensive restaurants, *mariachis* and splendid murals that bring even more color to its streets.

East of Whittier Blvd. is the town of **Whittier**, birthplace of former President Richard Nixon. The local Chamber of Commerce can provide a map of Nixonian sights. Farther E in La Puente is one of the city's priceless, vulgar, only-in-LA architectural landmarks, the DONUT HOLE, a snack-bar where customers drive through two gigantic donuts to place and collect their orders.

MOUNTAINS (*maps 3 B1-4*B5 and 10I6)

Two mountain ranges contain Los Angeles: the **San Gabriels** to the N and E and the **Santa Monicas** to the NW. The Santa Monicas run E-W for about 50 miles right through the city, from the Los Angeles River to the Oxnard plain, and are easily accessed via Mulholland Dr. Ranging up to 2,000 feet, the largely uninhabited chaparral-clad hills, administered by the National Park Service, offer stunning views and excellent trekking, though creeping residential development makes them something less than pristine wilderness. Near the junction of Freeways 5 and 14 are a number of man-made attractions, notably the 260-acre SIX FLAGS MAGIC MOUNTAIN amusement park with its breathtaking rides.

The San Gabriels to the E are wilder, much higher (up to 10,000 feet), and less accessible. The major routes from the S are the Angeles Crest Highway, the Angeles Forest Highway and San Gabriel Canyon. There are excellent campgrounds, and access to hiking through vast unspoiled areas. From the 5,710-foot summit of **Mt. Wilson** it is possible to overlook LA as far as the Pacific. Farther E are even higher peaks, such as the 10,080-foot **Mt. Baldy**, which offers exciting skiing in winter and climbing at other times.

DESERT (*map 10 H6-I7*)

Barely 100 years ago much of what is now lush Los Angeles was desert. Today the city's hinterlands to the E, SE and NE, in fact one-third of California, and almost all of neighboring Nevada, remains just that — desert. Of most interest are the **Colorado**, low desert; the **Mojave**, high desert; and the **Trans Sierra**, a mix of mountains and basins including **Death Valley.**

Some areas are little more than relentless badlands: flat, arid and with little charm beyond their possible novelty. But the high desert of **Antelope Valley**, above the San Gabriel Mountains in northern LA County, has some attractive parks and a 2,000-acre poppy reserve where the state's official flower grows wild.

Farther E in the San Bernardino Mountains are two of LA's most popular playgrounds, exclusive **Lake Arrowhead** and rather less exclusive **Big Bear Lake**. The Mojave, to the E and NE, is overlooked by the ragged peaks of the Sierra Nevada. Highway 15, running N and E from

San Bernardino to **Las Vegas** (see page 182), gives a taste of the desert's stark realities, and encounters with them by pioneers are fossilized in the ghost town of Calico. Due N of Route 15 is **Death Valley**, which in the cooler months is a not-to-be-missed experience. To the S, straddling the high and low deserts, is the **Joshua Tree National Monument** (see page 176), an 870-square-mile reserve populated almost exclusively by the giant, curiously-shaped Yucca trees named "Joshua" by Mormon pioneers, and the rare desert bighorn sheep.

South of the Joshua Tree, just off the San Bernardino Freeway 10 and roughly two hours' drive from Downtown LA, is the opulent oasis resort of **Palm Springs** (see page 175), dubbed by enthusiasts "Golf capital of the world." Californian hyperbole notwithstanding, they could be right; Palm Springs hosts over 100 tournaments a year. It is, all in all, a case of Beverly Hills in the desert, with the bonuses of clean air, hot springs, innumerable tennis courts, and a swimming pool for every five residents. In keeping with the town's upscale image, restaurants, shopping and cultural diversions are all topnotch. High season is November to March; April to May, and September to October, are the next most popular times of the year to visit.

Thirty miles S of Palm Springs in San Diego County is the **Anza-Borrego Desert State Park**, $\frac{1}{2}$ million acres notable for striking rock formations. To the E lies the **Salton Sea** (see page 177), at 30 miles in length California's largest lake and, at 235 feet below sea level, probably its saltiest. Fishing, bird-watching and boating are the principal attractions.

CENTRAL COAST *(map 9 H4-10 I5)*

From the northern extremity of LA as far as newspaper tycoon William Randolph Hearst's magnificent folly at **San Simeon** runs the Central Coast. Easily accessible via Highway 101 and the Pacific Coast Highway 1, the coast is characterized by wonderful beaches, dramatic cliff-top drives and mile after mile of unspoiled countryside.

Of the major towns from S to N, picture-postcard-pretty **Santa Barbara** (see page 178), fronting a 5-mile-long sandy beach and fringed by the Santa Ynez mountains, is a well-heeled study in Mission-style architecture and the laid-back California way of life. The town has just about everything by way of outdoor pursuits, attractive lodgings and restaurants, and a lively cultural life.

Santa Barbara's own historic Spanish mission is attractive enough, but some 50 miles NE, along Highway 1, is **La Purísima**, possibly the most beautiful of California's 21 missions. Between the two, in the Santa Ynez Valley, is the surprise of **Solvang**, translated as "sunny field," a quaint Danish village of startling architectural and atmospheric authenticity founded by immigrants from Denmark in the early years of the century.

Farther N, set against the steep coastal hills of the Santa Lucia Mountains and at an intersection of Highways 1 and 101, is **San Luis Obispo**, local center for the nearby ranching country and some fine wineries developed in recent years (see page 197). The town, a pleasant half-way stop between LA and San Francisco, is a good base for exploring Avila Beach, Morro Bay, San Simeon and other shoreside places.

Seven miles s of San Luis Obispo, **Avila Beach** is an unusually compact resort town, with fishing from the pier, charter boats, golf and volleyball on the white sandy beach. **Morro Bay**, 12 miles NW, is a working fishing port noted for its clams and the 576-foot volcanic rock formation known as Morro Rock. Nearby are two state parks with camping, hiking and golf.

Hearst Castle, to the NW, contrasts sharply with such wholesome recreations. Newspaper baron William Randolph Hearst's massive hilltop retreat serves primarily to show what colossal amounts of money can achieve when married to supreme bad taste. But there is nothing quite like it anywhere (save perhaps "Xanadu" in the movie *Citizen Kane,* a thinly-veiled fiction on Hearst's life and times), and it is now the **Hearst San Simeon State Historical Monument** (see page 178), which is open to the public. Visitors will be able to dine out for years to come on a day spent there.

ORANGE COUNTY *(map 10 J6, and ORANGE COUNTY map on page 170)*
South of LA County, running N-S along the coast between Seal Beach and San Clemente, and E as far inland as the Santa Ana Mountains, Orange County (see page 169) is the second most populous county in California, and often cited as its most conservative. Most of the fragrant orange groves were torn up between 1955 and 1965 to make way for residential and industrial development, and nowadays the county is best know for its wealth, its exclusive beach communities, and Disneyland, its top attraction and the catalyst for Orange County's recent spectacular growth.

The entire county has a web of freeways and major boulevards, and lies within easy reach of LA via the Pacific Coast Highway 1 and the two N-S freeways, San Diego 405 and Santa Ana 5. It is also well served both by bus services and Amtrak. Around the I-5 between Buena Park and Anaheim, **Disneyland** and **Knott's Berry Farm** (see pages 166 and 172) anchor a series of parks and entertainments. However, apart from these, the industrial-residential towns of Orange County's flat northern interior are of limited interest to visitors.

To the SW via Harbor Blvd., **Newport Beach** (see page 173) is the most fashionable playground in Orange County. Marinas, beachside homes, shops and restaurants are crowded onto a long, low-lying peninsula, which is said to be the most affluent concentration of boat people anywhere on the Pacific coast. The mainland shore and man-made islands inside the small bay have more of the same. Adjoining **Corona del Mar** is the tennis and golf suburb. The beach and the seafood at Newport Beach are first-rate, there are comfortable hotels and motels, and the area is within easy reach of Disneyland and John Wayne-Orange County Airport.

Farther s down the coast and more remote, **Laguna Beach** began as an artists' colony and, although few artists can now afford to live there, it retains some of the flavor, not least in the **Laguna Museum of Art**. Shopping streets lined with galleries and craft studios, and a coastline of coves, rocky promontories and sandy beaches, give it the feel of a small southern European seaside town. The **Laguna Hills** behind the town offer some marvelous views.

Other beach towns N and S beg not to be overlooked: **Huntington Beach** for surfing; **Capistrano** for its beach; **Dana Point** (named after 19thC sailor-author Richard Dana) for beaches and boating, and The Ritz-Carlton, Laguna Niguel, consistently voted the best resort hotel in the United States; and **San Clemente** (best known from the days of Richard Nixon's Western White House), also for its beach.

Just off the I-5, E of Dana Point, is **San Juan Capistrano** and its mission, famed for returning swallows, tranquility and ruggedly beautiful buildings dating from 1777. It is said to be California's oldest. The commercial possibilities are not lost on the heritage industry, and the area around the mission is swamped with gift stores. Nevertheless, San Juan Capistrano is generally thought to be a must for visitors keen on exploring California's past.

SAN DIEGO *(maps 7-8 and 11 J7)*

Down the Golden State Freeway 5, 120 miles S of LA, San Diego is too often regarded as the big city on the right that visitors pass en route to **Tijuana** (see page 185), 20 miles farther S. If it comes to a case of either/or, most visitors would be best advised to opt for the stylish, manicured and monied Southern Californian city. On offer is a unique combination of a Riviera climate, chic beach resorts, fine lodgings and shopping, a lively gastronomic and cultural life, several major visitor attractions, and a well-developed civic pride.

San Diego forms the subject of the final part of this book, starting on page 201.

Sights and places of interest

Like Los Angeles itself, the city's visitor attractions are spread out. This need not be daunting. Rather it calls for a little more planning and map-reading than a more compact city would require. And it is often wise to telephone ahead to make sure that the place(s) you want to visit are going to be open or, in the case of world-famous institutions such as the Getty Museum, to make the advance reservation upon which they insist.

One straightforward way to tackle the wide range of attractions scattered across Greater LA is to select a major boulevard, such as Sunset, Santa Monica or Wilshire, and target destinations located on or near it.

Sights listed by area

★   Recommended sight   ☆ Worth a detour
◅€ Good view
血 Building of architectural interest
✹ Special interest for children

CENTRAL
Aerospace Building 血 ✹
California Afro-American
  Museum
California State Museum
  of Science and Industry ☆ ✹
Exposition Park
Great Western Forum
Los Angeles County Museum
  of Natural History ✹
Memorial Coliseum and
  Sports Arena
Mitsubishi IMAX Theater ✹
Watts Towers ★

COASTAL
Gehry House 血
J. Paul Getty Museum 血 ☆ ◅€
Santa Monica Pier ✹
Venice ✹
Wayfarers' Chapel 血
Will Rogers State Historic
  Park ◅€

DOWNTOWN
Bradbury Building 血
Chinatown(s)
City Hall 血 ◅€

Dodger Stadium
Echo Park ✹
Elysian Park ✹ ◅€
Hebrew Union College
  and Skirball Museum ✹
Herald Examiner Building
  血
Heritage Square 血
Japanese American National
  Museum
Koreatown
Little Tokyo
Los Angeles Children's
  Museum ✹
Los Angeles Times Building
Macarthur Park ✹
Museum of Contemporary
  Art 血 ★
Music Center of Los Angeles
  血
Olvera Street
El Pueblo de Los Angeles
  State Historic Park 血
St Vincent de Paul Roman
  Catholic Church
The Temporary
  Contemporary 血
Union Passenger Station 血

But remember that the distances and driving time between attractions can be long. So, be selective rather than over-ambitious.

As is only to be expected in the USA's Entertainment Capital, LA's rich mix of sights and attractions is almost always welcoming and well managed. There's more history than one has the right to expect in such a youthful metropolis, there are the echoes and the substance of Hollywood's dream machines, and there is an almost embarrassing wealth of fine art, ancient and modern, to be viewed. Culture, including imaginative architecture, is high on the agenda of those well-heeled city fathers who aim to have LA taken seriously as a major world city.

The following A to Z pages list an extensive selection of LA's sights: the most fascinating, revealing, exciting, unmissable, and more.

EAST LA
Donut Hole ✷

HOLLYWOOD
Barnsdall Park
Capitol Records Building
Farmers Market
Hollyhock House
Hollywood Bowl
Hollywood Memorial
  Cemetery
Hollywood Sign ★
Los Angeles Municipal Art
  Gallery
Mann's Chinese Theater 🏛 ★
George C. Page Museum
  of La Brea Discoveries ✷
Paramount Studios
Sunset Strip
Tail o' the Pup 🏛
Television shows
Walk of Fame ★

VALLEYS
Gene Autry Western
  Heritage Museum ✷
Burbank Studios ✷
Descanso Gardens
Forest Lawn Memorial Park
Gamble House 🏛 ★
Greek Theater
Griffith Observatory,
  Planetarium and Laserium
  🏛 ✷ ◁€
Griffith Park ★ ✷ ◁€

Huntington Library, Art
  Gallery and Botanical
  Gardens ★
Los Angeles State and
  County Arboretum
Los Angeles Zoo ✷
Mission San Fernando Rey
  de España
Mission San Gabriel Arcángel
National Broadcasting
  Co. Television Studio ✷
Pacific Asia Museum 🏛
Norton Simon Museum
  of Art ★
Six Flags Magic Mountain ✷
Southwest Museum 🏛
Television shows
Travel Town ✷
Universal Studios ★ ✷

WESTSIDE
ABC Entertainment Center
Academy of Motion Picture
  Arts and Sciences
Armand Hammer Museum
  of Art 🏛
Hancock Park
Los Angeles County Museum
  of Art 🏛 ★ ✷
Miracle Mile
Pacific Design Center 🏛
Virginia Robinson Gardens
Rodeo Drive ★
University of California,
  Los Angeles

GETTING THERE

As ever, the best way to get around is by car. Attractions almost always have their own parking facilities for visitors. On the rare occasions that they do not, there is usually parking space to be found nearby.

For those who don't or won't drive there are alternatives. Buses of the **RTD** (Southern California Rapid Transit District) provide comprehensive, if slow and infrequent, coverage of LA and adjacent areas, and among scheduled stops are around a hundred visitor attractions. Free brochures detailing services are available from RTD Customer Centers.

The Downtown area is served by **DASH** (Downtown Area Short Hop), whose minibus routes pass major hotels, shopping districts, and some of Downtown's sights and attractions. Both DASH and RTD are inexpensive.

Pricier, but more predictable and usually including an informed and amusing commentary, are sightseeing tours. These can be a good way for first-time visitors to orient themselves. Though they obviously lack the flexibility of self-guided tours, they can be a comfortable and efficient way of seeing at least some of what LA has to offer.

HOW TO USE THIS A TO Z SECTION

In the following pages, LA's sights are arranged alphabetically. Look for the ★ symbol against the outstanding, not-to-be-missed sights. If you have a little more time, look for the ☆ symbol, indicating places that in our view are definitely worth a visit.

Places of special interest for children (♣) and with outstanding views (◀€) are also indicated, as are buildings of architectural interest (Ⅲ). **For a full explanation of symbols, see page 7.**

A classified list of visitor attractions with headings in this chapter, arranged by area, appears on the two pages preceding this one.

Some lesser sights do not have their own entries but are mentioned within other entries: it is easiest to look for these in the INDEX.

Bold type is mostly employed to indicate monuments, buildings or other highlights. Places mentioned without addresses and opening times are often described more fully elsewhere: check whether they are **cross-references** to other headings, which are printed in SMALL CAPITALS.

LA's sights A to Z

ABC ENTERTAINMENT CENTER

Ave. of the Stars, Century City (directly S of Beverly Hills, between Santa Monica Blvd. and Pico Blvd.). Map ***3****D2.*

The center contains the **Shubert Theater**, movie theaters, nightclubs, fine restaurants, an astonishing car dealership and other commercial enterprises. ABC's television studios are elsewhere (see TELEVISION SHOWS).

Just to the E of the ABC Center are Minoru Yamasaki's **Century Plaza Towers** (1969-75). Two tall towers, each of the same height and with the same triangular base, they are regarded as the hub of Century City. Certainly they are more noteworthy than most of the undistinguished Modernist hulks nearby. Watch out for them from the Santa Monica Freeway; at sunset they resemble nothing so much as twin pillars of gold.

Opposite is the semicircular **Century Plaza Hotel** (1966), also by Yamasaki, and much favored by Ronald Reagan during his Presidency (see WHERE TO STAY). The hotel has a valuable collection of artworks on public display. Ask for a catalog.

ACADEMY OF MOTION PICTURE ARTS AND SCIENCES

8949 Wilshire Blvd. (Wilshire Blvd., E of Doheny Dr.) ☎(310) 652-8526. Map ***3****D4. Library open Mon-Tues, Thurs-Fri 9am-5pm. Closed Wed, weekends, major holidays.*

Los Angeles' most important Academy — the one that awards the annual Oscars that can make or break careers in motion pictures. In addition, the superb 1,000-seat theater stages occasional public screenings, there are changing lobby exhibitions, and the Academy library is unequaled in movie literature.

AEROSPACE BUILDING 🏛

Frank Gehry's enormous hangar is part of the complex of displays at the **California State Museum of Science and Industry** in EXPOSITION PARK.

ARMAND HAMMER MUSEUM OF ART 🏛

10899 Wilshire Blvd., Westwood (Wilshire Blvd. and Westwood Blvd.) ☎(310) 443-7000. Map ***3****D1 Open Mon, Wed-Fri noon-7pm; Sat-Sun 11am-6pm. Closed Tues, major holidays.*

The legendary wheeler-dealer and Occidental oilman died in 1990, less than a month after the museum opened. But the museum is everything he hoped it would be. The collection, housed in a $100-million striped marble cube designed by New York architect Edward Larrabee Barnes, covers five centuries of European art, including 10,000 works by the French satirist Daumier, rare writings by Leonardo da Vinci, Old Masters and Impressionist works from Hammer's private collection. Even if you are short of time, it is worth a visit just to view the building and to see Van Gogh's *Hospital at Saint-Remy* and Gustave Moreau's *Salome Dancing Before Herod.*

GENE AUTRY WESTERN HERITAGE MUSEUM

4700 Zoo Dr., Griffith Park (via Zoo Dr. exit from Ventura Freeway/SR-134 or Golden State Freeway/I-5) ☎*(213) 460-5698. Map 1B2* ⬛ ⚹ ☕ 𝒳 *(for information* ☎*(213) 667-2000)* ▆ ━ *Open Tues-Sun 10am-5pm. Closed Mon; Thanksgiving; Dec 25; Jan 1.*

Among recent additions to Los Angeles's heritage industry, the museum, located in GRIFFITH PARK, explores the history and legends of the American West, although it probably owes rather more to Hollywood imaginings than tooth-and-claw reality. Visitors are invited to "Return to those exciting days of yesteryear when radio, motion pictures, and television featured good guys and bad guys in a struggle to win the West." No relativism or political correctness here.

Still, the showmanship is faultless. Exhibits, appropriately, are designed by Walt Disney Imagineering, and organized into separate "spirits" — of discovery; of opportunity; of conquest; of community; of the cowboy; of romance; of imagination. Films and presentations, with dazzling special effects, are offered in the museum's two theaters. Among the artworks on show are Thomas Moran's *Mountain of the Holy Cross,* Guy Deel's *Spirits of the West* mural, plus work by Frederic Remington, Charley Russell, Albert Bierstadt and others.

Watch out for movie cowboy Tom Mix's Stetson. This spotless white hat is an important relic of Hollywood's iconography of the old West. The cowboy kitsch is reflected in the museum building, a squat, tan and ocher affair, with stucco walls and red roof tiles, best described as Post-Modern Mission Revival. The local chapter of the American Institute of Architects awarded it a lemon in their oranges and lemons guide to the best and worst of recent LA architecture.

BARNSDALL PARK

4800 Hollywood Blvd. (NW of Downtown, two blocks w of Vermont Ave.). Map 5B7. There are two points of artistic interest in the park. **Hollyhock House** *(* ☎*(213) 662-7272* ⬛ 𝒳 ━ *open Tues, Thurs 10am-1pm, also first and third Sat and first Sun of each month noon-3pm)* was Frank Lloyd Wright's first (1921) Los Angeles private building, commissioned by oil heiress Aline Barnsdall. It has been restored to its original condition and is used as a residence and cultural center. The **Los Angeles Municipal Art Gallery** *(* ☎*(213) 485-4581* ⬛ 𝒳 ━ *open Tues-Sun 12.30-5pm, closed Mon, major hols)* has a lively program of changing exhibitions of contemporary art and films by Southern Californians.

BRADBURY BUILDING ▥

Downtown at 304 S Broadway ☎*(213) 489-1411. Map 6D9* ⬛ ━ *Open Mon-Sat 10am-6pm. Closed Sun.*

This is one of the few surviving examples of Victorian architecture in Downtown LA, and the building's plain, only slightly Romanesque brick exterior hides a magical interior, thought by some to be among the most thrilling spaces in North America.

The most striking feature of the five-story-high building is its magnificently detailed central atrium, lined with ornate iron railings around tiered open balconies and rising to a skylight 100 feet above. Staircases and floors are of marble, the tiling was handmade in Mexico, the walls are of yellow glazed brick and the paneling of rich polished hardwoods. The two open-cage elevators are remarkable, as is the quality of the light filtered through the skylight.

Built in 1893 for Louis Bradbury, who made his fortune in Mexican silver mining, and designed by George Herbert Wyman, the Bradbury is often used as a movie location, most famously in *Bladerunner,* a futuristic LA nightmare.

BURBANK STUDIOS
4000 Warner Blvd., Burbank (four blocks s of Ventura Freeway/SR-134 via Olive Ave.) ☎*(818) 954-1744. Map* **1**B2 ▆ ✱ 𝒦 *compulsory, by appointment only (reserve 1 week in advance), limited to 12 people: Mon-Fri 10am, 10.30am, 2pm, 2.30pm in summer; 10am, 2pm in winter; no children under 10* 🎥 ⊷ *Closed weekends, major holidays.*

Warner Bros. and Columbia Pictures offer highly instructive two-hour tours showing day-to-day work on a movie set and sound stage at their shared premises. For an extra fee, and by separate appointment, visitors may eat with actors and technicians in a company restaurant.

CALIFORNIA AFRO-AMERICAN MUSEUM
The history, art and culture of the Afro-American community in LA is celebrated at this museum in EXPOSITION PARK.

CAPITOL RECORDS BUILDING
1750 Vine St., Hollywood (just N of legendary Hollywood and Vine intersection). Map **5**B6.

Not open to the public, but visitors are likely to notice and wonder about this 14-story building, especially in December when it is lit up like a Christmas tree. Built in 1954, the world's first circular office building looks like a stack of 45rpm records with a stylus on top. It was meant to: what could be more appropriate for a record company's HQ? Younger visitors, brought up on CDs and digital audio tape, will probably be completely baffled.

CALIFORNIA STATE MUSEUM OF SCIENCE AND INDUSTRY ☆
A hands-on museum for children young and old: everything from animal husbandry to aerospace. See EXPOSITION PARK.

CHINATOWN(S)
New Chinatown: centered around 700-1000 N Broadway in between N Alameda, Yale, Bernard and Ord Sts. Map **6**D9.

Southern California's Chinese community dates back to gold rush days, but "Old" Chinatown on Alameda was displaced in 1930 by the construction of Union Station. The "New" Chinatown recognized the tourist potential of chinoiserie, and the exaggerated architectural forms — all sweeping tiled roofs, elaborate decoration and pagoda-style telephone booths — reflect those early theme-park decisions. **Gin Ling**

Way pedestrian mall running between Broadway and Hill St. has the best examples.

However, Chinatown is much more than that. It is the cultural and commercial center for some 20,000 people of Chinese ancestry who live and work in the area, and many more throughout Southern California. The shops, markets, restaurants and recreational facilities aim first and foremost to serve them. But visitors are welcome to wander, browse, eat and shop, or to take in the colorful celebrations that mark the Chinese New Year.

"Even Newer" Chinatown
Monterey Park, around Atlantic Blvd., bounded by San Bernadino Freeway/I-10 to N, Pomona Freeway/I-60 to S and Long Beach Freeway/I-710 to W. Map 1C3.

Although by no means such a uniform or concentrated community as Downtown's Chinatown, in recent years Monterey Park has won the sobriquet "Little Taipei" as a result of its popularity with immigrants from Taiwan. As in Chinatown proper, the area's shops, restaurants, even video rental outlets and newsstands, reflect the population shift. Less visually interesting than Chinatown, but some excellent eating.

CITY HALL   🏛
200 N Spring St. (Downtown, between 1st St. and Temple St.) ☎(213) 485-2121. Map 6D9 ▣ ◂€ ✗ by reservation only (see below for details). Observation deck open Mon-Fri 8am-1pm.

From its completion in 1928 until height restrictions were lifted in 1957, the 454-foot, 28-story tower of Albert C. Martin's monumental building was the city's tallest. Today it is dwarfed by taller modern buildings but retains its architectural and symbolic importance.

An image of the building appears on official documents, LAPD badges and in countless TV and movie dramas: those of us who were conscious in the 1950s will remember *Dragnet*. Drivers on the nearby Harbor, Hollywood and Santa Ana freeways still take their downtown bearings from it. Clearly, there was no serious question of the cash-strapped City failing to find the money to fund the recent painstaking renovation of this old trouper.

When it was built it was described as "Italian Classic." But the building itself is such an amalgam of borrowed styles that its architectural progenitors are hard to pin down: Greek here, a Romanesque forecourt there, a Byzantine rotunda, part skyscraper, part Classical temple, topped with a pyramid, and all adding up to what might be dubbed Hollywood Metropolitan. LA's ideology was inscribed onto it . . . "The city came into being to preserve life, it exists for the good life."

Certainly it is authentically Californian. The builders took the conscious decision to use materials from within the State: California granite for cladding, mortar using sand from each county, cement from each cement factory, water from each and every mission, bronze doors cast from California ores. Inside are marble columns and the four-story rotunda, inlaid with colorful mosaics. The flamboyantly patterned floor can be viewed from the balcony that rings it.

The 45-minute guided tour is a useful introduction to LA and Califor-

City Hall

nia, but reservations must be made two weeks ahead. No reservations are needed for the 27th-floor **observation deck**, which, on a clear day, affords a spectacular 360° view of the city. Exterior views of City Hall are most striking at night, when the building is tastefully illuminated.

DESCANSO GARDENS

1418 Descanso Dr., La Canada (via Verdugo Blvd. from either Glendale Freeway/SR-2 or Foothill Freeway/I-210) ☎*(818) 790-5571. Map* **1B3** 📧 ✗*MI on weekend afternoons* 🚻 💺 *Open 9am-5pm. Closed Dec 25. Persons under 18 must be with an adult. Pets, radios and bicycles not permitted.*

The 165 acres of oak-shaded gardens are famed for their 100,000 camellia plants representing some 600 varieties, said to be the world's biggest collection. The camellias bloom from late December to early March. Lilacs and outdoor orchids are best viewed in April. There are also striking collections of roses, azaleas, flowering shrubs, displays of bulb flowers and assorted annuals. So, whatever the season, something is sure to be in bloom, and there are shows throughout the year.

Horticultural events, lectures and demonstrations are staged in **Georgie Van de Kamp Hall**. Guided streetcar tours around the grounds depart on the hour. Refreshment is available in the **Japanese garden**, where there is a tea house.

DODGER STADIUM

1000 Elysian Park Ave. (directly N of Downtown in the angle formed by the Pasadena Freeway/SR-11 and Golden State Freeway/I-5 and accessible from either via Stadium Way) ☎*(213) 224-1400. Map* **6C9** 🚗 *Ticket office in parking lot open Mon-Sat 8.30am-5.30pm.*

81

The 56,000-seat cantilevered stadium on the s edge of ELYSIAN PARK, built in 1962 and home to the Los Angeles Dodgers baseball team, occasionally hosts special events. Hot dogs and merchandise are sold during games.

DONUT HOLE

15300 Amar Rd., La Puente (on E corner of Elliot Ave., one block w of Hacienda Blvd., N of Pomona Freeway). Map 2C4 ✷

Typical Los Angeles: Pop Art, symbolism and functionalism at its best/worst in the form of giant, drive-through fiberglass donuts. Needless to say, Donut Hole sells donuts in hundreds of different varieties. Drive through anytime, day or night.

ECHO PARK

Glendale Blvd. and Park Ave. (via Hollywood Freeway/US-101, Alvarado St. exit, then E) ☎(213) 250-3578. Map 6C8 ✷

The 26-acre park is one of the city's oldest and most attractive. Donated in 1891, it comprises landscaped and forested areas, a lotus pond, and a 15-acre palm-fringed lake with paddle boats for rental by the hour. At the NW end of the park is the domed 5,000-seat **Angelus Temple** *(1100 Glendale Blvd.* ☎*(213) 484-1100),* where evangelist Aimee Semple McPherson preached in the 1920s and '30s.

ELYSIAN PARK

1880 Academy Dr. (near the intersection of Golden State Freeway/I-5 and Pasadena Freeway/SR-110) ☎(213) 225-2044. Map 6C9 ◁€ ≈⅍ ✤ ▣

At 575 acres the city's second largest park, this was originally established during the 1880s, taking in rolling hills and several valleys. Much of it has been preserved in its natural state, with numerous nature trails across the chaparral-covered slopes. **Chavez Ravine Arboretum** *(on Stadium Way between Scott Ave. and Academy Rd.)* is noted for rare trees planted at the end of the 19thC. There are good views of Central LA and the San Gabriel Valley.

DODGER STADIUM is on the s edge of the park.

EXPOSITION PARK

Bounded by Exposition Blvd., Figueroa St., Santa Barbara Ave. and Menlo St. (one block w of Harbor Freeway/SR-11, Exposition Blvd. exit). Map 5F7.

The park covers 114 acres, including a 7-acre rose garden, within the urban heart of Los Angeles. But it is known primarily as the site of major museums, a theater, track-and-field facilities and, nearby, the redbrick and ivy University of Southern California (USC).

It wasn't always thus. In 1872 it was an agricultural park, the venue for fairs and shows for farmers and the Southern California Agricultural Society. Later, it hosted horse-racing, bicycle and auto-racing, even, in its time, camel-racing. Its transformation into cultural playground began only in 1910.

On the whole, the fauna is now more interesting than the flora, which is formally landscaped. The sunken rose garden, which boasts some

16,000 rose bushes of 190 varieties, is so delightful that it's a popular venue for weddings. The roses bloom between March and November.

Within the park are located a number of major attractions:

California Afro-American Museum
600 State Dr. ☎*(213) 744-7432* ☒ ✗ ⬤ *Open 10am-5pm. Closed major hols.*
Afro-Americans were among the first settlers in El Pueblo de Los Angeles, and this museum celebrates the community's achievements with changing exhibits on the history, art and culture of Black Californians, plus the work of Black artists from around the world displayed in bright, airy galleries. At the front of the museum is a 13,000-square-foot glass-covered sculpture court. There is also a research library, a theater and a gift shop.

California State Museum of Science and Industry ☆
700 State Dr. ☎*(213) 744-7400* ☒ ✱ ▣ ⬤ *Open 10am-5pm. Closed Jan 1; Thanksgiving; Dec 25.*
Here, behind a Beaux Arts Classical face, are 14 halls of touchable displays, many of them elegantly mounted by major industrial companies, all of them designed for pleasurable learning. Bilingual computers use speech to explain their own history and capabilities. Soap bubbles are used to teach lessons in mathematics. Electricity, internal combustion, communications (especially film) and animal husbandry, earthquakes, wine-making and economics are among the subjects covered in surprising ways in the main museum building. There are also health checks on offer, in the **Hall of Health**, whose star attraction is a transparent woman named "Clearissa."

The **Aerospace Complex** includes the **Aerospace Building** (🏛 ✱), a vast hangar designed by top LA architect Frank Gehry to dramatize the hi-tech exhibits. A Lockheed F-104 Starfighter is pinned to the wall, and other airplanes and space craft, including a 1920 Wright glider and the capsule of Gemini II, are suspended from the ceiling, allowing close-up views from an aerial walkway.

Right next door is the octagonal 430-seat **Mitsubishi IMAX Theater** (☎*(213) 744-2014* ✱), also Gehry-designed. The IMAX films, projected onto a huge 50-foot by 70-foot screen, successfully create an exciting 3-D illusion of travel across land and water and through air and space.

Los Angeles County Museum of Natural History
900 Exposition Blvd. ☎*(213) 744-3414, recorded information (213) 744-3411* ☒ *(but* ☒ *first Tues of each month noon-9pm)* ♿ ✱ ▣ *Open Tues-Sun 10am-5pm (summer Sat-Sun 10am-6pm). Closed Mon; Jan 1; Thanksgiving; Dec 25.*
The museum, housed in a fine refurbished building, dubbed "Spanish Renaissance" by its turn-of-the-century designers, takes an uncommonly broad view of natural history. In addition to major halls dealing with mammals (outstanding), paleontology, living mammals, insects and birds, there are exhibits of South Pacific ethnology, Indians, and American and Californian history.

The latter section in **Lando Hall** covers the era 1540-1940 in strict chronology. Exhibits include a stage coach, a superb turn-of-the-century fire engine and a model of Downtown Los Angeles as it was in 1940. The displays, often arranged as dioramas, represent detailed habitats of North

American mammals, dinosaurs and other prehistoric animals, along with impressive collections of fossils, minerals and cut gemstones. Then there is Megamouth, the world's rarest shark.

The **Discovery Center** has hands-on exhibits for children. A recent addition is the **Hall of Birds**, with uncannily realistic animation and authentic bird song. On top of all this, there are free travel films *(each Sat at 2pm)* and free chamber music concerts *(each Sun at 2pm).* The museum gift shop is especially good for dinosaur-related books and trinkets.

(Dinosaur enthusiasts will also head for the **George C. Page Museum** in HANCOCK PARK.)

Memorial Coliseum
☎*(213) 747-7111. Map 1C2.*

A 91,000-seat stadium, it was the major site for track and field events at the 1932 and 1984 Olympic Games. Robert Graham's **Olympic Arch** in front of the Coliseum is a permanent reminder of the 1984 games. Other sports events and concerts are regularly scheduled here.

Memorial Sports Arena
Next to the Memorial Coliseum ☎*(213) 748-6131.*

Its 17,000-seat main hall is the home base of the Los Angeles Clippers and USC basketball teams. It also hosts ice shows, concerts, rodeos and conventions, and is used for a variety of sports and entertainment events.

FARMERS MARKET
6333 W Third St. (at Fairfax Ave.) ☎*(213) 933-9211. Map 4C5* 🚗 ➡ *Open 9am-8pm summer, 9am-6.30pm winter.*

Opened in 1934 as a genuine farmers' market, it is now an improvised center of 160 stalls and stores dealing especially in food, from produce to fast food, but also in general merchandise. Excellent butchers, pastry stores and green grocers, along with al fresco dining at a range of food stalls, from Cajun to Japanese. See also page 150.

FOREST LAWN MEMORIAL PARK
1712 S Glendale Ave., Glendale (E of I-5 via Los Feliz Ave.) ☎*(818) 254-3131. Map 1B3* 📷 ✗ ➡ *Open 9am-5pm.*

This is the cemetery that provoked Evelyn Waugh to write *The Loved One* (in 1965 Liberace played a funeral director in the movie adaptation). The well-manicured 340-acre park, just w of Griffith Park, is a mixture of necropolis and theme park. Its founder, Dr. Hubert Eaton, said his aim was to make Forest Lawn " . . . as unlike other cemeteries as sunshine is unlike darkness, as Eternal Life is unlike death." His aim, in that respect, was certainly true.

The grounds are dotted with architectural and artistic attractions. There are innumerable copies of Michelangelo statues, including a life-sized *David,* and a replica of Boston's Old North Church. Among other life-sized replicas are the Church of the Recessional, after a 10thC English church in Rudyard Kipling's home town of Rottingdean, Wee Kirk o' the Heather, after a 14thC Scottish church, and the Little Church of the

Flowers, imagined from the Stoke Poges church in Thomas Gray's poem *Elegy in a Country Churchyard.* Jan Stykam's *The Crucifixion,* which at 195 feet by 45 feet is said to be the world's largest religious painting, is displayed in the Hall of the Crucifixion, every hour on the hour, along with Robert Clark's almost as huge painting *The Resurrection,* displayed on the half hour every half hour.

Other curiosities include a collection of originals of every coin mentioned in the Bible. A 15-acre Court of Liberty has a replica of the Liberty Bell, Thomas Ball's 60-foot bronze and marble Washington Memorial, a 30-foot by 165-foot mosaic entitled *The Birth of Liberty,* and a smaller mosaic copy of John Trumbull's *The Signing of the Declaration of Independence.* An outdoor plaza contains replicas of ancient Mexican sculptures.

In what may be its only concession to good taste, Forest Lawn refuses to reveal the exact sites of its more famous graves. Among stars buried here are Jean Harlow, Nat King Cole, Clark Gable and W.C. Fields. One suspects that Fields would rather be in Philadelphia.

GAMBLE HOUSE ▥ ★

4 Westmoreland Pl., Pasadena (Ventura Freeway/SR-134 to Colorado Blvd. exit, then N on Orange Grove Blvd.) ☎*(818) 793-3334. Map 1B3* ▨ ✗ *Open Tues, Thurs 10am-3pm; Sun noon-3pm. Closed Mon; Wed; Fri-Sat.*

Built in 1908 for David B. Gamble, heir to the fortune of Cincinnati company Proctor & Gamble, but now owned by the University of Southern California, the house is an immaculate legacy of the Craftsman Movement in California. Lovingly finished teak, Tiffany glass, overhanging roofs, low ceilings, cleverly articulated interior and exterior spaces, and much of the original furniture and fittings may be seen. The overall effect can be viewed as the refinement of a host of influences, from northern Europe to Japan, on the architects Charles and Henry Greene.

GEHRY HOUSE ▥

1002 22nd St., Santa Monica (S corner of Washington Ave.). Map 1C1. Private residence viewable only from street.

This is an important shrine on any architectural pilgrimage. Frank Gehry is one of California's most highly regarded architects, responsible for, among others, the Aerospace Building (see EXPOSITION PARK), the TEMPORARY CONTEMPORARY museum and the Loyola University Law School.

His own house began life as an ordinary Dutch Colonial-style cottage. Gehry has torn bits down, uncovered things that were hidden, and created a new shell using materials he likes, such as exposed two-by-four studs, corrugated metal, chain-links, lots of glass, and an asphalt floor in the kitchen.

GEORGE C. PAGE MUSEUM OF LA BREA DISCOVERIES

Set amid the **Rancho La Brea Tar Pits**, this is at the eastern end of HANCOCK PARK.

A South Porch
B Bookstore
C Orientation Theater
D Entrance Vestibule

Information C

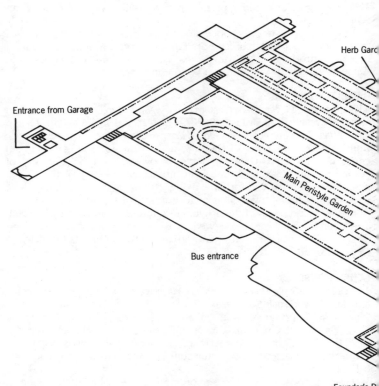

Herb Gard

Entrance from Garage

Main Peristyle Garden

Bus entrance

Founder's R

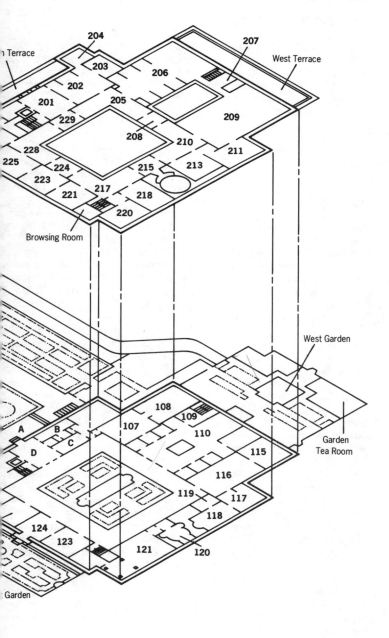

Terrace

204

207

West Terrace

203

206

202

201

205

209

229

208

210

228

211

225

224

215

213

223

221

217

218

220

Browsing Room

West Garden

108

107

109

110

A   B

115

D   C

116

119

117

118

124

123

121

120

Garden

West Garden

Garden
Tea Room

J. PAUL GETTY MUSEUM

J. PAUL GETTY MUSEUM ⅲ ☆
17985 Pacific Coast Highway, Malibu (w of intersection with Sunset Blvd.)
☎*(310) 458-2003* 🅵*(310) 454-6633. Map 10|6* 🔲 ■ 𝑟 *(see details below)*
🚻 ⚲ ⇐ ➡ *by reservation only for visitors arriving by car with admission to museum, but dependent on parking space. RTD bus 434 will drop visitors at the gate: passes are available from drivers. Open Tues-Sun 10am-5pm. Closed Mon; major holidays.* **See floor plan on preceding two pages.**

On a remote shelf overlooking the Pacific, oil millionaire Paul Getty built in 1974 a copy of the Villa dei Papiri, a 1stC Roman seaside villa and its gardens, to house his extensive art collection.

The museum has seven departments devoted mainly to European art from before 1900: **Antiquities** (including the 5thC BC bronze Etruscan *kouros,* the provenance of which has been questioned by some authorities), **Paintings**, **Decorative Arts**, **Drawings**, **Manuscripts**, **Photographs**, and **Sculpture and Works of Art**.

The 38 galleries are filled with Greek and Roman antiquities from 2000BC to AD300; Old, Renaissance and 19thC masters, with French, Dutch and Italian Schools well represented; impressive collections of drawings, especially by modern masters, illuminated manuscripts including important Italian, French, German, Flemish, English, Polish, Byzantine and Armenian works, and photographs from the early 1840s to the 1950s; fine furniture, tapestries, rugs, ceramics and gilt bronzes, all from the mid-17thC to the early 19thC; silver, especially French work from the 17th and 18thC; and porcelain.

The museum is the world's wealthiest, with an endowment of $2.2 billion, of which 4.2 percent must be spent each year. One consequence is that it is not always possible to predict with confidence precisely what will be hauled out of the ever-expanding Aladdin's cave for public display. The museum stages what it calls "changing exhibitions from the permanent collection."

It might be easier after inevitable expansion into new galleries in a complex designed by award-winning architect Richard Meier, which is planned to open on a 110-acre site in Brentwood in 1996. After this the Malibu museum will be devoted exclusively to Greek and Roman Antiquities: everything else will move to Brentwood.

For now, visitors are advised to search out the stunning **Ludwig collection** of illustrated manuscripts spanning the 8th-20thC. In addition there is the splendid **gallery of European silver**, including a collection of pre-revolutionary French silver in the Regency, Rococo and Neoclassical styles. It is also worth calling first to inquire what is currently on display. The range is so extensive that it defies a comprehensive listing. But a brief taster includes works by da Vinci, Raphael, Tiepolo, Bernini, Poussin, Watteau, David, Rembrandt, Rubens, Van Dyck and Ensor.

There are public lectures and films on Thursday evenings in the **Auditorium** *(lectures 8pm, films 7pm* 🔲 *but reservations essential* ☎ *(310) 458-2003).* Lectures are by resident experts and visiting scholars. Films are often of the hard-to-see variety: one notable season included a screening of three movies covering Euripides' Trojan cycle.

There are two guided tours: a 15-minute orientation talk, available to all visitors, and fuller talks for groups of up to 25 affiliated with art or academic departments, which must be arranged six weeks in advance.

GREAT WESTERN FORUM

3900 Manchester Blvd., Inglewood (1½ miles E of San Diego Freeway/I-405 in the vicinity of Los Angeles International Airport) ☎(310) 674-6000. Map 1C2.
This 17,000-seat arena, which bears little resemblance to the real Roman thing, is the in-season home from October to April of the National Basketball Association's Los Angeles Lakers and the National Hockey League's Los Angeles Kings *(☎(310) 673-1300 for both).* Tennis tournaments, boxing matches, ice shows, rodeos and concerts also take place here.

GREEK THEATER

A natural amphitheater in GRIFFITH PARK.

GRIFFITH PARK ☆

Visitor Center, 4730 Crystal Springs Rd. ☎(213) 665-5188. Map 5A7 ◁ ☞ ✹
General park hours 5am-10.30pm; hours for specific attractions noted below.
Four major entrances permit direct access to areas of interest: Western Canyon Rd., Crystal Springs Drive, Ventura Freeway at junction with Golden State Freeway, and Vermont Ave.
With 4,063 acres draped across the Hollywood Hills, the largest city park in the US has most of its major development on relatively gentle slopes toward its E boundary. Located in this area are the GENE AUTRY WESTERN HERITAGE MUSEUM (see entry on page 78), **Greek Theater, Los Angeles Zoo**, a transportation museum called **Travel Town**, most of the park's 18 picnic grounds, its golf courses, tennis courts, pony and train rides, and its games fields (see OUTDOOR ACTIVITIES). The **Griffith Observatory, Planetarium and Laserium** is high on Mt. Hollywood. Steeper hills still farther w have been kept in their natural state except for roads and trails.

Griffith Observatory, Planetarium and Laserium �

2800 E Observatory Rd., at the N end of N Vermont Ave. ☎(213) 664-1191. Map 5A7 ▣ ◁ ⬌ ✹ Open summer Sun-Fri 1-10pm, Sat 11.30am-10pm; winter Tues-Fri 2-10pm, Sat 11.30am-10pm. Closed Thanksgiving; Dec 24-25; Mon in winter.

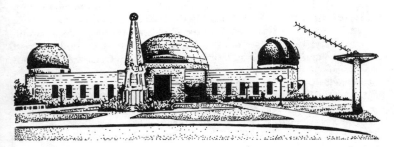

Inside the copper-domed 1935 observatory building, a dramatic landmark on the high ground of Griffith Park, are conventional star shows, as well as simulated eclipses, auroras and space voyages three or four times daily in the **Planetarium Theater** between 1-8pm. The **Hall of Science** has a weather satellite, a Foucault pendulum and other displays on meteorology and astronomy. Visitors may look through the telescope when weather permits. Late-evening shows in the **Laserium** accompanied by sci-fi rock music follow the star shows (**▨** **☎***(213) 997-3624 for schedules and programs).*

This spot, on the s slopes of Mt. Hollywood, is popular for viewing the lights of LA as well as the stars.

Greek Theater
2700 N Vermont Ave. ☎*(310) 410-1062. Map* **5A7** **▨** **⬤**
This has picnic tables and 6,000 seats in a natural amphitheater facing an open-air stage used between June and October for pop, rock and classical music and dance programs. Picnics, wine and beer may be bought at the site or brought along.

Los Angeles Zoo
5333 Zoo Dr., via Zoo Dr. exit from the Ventura Freeway/SR-134, directly w of its intersection with I-5 ☎*(213) 664-1100. Map* **1B2** **▨** *✗* **⬤** *✻* **⬤** *Open 10am-6pm summer; 10am-5pm winter. Closed Dec 25.*
Built in 1966, the zoo follows the modern trend toward natural enclosures without bars for its 2,000 animals, including 78 endangered species, which are grouped according to their continent of origin. The main zoo, including the picnic area, covers about 80 landscaped acres. A streetcar tour is available for an extra fee. There is also a new Children's Zoo called **Adventure Island,** which uses hi-tech participatory exhibits to teach about animals and their habitats, and an Animal Nursery for newly-born animal babies.

Travel Town
5730 Crystal Springs Dr., via the same freeway exit as for the zoo, then w ☎*(213) 662-5874. Map* **1B2** **▨** *✻* **⬤** *Open 9am-5.30pm. Closed Dec 25.*
An open-air transport museum with antique airplanes, locomotives and vintage railroad cars as its primary treasures. Children are welcome to climb upon many of the exhibits. Miniature train rides are inexpensive.

HANCOCK PARK
At the 5900 block of Wilshire Blvd., E of Fairfax Ave. Map **4D5.**
A modest picnic park, but it also contains the **Los Angeles County Museum of Art,** the **Rancho La Brea fossil pits** and the **George C. Page Museum of La Brea Discoveries**. Around the museums and between the fossil pits, Hancock Park also has picnic tables, street musicians, and a parking lot that is accessible from Curson Ave., opposite Wilshire Blvd.

Los Angeles County Museum of Art **血** ☆
5905 Wilshire Blvd., two blocks E of Fairfax Ave. ☎*(213) 937-2590 for recorded calendar, (213) 857-6111. Map* **4D5** **▨** *(but* **▣** *on second Tues of each month noon-9pm)* *✗* **⬤** *&* **⬤** *Open Tues-Fri 10am-4.30pm; Sat-Sun 10am-5.30pm. Closed Mon; Jan 1; Thanksgiving; Dec 25.*

This is one of California's best collections, housed in a series of provocative buildings, including Hardy Holzman Pfeiffer's glass and limestone **Robert O. Anderson Building** and, the most recent addition, Bruce Goff's **Pavilion for Japanese Art**. The latter features white window panels that eliminate glare and mimic the subdued lighting effect of traditional Japanese paper screens. Critical response to the building has been anything but subdued; many people hate it.

Still, there's plenty more to see. The Anderson 20thC wing is a showcase for contemporary and almost contemporary art, featuring the work of such as Picasso, Matisse, Kandinsky, Rivera, Hockney and others in permanent and changing exhibitions. Most of the museum's resident collections are housed in the **Ahmanson Building**, with paintings, sculptures, costumes, textiles and decorative arts from a wide range of cultures and periods. Among them are the Heeramaneck collection of Indian, Tibetan and Nepalese art objects, much prized by critics.

Also of note are a strong collection of pre-Columbian Mexican pottery and textiles, the Gilbert Collection of mosaics and monumental gold and silver, a series of Rodin bronzes, one of the country's largest collections of textiles and costumes, and an exhibition of glass work from Roman to modern times. Loan exhibitions are staged in the **Hammer Building**, where there are also galleries for prints, drawings and photography. The Pavilion for Japanese Art features the museum's collection of Japanese sculpture, paintings, ceramics and lacquerware, including the internationally renowned Shin'enkan collection of Japanese paintings and the Raymond and Francis Bushell collection of netsuke.

The **Leo S. Bing Center** to the E has a 600-seat theater and a 100-seat auditorium for lectures, concerts and films, both educational and Hollywood-retrospective. Two sculpture gardens, one with Rodin bronzes, the second with contemporary works, connect the pavilions.

George C. Page Museum of La Brea Discoveries

5801 Wilshire Blvd. ☎*(213) 936-2230, (213) 857-6306. Map* **4D5** �︎ ⅋ ✳ ⬳
Open Tues-Sun 10am-4.45pm. Closed Mon; Jan 1; Thanksgiving; Dec 25.

This is set amid the famous **Rancho La Brea Tar Pits** from which paleontologists have recovered tons of fossilized remains of Pleistocene creatures and plants. Imaginative displays show not only the individual bones, but reconstructions of complete animals, as well as the techniques of the science of paleontology. An observation deck around the outside of the building gives a good view across the fossil pits, which may also be seen at close range. Exploration continues on the site.

HEBREW UNION COLLEGE AND SKIRBALL MUSEUM

3077 University Ave. (Harbor Freeway/SR-110, Jefferson Blvd. exit, then N via Hoover Blvd.) ☎*(213) 749-3424. Map* **6E8** 🖭 ✳ ⬳ *Open Tues-Thurs 8.15am-5pm; Fri 8.15am-4.30pm; Sun 10am-5pm. Closed Mon; Sat.*

Opened in 1954, the museum has archeological and biblical exhibits relating to the Torah and Jewish holy days, ritual objects, coins, and textiles, along with artifacts and folk art displays. Children especially seem to enjoy the gallery called *A Walk Through the Past,* and the ten arches representing the Ten Commandments. Also of interest is the **Library of Judaica**, which includes a wide-ranging collection of works on the American Jewish experience.

HERALD EXAMINER BUILDING ⌂

1111 S Broadway (s of junction with 11th St.) ☎*(213) 744-8000. Map 6E8.*
This imposing, block-long Mission Revival-style building was commissioned in 1912 by newspaper baron William Randolph Hearst. Hearst chose architect Julia Morgan, the first woman graduate of the Paris École des Beaux-Arts and someone closely involved in the evolution of his fairytale San Simeon retreat, to design the home of his Los Angeles flagship publication.

The results remain impressive, and the building is a classic of the genre, marred only by the more recent closing in of its ground-floor arches. There are those who want to see the building demolished entirely and the site "re-developed." But there is fierce opposition from conservationists, and the debate is likely to continue for some time yet.

HERITAGE SQUARE ⌂

3800 N Homer St. (Ave. 43 exit from Pasadena Freeway/SR-110) ☎*(818)*
796-2829, recorded information (818) 449-0193 ▨ *𝄞 ⟶ Map 1B3. Open*
Sat-Sun noon-5pm in summer; Sun 11am-4pm in winter. Closed Mon-Fri in
summer; Mon-Sat in winter.
In an attempt to preserve at least a portion of Los Angeles' architectural heritage from the path of the developers, a kind of rest home for threatened Victorian buildings was created here by the Los Angeles Cultural Heritage Board. Others, somewhat unkindly, have called it an architectural petting zoo.

Rescued and relocated onto this 10-acre site next to the Pasadena Freeway are the 1886 **Palms Railroad Depot** from near to Century City; the 1898 Gothic **Lincoln Avenue Methodist Church** from Pasadena; the 1876 **Perry House**, an Italianate villa from Boyle Heights that was once considered LA's finest house; and several other striking Victorian homes. It is hoped that more will follow.

HOLLYHOCK HOUSE

Frank Lloyd Wright's first house in LA, in BARNSDALL PARK.

HOLLYWOOD BOWL

2301 N Highland Ave., Hollywood (w of Highland Ave. exit from the Hollywood
Freeway/US-101) ☎*(213) 850-2000. Map 5B5* ▣ *except during concerts*
▪ *before concerts ⟶ Grounds open daily July-Sept 9am-dusk.*
Frank Lloyd Wright's magnificent 100-foot-wide shell-shaped bandstand faces a 17,619-seat amphitheater surrounded by trees. The acoustics are less than perfect, but from July to September, in a tradition dating back to 1922, the Los Angeles Philharmonic plays light summer evening concerts, and other performers include pop, jazz and rock groups. The Easter sunrise service is held here, and the annual 4th of July concert climaxes with a firework display. Before the concerts,

grand al fresco picnics are a great tradition. Seats are hard wooden benches, so it pays to bring cushions. Evenings become cool, requiring a sweater or coat.

The **Hollywood Bowl Museum** *(near the entrance to the Bowl grounds, open 9.30am-8.30pm on concert days)* has displays on the Bowl and its sometime conductors, 3-D dioramas of the Bowl, Frank Lloyd Wrights original drawings, plus changing exhibitions on Southern California's musical and visual arts. Tapes of outstanding Bowl performances are available to be listened to in booths.

HOLLYWOOD MEMORIAL CEMETERY
6000 Santa Monica Blvd., Hollywood (between Santa Monica Blvd., Melrose Ave. and Gower St., behind Paramount Studios) ☎*(213) 469-1181. Map 5C6. Open Mon-Fri 8am-5pm; Sat-Sun 9am-4pm.*

A host of Hollywood legends lies behind the high walls of this 65-acre palm-fringed cemetery, including idol of the silent screen Rudolph Valentino, godfather of the movie epic Cecil B. De Mille, motion pictures' original swashbuckler Douglas Fairbanks, Peter Lorre, Tyrone Power, Peter Finch and many more. The mausoleums, statues and adornments are everything one would expect.

HOLLYWOOD SIGN ★
Durand Dr., off Beachwood Dr., Hollywood. Map 5A6.

Possibly LA's best-known landmark, the Hollywood Sign, near the summit of Mt. Lee overlooking the city of Hollywood, was erected by real-estate developers in 1923, when it spelled out "Hollywoodland" in 50-foot-high letters. The site and the sign were donated to the city in 1945 and the last four letters were removed.

In 1978 the original dog-eared sign was replaced with a new $250,000 sign paid for by celebrities: Playboy's Hugh Heffner bought the "Y," rock star Alice Cooper sponsored an "O."

HUNTINGTON LIBRARY, ART GALLERY AND BOTANICAL GARDENS ★
1151 Oxford Rd., San Marino (from Pasadena Freeway/Arroya Parkway, E on California Blvd. to Allen Ave., then s to grounds) ☎*(818) 405-2100. Map 1B3*
🖼 ⚟ 🖳 ⚹ ➳ *Open Tues-Sat 1-4.30pm, and Sun 1-4.30pm by reservation only (write for Sunday tickets to above address, or* ☎*(818) 405-2273 during preceding week). Closed Mon; Oct; hols.*

Once the home of railroad tycoon Henry E. Huntington (1850-1927), the 207-acre hilltop estate was developed and the collections begun between 1910 and 1925. Today, as a privately endowed museum and study center of international stature, it continues to grow in both scope and quality.

The art gallery, in what was formerly the Huntington mansion, focuses on 18th and early 19thC European painters, most notably works of Gainsborough (including *Blue Boy*), Turner, Reynolds and Romney. But there are important 17thC works by Claude Lorraine and Van Dyck, 18thC French paintings by Boucher, Nattier and Watteau, and 18th-20thC American art by Cassatt, Copley and Hopper.

The library contains rare books and manuscripts from the 11thC to the present. Items on public display include a Gutenberg Bible, the Ellesmere manuscript of Geoffrey Chaucer's *Canterbury Tales,* and a first folio of Shakespeare's plays.

Among the most recent additions is a permanent exhibition entitled *Greene & Greene and the Arts and Crafts Movement in America*. On display are furniture and decorative artworks by brothers Charles and Henry Greene, who lived and worked in Pasadena from 1893 and were highly respected for their architecture, furniture and landscape design.

The vast surrounding gardens, dating from 1904, include a 12-acre desert succulent and cacti collection filled with rarities, including the largest cacti in the world; a rose garden with more than 1,000 varieties; 1,500 varieties of camellia; and a Japanese garden with a 16thC teahouse and a Zen rock garden.

KOREATOWN

Mid-Wilshire district between Vermont Ave., Pico Blvd., Western Ave. and 8th St. Map 5D7.

Most of California's 200,000-plus people of Korean origin live in Los Angeles, many of them in Koreatown. Anchored by the lively, colorful market at the corner of 8th St. and Normandie Ave., the still-expanding *quartier* is characterized by Korean (as well as Chinese and Japanese) restaurants, food stores, bakeries, small shops and boutiques. The distinctive phonetic calligraphy is hard to miss.

LA BREA TAR PITS

La brea means "tar" in Spanish, so "La Brea Tar Pits" is tautologous. But that's firmly what Angelenos call them. See HANCOCK PARK, where the **George C. Page Museum of La Brea Discoveries** is located.

LITTLE TOKYO

Downtown between 1st St., 3rd St., Los Angeles St. and Alameda St., E of Civic Center ☎(213) 628-2725 (Japanese American Cultural and Community Center) for information. Map 6D9.

Southern California's Japanese-American population numbers considerably more than 100,000, and its cultural focus is Downtown's Little Tokyo, centered around the **Japanese Village Plaza**, built in 1979. It feels like Japan — clean, compact, with Japanese-influenced architecture, authentic restaurants complete with window displays of plastic food and largely Japanese clientele, bookstores, and shops selling most things Japanese, from groceries to art works, furniture, clothes and cosmetics.

The **Japanese American Cultural and Community Center** orchestrates major events and festivals such as the Nisei Week in August (☎ *(213) 687-7193 for details)*, which includes a huge, noisy parade, street dancing, public demonstrations of Japanese arts and crafts, and festival food. ("Nisei" means "second-generation Japanese.")

Notable in the area are the **Japan American Theater** (☎ *(213) 680-3700)*, which stages Asian theater, including Noh and Kabuki, dance and music; the **Higashi Hongwanji Buddhist Temple**, with its traditional blue-tiled roof (☎ *(213) 626-4200)*; and the *JACCC Plaza*, a plate-glass and concrete construction by Buckminster Fuller and Isamu Noguchi.

The newest feature of the area is the **Japanese American National Museum** *(369 E 1st St.* ☎ *(213) 625-0414)*, a collection of artifacts, many of them personal possessions passed down the generations, which record the Japanese experience in the US since the 1920s.

LOS ANGELES CHILDREN'S MUSEUM

310 N Main St. (at street level of Los Angeles Mall in the Civic Center) ☎(213) 687-8800. Map 6D9 💺 ☀ 🚗 *(for a fee). Open Mon-Fri noon-5pm; Sat-Sun 10am-5pm summer; call for winter hours.*

The emphasis is on exploring the senses with sticky stuff, strobes, old clothes, butter churns and other familiar or rare items. Some of these whimsical lessons are scheduled classes and workshops; others are for those who just drop in. A children's TV studio, where they put on their own news shows, is a highlight. Birthday party programs are available.

LOS ANGELES COUNTY MUSEUM OF ART 🏛 ☆

One of the finest art collections in the US can be found in HANCOCK PARK.

LOS ANGELES COUNTY MUSEUM OF NATURAL HISTORY

Located in EXPOSITION PARK, this is the fourth-largest natural history museum in the US.

LOS ANGELES MUNICIPAL ART GALLERY

A gallery and theater for contemporary art and film, in BARNSDALL PARK.

LOS ANGELES STATE AND COUNTY ARBORETUM

301 N Baldwin Ave., Arcadia (s of Foothill Freeway/I-210, via Baldwin Ave. exit directly across from Santa Anita Park thoroughbred race course) ☎(818) 446-8251. Map 2B4 💺 *(but* 🚗 *on 3rd Tues of each month). Streetcar tours available for extra fee* ✗ 🍽 🚗 *Open 9am-4.30pm. Closed Dec 25.*

This horticultural research center covers 127 acres of the property that once belonged to legendary silver miner and rancher Elias Jackson (Lucky) Baldwin, whose ornate Queen Anne cottage still stands.

Among plants from every continent are rarities from Australia and South Africa. Remember the *African Queen?* The lake that Humphrey Bogart hauled the boat through is here. Giant palm trees and the orchid collection are well regarded.

LOS ANGELES TIMES BUILDING

202 W 1st St. (Downtown, near intersection with Main St.) ☎*(213) 972-5757. Map* **6D9** ✗ *Mon-Fri 3pm* ▣ *Children must be aged at least 10.*
Los Angeles' premier daily newspaper inhabits this monumental 1935 Moderne beige limestone block, and a less distinguished 1973 glass-box addition. Free tours offer a rare opportunity to see a newspaper produced, from newsroom to printing press.

LOS ANGELES ZOO

Noted for its breeding of endangered species, this is one of the major zoos in the United States. See GRIFFITH PARK.

MACARTHUR PARK

Wilshire Blvd., between Alvarado St. and Park View. Map **6D8** ✿
Laid out in 1890 and originally named Westlake Park, the 32-acre public space was renamed after General Douglas MacArthur in 1942. In addition to some 80 rare plants and trees, a small boating lake, a bandstand, picnic areas and a children's playground, the park has a number of specially commissioned works of art. These include a 500-foot water spout, a clock tower and two pyramids. Visitors are not advised to visit the park after dark.

MANN'S CHINESE THEATER ▥ ★

6925 Hollywood Blvd., Hollywood (one block w of Highland Ave.) ☎*(213) 464-8111. Map* **5B5** ➤ *Open daily.*
Originally Grauman's Chinese Theater, it has the famous courtyard with handprints and footprints of 150 movie stars pressed into concrete. The courtyard is open to passers-by without charge; the building, a functioning movie theater, is a real Hollywood-style fantasy of Chinese architectural themes.

MEMORIAL COLISEUM AND SPORTS ARENA

The Olympic stadium and its sister facility (the home base of the LA Clippers and USC basketball teams) in EXPOSITION PARK.

MIRACLE MILE

Wilshire Blvd. (between Sycamore and Fairfax Aves.). Map **4D5**.
Among the first Los Angeles strips developed with drivers in mind, Miracle Mile was so named because, at first, most people thought A.W. Ross was crazy when in 1920 he began the development of a commercial center along a dirt road surrounded by farmland and several miles from anywhere. But the visionary Mr Ross foresaw the commuter age, turned his piece of Wilshire into a six-lane boulevard with off-street parking, and ensured that the buildings were attractive, interesting and

literally arresting. Those who had doubted the scheme pronounced its success a miracle. Many of the mile's Art Deco buildings have survived, making it one of the more engaging drives/walks in the city.

MISSION SAN FERNANDO REY DE ESPAÑA

15151 San Fernando Mission Blvd., Mission Hills (in San Fernando Valley between San Diego Freeway/I-405 and Golden State Freeway/I-5 via San Fernando Mission Blvd. exit) ☎*(818) 361-0186. Map 10l6* ▨ ◀ *Open Mon-Sat 9am-5pm, Sun 10am-5pm.*

Founded in 1797, 17th of the 21 missions, San Fernando Rey was one of the most successful; it exported goods to Mexico and Spain and even experienced a mini-gold rush when deposits were found on mission land in 1842. California's first Bishop lodged here. An earthquake in 1812 demolished all save the Convento and an outbuilding. But various efforts since 1879, including wholesale demolition and rebuilding following the 1971 earthquake, have seen the reconstruction of the **Convento** (accommodation building), the old adobe church, the campanario (belfry) and Mission shops, with a tableau of everyday 19thC life.

All this re-working means that the Mission looks, indeed is, very new. The thick walls, Moorish windows, semicircular arches, high-ceilinged rooms, moldings and *trompe l'oeil* niches are impressive. But much of the honest simplicity of the original has been overwhelmed by rather too enthusiastic embellishments; gilt triumphal arches, for instance. Critics say it has been restored beyond credibility.

The **cemetery**, just N of the church, is intact and still contains the graves of early settlers and converts. Perhaps the most engaging features of the Mission are the courtyard planted with olive trees and the **Memory Garden** opposite the Convento. It has grape arbors, olive trees, a fountain modeled on an original in the Spanish city of Córdoba, and a statue of Fra Junipero Serra, the Majorca-born Franciscan who founded the first nine missions.

For further details of the Spanish missions see page 37.

MISSION SAN GABRIEL ARCÁNGEL

537 W Mission Dr., San Gabriel (E from Los Angeles via San Bernardino Freeway/I-10 to New Ramona Ave. exit, then N) ☎*(818) 282-5191. Map 2B4* ▨ ◀ *Open 9.30am-4pm.*

Founded in 1771, fourth of the missions, San Gabriel moved to its present site in 1775. It achieved distinction as the most productive mission, with the biggest crops and a legendary vineyard and winery, California's oldest.

The church, rebuilt after the 1812 earthquake, is thought to be styled after the cathedral of Córdoba in southern Spain, the hometown of its designer Fra Antonio Cruzado. The mission is of heavy Moorish construction, long and narrow with tall, thick stone walls and high oblong windows set between capped buttresses. The bell tower on the N wall has three rows of arched openings that represent the classic Mission image. All in all, however, it has the air of a fortress.

The grounds are less mournful. There are olive trees planted in the mid-19thC, grapevines dating from the 1930s and a cactus garden. What was the winery has been restored to give an idea of the original. It also houses a museum of religious and Indian artifacts, and there is a gift store.

MUSEUM OF CONTEMPORARY ART ▥ ★

250 S Grand Ave. (Downtown at California Plaza, one block s of Music Center) ☎*(213) 62-MOCA-2, (213) 626-6828. Map* **6D9** ▨ *(but* ▣ *Thurs 5pm-8pm)* ♿ ☕ 🚶 *Open Tues, Wed, Sat, Sun 11am-6pm; Thurs-Fri 11am-8pm. Closed Mon; Thanksgiving; Dec 25; Jan 1.*

When MOCA opened in 1986, Japanese architect Arata Isozaki's dazzling red-sandstone-clad geometric building, with its pyramidal skylights, attracted as much attention as the exhibits. It still does, and the museum is arguably the most important addition to Downtown architecture in decades. The permanent and the changing exhibitions of both paintings and sculpture, all of them displayed in generous well-lit spaces that open off a sunken courtyard, tend to be equally modern and avant garde.

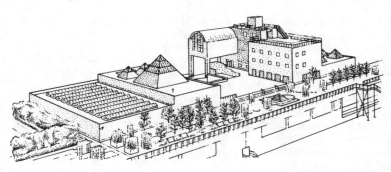

The museum is especially strong on Pop Art and Minimalism. Notable are works by Roy Lichtenstein, Robert Rauschenberg, Claes Oldenburg and Mark Rothko. In its 200-seat auditorium MOCA also presents regular Art Talks (☎ *(213) 621-1751),* slide presentations giving an overview of exhibitions (☎ *(213) 621-1751),* and occasional symposiums.

Admission is also valid for sister facility THE TEMPORARY CONTEMPORARY.

MUSIC CENTER OF LOS ANGELES ▥

135 N Grand Ave. (Downtown adjoining Civic Center at 1st St., one block s of Hollywood Freeway) ☎*(213) 972-7211. Map* **6D9** ▣ ✗ *compulsory* 🚶 *Open for tours May-Oct Mon 10am-2pm, Tues, Fri 10am-5pm; Nov-Apr Mon-Thurs 10am-2pm; Sat 10am-noon year round.*

Guided tours focus on the architecture of the center's **Dorothy Chandler Pavilion** (a 3,197-seat concert hall), **Ahmanson Theater** (a 2,100-seat theater and concert hall) and **Mark Taper Forum** (a 750-seat theater), and the art adorning it. Some love the late-1960s marble-clad rectangles and central cylinder; others hate them. What it lacks in accessibility and warmth it compensates for with extensive basement parking and some impressive sculptures in an otherwise unwelcoming plaza. However, the interior is luxuriously appointed, and the center is home to the **Los Angeles Philharmonic** and the **Center Theater Group** (for further details see PERFORMING ARTS). It is also the site of special music and theater performances all year round.

A promised addition, expected to open for the 1995 music season, is the **Disney Concert Hall**. The commission for the new auditorium, to be built across 1st St. from the Dorothy Chandler Pavilion, has gone to Frank Gehry, perhaps LA's most celebrated architect. It will be the future home of the Los Angeles Philharmonic.

NATIONAL BROADCASTING COMPANY TELEVISION STUDIO

3000 W Almeda Ave., Burbank (via Hollywood Way exit from Ventura Freeway/ SR-134) ☎*(818) 840-3537. Map 1B2* 🔄 ♣ ✗ *compulsory* ⬤ *Open Mon-Fri 9am-4pm; Sat 10am-4pm; Sun 10am-2pm. Closed Jan 1; Thanksgiving; Dec 25.*
The long-running *The Tonight Show* comes from here. Guides take visitors on a 75-minute tour through set construction, special effects, wardrobe departments, prop warehouses and sound stages — including **Studio 1**, where they can stand on Johnny Carson's mark: a star. Johnny's retirement notwithstanding, it will always be his star.

Tours do not include tickets to taping sessions: for tickets see TELEVISION SHOWS.

OLVERA STREET

This is the heart of EL PUEBLO DE LOS ANGELES STATE HISTORIC PARK.

PACIFIC ASIA MUSEUM 🏛

46 N Los Robles Ave., Pasadena (via Ventura Freeway/SR-134, Colorado Blvd. exit, then w) ☎*(818) 449-2742. Map 1B3* 🔄 *Open Wed-Sun noon-5pm. Closed Mon-Tues.*
Housed in a delightfully ornate replica of a traditional Northern Chinese building (1924), originally home and shop for Oriental art dealer Grace Nicholson, the museum stages changing exhibitions of Asian art, both ancient and contemporary. The scope is wide-ranging, from Afghanistan to the California Coast. Among outstanding exhibits are a 4thC Buddha from Kashmir, a 15thC Ming Dynasty painting and a series of Tibetan dolls. It also has a peaceful courtyard garden, and a gift store selling kitchenware and household objects.

PACIFIC DESIGN CENTER 🏛

8687 Melrose Ave., West Hollywood (NE corner of San Vicente Blvd.) ☎*(310) 657-0800. Map 4C4.*
Conceived as a headquarters for Melrose's fashionable interior design trade, the aircraft-hanger-sized, blue-glass design center (illustrated on page 39) was likened by its critics to a beached blue whale. However, the stark elegance of the 1975 Cesar Pelli building and its landmark massiveness have won over most of the critics. A Green Whale and a Red Whale now keep the Blue Whale company, providing 1.2 million

square feet of display space. However, this is a working building and the best that visitors can expect is the exterior view, or a visit to the **Melrose Bar & Grill** in the Blue Whale.

PARAMOUNT STUDIOS

5555 Melrose Ave. (Marathon St. and Bronson Ave., between Gower St. and Van Ness Ave.) ☎*(213) 468-5575. Map* **5***C6. Not open to the public.*

Paramount's famous **iron gates**, immortalized in the movie *Sunset Boulevard,* are actually to be found on Bronson Ave. Those on Melrose Ave. are new. Dating from the silent movie era, and featuring stars such as Rudolph Valentino, Marlene Dietrich, Bob Hope and Dorothy Lamour, Paramount is the only great movie studio to have stayed on in Hollywood. It's worth the visit just to see those gates.

EL PUEBLO DE LOS ANGELES STATE HISTORIC PARK 血

*622 N Main St. (*N *of Downtown between Temple St. and Sunset Blvd.)* ☎*(213) 628-0605. Map* **6***D9* ⊡ *⚲ Open 10am-10pm summer; 10am-8.30pm winter.*

Here, where the City of Los Angeles was founded, the park preserves Los Angeles' Spanish-American beginnings in the form of restored buildings, especially the Mexican rustic-style **Plaza Church** (1818), the city's oldest religious building, **Avila Adobe** (1818), the oldest house in Los Angeles, and **Pico House** (1869), which in its prime was the city's finest hotel. Other early buildings include the **Victorian Fire House No. 1** (1886), the Italianate **Masonic Lodge** (1858), and LA's first theater, the **Merced Theater** (1870); under it ran labyrinthine tunnels, hide-outs for oppressed 19thC Chinese.

However, the park's most visited part is **Olvera Street,** built in the 1920s as a tourist-oriented, block-long marketplace for Mexican restaurants, trinket shops and stalls selling candies. Many consider it to be California's first theme park. This miniature forerunner of Disneyland has a bandstand that serves as the site of *mariachi* concerts throughout the summer. The whole street erupts in fiesta at **Cinco de Mayo** *(May 5; for information* ☎*(213) 688-7330).*

A map of the four-block park is available at park headquarters next to the Fire House on the plaza E of Main St.

VIRGINIA ROBINSON GARDENS

Beverly Hills. Map **3***C2* ☎*(310) 276-5367* ▨ *Only open for ⚲ Tues-Fri 10am-1pm, by advance reservation only* ⬸ *for cars and vans only, no buses.*

Built in 1911, the Robinsons' Beaux Arts house is said to be Beverly Hills' oldest, and it provides a glimpse of the early years of the Los Angeles good life. The 6-acre landscaped estate features terraced hillsides and groves of king palms, azaleas and camellias, the whole crisscrossed by interlocking footpaths.

RODEO DRIVE ☆

Beverly Hills, between Wilshire Blvd. and Santa Monica Blvd. Map **3***C3.*

Rodeo Drive is the apotheosis of Los Angeles' consumer culture. Designer fashions, designer jewelry, designer perfumes, designer adult toys, designer salads, designer people; pricey, but *the* place to see and be seen. (See SHOPPING, pages 152-3.)

ST VINCENT DE PAUL ROMAN CATHOLIC CHURCH

621 W Adams Blvd. (intersection of Adams Blvd. and S Figueroa St.). Map 6E8.

One of Southern California's most beautiful churches, St Vincent's, designed by Albert C. Martin, is a splendid example of the ornate Spanish-Mexican Churrigueresque style. Built between 1923 and 1925 with money donated by wealthy oilman Edward Doheny, its most notable features are an entrance screen of Indiana limestone and a brilliantly tiled 45-foot-diameter dome. (See illustration on page 36.)

SANTA MONICA PIER

At the foot of Colorado St., one block from the end of Santa Monica Freeway/I-10, Santa Monica. Map 10I6 ✱

Constructed in 1908, this is the oldest pier on the West Coast, and the only surviving turn-of-the-century pier in California. Following storm damage in 1983, it was slated for demolition, but outraged residents voted the officials responsible out of office. Instead the city approved $10 million for strengthening and restructuring, completed in 1990, since when a $30-million wholesale renovation has begun.

For now it retains a pleasing raffishness, with arcades, restaurants, small cafés, snack bars, curio stores and bait shops. There is now also an English pub and a fortune teller. The historic carousel (featured in the motion picture *The Sting* with Newman and Redford), with its 46 hand-crafted gilt and painted prancing horses, is fully restored and has been designated a national monument by the US government. New attractions include bumper rides and a park and play area for children. Old attractions include sea breezes and breathtaking sunsets.

During the summer months the pier stages the Twilight Dance Series, a free music and dance festival that showcases local talent. Nearby are more avant-garde attractions. On the beach immediately to the N and S of the Pier is the **Natural Elements Sculpture Park** featuring, among others, Doug Hollis' *Singing Chairs* (the wind makes the steel and aluminum chairs sing) and Carl Cheng's *Santa Monica Art Tool*, a giant steel and concrete roller that performs monthly roll-outs on the sand.

Farther N and E, behind the Pacific Coast Highway and overlooking the ocean, is **Palisades Park**, a palm-lined green space which also hosts some wacky and provocative public art. The Visitors Center is located in the park. The pier and the beach are open 365 days a year, admission free.

NORTON SIMON MUSEUM OF ART ☆

411 W Colorado Blvd., Pasadena (s side of Ventura Freeway/SR-134 at Orange Grove Blvd.) ☎ (818) 449-3730. Map 1B3 📷 𝙆 ➾ *Open Thurs-Sun noon-6pm. Closed Mon-Wed; major holidays.*

Many art lovers consider this to be one of the finest collections in the western United States both for its quality and for the personal vision of the man who assembled it at an estimated cost of $100 million. This is very much a personal collection; Norton Simon's taste and eye applied across seven centuries of European paintings, and several millennia of Asian art. Simon only began acquiring Asia art in 1971, after a visit to India with his new wife, the actress Jennifer Jones. After 20 years the collection includes work from India, Thailand, Cambodia and Nepal, filling three galleries and a sculpture garden outside.

Rodin's *Burghers of Calais* adorn the forecourt. Inside the handsomely laid out galleries are Old Master paintings and drawings including Canaletto's *Piazzetta Venice, Looking North;* Rembrandt's *Titus, Bearded Man in Wide-Brimmed Hat* and *Self Portrait;* works by Rubens, Raphael, Goya and Breughel; Francisco Zurbarán's stunning *Still Life — Lemons, Oranges and a Rose;* a superb range of Impressionist and Cubist works including Cézanne's *Tulips in a Vase,* Renoir's *Pont des Arts* and Van Gogh's *Portrait of a Peasant;* a roomful of Degas paintings and sculptures; Picassos, including *Woman with Book;* works of the German Expressionists; and some fine examples of other 20thC painters such as Klee, Kandinsky and Braque.

It seems to be increasingly the case in LA that at any one time museums and galleries have many more works under lock and key than they are able to display on public view. So, apart from the permanent collection, there are changing special exhibitions that can usually be relied upon to excite interest. Among things to watch out for here are: paintings and lithographs by Toulouse Lautrec; Japanese woodblock prints; prints and etchings by William Hogarth; etchings and aquatints by Picasso; and the works of Marcel Duchamp and other exponents of Dadaism and Surrealism, notably Dalí, Giacometti, Magritte, Miró and Man Ray.

There is also an excellent museum shop selling one of Los Angeles' broadest selections of art books, prints and cards.

SIX FLAGS MAGIC MOUNTAIN
26101 Magic Mountain Parkway, Valencia, w of I-5 at Magic Mountain Parkway exit ☎(805) 255-4100, from Los Angeles (213) 367-5965. Map 10I6 ▨ ▣ ✱ ♫ ⇦ AE CO VISA Open mid-May to mid-Sept Sun-Thurs 10am-10pm, Fri-Sat 10am-midnight; weekends and hols (except Christmas) all year.

Set in 260 landscaped acres in hilly Valencia, the newest of the big amusement parks in Southern California is something of an anthology of all the rest. Key among its permanent attractions are its 100 rides, and especially the thrill rides. No other place in California has as much equipment for shaking the boredom out of travel-weary, school-age children. The price of admission covers all rides.

The premier white-knuckle trips are on **Viper**, a looping roller coaster boasting speeds of up to 70mph and seven upside-down spirals, and its newest attraction, **Flashback**, which features a 540˚ spiral. Also recently added was **Psyclone**, a wooden coaster that is a replica of the legendary Coney Island Cyclone. It even features the sound of creaking wood to add to the thrill, but it is only the centerpiece in a collection of heart-stoppers. The park also has a loop roller coaster, a pirate ship that makes vertical swings at speeds useful for training astronauts to live through rocket launches, and the highest double-arm Ferris wheel in the world.

Carousels and other more sedate devices suit small children. Still other variations on roller coasters and spinning rides fit between the extremes.

In addition to rides, the spacious park has a dolphin show, a diving exhibition modeled after the famous cliff dives at Acapulco, a petting zoo, and a tots' playground called **Children's World** that features rides for little people, Warner Bros. cartoon characters and a participatory circus. A section called **Spillikin's Handcrafters Junction** has artisans in residence demonstrating turn-of-the-century techniques of candy-making, basket-weaving, wood-carving and glass-blowing. Last but not least, the park has regular live music, mime and magic performances, plus occasional major shows by big-name entertainers on summer evenings.

Like other theme parks, Six Flags Magic Mountain has a number of restaurants with menus ranging from fast-food to fairly elaborate, and from all-American through several national cuisines.

For those who prefer not to make the fairly long drive from Los Angeles, **Gray Line** runs tour buses from both LA and Orange County, and **Greyhound** provides a regular bus service.

SOUTHWEST MUSEUM 血
234 Museum Dr., Highland Park, N of Pasadena Freeway/SR-11, via Pasadena Ave. exit, then Marmion Way, about 2 miles E of Dodger Stadium and Elysian Park ☎*(213) 221-2163. Map 1B3* 🚃 ➡ *Open Tues-Sat 11am-5pm; Sun 1-5pm. Closed Mon; major holidays.*

This is LA's oldest museum. Greatly transcending its name, the Mission-style museum, begun in 1912, houses a wealth of material on Native Americans from Mexico to northernmost Alaska. Major displays cover the cliff-dwellers of the southwest, the Plains Indians, the North Coast Indians of British Columbia and Alaska, and the Inuit.

At an institution highly regarded for its anthropological and archeological research, several excellent dioramas depict the rich variety of Indian ways of life. A reminder of the European intrusions that destroyed those ways of life is provided by a depiction of Custer's Last Stand by an Indian participant. Perhaps the strongest collection of artifacts is basketry from every part of the American continent W of the Mississippi River. Materials in this and other collections date from 10,000 years ago to near-contemporary.

The museum hosts a **Festival of Native American Arts** every October. The adjacent **Casa de Adobe**, a pre-1850s-style ranch house built in 1918, provides galleries for the museum's collection of Hispanic art and artifacts. Also on show are period furnishings.

SUNSET STRIP
Sunset Blvd., West Hollywood, between Crescent Heights Blvd. and Doheny Dr. Map 4B-C4.

Running for almost two miles between Hollywood and Beverly Hills, Sunset Strip was once Hollywood's glossy playground. In the 1930s and '40s stars and starlets flocked by limousine to chic nightclubs such as Ciro's, the Mocambo and the Trocadero. The Strip has undergone several metamorphoses since then, hitting rock-bottom in the 1970s when it was characterized by porno theaters, prostitutes and drug addicts. Nowadays it is peopled by record companies, agents and managers, and movie producers. Fashionable hotels, trendy stores and restaurants, and nightclubs serving up rock-'n'-roll and comedy make for a nightlife almost as lively as the halcyon days.

Château Marmont *(8221 Sunset Blvd.* ☎ *(213) 656-1010)* was built in 1929 along the lines of a Norman castle and is as popular as ever with movie and music stars; Humphrey Bogart and Greta Garbo stayed here (see WHERE TO STAY). **St James's Club** *(8358 Sunset Blvd.* ☎ *(213) 654-8964)* is a beautifully restored 1931 Art Deco classic. Even harder to miss are the Strip's "vanity boards," enormous elevated billboards advertising who and what's new and hot in entertainment. Each is hand-painted and merits attention as great popular art.

TAIL O' THE PUP 🏛

329 N San Vicente Blvd., NW of Beverly Center. Map 4C4.

Displaced from its original site in 1988 by the new Ma Maison Sofitel hotel, the hot dog and hamburger stand constructed in 1946 in the shape of a hot dog, complete with yellow mustard, is regarded as a Pop Art classic. The hot dogs are so so, but most people are pleased that it has found a new home.

TELEVISION SHOWS

The major networks tape a number of shows before live audiences. Tickets to them are free.

Networks make some tickets available at their offices on the day of taping. **The Los Angeles Visitors and Convention Bureau Visitor Center** *(Arco Plaza, Level B, 6th and S Flower St., map 6D9)* has daily rations of tickets to many of the popular shows, which are also available on the day of taping. Other tickets are available from **Audiences Unlimited** *(* ☎ *(818)506-0067)*, which handles *Married with Children, Golden Girls, Roseanne* and *Major Dad,* among others.

Each show or studio has its own minimum age limit for audience guests — the range is 12-18 years — so families should check in advance. Few shows are taped between March and June.

ABC-TV Ticket Office

4151 Prospect Ave., Hollywood, an eastward extension of Hollywood Blvd.
☎ *(310) 557-4103. Map 6B8. Open Mon-Fri 9am-1pm, 2-5pm. Closed Sat-Sun. Tickets also available at ABC Entertainment Center, Plaza level, 2040 Ave. of the Stars, Century City. Map 3D2. Open Mon-Sat 10am-10pm. Closed Sun.*

CBS-TV Ticket Office

7800 Beverly Blvd., Hollywood, at Fairfax Ave. ☎ *(213) 852-4002. Map 4C5. Open Mon-Fri 9am-5pm; Sat-Sun 10am-5pm.*

Shows include *Wheel of Fortune, The Price is Right* and *Family Feud.*

Fox Television Ticket Office

5746 W Sunset Blvd., Hollywood ☎ *(213) 856-1520; for recorded information (818) 506-0067. Map 5B6. Open Mon-Fri 8.30am-5.30pm. Closed Sat-Sun.*

NBC-TV Ticket Office

3000 W Alameda Ave., Burbank, via Hollywood Way exit from Ventura Freeway/

SR-134 ☎*(818) 840-3537. Map* **1**B2. *Open Mon-Fri 8.30am-5.30pm; Sat-Sun 9am-4pm.*

The Tonight Show is taped here. Note that tickets are only posted within California, but if you live outside you will be sent, upon application, a letter of priority, providing a first chance in the line on the day.

Paramount Television Audience Shows
780 N Gower St. ☎*(213) 468-5575 for information. Map* **5**C6.

Shows include the top-rating comedy *Cheers* and *The Arsenio Hall Show.*

Hollywood on Location
8644 Wilshire Blvd., Beverly Hills ☎*(310) 659-9165. Map* **4**D4. *Open Mon-Fri 9.30am-5pm. Closed Sat-Sun.*

This provides daily location lists of which TV shows, movies and rock videos are shooting around the city, along with maps of how to find them and lists of stars likely to be on set. However, the service is expensive.

THE TEMPORARY CONTEMPORARY Ⅲ
152 N Central Ave. (Downtown, near junction with 1st St.) ☎*(213) 626-6222. Map* **6**D9 ▨ *(but* ▣ *Thurs 5pm-8pm)* ﴾ ➤ *Open Tues-Wed, Sat-Sun 11am-6pm; Thurs-Fri 11am-8pm. Closed Mon; Thanksgiving; Dec 2; Jan 1.*

In 1983 architect Frank Gehry renovated two warehouses to create a lofty space of 70,000 square feet. Initially the Temporary Contemporary was envisaged as just that, a temporary home for the MUSEUM OF CONTEMPORARY ART before its California Plaza home was built. But its imaginative exhibitions have given the Temporary a life of its own, working in harness with its sister museum. The admission fee covers MOCA as well.

TRAVEL TOWN
An open-air museum of transport in GRIFFITH PARK.

UNION PASSENGER STATION Ⅲ
800 N Alameda St. ☎*(213) 683-6873. Map* **6**D9 ▣

The last (1939) grand-scale railroad station to be built out West, this was once the opulent end of the line for passengers chasing the setting sun. Working jointly for the Union Pacific, Southern Pacific and Santa Fe companies, architects John and Donald Parkinson overlaid basic Spanish Colonial Revival with touches of Streamline Moderne and Moorish design, achieving a handsomely proportioned structure where inside and out are interwoven. With its ceramic-tiled floors, wood-beamed ceilings and the many original furnishings still in place, the station is a stylish evocation of Southern California's prewar era. The surrounding courtyards provide travelers with an accurate and imaginative reflection of the vivid variety of flora that awaits them.

UNIVERSAL STUDIOS ★
100 Universal City Plaza, Universal City (at Lankershim/Universal City exit from Hollywood Freeway/US-101) ☎*(818) 777-3794. Map* **1**B2 ▨ ✗ *compulsory*

📺 ✱ 🚃 *Open daily for tours late May-late June 9am-4pm; late June-early Sept 8am-6pm; early Sept-late May Mon-Fri 10am-3.30pm, Sat-Sun 9.30am-4pm. Closed Thanksgiving; Dec 25.*

Carl Laemmle moved his studio here from Hollywood in 1915, and soon recognized that the public would pay for a behind-the-screen look at movies; the very first visitors paid 25¢. He was right; but could scarcely have guessed that it would become the sixth most popular attraction on earth, with well over 4 million visitors a year.

Nowadays it is pricier, but wittily commentated streetcar tours take in tantalizingly familiar sets for Westerns, monster thrillers, sci-fi and every other movie genre. Visitors see through the illusion of some amazing action sequences — for example, a collapsing bridge, the parting of the Red Sea, and an alpine avalanche — and visit back-lot departments that reveal yet more of the tricks used in movie-making. Expect close encounters with King Kong, Jaws and the Bates mansion from Hitchcock's *Psycho,* and to be caught in a spectacular man-made Earthquake registering 8.3 on the Richter Scale, as well as the crossfire of a space-age laser gunfight.

After the tour, the **Entertainment Center** offers a variety of spectacles, including the taping of an episode from *Star Trek,* with members of the audience invited to play starring roles and the results played back on video; the $5 million *Adventures of Conan* sorcery show; an action-packed scene from *Miami Vice;* Cowboy Stuntmen in action; and Animal Actors doing their things.

Among new attractions following a $100 million facelift are *E.T. Adventure,* a hi-tech ride employing robotics, fiber optics, and other wizardry to carry the visitor to E.T.'s home planet; and the **Tribute to Lucy Museum** focusing on the ever-popular comedienne Lucille Ball.

Frankenstein's Monster, Charlie Chaplin and other movie-star look-alikes tour the grounds and will pose for pictures. Allow at least five hours overall.

UNIVERSITY OF CALIFORNIA, LOS ANGELES (UCLA)

405 Hilgard Ave., Westwood (between Sunset Blvd., Hilgard Ave., Le Conte Ave., Gayley Ave. and Veteran Ave.). Visitor Center ☎(310) 206-8147. Map 3C2 📷 ✗ 📺 🚃

The first buildings went up in 1929. Since then UCLA has expanded across more than 400 acres to comprise 13 colleges and 69 departments. The campus grounds are beautifully landscaped and include a traditional **Japanese rock garden**, a delightful **botanical garden** thick with tropical and subtropical plants, and a five-acre **sculpture garden** peppered with some 50 works by artists such as Rodin, Moore and Matisse.

The buildings are, on the whole, less distinguished. The exceptions include the four original buildings: **Powell Library, Kinsey Hall, Haines Hall** and **Royce Hall**. All are a combination of red brick and beige stone in Italian Romanesque style. Also on campus are the **Museum of Cultural History** (☎ *(310) 206-1459),* the **Wight Art Gallery** (☎ *(310) 825-9345)* and, best of all, the **Film and Television Archive**

(☎ *(310) 206-8013)*, an impressive collection of material dating back to the earliest days of cinema, although requests to view must be made well in advance.

VENICE
s of Santa Monica via Pacific Ave., or at the w end of Venice Blvd. Map 1C1.

For some years now the beach town of Venice has been regarded as *the* place for an authentic taste of legendary West Coast libertarianism, zaniness, excess, eccentricity and exhibitionism. Ocean front acts as a magnet for all sorts of good-natured oddballs eager to strut, or often roller-skate, their stuff.

It wasn't always thus. The town was originally created early this century by tobacco magnate Albert Kinney. His dream was to mirror the original. Sixteen miles of canal were dug, narrow bridges straddled them and elegant houses and hotels lined them. Fires, storm damage and bad engineering soon caused problems. The dream was finally sullied after oil was discovered and the polluted canals were filled in. It became a slightly disreputable place, most notable for anything-goes clubs and divers entertainments.

Bohemians first colonized the then run-down town in the 1950s, further entrenching the rapscallion reputation that Venice still retains, though nowadays it is scarcely justified. Rich, fashionable people and retirees have moved in and real estate located near the beach is now expensive.

Still, there are narrow streets, probably a greater concentration of art galleries than anywhere else in LA — and then there's the boardwalk, officially known as **Ocean Front Walk**. It tends to get very crowded, especially on holidays and weekends, and competition for attention is fierce. So, unless you're built like a Playboy, or Playgirl centerfold, walk on stilts, ride a penny-farthing, or juggle chainsaws, don't expect any. However, ogling is free, and the bizarre and beautiful people crave it.

The street performers working the Walk are pretty impressive too. At Muscle Beach, where budding Schwarzeneggers, male and female, work out with weights in the open air, hawkers sell seaside gewgaws and inexpensive leisurewear, and there are fast food and drink stalls. Bring your skateboard.

WALK OF FAME ☆
Hollywood Blvd. between Gower St. and Sycamore Ave., and Vine Street between Yucca St. and Sunset Blvd. Map 5B6.

Since 1958 almost 2,000 brass-edged stars, inlaid with the names of entertainment industry celebrities, have been embedded in the sidewalk. The street is seedier than in its heyday but improving, and volunteer fans polish the stars; Marilyn Monroe has a waiting list.

WATTS TOWERS ★
Willowbrook Ave. and 107th St., midway between Long Beach and Harbor Freeways in Watts district. Map 1D3 🖾 *Open for ✗ only, on Sat, from 10am-3pm (☎ (310) 271-9711), but towers visible from all sides.*

Rodia's lifetime work and folk-art masterpiece, constructed from the affluent city's scraps.

Sabbatino (Simon) Rodia, a tile-setter by trade, spent three decades (from 1921 to 1954) building this giant, magical, *objet trouvé* sculpture. The towers — the tallest central tower is 107 feet — are made of salvaged steel rods and scrap metal coated with concrete, and decorated with ceramic and glass fragments and 70,000 sea-shells. Once threatened by vandals and demolition plans, the towers are now administered by the Los Angeles Department of Cultural Affairs. Restoration work is now complete.

WAYFARERS' CHAPEL 🏛

5755 Palos Verdes Dr. S, Rancho Palos Verdes ☎*(310) 377-1650. Map **1**E2*
📷 ☞ *Open 11am-4pm.*
Lloyd Wright, son of Frank Lloyd Wright, designed this famous glass-and-redwood church erected in 1949 in tribute to theologian and mystic Emanuel Swedenborg. Blending in with the surrounding forest, the church, which overlooks the ocean, is open to all.

WILL ROGERS STATE HISTORIC PARK

14325 Sunset Blvd. ☎*(310) 454-8212. Map **10**l6* 📷 ☞ ◄€ *Park open 8am-7pm summer, 8am-5pm remainder of the year; house open 10am-5pm. Closed Jan 1; Thanksgiving; Dec 25.*
The estate of the cowboy philosopher and humorist is one of the finest remaining opportunities to see how movie stars of the grand era lived. Will Rogers' 187-acre property has its own polo field, still in use. There is a collection of memorabilia, including valuable paintings by Morgan Russell and Frederic Remington, Navajo rugs and cowboy things, inside the Spanish Revival-style house.

Where to stay

Making your choice

In hotels, as in everything else, Los Angeles is a great shopper's bazaar for anyone willing to spend. Beyond its vast number of comfortable, conventional modern towers, it has a remarkable supply of unusual places. Some are merely distinctive, but others — including a cluster of high-rise glass-walled cylinders, a Norman castle, and a tropical garden hideaway — are unique. And, because the city is acutely aware of its hi-tech hinterland, there is competition not only to provide comfort and service, but also the latest in technological aids to allow the mobile executive to keep in touch via phone, fax and computer modem. The newest hotels often go even further, offering an in-room CD-player and VCR, not to mention a score of cable TV channels, and rapid in-room checkout via the TV.

For all the variety, some types of accommodation are lacking. Small bed-and-breakfast establishments of the type commonplace in San Francisco are rare in Los Angeles: in our selection, SALISBURY HOUSE is a worthy representative of this scarce breed. Although **Santa Monica** has a range of hotels and motels near its beach, beach resorts as such are uncommon. **Downtown** has few relatively small, moderately priced old hotels. Most districts have none.

In an area where budget-conscious travelers do not find easy pickings, good rooms can be difficult to find in many districts of prime interest to visitors. Alternatives are to shop for weekend or off-season special rates in business-oriented hotels, or to seek out the better chain motels. For longer stays of a month or more, investigate the very competitively priced efficiency (self-catering) apartments: we include the OAKWOOD APARTMENTS in our selection as a good representative example.

CHOOSING BY DISTRICT

There are tight clusters of hotels **Downtown**, in **Mid-Wilshire** and especially at the entrance to **Los Angeles International Airport**. But only visitors doing business or in a hurry, or both, are likely to be attracted to Downtown or airport areas; neither is especially lively or interesting, especially after dark.

Otherwise, in keeping with the general nature of Los Angeles, hostelries are usually scattered throughout districts as well as across the length and breadth of the basin. The districts already named, along with **Westside** (Beverly Hills-Westwood-Bel Air-Brentwood), **Hollywood**, Coastal centers such as **Marina del Rey** and **Santa Monica**, as well as Valley towns such as **Pasadena** and **Burbank**, are the most likely headquarters for visitors. When shopping around for bargain rates in less central districts, consider easy access to a freeway as an important advantage.

CHAIN HOTELS

Many hotels are of course members of a chain. In the following pages, pressure of space prevents description of more than one outstanding member of such leading chains as BEST WESTERN, HILTON, HYATT, SHERATON and HOLIDAY INN. Following this landmark entry will be found a short list of other representative hotels in the chain, with their locations, telephone numbers and price categories, and a central reservations telephone number where appropriate.

BUDGET ACCOMMODATIONS

Ending this chapter is a selection of pleasant low-cost accommodations for younger travelers.

ADVANCE RESERVATIONS

Contact the **Southern California Hotel Reservations Center** *(P.O. Box 4569, Anaheim, CA 92803-4569* ☎ *(714) 772-7507),* which also handles motels and inns. The service is free.

TAXES

A hotel tax will be added to quoted rates. The percentage varies by municipality. Los Angeles charges 7.5 percent, Beverly Hills 8.2 percent, Redondo Beach 5 percent. Others fall within that range.

HOW TO USE THIS CHAPTER

The following alphabetical list of hotels is selective, covering a broad spectrum of size, price, area and character. Addresses, telephone and fax numbers are given, and other symbols denote many categories of information, from ☎ (quiet hotel) to ✪ (conference facilities). The luxury hotel (🏨) and good-value (♣) symbols are awarded in only a small number of cases.

See HOW TO USE THIS BOOK **on page 7 for a full list of symbols.**

Price categories for hotels listed on the following pages are intended only as guidelines to average prices. There are four bands: inexpensive (▥), moderate (▦), expensive (▨) and very expensive (▩). They are based on the approximate cost, in fall 1992, of a double room with bathroom, including the cost of breakfast. Single rooms are not much cheaper. Even with cost inflation, hotels will normally remain in the same price category.

Symbol	Category	Current price
▩	very expensive	over $210
▨	expensive	$160–210
▦	moderate	$100–160
▥	inexpensive	$50–100

HOTELS CLASSIFIED BY AREA

CENTRAL
Los Angeles Airport Marriott ▥
Salisbury House ▣

COASTAL
Barnaby's ▥ to ▥
Best Western Jamaica Bay Inn ▥ to ▥
Cadillac Hotel ▢
Holiday Inn–Los Angeles International Airport ▥
Hotel Queen Mary ▥ to ▥
Huntley ▥ to ▥
Hyatt at Los Angeles Airport ▥
Interclub Hostel ▢
Loews Santa Monica Beach ▥ to ▥
Ritz Carlton, Laguna Niguel ▥ to ▥
Marina del Rey ▥ to ▥
Oakwood Apartments Marina del Rey ▢ to ▥
Ritz Carlton, Marina del Rey ▥ to ▥
Shangri-La ▥ to ▥
Sheraton Plaza–La Reina ▥ to ▥
Venice Beach Cotel ▢

DOWNTOWN
Biltmore ▥
Checkers ▥ to ▥
Figueroa ▥
Holiday Inn–Convention Center ▥ to ▥
Holiday Inn–Downtown ▥
Hyatt Regency–Los Angeles ▥
Los Angeles Hilton and Towers ▥
Miyako Inn ▥
Mayfair ▥ to ▥
New Otani Hotel & Garden ▥
Sheraton–Grande ▥
Westin Bonaventure ▥

HOLLYWOOD
Le Bel Age ▥
Best Western Hollywood Plaza Inn ▥
Best Western Sunset Plaza ▥
Château Marmont ▥ to ▥
Le Dufy ▥ to ▥
Hollywood Roosevelt ▥ to ▥
Hyatt on Sunset ▥ to ▥
Ma Maison Sofitel ▥
St James's Club ▥
Sunset Marquis Hotel & Villas ▥

VALLEYS
Burbank Airport Hilton ▥
Ritz-Carlton, Huntington ▥ to ▥
Oakwood Apartments Toluca Hills ▢ to ▥
Oakwood Apartments Woodland Hills ▢ to ▥
Safari Inn ▥ to ▥
Sheraton–Universal ▥
Sportsmen's Lodge ▥
Universal City Hilton ▥

WESTSIDE
Bel-Air ▥
Bel-Air Sands ▥
Bel-Air Summit ▥
Beverly Hills ▥
Beverly Hilton ▥
Beverly Terrace ▢ to ▥
Beverly Wilshire ▥
Century Plaza ▥
L'Ermitage ▥
Four Seasons ▥
Hotel Nikko ▥ to ▥
Miramar–Sheraton ▥
Oakwood Apartments Mid Wilshire ▢ to ▥
Westwood Marquis ▥
Westwood Plaza (Holiday Inn) ▥

LA's hotels A to Z

BARNABY'S

3501 N Sepulveda Blvd., Manhattan Beach 90266 ☎*(310) 545-8466, (800) 732-1540* ⊠*(310) 545-5849. Map 1D2* ▥ to ▥ *128 units* ⊶ ⇌ AE ⊙ CD VISA ▢ ⊡ ✿ ⚓ ∿ ☂ ♫ ⚓

Location: 2 miles s of LAX, half a block s of Rosencrans Ave. A family-run hotel of European charm and elegance set incongruously in surfuria. Barnaby's decor is hard to pin down, lying somewhere between Victorian England and turn-of-the-century Vienna. Nevertheless the result is engaging, and the rooms, both private and public, are a successful blend of antique decor and modern amenity. Service is friendly, the enclosed gardens are especially pleasant, and the restaurant serves good traditional Viennese cuisine. Complimentary London black cabs are available for guests.

LE BEL AGE ⌸

1020 N San Vicente Blvd., West Hollywood 90069 ☎*(310) 854-1111. Map 3C3* ▥ *198 units* ⊶ ⇌ AE ⊙ CD VISA ‡ ▢ ⊡ ✿ ∿ ☂ ♫

Location: Half a block s of Sunset Strip. From the outside just another undistinguished Los Angeles building. Inside is a different story: pure luxury. No rooms here, only suites, all of them lavishly done out with original art and fine furniture, three telephones, extra-large TV, and private balcony. Public rooms are equally tasteful, and the atmosphere is one of discretion and exclusivity. Le Bel Age also offers secretarial and limousine services and boasts a fine Franco-Russian restaurant.

BEL-AIR ⌸

701 Stone Canyon Rd., Los Angeles 90024 ☎*(310) 472-1211.* ⊠*(310) 476-5890. Map 3C1* ▥ *92 units* ⊶ ⇌ AE ⊙ CD VISA ⌸ ▢ ⊡ ✿ ⚓ ∿ ☂ ♫

Location: Directly n of UCLA campus, accessible from Sunset Blvd. All the clichés of the well-heeled Southern California style of life are summed up by home-away-from-home Spanish Mission-style haciendas snuggled into 10 acres of fairytale semitropical gardens in a remote-feeling part of residential Bel-Air. Many of the legendary names of Hollywood hide away here. Suites are luxuriously furnished with antiques; rooms are simpler. The staff cossets guests with skill but without stuffy formality. No conventions or tour groups are allowed. Advance deposits are required.

BEL-AIR SUMMIT

11461 Sunset Blvd., Los Angeles 90049 ☎*(310) 476-6571, (800) 352-6680. Map 1C1* ▥ *181 units* ⊶ ⇌ AE ⊙ CD VISA ⌂ ‡ ▢ ⊡ ✿ ⚓ ∿ ♪ ☂ ☂

Location: One block w of San Diego Freeway/I-405, Sunset Blvd. exit. Two modern 2-story buildings in a steep hillside garden setting. Lanais (balconies) help bring the outdoors into the large rooms or suites, boldly decorated in sunny colors. Many units have separate dining nooks. The bar and pool area are popular with locals. Free limousine service to Westwood and Beverly Hills is only one of the extra touches provided by this hotel.

BEST WESTERN JAMAICA BAY INN

4175 Admiralty Way, Marina del Rey 90291 ☎*(310) 823-5333. Map 1C1* ▥ to ▥ *42 units* ⊶ ⇌ AE ⊙ CD VISA ‡ ▢ ⊡ ✿ ◁ ∿ ⊞ ☂ ☂ ♫

Location: On the Marina del Rey Yacht harbor, one block from Washington St. A comfortable two-story motel adjoins a white-sand beach by the sheltered waters of the yacht harbor. Many rooms have patios overlooking the beach and harbor. Advance deposit required.

OTHER BEST WESTERNS

Best Western Hollywood Plaza Inn (☎*(213) 851-1800* ▥*)*, convenient for the Hollywood Freeway; **Best Western Sunset Plaza** (☎*(213) 654-0750* ▥*)*, close to Sunset Strip.

For information on other Best Westerns and reservations in the LA area ☎(800) 528-1234.

BEVERLY HILLS HOTEL

9641 Sunset Blvd., Beverly Hills 90210
☎*(310) 276-2251, (800) 792-7637. Map*
3C3 📶 *263 units* 🚗 🍴 AE ◉ ◉ VISA
🏨 ✦ 🖥 🖨 ✂ ⚓ ♨ ℘ 🏋 ❤ 🎵

Location: In a residential area, less than a mile N of Wilshire Blvd. via Cañon Dr. or Rodeo Dr. All of the mythical big deals by Hollywood tycoons, and some of the real ones, have been fixed over breakfast in the **Polo Lounge** (see page 144) of this grand garden hotel, first opened in 1912. The Polo Lounge feels perhaps a little tired these days, but the hotel still provides a perfect atmosphere for a Hollywood deal or for a dip into the milieu. On 12 acres, it has fine gardens with royal palms, banana and jacaranda trees, a huge pool, and floodlit tennis courts. Rooms in the rosy pink, Spanish Colonial-style main building are immense and are furnished with quiet luxury. Many of them have fireplaces, and most have bars.

Rooms in 20 bungalows dotted around the property are more variable in size, but no less richly furnished. Conventions are not accepted. The hotel is owned by the Sultan of Brunei. Reservation deposit required.

BEVERLY HILTON

9876 Wilshire Blvd., Beverly Hills 90210
☎*(310) 274-7777* 📠*(310) 285-1313.*
Map *3D3* 📶 *592 units* 🚗 🍴 AE ◉ ◉
VISA ✦ ♿ 🖥 🖨 ⚓ ♨ 🏋 ❤ 🎵 ♫

Location: Near the intersection of Wilshire Blvd. and Santa Monica Blvd. The traditional home of the Academy Awards ball is not exactly a typical Hilton. Both public and guest rooms are decorated less functionally than the norm for this far-ranging chain. The lobby is nondescript, but the **International Ballroom** has a glittering opulence that attracts conventions and gala events. All guest rooms are bright, informal and remarkably varied in decor. However, many are small, so visitors wanting a larger room need to ask for one. Rooms facing away from Wilshire Blvd. have private balconies; quite a few overlook a spacious pool

and lounge area. Among the Beverly Hilton's restaurants is a well-regarded branch of **Trader Vic's**.

OTHER HILTONS

The **Los Angeles Hilton and Towers** (☎ *(213) 629-4321* 📶), in the Downtown area; the **Burbank Airport Hilton** (☎ *(818) 843-6000* 📶), opposite the airport; the **Universal City Hilton** (☎ *(818) 506-2500* 📶), near Universal Studios (previously called The Registry).

BEVERLY TERRACE

469 N Doheny Dr., Beverly Hills 90210
☎*(310) 274-8141, (800) 421-7223. Map*
3C3 📶 *to* 📶 *39 units* 🚗 🍴 AE ◉ ◉
VISA ⚓ 🖥 🖨

A small, intimate hotel, unremarkable save for its moderate rates and upscale location. Popular with the design set, supremely convenient for Westside shopping, theaters and restaurants, and so sought after that it's necessary to reserve well in advance.

BEVERLY WILSHIRE

9500 Wilshire Blvd., Beverly Hills 90212
☎*(310) 275-5200, (800) 282-4804*
📠*(310) 274-2851. Map 3D3* 📶 *380 units* 🚗 🍴 AE ◉ ◉ VISA ✦ 🖥 🖨 ✂
《 ⚓ 🏋 ❤ 🎵 ♫

Location: At the intersection of Wilshire Blvd. and Rodeo Dr. Of all the grand hotels in Los Angeles, the Beverly Wilshire clings most faithfully to the starchy era of grand manners. In both the original hotel (the **Wilshire Wing)** and in a modern tower (the **Beverly Wing**), opulence remains the watchword. Rooms in the tower are decorated floor by floor, tracing California history from Spanish beginnings to trendy modern, with plenty of luxury and marble bathrooms in evidence.

The older wing is more spacious and traditional, suited to the tastes of the hotel's established guest list, which includes kings, presidents and legendary movie stars. Among the restaurants and bars, **El Padrino** is famous as a meeting place of movie moguls and leading businessmen.

BILTMORE 🏨 ♨ 🏛

506 S Grand Ave., Los Angeles 90071
☎*(213) 624-1011, (800) 421-8000, (800)*
252-0175 🖷*(213) 612-1545. Map* **6**D9
🎞 *700 units* [AE] [●] [●●] [VISA] ‡ ⓺ □ ⌂
🌿 ➰ 🍸 ♨ ☕ 🍽 ☀ ♨ ♨

Location: Downtown at 5th St., across from Pershing Sq. A grand old Downtown landmark restored to its 1920s glories. Externally the style is Beaux-Arts; internally it draws upon a host of traditions, most notably Italian-Spanish Renaissance. The old lobby and **Main Galeria** are magnificent, with acres of marble and lofty hand-painted and gilded ceilings. Some of the suites are as rich in material and detail as the Galeria, although not quite as large. Guest rooms maintain the level of quality but in more modern style. The attached pâtisserie is excellent, and **Bernard's**, the Biltmore's formal restaurant, still has its fans.

CENTURY PLAZA 🏨

2025 Ave. of the Stars, Los Angeles 90067
☎*(310) 277-2000, (800) 228-3000. Map* **3**D2 🎞 *1,072 units* ⛟ ➰ [AE] [●] [●●] [VISA]
‡ ⓺ □ ⌂ ⋘ ➰ ♨ ♨ ☕ ♪ ♨

Location: Century City, opposite ABC Entertainment Center. A member of the uniformly excellent Westin chain, and still popular with Ronald Reagan and his friends, the Century Plaza collects awards annually for its comfort and service. Spacious guest rooms are expensively furnished and have private balconies, some with marvelous views. However, the great curving mass of concrete and glass was designed as an efficiently elegant convention hotel — its primary function — and it lacks some warmth and character as a result.

CHÂTEAU MARMONT

8221 Sunset Blvd., Hollywood 90046
☎*(213) 656-1010, (800) 242-8328. Map* **4**B4 🎞 *to* 🎞 *63 units* ⛟ [AE] [●] [●●] [VISA]
⌂ ‡ ☀ ➰ ⋘ ➰

Location: In Hollywood Hills, w of Fairfax Ave. at the E end of Sunset Strip. Even in Hollywood a gray-walled Norman castle with a Mediterranean lobby looks a shade curious, but Château Marmont is prized all the same, or perhaps all the more. The 1920s building has been a favorite haunt of actors of widely separated generations. Carole Lombard and Jean Harlow favored it when it was new, Greta Garbo and Humphrey Bogart stayed here before it declined, and since its 1976 renovation Al Pacino and other New York actors have revived the glamor. The pool-side bungalows are popular, and there are good views from the main balconies.

CHECKERS 🏨

535 S Grand Ave., Los Angeles 90020
☎*(213) 624-0000* 🖷*(213) 626-9906. Map* **6**D9 🎞 *to* 🎞 *205 units* [⌂] ➰ [AE]
[●] [●●] [VISA] ➰ 🍸 ‡ □ ⌂ ♨ ☕ 🍽

Location: Central Downtown. Opened in 1989 after a tasteful, luxurious $49 million remodeling of what was the 1927 Mayflower Hotel, Checkers has an intimacy and refinement more usually found in Beverly Hills than Downtown. Interior design, by Richard Northcutt, and service are exceptional, as is the largely chinoiserie artwork displayed in rooms and public areas. The innovative restaurant is already a popular venue, especially for lunch, and there are special weekend packages.

LE DUFY

1000 Westmount Dr., West Hollywood 90069 ☎*(310) 657-7400. Map* **4**C4 🎞 *to* 🎞 *121 units* ⛟ [AE] [●] [●●] [VISA] ⌂ ⋘
➰ ‡ □ ⌂ ♨

Location: Three blocks s of Sunset Blvd, one block s of Holloway Dr. A more affordable cousin of LE BEL AGE, Le Dufy is a modern hotel with the feel of an apartment building on a quiet residential street within striking distance of Beverly Hills. Most suites have a living room with living gas fire and a balcony; some have small kitchens. As well as the pool, there's a rooftop Jacuzzi, self-service laundry and baby-sitting service.

L'ERMITAGE 🏨

9291 Burton Way, Beverly Hills 90210
☎*(310) 278-3344, (800) 282-4818. Map* **3**C3 🎞 *112 units* ⛟ ➰ [AE] [●] [●●] [VISA]
‡ □ ⌂ 🌿 ♨ ⋘ ➰ ♨ ♪

Location: On a residential boulevard five blocks E of Rodeo Dr., between Santa Monica Blvd. and Wilshire Blvd. L'Ermitage has been called the finest hotel in the US, and given the prices and the staff-to-guest ratios it ought to be. The frontage has something of the air of an embassy about it and, although the Braques, Dufys and Renoirs on the walls are not originals, the decor throughout is immaculate. Privacy is guaranteed, service is impeccable, and a French chef presides over a private dining room for residents and their guests. A limousine is at one's disposal at no extra charge. A reservation deposit is required.

FIGUEROA
939 S Figueroa St., Los Angeles 90015
☎(213) 627-8971, (800) 331-5151. Map
6E8 █ 280 units ⬅ ⇌ AE ◆ ◯ VISA
⬇ ⋙ ✦ ☐ ◿ ⚡ ♈

Location: Downtown, one block from Convention Center. This is a charming Spanish-style hotel dating from 1927, with a beautiful lobby, huge swimming pool and palm-fringed courtyard. Rooms are of a generous size. The hotel is popular with performing arts companies on tour.

FOUR SEASONS ⌂
300 S Doheny Dr., Beverly Hills 90048
☎(310) 273-2222, (800) 332-3442
ⒻⓍ(310) 859-3824. Map 3C3 █ 285
units ⬅ ⇌ AE ◆ ◯ VISA ⌂ ✦ ☐ ◿
⋙ ♈ ♈

Location: Corner of Burton Way. An attractive recent addition to LA's range of hotels, the Four Seasons is a relatively small European-style establishment. Rooms and suites are large and elegantly furnished, and each has a balcony. Public areas are tastefully decorated with marble, original art and fresh flowers. There are all the refinements and amenities one would expect, including 24-hour concierge, baby sitting, and complimentary limousines to Rodeo Dr.

HILTONS
See after **BEVERLY HILTON**.

HOLIDAY INNS
See after **WESTWOOD PLAZA**.

HOLLYWOOD ROOSEVELT
7000 Hollywood Blvd., Hollywood 90028
☎(213) 466-7000, (800) 858-2244. Map
5B5 █ to █ 400 units ⬅ ⇌ AE ◆
◯ VISA ⬇ ⋙ ✦ ☐ ◿ ⚡ ♈ ♈ ⋒

Location: Across from Mann's Chinese Theater. Reopened in 1985 after a $35-million face-lift, the Roosevelt is back to something like its former self. Site of the first Academy Awards, it was once a favorite with celebrities such as Errol Flynn, Clark Gable, Carole Lombard, Ernest Hemingway and Salvador Dalí. Nowadays, movie, TV and music industry types enjoy the echoes. The high-ceilinged Spanish Colonial-style lobby, the Olympic-sized swimming pool and the stylish **Cinegrill Supper Club** are all fashionable places in which to see and be seen.

HOTEL NIKKO ⌂
465 La Cienega Blvd., Los Angeles 90048
☎(310) 247-0400. Map 4C4 █ to █
304 units ⌂ ⇌ ⋙ AE ◆ ◯ VISA ⚹ ⋙
♈ ✦ ☐ ◿ ♈ ⋒ ⟨ ▣

Location: Near the Beverly Center, Wilshire Blvd., the Pacific Design Center and Melrose Ave. Opened in December 1991, the Nikko is a welcome addition to this up-and-coming stretch of La Cienega. Further stylish developments are planned around here, and already there's plenty that is of interest within walking distance. As befits a hotel whose parent company hails from Tokyo, Nikko designer Frank Mingis has successfully fused hi-tech American design with Japanese simplicity, notably in the strikingly beautiful lobby, laid out like a Japanese garden. The spacious rooms are distinguished by tasteful furnishings and lots of useful gadgetry, while the bathrooms are equipped with deep Japanese soaking tubs and separate power showers. There are Club floors for special pampering, and room service and restaurants feature Japanese cuisine. There's also an up-to-the-minute business center.

115

HOTEL QUEEN MARY

Pier J, PO Box 8, Long Beach 90801
☎*(310) 435-3511. Map 1E3* ▥ *to* ▥▥
365 units ⛵ ≈ 🆎 ⊡ ⊙ 🆅🆂🅰 ⅃ ♨ ☐
◲ 🕷 ♈ ♫ ⅋

Location: Harborside, at the s end of Long Beach Freeway/I-710. 1930s-style Art Deco luxury aboard one of the greatest ever ocean liners, and a chance to experience how the wealthy traveled before the jet plane. Although restored and kitted out with modern necessities such as telephones and TVs, many of the rooms and suites retain their original furnishings and decoration. The outside rooms, with portholes, are pricier but preferable.

At the time of writing, the future of this grand old institution was uncertain. See also page 169.

HUNTLEY

1111 Second St., Santa Monica 90403
☎*(310) 394-5454. Map 1C1* ▥ *to* ▥▥
210 units ◲ ≈ 🆎 ⊡ ⊙ 🆅🆂🅰 ▱ ♨ ☐
◲ 🕷 ◈ ♈ ♫ ⅋

Location: Two blocks from the beach near Wilshire Blvd. The rooms, in a tower with fine views across the bay, are tastefully decorated and furnished.

HYATT REGENCY–LOS ANGELES

711 S Hope St., Los Angeles 90017
☎*(213) 683-1234, (800) 228-9000. Map 6D9* ▥▥ *480 units* ◲ ≈ 🆎 ⊡ ⊙ 🆅🆂🅰
♨ ☐ ◲ 🕷 ◈ ♛ ♈ ♫

Location: Downtown at 7th St. A conventional modern tower much improved by a $30-million facelift. One floor is set aside for nonsmokers. Another floor is titled the **Regency Club**, which has richly comfortable library lounges, a butler to attend to personal needs and to put out afternoon hors d'oeuvres and cocktails, and a concierge to arrange such things as transportation. Throughout the hotel, spacious rooms are furnished in expensive good taste.

OTHER HYATTS

The **Hyatt at Los Angeles Airport** (☎*(310) 670-9000* ▥▥), at the front entrance to Los Angeles International

Airport; the **Hyatt on Sunset** (☎*(213) 656-4101* ▥▥ *to* ▥▥), in Hollywood; the **Hyatt Wilshire** (☎*(213) 381-7411,* ▥▥), in Mid-Wilshire.

For central Hyatt information ☎(800) 228-9000.

LOEWS SANTA MONICA BEACH ☖

1700 Ocean Ave., Santa Monica 90401
☎*(310) 458-6700* 🅵🆇*(310) 458-6761. Map 10I6* ▥▥ *to* ▥▥ *349 units* ◲ ≈ 🆎
⊡ ⊙ 🆅🆂🅰 ◈ ⋙ ♜ ♈ ♛ ♨ ◲ ♈ ⚓
▤

Location: On the Santa Monica beachfront, s of the pier. A notable addition, not least because beachside accommodations for visitors are so rare. Opened in 1989, the hotel itself is distinguished by Southern California pastel colors and a soaring central atrium. Not all rooms front the Pacific, so if you want to enjoy the view and the sunsets be sure to ask for "oceanside." As well as the beach, Loews is just a walk or short drive from Santa Monica's other main attractions.

LOS ANGELES AIRPORT MARRIOTT

5855 W Century Blvd., Los Angeles 90045
☎*(310) 641-5700. Map 1D2* ▥▥ *1,019 units* ⛵ ◲ ≈ 🆎 ⊡ ⊙ 🆅🆂🅰 ♨ ⅃ ☐
◲ 🕷 ⋙ ♫ ♈ ♫ ⅋

Location: Near the front entrance to LAX. Spanish overtones in the lobby and subtle earth tones in spacious rooms give real warmth to a modern tower hotel aimed primarily at executive travelers. Suites are luxurious. A four-story wing surrounds a large swimming pool with gardens and ample terraces around it, suitable for gentle strolls.

MA MAISON SOFITEL ☖ 🏛

8555 Beverly Blvd., Los Angeles 90048
☎*(310) 278-5444, (800) 221-4542*
🅵🆇*(310) 657-2816. Map 4C4* ▥▥ *311 units* ⛵ ≈ 🆎 ⊡ ⊙ 🆅🆂🅰 ♨ ▱ ⅃ ⋙
♛ ♈ ☐ ◲ ♈

Location: At the intersection of Beverly and La Cienega Blvds., opposite the Beverly Center. This made quite a splash when it opened in December 1988. The Post-Modern architecture, with hints of French Château and Spanish Colonial Revival, is matched by the understated pastel elegance of the interiors and a European sense of intimacy. The location is hard to beat for shopping, dining and nightlife. The name points to what could be its major attraction: the justly famous MA MAISON restaurant (see WHERE TO EAT) is relocated here, along with its French/California cuisine. There is also a promising brasserie patterned after La Coupole in Paris.

MARINA DEL REY
3534 Bali Way, Marina del Rey 90292
☎*(310) 301-1000, (800) 862-7462. Map*
1C1 ▥ *to* ▥ *160 units* ⊨ ≈ AE ◉
◎ VISA ◀≣ ⋘ ⋐ ✿ ☐ ⌖ Ⴤ
Location: 5 miles N of LAX, $\frac{1}{4}$ mile w of Lincoln Blvd. Surrounded on three sides by water and with its own boat slip, the hotel is perfect for sailor visitors. Rooms, and the **Crystal Seahorse** restaurant, have excellent views across the marina.

MAYFAIR
1256 W 7th St., Los Angeles 90017
☎*(213) 484-9789. Map 6D8* ▥ *to* ▥
300 units ▦ ≈ AE ◉ ◎ VISA ✿ ☐ ⌖
⅜ Ⴤ
Location: Four blocks w of Figueroa St. Among the few LA hotels of a type now common in San Francisco, this is a well-remodeled, middle-sized older building with every comfort in its guest rooms, but not all the public rooms and personal services that are expected of a grand hotel. Some guest rooms are reserved for nonsmokers. The hotel is sited well nigh perfectly for Downtown visitors. Its restaurant, the **Orchid Court**, is useful.

MIYAKO INN
328 E First St., Los Angeles 90012
☎*(213) 228-8888, (800) 528-1234. Map*
6D9 ▥ *174 units* ▦ ≈ AE ◉ ◎ VISA
⋘ ✿ ☐ ⌖ Ⴤ Ⴤ
Location: Little Tokyo area, just w of Alameda St. Previously this was the Best Western Hotel Tokyo, and it retains the clean and neat Japanese air, and the Japanese-speaking staff, that is

to be expected in the heart of Little Tokyo. Convenient for Downtown and major freeways.

NEW OTANI HOTEL & GARDEN ▥
120 S Los Angeles St., Los Angeles 90012
☎*(213) 629-1200, (800) 252-0917. Map*
6D9 ▥ *448 units* ▦ ≈ AE ◉ ◎ VISA
⋆ ⋘ ☐ ⌖ ◀≣ ✸ Ⴤ ♫
Location: N of Downtown in Little Tokyo at 1st St. The 21-story, ultramodern tower hotel is full of surprises. A rooftop terrace has a half-acre impression of the original Otani garden. On one side of it there is an exquisite, glass-walled Japanese restaurant (see A THOUSAND CRANES in WHERE TO EAT). On the other side is a bar decorated in modern Japanese style but dedicated to jazz. In the 3-story lobby/lounge, classical soloists or duettists play beneath imposing paintings by Nong. Large rooms are expensively furnished with only faint nods to Japan. Suites have Japanese bathrooms and bedrooms, but Western living rooms.

OAKWOOD APARTMENTS MID WILSHIRE ✿
209 S Westmoreland Ave., Los Angeles 90004 ☎*(213) 380-4221, (800) 421-6654. Map 5D7.*
Location: Handy for Olympic Blvd. and Santa Monica Freeway.
OAKWOOD APARTMENTS TOLUCA HILLS ✿
3600 Barham Blvd., Los Angeles 90068
☎*(213) 851-3450, (800) 421-6654. Map 1B2.*
Location: S of Universal City, E off US-101, Barham Blvd. exit.
OAKWOOD APARTMENTS MARINA DEL REY ✿
4111 S Via Marina, Marina del Rey 90292
☎*(310) 823-5443, (800) 421-6654. Map 1C1.*
Location: Just s of Washington Blvd.
OAKWOOD APARTMENTS WOODLAND HILLS ✿
22122-22222 Victory Blvd., Woodland Hills 91367 ☎*(818) 340-5161, (800) 421-6654. Map 1B1.*
Location: Near intersection with Topanga Canyon Blvd.

Common to all Oakwood Apartments are
▬ ▯ to ▥ ☘ ♨ ♈ ♙ ‡ ▢ AE ⊙ ⊡ VISA

Visitors staying in LA for 30 days or more could do far worse than investigate these short/long-stay apartments. Oakwood have several thousand units in total, and the choice ranges from studios with Murphy bed, kitchenette and bathroom, to family-sized units with living room, two bedrooms, kitchen and bathroom. All come fully equipped with linen and kitchenware, most have a balcony, and communal facilities include pools, clubhouse, gymnasiums, barbecues and coin-laundry. Electricity and cleaning are extra, but the deal is still hard to beat, and what the Oakwoods lack in architectural distinction they make up for with their friendliness. The only drawback is that guests must make their own arrangements with the telephone companies to have telephones connected and pay the bill. Unless a friend on the spot can arrange it for you beforehand, this can take a few days.

RITZ-CARLTON, HUNTINGTON ▦ ⌂

1401 South Oak Knoll Ave., Pasadena 91106 ☎*(818) 568-3900* ℻*(818) 568-3159. Map 1B3* ▥ to ▥ *383 units*
▬ ⇌ AE ⊙ ⊡ VISA ▭ ♿ ☘ ◁ ♨ ℘
♈ ♟ ‡ ▢ ▤ ♇ ♄ ♠ ⤢ ▣

Location: At the foot of the San Gabriel Mountains, 15 minutes by freeway from Downtown. This is an updated reincarnation of the Huntington Hotel, a Pasadena institution first opened in 1906 and closed down following the massive earthquake of 1985. The re-creation is authentic and, truth be told, probably improves upon the original. The Hotel, set in 23 acres, has all the usual Ritz Carlton qualities, plus peaceful gardens, great views across the Picture Bridge, poolside terraced rooms, exclusive cottages, and that indefinable sense of well-bred exclusivity that Pasadena still cherishes. The neighboring area is both well-groomed and affluent, and there isn't much of interest within walking distance. But it is a short drive to the refined delights of downtown

Pasadena, the NORTON SIMON MUSEUM or Santa Anita Racetrack.

RITZ-CARLTON, LAGUNA NIGUEL ▦ ⌂

33533 Ritz-Carlton Dr., Dana Point 92629 ☎*(714) 240-2000* ℻*(714) 240-1061. Map 10J6* ▥ to ▥ *393 units* ▬ ⇌ AE ⊙ ⊡ VISA ▭ ♿ ☘ ◁ ♨ ♠ ℘ ⤢ ♈ ▤ ‡ ▢ ▤ ♟ ♄ ♇ ⤢ ▣

Location: On the coast midway between Los Angeles and San Diego. Since it opened in 1984, set in 18 acres atop a 150-foot bluff overlooking the Pacific Ocean and Catalina Island, this outpost of laid-back luxury, the only holder in California of 5-Star and 5-Diamond ratings, has regularly been voted the country's number one resort hotel. It has also become a firm favorite with weekending Angelenos — especially those in the entertainment industry. With good reason: the location and views are breathtaking, the decor immaculate, the service impeccable, the restaurants and wines on a par with just about anything LA can offer, and the recreational facilities as good as they come. They include an 18-hole golf course, 2 miles of beachfront, four tennis courts, volleyball and croquet. Appropriately, given its setting on the California Riviera, the four-story building itself, in pastel stucco with red-tiled roofs, is a mix of California Mission and Mediterranean villa. Displayed around the hotel is an impressive collection of 18th and 19thC European and American paintings. For those who can tear themselves away from the hotel, a wide range of attractions lie within short driving distance. They include Mission San Juan Capistrano, Laguna and Newport Beaches, Disneyland, South Coast Plaza Shopping, and the Orange County Performing Arts Center (see ORANGE COUNTY, page 169).

RITZ-CARLTON, MARINA DEL REY ▦

4375 Admiralty Way, Marina del Rey 90292 ☎*(310) 823-1700* ℻*(310) 823-2403. Map 1C1* ▥ to ▥ *306 units* ▣ ⇌ AE ⊙ VISA ♿ ☘ ◁ ♨ ♠ ℘ ⤢ ♈ ▤ ‡ ▢ ▤ ♟ ⤢ ▣

Location: On the Marina, 5 miles N of

LAX. Opened in 1990 overlooking the world's largest man-made marina, the Ritz Carlton effortlessly combines European-style comforts and elegance with a prime California location. Those arriving by yacht can moor in a hotel berth. Those not doing so can always charter a hotel boat. There are great views, not least of magnificent sunsets, from the balconies, marina-side walks, jogs or bicycle rides, plus on-the-spot recreations and two splendid but reasonably-priced restaurants. For those who want extra cosseting, two exclusive "Club" floors are available.

SAFARI INN

1911 W Olive Ave., Burbank 91356
☎(818) 845-8888, (800) 845-5544
Ⓕ(818) 845-0054. Map 1B2 ▥ to ▥▥▥
110 units ➡ ⇌ AE ⊡ ⊙ VISA ≋ ‡ ⊡
⊡ � Ⓨ
Location: sw of I-5, Olive Ave. exit. A popular 1950s motel with character, pleasant rooms and a perfect location for Burbank's entertainment industry. Universal Studios, NBC, Disney and Warner Bros are all near.

ST JAMES'S CLUB ⌂

8358 Sunset Blvd., Los Angeles 90069
☎(213) 654-7100, (800) 225-2637. Map
4B4 ▥▥▥ 74 units ➡ ⇌ AE ⊡ ⊙ VISA ≋
Ψ ⊡ ⊡ Ⓨ
Location: On Sunset Strip. Just a few years ago this landmark 1931 Art Deco delight was dilapidated and inhabited only by squatters. The new British owners spent $40 million restoring it, and the result is an exclusive, lavishly furnished club/hotel popular with the traveling glitterati.

SALISBURY HOUSE

2273 W 20th St., Los Angeles 90018
☎(213) 737-7817. Map 5E6 ▥ 5 units
AE ⊙ VISA ✗
Location: Two blocks n of I-10, two blocks w of Western Ave. One of only a handful of small bed-and-breakfast establishments in LA, it has the added attraction of being an historic Craftsman-style bungalow built in 1909. Weekly rates are available.

SHANGRI-LA

1301 Ocean Ave., Santa Monica 90401
☎(310) 394-2791. Map 1C1 ▥ to ▥▥▥
55 units ➡ AE ⊡ ⊙ ⊙ VISA ‡ ⊡ ⊡ ✗ ☎
Location: One block s of Wilshire Blvd., across from Palisades Park. This is a refurbished 1939 Art Deco hotel, with splendid ocean views and sea breezes. Rooms are decorated in period style, and most have fully equipped kitchenettes. The hotel is well placed for Santa Monica's many attractions, not least the beach.

SHERATON–GRANDE ⌂

333 S Figueroa St., Los Angeles 90071
☎(213) 617-1133, (800) 325-3535. Map
6D9 ▥▥▥ 470 units ⊡ ⇌ AE ⊡ ⊙ VISA
‡ ⊡ ⊡ ✗ ✿ ⎔ ≋ ⌖ Ⓨ ♪ ✦
Location: Adjoining the Harbor Freeway near 3rd St. The grandest of Sheraton's LA hotels has benefited from a major overhaul. The amazing mass of glass that is its front elevation hides not only a soaring atrium lobby and luxury rooms, but a splendid four-movie theater (the first new one in Downtown in four decades) and several fine restaurants (particularly **Ravel**). The emphasis throughout is on personal service, with a butler for each floor, and multilingual concierges. Subtly decorated guest rooms are tranquil retreats; 65 of them are suites. The Downtown location is good for business and the highbrow arts venues, but expect to feel isolated from real life.

OTHER SHERATONS

Miramar–Sheraton (☎(310) 394-3731 ▥▥▥), facing the beach at the foot of Wilshire Blvd.; **Sheraton Plaza–La Reina** (☎(310) 642-1111 ▥▥ to ▥▥▥), a dramatic 1981 tower close to Los Angeles International Airport; **Sheraton–Town House** (☎(213) 382-7171 ▥▥▥), a stately, comfortably old-fashioned 1929 tower in Mid-Wilshire; **Sheraton–Universal** (☎(818) 980-1212 ▥▥▥), at Universal Studios, Universal City.

The last of these runs complimentary buses up the hill to the UNIVERSAL STUDIOS tour. Actor Telly Savalas, a.k.a.

Kojak, keeps a permanent suite at the recently refurbished hotel and often hangs out in **"Telly's,"** the lively sports bar named after him.

For Sheraton central information ☎(800) 325-3535.

SPORTSMEN'S LODGE

12825 Ventura Blvd., North Hollywood 91604 ☎*(818) 769-4700. Map **1**B2* ⬜ *196 units* ⬛ ═ 🏠 AE 💠 CB VISA ♨ ≈ ♈ ‡ ☐ 🗋 ⚡ ♈ ⚓

Location: One mile s of US-101 Coldwater Canyon exit. Almost the countryside in the city; greenery, waterfall and ponds around a charming, moderately priced hotel. About 20 minutes N of Downtown, and supremely convenient for the Valley, Universal City, Beverly Hills and Burbank Airport. A good restaurant and a coffee shop are attached.

SUNSET MARQUIS HOTEL & VILLAS

1200 N Alta Loma Rd., West Hollywood 90069 ☎*(310) 657-1333. Map **4**B4* ⬜ *120 units* ⬛ ═ AE 💠 CB VISA 🖼 ≈ ♈ ‡ ☐ 🗋 ⚡ ♈ ⚓

Location: Half a block s of Sunset Blvd. An intimate and fashionable hotel popular with visiting entertainers; Mick Jagger has been known to stay here. All you would expect of an upscale hotel conveniently placed for Hollywood nightclubs, theaters, restaurants and shops. Most suites have decently equipped kitchens.

WESTIN BONAVENTURE 🏨 🏛

404 S Figueroa St., Los Angeles 90071 ☎*(213) 624-1000, (800) 228-3000* ☒*(213) 612-4800. Map **6**D8* ⬜ *1,474 units* ⬛ ═ 💠 CB VISA ‡ ⚡ ☐ 🗋 ⚔ ≈ ⚱ ⚒ ♈ ⚓ ⚘ ⚲

Location: Downtown at 5th St. Five clustered cylinders sheathed in glass look like a 35-story, multistage rocket waiting for its nose cone. Dating from 1976, John Portman's building symbolizes Los Angeles perfectly as a city of the future. The medium-sized rooms, aside from having nonparallel side-walls and slightly curved window walls, are conventional in design and decor. The six-story lobby is striking: Portman used cast concrete to achieve such astonishing effects as miniature cocktail lounges cantilevered into space and called, appropriately, cocktail pods. Six levels of shops and several interesting restaurants rim the walls (see SHOPPING, page 149), and a revolving restaurant on the 35th floor provides stunning views of the city.

WESTWOOD MARQUIS 🏨

930 Hilgard Ave., Los Angeles 90024 ☎*(310) 208-8765, (800) 352-7454* ☒*(310) 824-0355. Map **3**D2* ⬜ *258 units* ⬛ ═ AE 💠 CB VISA 🖼 ‡ ⚡ ☐ 🗋 ⚔ ≈ ⚒ ♈ ⚓

Location: In Westwood village, adjoining UCLA campus to the E. This is an excellent example of something Los Angeles seems to do particularly well: a modern tower filled with rooms evoking the past. All suites, the Westwood is in every sense a luxury hotel. Furnishings are antique, eclectic as to period and style, but reliably comfortable and tasteful. Public rooms are sunny and cheerful. The pool and surrounding garden are pleasantly private. High tea and Sunday brunch are popular.

WESTWOOD PLAZA (HOLIDAY INN)

10740 Wilshire Blvd., Los Angeles 90024 ☎*(310) 475-8711, (800) 238-8000. Map **3**D2* ⬜ *300 units* ⬛ ═ AE 💠 CB VISA ‡ ⚡ ☐ 🗋 ⚔ ≈ ⚒ ♈ ⚓

Location: E of Westwood Blvd. A modern 19-story tower, the hotel is set apart from standard Holiday Inns by a number of grace notes. Guest rooms are fairly spacious, with well-appointed, modern bathrooms. The largely European staff offers concierge and other extra services.

HOLIDAY INNS

All the hotels in this reliable chain can be expected to have comfortable, conventionally modern rooms of very similar decor. Those listed opposite are in useful locations for tourists. For central reservations for these and eight other Holiday Inns in the Greater LA area, plus eight more in Orange County ☎(213) 688-7313.

Holiday Inn–Convention Center (Los Angeles) (☎ *(213) 748-1291* ▥ *to* ▥ *)*, in LA's Downtown area; **Holiday Inn–Convention Center (Pasadena)** (☎ *(213) 449-4000* ▥ *)*, in downtown Pasadena; **Holiday Inn– Downtown** (☎ *(213) 628-5242* ▥ *)*, in LA's Downtown area; **Holiday Inn– Los Angeles International Airport** (☎ *(310) 649-5151* ▥ *)*, near the entrance to Los Angeles International Airport.

Budget accommodations

The following are clean, no-frills ho(s)tels catering primarily to young, low-budget travelers and featuring shared or private rooms, many with ocean views:

- **Belair Bed and Breakfast**   941 Frederic Ave., Burbank ☎(818) 848-9227, map **1**B2. Small, cozy and well equipped, near Universal Studios.
- **Cadillac Hotel**   401 Ocean Front Walk, Venice 90291 ☎(310) 399-8876, map **1**C1. A beachfront bargain for gregarious travelers and party animals.
- **Colonial Inn Youth Hostel**   9421, 8th St., Huntington Beach ☎(714) 536-3315, map **2**F4. Shared rooms; wash your own clothes; walk to the beach; take a bus to Disneyland.
- **Interclub Hostel**   2221 Lincoln Blvd, Venice 90291 ☎(310) 305-0250, map **1**C1. Cheap, very cheerful, and popular with young visitors.
- **Santa Monica International AYH-Hostel**   1436 2nd St., Santa Monica ☎(213) 393-9913, map **1**C1. The largest hostel on the w coast, with 200 rooms, just two blocks from the beach and pier.
- **Venice Beach Cotel**   25 Windward Ave., Venice 90291 ☎(310) 399-7649, map **1**C1. A restored landmark hotel on Venice Beach, with private and shared rooms.

Where to eat

Dining out

The amazing range of cuisines, along with top-quality ingredients and boundless enthusiasm for experiment, ought to make Los Angeles a strong contender for the title Culinary Capital of the United States. And if it isn't the best, it is certainly the most interesting.

This wasn't always the case. Not so many years ago San Francisco and every other US city with a culinary tradition looked down their noses at LA. How things have changed in recent years! Now some influential food critics are ranking LA ahead of San Francisco and New York.

This is scarcely surprising, given a population that hails from the four corners of the globe, loves food and the dining experience, and has the wherewithal to pay for it — and the top-flight chefs to prepare it. None of which is to say that the food is universally good, even now. Indeed, it can be very bad indeed. For every restaurant of note there are dozens that can disappoint. Quality is not always determined by the size of the bill, just most of the time, and it is remarkably easy for two people to spend $100 and more for dinner with wine. Still, the better chain restaurants and fast-food joints succeed in satisfying most people for under $20 for two.

If Los Angeles is short of anything, it is distinctive, small, moderately priced restaurants. This could have something to do with the cornucopia of both ingredients and ready-cooked dishes available in the better supermarkets. With everything on offer from barbecued chicken to exotic salads, to live lobster and freshly baked breads, it can be cheaper and more rewarding to eat at home. Or it may be that, in the niche between the highly advertised, easily affordable chain restaurants on the one hand, and the ultra-fashionable bistros on the other, it's just too tough to survive. Certainly LA restaurants come and go with disconcerting speed.

WHAT'S HOT?
One heady complication in choosing among famous places is star-gazing. If the probable presence of movie celebrities and other glitterati is a factor, remember that movie stardom does not necessarily confer a great palate.

Put another way, not all of the stars' favorite haunts serve great food, and not all great restaurants are haunted by stars. Furthermore, today's hottest spot could be stone-cold tomorrow.

Angelenos are frequently seduced by novelty, sometimes with spectacular consequences. But for the visitor, the tried, tested, and consistent may be a better bet than the latest gimmicky fashion.

CALIFORNIAN AND ETHNIC CUISINE

With or without famous and fashionable faces, the range is dazzling. Perhaps the most novel experience awaiting visitors is home-grown California cuisine. The underlying characteristic is the use of fresh, in-season ingredients lightly cooked. If this sounds suspiciously like *nouvelle cuisine,* that's no mistake. Many of the techniques, though by no means all, find their antecedents in French cooking.

But the ingredients — and especially the combinations of ingredients — are peculiarly Californian. And such is the eclecticism of Los Angeles chefs that they feel free to draw upon any influences that take their fancy, be they Japanese, Chinese, Mexican, Italian, Thai or whatever.

There are many unprecedented results; from *la nueva cocina Mexicana,* with Mexican ingredients and French techniques, to *nouvelle Chinoise,* mixing ingredients and techniques from East and West. The most recently consummated marriage is between French and Japanese foods. Indeed, give the geographic orientation and the changing ethnic balance, **Cal-Asian**, the trendy synthesis of California ingredients and East Asian techniques, may turn out to be the city's most enduring innovation. They'll certainly not be constrained by local ingredients: if Los Angeles hasn't got it, they ship it in.

Chilis can be very hot indeed. In 1989 a Los Angeles
chili warehouse was destroyed by spontaneous combustion.
Stock worth $70,000 was lost.
(From a fact-sheet about . . . chilis)

In addition to the innovators, there are many who adhere to ethnic and national culinary traditions. There are excellent French, Italian and Mexican restaurants; good Chinese, Thai, Korean, Vietnamese and Jewish restaurants; and Greater Los Angeles is said to have more Japanese *sushi* bars than McDonald's outlets.

FAST FOOD

Connoisseurs of that other major southern California genre, fast food, will not be disappointed. Born out of the hamburger drive-in and multiplied to include fried chicken, fish and chips, *tacos,* pizza and barbecue, they are legion. Franchized fast-food joints are amusingly easy to spot. They have vast expanses of window glass, eye-catching signs, and roof-lines somewhere between mansard and Mayan.

WHERE TO LOOK

The geography of outstanding food is fairly predictable. The Wilshire Blvd. axis serves well, along with West Hollywood-Beverly Hills, where there is a dense concentration of famous places: the gastronomic heart of Los Angeles beats near the intersection of La Cienega Blvd. and Melrose Ave. But other hallowed names are found Downtown and in Santa Monica, Wilshire itself has some very good restaurants, and most districts can claim more than one establishment that should prove worth the drive.

USEFUL TO KNOW

Parking is a consistent, expensive problem. Most of the better restaurants have a valet parking system, but many cheaper places have no parking at all except on the street. **Reservations** are mandatory, unless noted otherwise in this chapter. As to **last orders**, visitors should note that Angelenos eat early by European or New York standards; it can be difficult to order food after 10pm.

Menus — or their frequent absence — speak volumes about the LA style. Serious restaurants often announce their choice of dishes not on a printed menu but posted on a blackboard or recited by the waiter. Waiters (and diners) in really serious restaurants often have to be able to memorize the equivalent of a three-act play. One likely explanation is that restaurants base their menus on the best produce available on a given day. Another is the seemingly tireless quest for novelty.

HOW TO USE THIS CHAPTER

The following alphabetical list of restaurants is selective, covering a broad spectrum of cuisine, price, area and character. Addresses and telephone numbers are given, and symbols denote other useful points of information, from ▰ (good wines) to ⌾ (open-air dining). The luxury restaurant (⬠) and good-value (♣) symbols are awarded in only a small number of cases.

See HOW TO USE THIS BOOK on **page 7 for a full list of symbols.**

Price categories for restaurants listed on the following pages are intended only as guidelines to average prices. There are four bands: inexpensive (▯▯), moderate (▯▯▯), expensive (▯▯▯) and very expensive (▯▯▯▯). They are based on the approximate cost, in fall 1992, of a meal for one with service, tax and house wine. Even with cost inflation, restaurants will normally remain in the same price category.

Symbol	Category	Current price
▯▯▯▯	very expensive	over $65
▯▯▯	expensive	$45–65
▯▯	moderate	$30–45
▯	inexpensive	under $30

RESTAURANTS CLASSIFIED BY AREA

DOWNTOWN TO MID-WILSHIRE
Bernard's ▦
Bicycle Shop Café ▦ to ▦
Cassis ▦ to ▦
Chan Dara ▦ to ▦
City Restaurant ▦ to ▦
Lawry's California Center ▦
The Original Pantry Café ▦
Pacific Dining Car ▦ to ▦
Rex, Il Ristorante ▦

DOWNTOWN/CHINATOWN
Mon Kee Live Fish Sea Food ▦ to ▦
See also INEXPENSIVE CHINATOWN on
  page 138.

DOWNTOWN/LITTLE TOKYO
Horikawa ▦
Oomasa ▦ to ▦
A Thousand Cranes ▦
Yagura Ichiban ▦ to ▦

HOLLYWOOD/WEST HOLLYWOOD/BEVERLY HILLS
Antonio's ▦
Benihana of Tokyo ▦ to ▦
The Bistro ▦
The Border Grill ▦
Carnegie Deli ▦ to ▦
Chan Dara ▦ to ▦
Chasen's ▦
Chianti Cucina ▦ to ▦
Citrus ▦ to ▦
Le Dôme ▦
El Torito Grill ▦
Gitanjali ▦ to ▦
Hampton's ▦
Lawry's The Prime Rib ▦
Ma Maison ▦
The Mandarin ▦ to ▦
Matsuhisa ▦ to ▦
Moustache Café ▦ to ▦
Musso & Frank Grill ▦ to ▦
L'Orangerie ▦

Patina ▦ to ▦
La Scala ▦ to ▦
Spago ▦
Tommy Tang's ▦ to ▦
La Toque ▦
Trumps ▦

WEST LA/WESTWOOD/BRENTWOOD
Harry's Bar and American Grill
  ▦ to ▦
Homer & Edy's Bistro ▦
Lew Mitchell's Orient Express
  ▦ to ▦
Peppone ▦
Studio Grill ▦
Toledo Restaurant ▦

COASTAL
Chinois on Main ▦
Famous Enterprise Fish Co. ▦ to ▦
Michael's ▦
Pioneer Boulangerie ▦
Rebecca's ▦
Sabroso ▦
St Estephe ▦ to ▦
72 Market Street ▦
Valentino ▦
West Beach Café ▦

VALLEYS
Benihana of Tokyo ▦ to ▦
Café Jacoulet ▦
The Chronicle ▦ to ▦
Dragon Regency ▦
L'Express (1) ▦ to ▦
L'Express (2) ▦ to ▦
Fragrant Vegetable ▦ to ▦
Hampton's ▦
Harbor Village ▦ to ▦
Holly Street Bar and Grill ▦ to ▦
Jerry's Famous Deli ▦ to ▦
Jitlada ▦
Katsu ▦ to ▦
Wonder Seafood ▦ to ▦

LA's restaurants A to Z

ANTONIO'S

7472 Melrose Ave., LA ☎(213) 655-0480.
Map 4C5 ▥ ▭ ▾ ⬤ by valet AE ⬤ VISA
Open Tues-Fri noon-2.30pm, 5-11pm;
Sat-Sun 5-11pm. Closed Mon; major hols.

Innovations at newer places have made
the once radical Antonio's look positively traditional. But among regular
dishes at this renowned restaurant, the
tamales are worth a drive, and special
goodies are offered in the list of daily
specials, all drawn from the area around
Mexico City. The bar serves excellent
Margaritas. *Specialties: Mole negro
Oaxaqueno; pollo en pipian; ropa
vieja; albondigon rebozado.*

BENIHANA OF TOKYO

38 N La Cienega Blvd. ☎(213) 655-7311,
map 4D4, and 16226 Ventura Blvd., Encino
☎(818) 788-7121, map 1B1 ▥ to ▥
▭ ▰ ▾ ⬤ by valet AE ⬤ ⬤ VISA Open
Mon-Thurs 11.30am-2pm, 5.30-10pm; Fri
11.30am-2pm, 5.30-11pm; Sat 5.30-11pm;
Sun 4.30-10pm.

The decor at this popular chain "Japanese" restaurant is very Japanese; the
food, truthfully, isn't. However, the
Westernized hybrids on offer are ge-
nuinely good, and the *teppan* chefs
provide one-man floor shows as they
work with lightning speed and skill at
the individual grills set inside horse-
shoe-shaped tables. With a few Japanese beers or jars of warm sake, it's lots
of fun. *Specialties: Hitachi steak; lobster
and chicken.*

BERNARD'S

515 S Olive St., LA ☎(213) 624-0183.
Map 6D9 ▥ ▭ ▰ ⬤ by valet AE ⬤
⬤ VISA Open Mon-Thurs 11.30am-1.45pm,
6-10pm; Fri 11.30am-1.45pm, 6-11pm; Sat
6-11pm. Closed Sun.

This grand old institution in the BILT-
MORE HOTEL (see WHERE TO STAY) has kept
its reputation as a fine French restaurant. Dim lights, plush furnishings
and a harpist make the room as romantic as one could hope. The staff is impeccably attentive. The emphasis is on
fish and inventive seasonings. *Special-*
*ties: Sole in lobster sauce; sea bass with
ginger and lime.*

BICYCLE SHOP CAFÉ ♣

12217 Wilshire Blvd., LA ☎(310)
826-7831. Off map 3D1 ▭ to ▥ ▭ ⬤
VISA Open Mon-Fri 7am-midnight; Sat-Sun
7am-1am. Closed Jan 1; Thanksgiving;
Dec 25.

A cloud of bicycles hangs from the ceiling to justify the name of a restaurant
that is a happy, noisy hangout for neighborhood regulars. Omelets, sandwiches and crepes are mainstays, but
the menu ranges into conventional entrées. *Specialties: Terrine of sweetbreads; Pacific red snapper in lemon
sauce; El Steak Bravo.*

THE BISTRO

246 N Canon Dr., Beverly Hills ☎(310)
273-5633. Map 3C3 ▥ ▭ ▰ ▾ ⬤ by
valet AE ⬤ ⬤ VISA Open Mon-Fri
noon-3pm, 6-11pm; Sat 6-11pm. Closed
Sun.

One of the summits of Beverly Hills chic
is usually crowded with movie people.
Although star-watching counts for
much here, the French and Continental
menu has more ups than downs. Daily
blackboard specials are of particular
interest. The mirrored downstairs room
is quite small but still one of the most
handsome around. *Specialties: Brains
beurre noir; calf's liver.*

THE BORDER GRILL

7407½ Melrose Ave., LA ☎(213)
938-2155. Map 4C5 ▥ ▭ AE ⬤ VISA
Open Mon-Sat 11.45am-11.45pm; Sun
noon-11.45pm.

Susan Feniger and Mary Sue Milliken's
kitchen is one of the ablest interpreters
of *la nueva cocina Mexicana,* but the
dining room is a particular LA type:
small and bare, full of local heavy-
weights who come in their grubbies to
spend considerable money on unusual
food. *Specialties: Grilled turkey; sa-
bana (very thin steak marinated in
lime juice, served with scallions and
jalapeno peppers).*

CAFÉ JACOULET

91 N Raymond Ave., Pasadena ☎*(818) 796-2233. Map 1B3* ▦ ☐ ☰ ◢ ◉ ◙ ▨ *Open for lunch Mon-Fri 11.30am-2.30pm, Sat noon-3pm; for dinner Mon-Thurs 6-9.30pm, Fri-Sat 6pm-midnight, Sun 5.30-9.30pm.*

A light, airy atmosphere matches a light, airy menu compounded from diverse sources. Jacoulet was a French painter who was much influenced by things Japanese; the food here reflects both of those cuisines plus those of California and Italy. *Specialties: Duck with raspberry sauce; lobster ravioli with spinach pasta; fresh salmon poêle with fresh spinach sauce.*

CARNEGIE DELI

300 N Beverly Dr., Beverly Hills ☎*(310) 275-3354. Map 3C3* ☐ *to* ▦ ☐ ❦ ▨ ◙ ▨ *Open Sun-Thurs 7.30am-11pm; Fri-Sat 7.30am-midnight.*

Remarkable value here in tinseltown's priciest shopping district. The familiar New York-style deli fare is done very well indeed. The main high-ceilinged dining room, designed by San Francisco's Pat Kuleto, has booths affording both a degree of privacy and window seating to take in the passing upscale sidewalk scene. There is also a busy, well-stocked counter for take-out food, and a catering service. Portions are enormous, so be warned. *Specialties: Overstuffed sandwiches; salads; cheesecake.*

CASSIS

8450 3rd St., LA ☎*(213) 653-1079. Map 4C4* ▦ *to* ▦ ☐ ◼ ☰ ◢ *by valet* ▨ ◉ ◙ ▨ *Open Mon-Fri 10.30am-3pm, 6-11pm; Sat 6-11pm. Closed Sun.*

This is a charming, romantic French restaurant. The structural interior is Art Deco; the decoration is an extension of the garden in the form of potted plants and cut flowers. A luncheon clientele anchored by neighborhood television and recording studio employees has the best of the atmosphere, but dinner patrons get the best of the menu. *Specialties: Duck in peppercorn sauce; rack of lamb in honey-vinegar sauce.*

CHAN DARA

1511 N Cahuenga Blvd., Hollywood ☎*(213) 464-8585, map 5B6, and 310 N Larchmont Blvd., Hancock Park* ☎*(213) 467-1052, map 5C6* ▦ *to* ▦ ☐ ❦ ◢ ▨ ◙ ▨ *Open Mon-Fri 11am-11pm; Sat-Sun 5-11pm.*

Long-established (by Los Angeles standards) and popular, Chan Dara's Thai cuisine is extremely good, and consistently so. Both locations can be crowded, so expect a wait. *Specialties: Barbecued chicken; sausage with lime and ginger; satay.*

CHASEN'S

9039 Beverly Blvd., West Hollywood ☎*(310) 271-2168. Map 4C4* ▦ ◢ ☐ ❦ ▨ *Open Tues-Sun 6pm-1am. Closed Mon.*

Chasen's seems to have been going as long as some of its celebrity customers, and they keep coming back. It's said that Ronald Reagan likes the chili, possibly the most expensive in town. Not exactly at the cutting edge of new California cuisine, this nevertheless offers a reliable formality. *Specialties: Hobo steak; banana shortbread.*

CHIANTI CUCINA

7383 Melrose Ave., LA ☎*(213) 653-8333. Map 4C5* ▦ *to* ▦ ☐ ◢ ▨ ◙ ▨ **Chianti** *open nightly 5-11pm;* **Cucina** *open Mon-Sat 11.30am-midnight, Sun 5pm-midnight.*

Chianti and Cucina are two rooms on either side of one Tuscan kitchen. Chianti is the quieter, darker and more expensive side. The food in both is the same, putting them at the head of the city's list of Italian restaurants. The menu changes every day or two to reflect what is freshest in the market.

CHINOIS ON MAIN

2709 Main St., Santa Monica ☎*(310) 392-9025. Map 1C1* ▦ ☐ ◢ ▨ ◉ ◙ ▨ *Open Mon-Sat 6-11pm; Sun 5.30-10.30pm.*

Wolfgang Puck — the still-youthful wonder who invented and still runs SPAGO (see page 135) — has reinvented Chinese cooking by mixing Asian and

French techniques with Californian ingredients, and built a startlingly original room in which to serve the results. Amid riveting expanses of copper, marble, and what the proprietors call "screaming art," diners confront *chèvre*-stuffed *bao*, *sashimi*-like Spanish mackerel, mandarin orange-flavored *crème brulée* and suchlike adventures. *Specialties: Sizzling catfish; Mongolian lamb*.

CITRUS

6703 Melrose Ave., Hollywood ☎*(213) 857-0034. Map 5C5* ▥ *to* ▥ 🖃 ▭ ▣ ⟁ ⟶ *by valet* ᴀᴇ ⒸⒹ 🚾 *Open Mon-Sat noon-3pm, 6.30-11pm. Closed Sun.*

Many hold Citrus, owned and run by Michel Richard, LA's premier *pâtissier*, among the city's top California/French restaurants. Its clean, chic lines are enlivened by a fashionable clientele, a kitchen visible through a glass wall, and exceptionally good *nouvelle* bistro food. The leafy patio is generally less crowded than the main dining room. *Specialties: Scallops with maui onions; lamb with ravioli; pear sorbet*.

CITY RESTAURANT

180 S La Brea Ave., LA ☎*(213) 938-2155. Map 4C5* ▥ *to* ▥ ▭ ᴀᴇ ⒸⒹ 🚾 *Open Mon-Sat 11.45am-2pm, 5.45-11.45pm; Sun 5-11pm.*

Created by Susan Feniger and Mary Sue Milliken (also the owner-chefs of THE BORDER GRILL — see page 126), City's menu is what one dazzled admirer calls "off-the-wall eclectic." Not everyone is dazzled but, if not exactly like anything else, the food is earthy and vital. Northwest razor clams come with Mexican sauces; flank steaks are tandoori baked; and so on. Preparations are impeccable, and the desserts are exceptional. The atmosphere, meanwhile, is stark hi-tech, or very close to it. The clientele is as off-the-wall as the food. *Specialties: Poona pancake; vegetable vermicelli*.

LE DÔME ⌂

8720 Sunset Blvd., LA ☎*(310) 659-6919. Map 4B4* ▥ ▭ 🍴 ⟶ *by valet* ᴀᴇ ⒸⒹ ⒸⒹ 🚾 *Open Mon-Fri noon-1am; Sat 6pm-1am. Closed Sun.*

Le Dôme is still a trendy hangout for recording stars and their companions. The decor remains an eccentric mishmash of Art Deco, chrome and velvet, with a scattering of Chinese pottery. But now, more than ever, Le Dôme is also a venue for seriously good food. Old timers will find the menu longer, but reassuringly familiar. *Specialties: Grilled shark with anchovy butter; boudin noir*.

DRAGON REGENCY

120 S Atlantic Blvd., Monterey Park ☎*(818) 282-1089. Map 1C3* ▥ ▭ ⟶ ⒸⒹ 🚾

Yet more evidence of Monterey Park's emergence as a center of Chinese culinary excellence. Neither the shopping mall location nor the decor are anything special. But the food, especially the seafood, is as good as any Chinese fare available in LA. *Specialties: Double-pleasure sole; pan-fried crab; salt-fried shrimp*.

EL TORITO GRILL

9595 Wilshire Blvd, Beverly Hills ☎*(310) 550-1599. Map 3D3* ▥ ▭ 🍴 ᴀᴇ ⒸⒹ 🚾 *Open daily 11am-11pm.*

The forest of cacti surrounding El Torito make it hard to miss in Beverly Hills "Golden Triangle," and it is almost invariably lively, loud and full, often with young(ish) singles. The decor and the food are Southwest, known locally as Cal-Mex. The food is not spectacularly good, but more enjoyable than the tasteless mush mostly served up as Mexican food in LA chain restaurants. The Margaritas are certainly good enough. *Specialties: Quesadilla with oven-smoked chicken; stuffed red corn taquitos; Texas sundae*.

L'EXPRESS

14910 Ventura Blvd., Sherman Oaks ☎*(818) 990-8683, map 1B1, and 3575 Cahuenga Blvd., Studio City* ☎*(213) 876-3778, map 1B2* ▥ *to* ▥ ▭ 🍴 ⟶ *by valet* ᴀᴇ ⒸⒹ 🚾 *Open daily 7am-2am.*

Fairly standard brasserie food in exceptional settings designed by Johannes van Tilburg. The clientele is a mix of local, young professional, and entertainment industry, who enjoy the chic ambience and the piped rock music. *Specialties: Duck salad; croque monsieur; pizza.*

FAMOUS ENTERPRISE FISH CO.
174 Kinney St., Santa Monica ☎*(310) 392-8366. Map 1C1* 🔲 *to* 🔲 ▀ ⚍ 🄰🄴 🄲🄳 🆅🅸🆂🄰 *Open Sun-Thurs 11.30am-10pm; Fri-Sat 11.30am-11pm.*

Grilled fresh fish is the basic dish in a big, comfortable converted warehouse where formality is forbidden. The cooking is no fancier than the decor, but anything listed on the blackboard is indeed fresh. Not only is it not overcooked, it will be brought undercooked on request. *Specialties: Snapper, shark and other freshly caught fish; Alaskan king crab.*

FRAGRANT VEGETABLE
108 N Garfield Ave., Monterey Park ☎*(818) 280-4215. Map 1C3* 🔲 *to* 🔲 ⚍ ⚍ 🄰🄴 🄲🄳 *Open Mon-Thurs 11am-9.30pm; Fri-Sun 11am-10pm.*

The Fragrant Vegetable is sited in an otherwise undistinguished shopping mall in what's fast becoming known as Little Taiwan. It offers vegetarian food with a difference, drawing on centuries of Chinese magic with vegetables, fungi and bean curds to produce flavor-full dishes, many of them artfully resembling meat or fish. The decor is tasteful and restrained and the service friendly, with patient waiters happy to explain dishes to the uninitiated. *Specialties: Eight precious assorted appetizer; Buddha's cushions; mixed mushrooms and water chestnuts.*

GITANJALI ♘
414 N La Cienega Blvd., LA ☎*(310) 657-2117. Map 4C4* 🔲 *to* 🔲 ⚍ ⚍ 🄰🄴 🄲🄳 🄲🄳 🆅🅸🆂🄰 *Open Mon-Thurs 6-10.30pm; Fri-Sat 6-11pm; Sun 5.30-10.30pm. Closed Thanksgiving; Dec 24-25; Dec 31.*

The decor sketches a mood of Northern India in a handsome room. The cooking is meticulous and the menu includes vegetarian dishes. Spicy fires range from faint glow to conflagration. *Spe-*

cialties: Lamb Kathmandu; tandoori chicken; tikka grills.

HAMPTON'S
4301 Riverside Dr., Toluca Lake ☎*(818) 845-3009, map 1B2, and 1342 N Highland Ave., Hollywood* ☎*(213) 469-1090, map 4B5* 🔲 🔲 ⚍ ⚍ *by valet* 🄲🄳 🆅🅸🆂🄰 *Open Sun-Thurs 11am-10pm; Fri-Sat 11am-11pm.*

Hampton's is said by many to serve the finest burgers in LA. Certainly they're fresh, cooked precisely to order, and come with all imaginable, and some unimaginable, toppings. There's also a help-yourself fresh salad bar. *Specialty: Hamburgers (natch!).*

HARBOR VILLAGE
Penthouse, Landmark Center, 111 N Atlantic Blvd., Monterey Park ☎*(818) 300-8833. Map 1C3* 🔲 *to* 🔲 ⚍ 🔲 ⚍ 🄰🄴 🄲🄳 🄲🄳 🆅🅸🆂🄰 *Open daily 10am-2.30pm, 5.30pm-11pm.*

After successes in Hong Kong and San Francisco, the Harbor Village has chosen "Little Taiwan" for its LA debut. The location, inside a featureless shopping mall, makes it hard to find, and the decor is much plainer than in SF, but then the largely Chinese clientele would argue that you can't eat fancy furniture. The standard of Cantonese cooking is way ahead of rivals in old Chinatown. It's not quite Hong Kong, but with the bustle and raucous enjoyment it's a good approximation. Sunday lunchtime offers the best choices of trolley-laden *dim sum*, and the biggest crowds. Make a reservation, and expect to be kept waiting even if you're on time. *Specialties: Lunchtime dim sum; seafood.*

HARRY'S BAR AND AMERICAN GRILL ♘
2020 Ave. of the Stars (lower level, ABC Entertainment Center), LA ☎*(310) 277-2333. Map 3D3* 🔲 *to* 🔲 ⚍ ⚍ 🄰🄴 🄲🄳 🆅🅸🆂🄰 *Open Mon-Sat 11.30am-11.30pm; Sun 4.45-10.30pm. Closed Jan 1; Labor Day; Dec 25.*

The staff says this Harry's is a precise copy of the one in Florence. A connoisseur swears it feels more like the one in Venice. Either way, unornamented dark wood, creamy white plaster and good paintings make an elegant setting for some proper Florentine cookery. *Specialties: Paglia e fieno; vermicelli all'Amatriciana; veal tonnato.*

HOMER & EDY'S BISTRO

2839 S Robertson Blvd., LA ☎*(310) 559-5102. Map 4E4* ▦ ▭ ➾ ▨ ⊕ ▣ ▨ *Open Tues-Fri 11.30am-3pm, 6-11pm; Sat 6-11pm; Sun 5-11pm. Closed Mon.*

Homer & Edy's is so far off the beaten track that it enjoys one of the rarest blessings in Los Angeles: free parking. It is even farther away from New Orleans, but hear the piano player and smell the food, and there is no room for doubt that this restaurant in a converted one-time residence is the real thing. *Specialties: Gumbo; oysters Bienville; southern fried frogs' legs.*

HORIKAWA

111 S San Pedro St., LA ☎*(213) 680-9355. Map 6D9* ▦ ▭ ▬ ➾ *by valet* ▨ ⊕ ▣ ▨ *Open Mon-Thurs 11.30am-2pm, 5.30-11.30pm; Fri 11.30am-2pm, 5.30-11pm; Sat 5-11pm; Sun 5-10pm.*

This all-purpose Japanese restaurant has one of the largest *sushi* bars in the city, a comparable *teppan* section, and a regular dining room. All three are well regarded. *Specialties — In the* **teppan** *section, where chefs give amazing tableside displays of cutting and chopping as part of the entertainment: lobster and filet mignon. In the* **dining room***: Iso-yaki; shabu-shabu.*

JERRY'S FAMOUS DELI

12655 Ventura Blvd., Studio City ☎*(818) 980-4245. Map 1B2* ▭ *to* ▦ ▭ ☲ ➾ ▨ ▣ ▨ *Open 24hrs.*

Like all LA delis, Jerry's staples, from pastrami on rye to cheesecake, seem to fall short of the same dishes served up in New York; this in spite of the fact that many of the ingredients here are imported from there. Maybe they lose something on the journey. Nevertheless, quality at Jerry's is high, service is brisk and helpful, and both the Valley clientele and the artworks covering the walls are stimulating. *Specialties: Overstuffed sandwiches; salads.*

JITLADA

11622 Ventura Blvd., Studio City ☎*(818) 506-9355. Map 1B2* ▦ ▭ ☲ ▣ ▨ *Open Tues-Thurs 11am-10pm; Fri-Sat 11am-11pm; Sun 4-11pm.*

Anyone who claims that the Thai food at this unpretentious restaurant in the Valley is superb hasn't been to Bangkok. Probably they're just reflecting the fact that Thai is among the hottest cuisines (figuratively and literally) in Los Angeles. Still, Jitlada is pretty good, and ranks highly among the rapidly increasing number of Thai restaurants on the West Coast. Most of the authentic ingredients appear to be on hand, although a few are obviously missing, service is friendly, prices reasonable, and there's excellent imported Thai beer. *Specialties: Stuffed chicken wings; mee krob; yam yai.*

KATSU

1972 N Hillhurst Ave., Los Feliz ☎*(213) 665-1891. Map 5B7* ▦ *to* ▦ ▭ ☲ ☲ ➾ *by valet* ▨ ⊕ ▣ ▨ *Open Mon-Fri noon-2pm, 6-10pm; Sat 6-10pm. Closed Sun.*

Minimalist black and white decor, avant-garde tableware, plus what may be the best *sushi* in Los Angeles. The dishes, employing only the freshest seafood, are a visual as much as a culinary delight. Arrive early or expect to wait. Reservations a must for tables. No reservations accepted for *sushi* bar. *Specialty: Sushi . . . .*

LAWRY'S CALIFORNIA CENTER

570 W Ave. 26, LA ☎*(213) 224-6850, (213) 224-5783. Map 6C9* ▦ ▭ ▬ ☲ ⬟ ☲ ♫ ➾ ▨ ▣ ▨ *Open daily 11am-3pm all year; plus May-Oct Mon-Fri 5-10pm, Sat-Sun 4-9pm. Call for holiday schedules. Also ✗ of food plant Mon-Fri 11.30am, 1.30pm, 2.30pm.*

Shops and a multifaceted restaurant that is mostly garden and patio adjoin Lawry's food-processing and packaging plant out among the warehouses lying E of Dodger Stadium. The restaurant menu is mostly Californian-Mexican, and the food is consistently good.

LAWRY'S THE PRIME RIB
55 N La Cienega Blvd., Beverly Hills ☎*(310) 652-2827. Map* **4**C4 ▥ ▢ ☖
━ ▣ ▣ ▨ *Open Mon-Thurs 5-11pm; Fri-Sat 5pm-midnight; Sun 3-11pm.*
The menu pretty much repeats the name of the place. The side dishes are Yorkshire pudding and salad. Otherwise, prime rib it is, and in such quantities that the staff takes it in its stride each year when the opposing Rose Bowl football teams come in and try to eat everything but the walls. No reservations are accepted.

LEW MITCHELL'S ORIENT EXPRESS
5400 Wilshire Blvd., LA ☎*(213) 935-6000. Map* **4**D5 ▥ *to* ▥ ▢ ☖ ♪ ━ ▣ ▣ ▨ *Open Mon-Fri 11.30am-3pm, plus daily 6-11pm or later.*
The dark rose and charcoal-gray interior of this great example of Los Angeles eclectic has severe lines and rich textures that make it look as if a contemporary Italian had designed it. The huge, happily uncrowded room makes a perfect backdrop for a collection of fine Chinese art. The menu, created by Mitchell's Chinese wife, reverses the East-West proportions. It is nearly all traditional Hunanese and Szechuan, with a small but thoughtful selection of Western dishes. *Specialties: Crab cake; whole rock cod; beef hunan.*

MA MAISON
8555 Beverly Blvd. (Ma Maison Sofitel Hotel), Mid-Wilshire ☎*(213) 655-1991. Map* **4**C4 ▥ ▢ ☖ ━ *by valet* ▣ ▣ ▣ ▨
Many credit Patrick Terrail and his original Ma Maison on Melrose Ave. (from 1973-85) with a central match-making role in LA's love affair with chic restaurants. The new setting is Hollywood French, with a garden feel and sliding glass roof. The restaurant in its new location hasn't yet attained the same mythic status as the original. Which is a shame, because the setting is a huge

improvement, and the food has settled down to reliable — with touches of brilliance. *Specialties: Smoked salmon; warm lobster salad; sautéed bass.*

THE MANDARIN
430 N Camden Dr., Beverly Hills ☎*(213) 272-0267. Map* **3**C3 ▥ *to* ▥ ▢ ☖ ☖ ━ ▣ ▣ ▣ ▨ *Open Mon-Fri noon-11pm; Sat 5-11pm; Sun 5-10.30pm.*
This is a clone of Cecilia Chiang's excellent San Francisco temple of imperial Chinese gastronomy. It is the equal of its forerunner in opulence of decor and breadth of menu. The Peking duck must be ordered in advance. *Specialties: Prawns Szechuan; Peking duck; noodles.*

MATSUHISA
129 N La Cienega Blvd., West Hollywood ☎*(310) 659-9639. Map* **4**C4 ▥ *to* ▥ ▢ ▣ ▣ ▣ ▨ *Open Mon-Fri 11.45am-2.30pm, 5.45-10.30pm; Sat-Sun 5.45-10.30pm.*
Another contender for the title "best *sushi* bar in town," Matsuhisa is small, nothing special to look at, and the service can be erratic. However, the seafood dishes, both cold and hot, are excellent, and the culinary provenance is extraordinary: an amalgam of Japan, California and Peru. Reservations are essential. *Specialties: Sushi rolls; bonito.*

MICHAEL'S ☖
1147 3rd St., Santa Monica ☎*(310) 451-0843. Map* **1**C1 ▥ ▢ ━ ▣ ▣ ▣ ▨ *Open Tues-Fri noon-2pm, 6.30-10pm; Sat-Sun 10.30am-2pm, 6.30-10pm. Closed Mon; Jan 2; Dec 24.*
One of the most ambitious and highest-priced restaurants in the Los Angeles basin, Michael's is generally French but particularly Californian. One of the motivations is a quest by owner Michael McCarty for perfect ingredients arrayed in striking new combinations. The spectacular wine list is revised twice weekly. As usual among perfectionists, the failures are almost as dramatic as the successes. Most of the tables are outdoors in a delightful garden. *Specialties: Poulet grillé – cresson nature et beurre*

d'estragon; pigeon grillé sur foie gras de canard au vinaigre de framboise; faux-filet de veau – citron caramelisé.

MON KEE LIVE FISH SEA FOOD 🍴 ♣

679 N Spring St., LA ☎*(213) 628-6717, (213) 628-1090. Map* **6**D9 ▦ *to* ▦ ▭ ▬ ◉ 💳 *Open daily 11.30am-10pm.*

The place is as bare and plain as only inexpensive Cantonese restaurants can be, but the claim of live fish is true. Tanks full of fish await the cooks, who work in the Hong Kong style. A few chicken, pork and beef dishes supplement five pages of fish on the menu. *Specialties: Bird's nest of grated potato with conch, squid, shrimp, scallops or rock cod; lobster or crab in gingery hoisin-style sauce.*

MOUSTACHE CAFE

8155 Melrose Ave., LA ☎*(213) 651-2111. Map* **4**C4 ▦ *to* ▦ ▭ 🛋 ◉ 💳 *Open Sun-Thurs 11.30am-midnight; Fri-Sat 11.30am-1am. Closed Mon; Jan 1; Thanksgiving; Dec 24-25.*

The place looks like a bistro: it has a café-style interior and a patio shielded from the street by tenting. The food includes undistinguished bistro fare anchored by sandwiches and crepes, and ranges into fuller meals more typical of a brasserie. But the heart of Moustache really is the clientele, which is pure Hollywood bent on a relaxed good time. *Specialties: Canard au Muscadet; daily meat and fish entrée; chocolate soufflé.*

MUSSO & FRANK GRILL

6667 Hollywood Blvd., Hollywood ☎*(213) 467-7788, (213) 467-5123. Map* **5**B5 ▦ *to* ▦ ▭ 🚗 nearby* ▣ ◉ ◎ 💳 *Open Mon-Fri 11am-10.45pm. Closed Sat-Sun; major holidays.*

While actors and directors parade through ultra-chic spots in Beverly Hills, writers hang out in the worn, warm confines of an old-fashioned Hollywood joint that resembles a stage set of a New York bar and grill, where the guy in the next booth looks like Philip Marlowe, private eye, and the waiters look just slightly cynical. Atmosphere is the main event. (A second room with tables has slightly less of it, but is easier to get into.) The kitchen produces satisfying but not stylish food from a long, New York-style menu. *Specialties (one each day): Corned beef and cabbage; sauerbraten; chicken pot pie; braised short ribs of beef.*

OOMASA

350 E 1st St., LA ☎*(213) 623-9048. Map* **6**D9 ▦ *to* ▦ ▭ ▬ ▣ ◉ 💳 *Open Tues-Sun 11.30am-10pm. Closed Mon.*

Scores of *sushi* bars in LA contend for top honors. But Oomasa is one of the best and has an appropriate location on Japanese Village Plaza. The restaurant also serves dinners in booths in a pale, paneled area to one side of the *sushi* bar. *Specialties: Sushi; sashimi; unikirage (sea urchin and jellyfish); unagi kabayaki (grilled freshwater eel with sweet sauce).*

L'ORANGERIE 🏛

903 N La Cienega Blvd., West Hollywood ☎*(310) 652-9770. Map* **4**C4 ▦ ▭ ▬ 🍷 🚗 *by valet* ▣ ◉ ◎ 💳 *Open daily 6-10pm.*

Hiding behind a stony facade, this temple of *nouvelle cuisine* manages to be at once beautiful, formal and welcoming. Service is splendid, and the French food, appreciably more distinctive and intense in flavor than typical *nouvelle*, can be among the best in Los Angeles. *Specialties: Eggs in shells with caviar; grilled sea bass with fennel; veal medallions in cream and mustard; apple tart.*

THE ORIGINAL PANTRY CAFÉ 🍴

877 S Figueroa St., LA ☎*(213) 972-9279. Map* **6**D8 ▦ ▭ ▬ *Open 24hrs.*

This big, plain barn of a place is worth knowing about for hearty breakfasts and nourishing if unimaginative main meals. No beer or wine, or other grace notes, and fast service is counted as good service. *Specialties: Steak with hash browns; selection of daily specials.*

PACIFIC DINING CAR ♣

1310 W 6th St., LA ☎*(213) 483-6000.*

Map 6D8 ▥ to ▥ ☐ ➤ ☿ ➧ *by valet* ▣ ▨ *Open 24hrs.*

Every city claiming greatness should have a round-the-clock restaurant serving properly grilled meats and fish in an atmosphere that permits conspiracy without encouraging it. LA has this one, dating back to 1921. Breakfast *(from 1-11am)*, lunch *(from 11am-4pm)* and dinner *(from 4pm-1am)* menus all have a selection of steaks and other grills. Reservations are advised at mealtimes. Incidentally, a small part of the premises is indeed a railroad dining car. The bar, in Stygian darkness, offers four whiskeys (The Glenlivet, Chivas Regal, Jack Daniels and Jim Beam), plus white spirits for the timid, and good California wines by the glass. *Specialties: Grilled beef; daily specials such as broiled rabbit or grilled sole.*

PATINA ⌂
5955 Melrose Ave., Hollywood ☎*(213) 467-1108. Map 5B6* ▥ to ▥ ➧ ➤ ▨ ▣ ▨ ☐ ➟ *Open Mon-Thurs 11.30am-2pm, 6-9.30pm; Fri 11.30am-2pm, 6-10.30pm; Sat 6-10.30pm; Sun 6-9.30pm.*
Patina is one of LA's most talked-about restaurants, despite the easily missed exterior and the interior with those small tables placed too close for privacy. The attraction is the food offered by German-born chef/owner Joachim Splichal, regarded as one of the most creative talents in town. Seafood and vegetables dishes are the main attraction and both can be strikingly inventive. The fixed-price lunch and dinner menus are unbeatable bargains. The California wines are well chosen, affordable and available by the glass, half-bottle or bottle. *Specialties: Corn blini with marinated salmon; John Dory with calf's feet and oysters; corn crème brulée.*

PEPPONE ⌂
11628 Barrington Ct., LA ☎*(310) 476-7379. Map 1C1* ▥ ☐ ➤ ☿ ➧ ▨ ▣ ▣ ▨ *Open Tues-Fri 11.30am-2.30pm, 5.30-11.30pm; Sat-Sun 5.30-11.30pm. Closed Mon; Sept 1-15; Thanksgiving; Dec 25.*

Frequently chosen as LA's best Italian restaurant, although critics believe it's been passed in recent years. Its owner-chef hopes guests will ignore the menu and give him instructions to extemporize, perhaps using one or two dishes from an encyclopedia-length list of daily specials. The style is southern, with subtle but unwavering enthusiasm for tomatoes and garlic. The room is dark, but not quite dark enough to hide the paintings of miserably weeping children, the only drawback. *Specialties: Fusili carbonara; green fettucine with anchovy and garlic sauce; sweetbreads Pompeii; calamari.*

PIONEER BOULANGERIE ♣
2012 Main St., Santa Monica ☎*(310) 399-7771. Map 1C1* ▥ ➧ ➤ ➟ ▣ ▨ *Open daily for breakfast 8-11am; lunch and dinner 11am-9pm. Closed Jan 1; Dec 25.*
First and foremost, this enterprise is a splendid bakery. Secondly, because baked-on-the-spot croissants, breads, cinnamon and other sweet rolls dominate and the espresso is rich, it is excellent for cafeteria breakfasts. The sunny patio is only an extra blessing. Thirdly, it is an inexpensive and hearty Basque dinner house with one seating nightly, Wednesday-Sunday by reservation only.

REBECCA'S
2025 Pacific Ave., Venice ☎*(310) 306-6266. Map 1C1* ▥ ➧ ☿ ☐ ▨ ▣ ▣ ▨ *Open Sun-Thurs 6pm-10.30pm; Fri-Sat 6pm-11.30pm.*
The decor from Frank Gehry is bizarre and provocative. The food from Mexico via France and California takes second place to the high-energy scene. Still, preparation is authentically south of the border, ingredients and combinations local and inventive. Owners Bruce and Rebecca Marder also claim the best Margaritas in town and attract a young, trendy crowd. *Specialties: Sea Bass taco; duck rellenos; chicken fajitas.*

REX, IL RISTORANTE ⌂
617 S Olive St., LA ☎*(213) 627-2300. Map 6D9* ▥ ☐ ➧ ➤ ☿ ☙ ➟ *by valet at dinner only* ▨ ▣ ▣ ▨ *Open Mon-Fri*

noon-2pm, 7-10pm; Sat 7-10pm. Closed
Sun; Sept 1-15.

The style is *nuova cucina,* the regional
touches mostly Roman. Rex's decor
announces that it is for serious eaters.
Walls have paneling, chairs are plush,
upholstered for long sitting. The center
of an uncrowded room is given over to
a display of food artful enough to go in
a museum. The effect of all this is mag-
nified by a gilded exterior. Reservations
are required, and with a single nightly
seating they are often difficult to make.
Up on the mezzanine there is an Art
Deco bar and a tiny floor meant for
cheek-to-cheek dancers. *Specialties:
Terrine of duck with pistachios and
small salad of cucumbers and duck
hearts; fettucine with porcini (wild
boletus mushrooms); baby red snapper
in tomato sauce; grilled entrecôte and
eggplant.*

SABROSO

1029 W Washington Blvd., Venice ☎*(310)
399-3832. Map 1C1* ▥ ☐ ❧ *Open
Tues-Fri noon-2pm, 6-10pm; Sat-Sun
6-10pm. Closed Mon.*

There's a jukebox playing Mexican hits,
cacti on the patio and an anarchic air.
The fare is *nouvelle* Mexican and the
menu, which changes often, is written
up on a large blackboard. The food
seldom disappoints. *Specialties: Ca-
zuela ranchera; cactus salad; chocolate flan.*

ST ESTEPHE

2640 Sepulveda Blvd., Manhattan Beach
☎*(310) 545-1334. Map 1D2* ▥ *to* ▥
☐ ◛ ▧ ▣ ▨ *Open for lunch Mon-Fri
11am-2pm; for dinner Tues-Sat 6-10pm.
Closed Sun.*

The name comes from an old bottle of
Cos d'Estournel that dazzled the
owners, but that is the most of the
French inspiration. The cookery of the
American southwest is the greater half
in a signal variation on *la nueva cocina
mexicana.* The presentation is stunning. *Specialty: Salmon painted dessert.*

LE ST GERMAIN ⌂

5955 Melrose Ave., LA ☎*(213) 467-1108.*

Map 5C2 ▥ ☐ ◛ ▽ ◛ *by valet* ▧ ▣
▨ ▨ *Open Mon-Fri noon-2pm, 6-10.30pm;
Sat 6-10.30pm. Closed Sun.*

A pleasant old building painted yellow,
a terrace full of flowers and rosy-hued
walls hung with pastoral paintings create a perfect illusion of a French country
restaurant right next to one of LA's busiest streets. Several small dining rooms,
plus tables on the terrace, sustain a
mood of intimacy. This triumph of imagination is equaled by one of the earliest, most intelligent weddings of
French culinary technique with fresh
California ingredients on a menu that
has been around so long it no longer
smacks of the experimental. *Specialties:
John Dory; rabbit in wine, cream and
mustard sauce; veal sautéed with
mushrooms and crayfish; California
salad.*

LA SCALA ⌂

410 N Canon Dr., Beverly Hills ☎*(310)
275-0579. Map 3C3* ▥ *to* ▥ ☐ ▬ ◛
▧ ▣ ▨ ▨ *Open Mon-Fri 11.30am-
2.30pm, 5.30pm-midnight; Sat 5.30pm-
midnight. Closed Sun.*

The funny, half-fancy, half-Chianti-
bottle decor of this durable restaurant
could probably double as a stage set for
some light-hearted opera, but it is apt
where it is. Since its beginnings, La Scala
has been both a showplace for celebrities (the bar is a good place for star-
gazing) and a good northern Italian
restaurant with, maybe, a few Spanish
touches. The menu has kept pace with
rising culinary standards without losing
its earthy vitality. A meal of pasta at an
off-peak hour is a bargain. The wine list,
Italian, French and Californian, is excellent. Proprietor Jean Leon has a less
formal place, **La Scala Malibu**, in a
shopping center called Malibu Country
Mart *(3835 Cross Creek Rd.).* Same
clientele in less fancy dress; similar
menu, but simpler and fresher. *Specialties: Mussels; Melanzane nostra; mig-
nonettes Rossini; veal scallopine
piccata.*

72 MARKET STREET

72 Market St., Venice ☎*(310) 392-8720.*

Map 1C1 🔲 🔲 ☍ ✦ *by valet* 🔲 🔲 🔲
Open Tues-Thurs 8-10.30am, 11.30am-
2.30pm, 6-10.30pm; Fri 8-10.30am,
11.30am-2.30pm, 6-11.30pm; Sat
6-11.30pm. Closed Sun-Mon.

Dudley Moore and Liza Minelli are
among the owners of this chic restaurant, where the architecture is as
noteworthy as the cuisine. The airy,
high-ceilinged space was once used as
a studio by architect Frank Gehry, and
the hi-tech conversion suits the arty
showbiz crowd who go for the all-
American food and the prospect of
hearing Moore tinkling the ivories,
something he does more often than
you'd expect. Good, long list of daily
specials. *Specialties: Meatloaf; chili;*
grilled fish.

SPAGO

8795 Sunset Blvd., LA ☎*(310) 652-4025.*
Map 3C3 🔲 🔲 ☍ ✦ *by valet* 🔲 🔲 🔲
Open daily 6pm-2am.

Wolfgang Puck was a legend before he
left the then ultra-chic MA MAISON to open
. . . . a pizzeria! He has become a bigger
legend since, as Spago has turned out
to be to pizzerias what Maseratis are to
Fiats. Dough is rolled to order; fresh
tomatoes replace tomato sauce; the galaxy of toppings includes artichokes,
eggplants and goat cheeses.

Not only that: this is where the hot
names of Hollywood come to see, to be
seen, and — not incidentally — to eat
Puck's spectacular reinventions of old
Italian standbys. If they're able to get a
table, mere passers-through eat pretty
well toward the back of the room,
where the views are modest but the fare
is every bit as good as it is out front
where the social lions lounge, and
where Puck still treats familiars pretty
much as if they were in his dining room
at home.

When he is not at Spago, he is at his
other place (CHINOIS ON MAIN — see page
127) shattering other culinary icons.

The name Spago is, incidentally, an
irreverent shorthand for spaghetti,
which also finds new levels here. *Spe-*
cialties: Pizza; pasta; Sonoma baby
lamb.

STUDIO GRILL

7321 Santa Monica Blvd., LA ☎*(213)*
874-9202. Map 4C5 🔲 🔲 ▬ ▬ ✦ 🔲
🔲 🔲 *Open Mon-Fri noon-2.15pm;*
Sun-Thurs 6-10.15pm; Fri-Sat 6-11.15pm.

This is almost beyond doubt the ultimate example of Los Angeles reverse
chic. The dusty white facade is in the
middle of a particularly dull-looking
stretch of Santa Monica Blvd., but the
room within is elegant and the eclectic
menu one of the finest in the city. The
style is light without being *nouvelle*.
Reservations are required. The list has
many well-aged wines at fair prices.
Specialties: Carpaccio; shrimp with
ginger and lime; roasted peppers with
anchovies.

A THOUSAND CRANES ⌂

120 S Los Angeles St. (New Otani Hotel),
LA ☎*(213) 629-1200. Map 6D9* 🔲 🔲
▬ ✦ 🔲 🔲 🔲 *Open daily 6-10.30pm.*

Because the menu is aimed largely at
Japanese guests in an elegant hotel, A
Thousand Cranes has a luxurious
breadth of dishes both in its à la carte
and set-dinner lists. The room could
hardly be lovelier. One side has Japanese tables (with welcome foot wells for
the less than limber), the other conventional Western furnishings. A glass wall
looks onto a garden with pools and
waterfalls. *Specialties: Salt roasted*
clams; shabu shabu.

TOLEDO RESTAURANT

11613 Santa Monica Blvd., LA ☎*(310)*
477-2400. Map 1C1 🔲 🔲 ▬ ▬ 🔲 🔲
🔲 *Open Tues-Thurs 11.30am-2.30pm,*
5.30-10.30pm; Fri 11.30am-2.30pm,
5.30-11pm; Sat 5.30-11pm; Sun 4-10pm.
Closed Mon.

The decor is worthy of an urbane restaurant in Spain, and so is the menu,
which has some hints of Castile and
many of Andalucía. Preparation and
service live up to appearances. Toledo's
long wine list also waves the Spanish
flag. *Specialties: Paella; pato Sevilla.*

TOMMY TANG'S

7473 Melrose Ave., LA ☎*(213) 651-1810.*
Map 4C5 🔲 *to* 🔲 ✦ 🔲 ☍ 🔲 🔲 🔲

VISA Open Mon-Thurs 11.30am-11.30pm; Fri-Sat 11.30am-midnight; Sun 5-10pm.
Stylish location for a stylish and unusual restaurant. Choose between the restaurant proper, with authentic and imaginatively modified Thai dishes, and the *sushi* bar. Tommy Tang's is at the smarter end of Melrose's and the youngish crowd who gather here reflect this; wear black and you'll feel at home. *Specialties: Duck and tiger prawns with cilantro sauce; bbq chicken; sushi.*

LA TOQUE

8191 Sunset Blvd., West Hollywood ☎(213) 656-7515. Map 4B4 ▦ ▦ ▭ �◼ ♈ ⬇ by valet ⬛ ⬛ ⬛ *VISA* Open *Mon-Thurs noon-2pm, 6.30-10.30pm; Fri noon-2pm, 6-10.30pm; Sat 6-10.30pm. Closed Sun.*
La Toque is a small restaurant with a big, deserved reputation. It avoids novelty for novelty's sake, serving only the freshest ingredients prepared in both classical and restrained *nouvelle* French fashion. The menu changes with the seasons, the fish dishes and puddings are especially good, and the ambience is quiet and charming. *Specialties: Sea bass rolled with crayfish; rabbit in mustard sauce; fresh fruit tarts.*

TRUMPS ⬆

8764 Melrose Ave., LA ☎(310) 855-1480. Map 4C4 ▦ ▭ ♈ ⬇ by valet ⬛ ⬛ *VISA* Open *Mon-Thurs noon-3pm, 6.30pm-midnight; Fri-Sat noon-3pm, 6.30pm-12.30am. Closed Sun.*
Among all the experimental kitchens in this open-minded city, trendy Trumps stands alone on a new frontier. Almost no combination is too outlandish to consider. The architecture echoes the menu. Late-night suppers are less bizarre and are a better value. *Specialties: Potato pancakes with goat cheese; cold lobster pesto; scallops with pine nuts.*

VALENTINO ⬆

3115 Pico Blvd., Santa Monica ☎(310) 829-4313. Map 1C1 ▦ ▭ ▭ ◼ ♈ ⬇ by valet ⬛ ⬛ ⬛ *VISA* Open *Mon-Sat 5.30-11.30pm; lunch Fri only 11.30am-2.30pm. Closed Sun.*

Recently revamped, Valentino's stylish decor is now worthy of its splendid Italian food and exceptional wine list. Ignore the à la carte and choose from a long list of daily specials, which include well-executed traditional dishes and more innovative creations.

WEST BEACH CAFE

60 N Venice Blvd., Venice ☎(310) 832-5396. Map 1C1 ▦ ▭ ◼ ⬛ ⬛ ⬛ *VISA* Open *10am-1am, except Mon lunch.*
One of the more versatile demonstrations of modern California changes the contemporary paintings on its walls each month, and changes its "*nouvelle* California" and/or "minimalist" menu weekly. Snow-white, rectilinear and skylit, this is every bit as good a restaurant as it is a gallery. *Specialties: They change seasonally and weekly, but typical are Hawaiian tuna with sea urchin sauce, and breast of turkey in vinegar and honey.*

WONDER SEAFOOD

2505 W Valley Blvd., Alhambra ☎(818) 308-0259. Map 1C3 ▭ to ▦ ▭ ⬛ *VISA* Open *daily 11.30am-10pm.*
Cantonese chefs have little if anything to learn about getting the best out of fresh seafood, and it doesn't come much fresher than at Wonder Seafood, where many of the live ingredients-in-waiting can be seen swimming about in large water tanks. The traditional Cantonese food is so authentic you could be in Hong Kong. *Specialties: Snake soup; crab with black beans; prawns baked in salt.*

YAGURA ICHIBAN

101 Japanese Village Plaza, LA ☎(213) 623-4141. Map 6D9 ▭ to ▦ ▭ ♈ ⬛ ⬛ *VISA* Open *Mon-Fri 11am-2.30pm, 5-10.30pm; Sat 11am-10.30pm; Sun noon-10.30pm. Closed 1st week of Jan.*
The dining rooms evoke Japanese country inns to the satisfaction of visiting Japanese. The most praised of several restaurants within a restaurant is the *robatayaki* bar, a sort of country barbecue style of cooking done in front of the diners.

Eating on a budget

Eating out is an integral part of the LA experience, but it isn't necessary to book months ahead, break the bank or behave like a style victim to enjoy the theater of it all, not to mention the food. Moderately priced establishments also offer, in their way, an authentic LA lifestyle experience. They can be fast and plastic, cozy and relaxed, noisy or sedate, one of a chain, one-of-a-kind, or mom-and-pop neighborhood favorites. There's plenty of junk food for those who crave it. But almost invariably the dishes on offer are wholesome and tasty, the portions more than adequate, the service friendly and attentive.

Moreover, children are usually welcomed. And the other customers? Well, they're regular people.

AMERICAN DINER
Cafe '50s   838 Lincoln Blvd., Venice ☎399-1955, map **1**C1, for 1950s decor, ambience, and good, simple food
Ed Debevic's   134 N La Cienega Blvd., Beverly Hills ☎(310) 659-1952, map **4**D4, an over-the-top '50s retro diner that's always crowded
Jan's   8424 Beverly Blvd., Beverly Hills ☎651-2866, map **4**C4, for meatloaf and 1950s retro
O'Shaughnessy's Downtown   505 S Flower St., ARCO Plaza ☎(213) 629-2568, map **6**D9, for LA Irish steaks
Stepps on the Court   330 S Hope St., Crocker Center ☎(213) 626-0900, map **6**D9, in the heart of the financial district, notable for huge back bar

BBQ
Dr. Hogly-Wogly's Tyler Texas BBQ   8136 N Sepulveda Blvd., Van Nuys ☎(818) 780-6701, map **1**B1: expect to line up for giant Texan portions of delicious downhome spareribs and hot links

BREAKFAST PLACES
Croissants USA   9536 Brighton Way, Beverly Hills ☎(310) 271-2535, map **3**C3, pastries and more
Konditori Patio Cafe   230 S Lake Ave., Pasadena ☎(818) 792-6600, map **1**B3, friendly Scandinavian café
Old World Restaurant   1019 Westwood Blvd., LA ☎(310) 208-4033, map **3**D2, a UCLA favorite, with health foods and burgers too
Vickman's   1228 E 8th St., LA ☎(213) 622-3852, map **6**B8, big breakfasts from 3am

DELICATESSENS
Art's Deli   12224 Ventura Blvd., Studio City ☎(818) 769-9808, map **1**B2, no-frills decor, abrupt service, but excellent sandwiches
Canter's   419 N Fairfax Ave., Hollywood ☎ 651-2030, map **4**C5, 24-hour deli with New York-style service and decor, LA-style food
Deli Malibu   3894 Cross Creek Rd., Malibu ☎456-2444, for all the deli favorites done well

Pico Kosher Deli   8826 W Pico Blvd., Ranco Park ☎273-9381, map **3**D3, for toothsome, really kosher, pastrami and corned beef
Stage Deli   Century City Marketplace, 10250 Santa Monica Blvd. ☎(310) 553-DELI, map **1**C2, a range of fast-food outlets from pizza to Chinese to salads
Starkey's Deli   Beverly Center, 8500 Beverly Blvd., West Hollywood ☎659-1010, map **4**C4, for deli sandwiches between shopping

FISH & CHIPS
H. Salt   4795 Vineland Ave., North Hollywood ☎(818) 761-1750, map **1**B2, a takeout that's so unassuming you'd think you're in Britain

HAMBURGERS AND HOT DOGS
Cassell's   3300 W 6th St., Mid-Wilshire ☎(213) 480-8668, map **5**D7, superb no-nonsense burgers
Hard Rock Café   Beverly Center at 8600 Beverly Blvd., Mid-Wilshire ☎(310) 276-7605, map **4**C4. reliably the same as all the other Hard Rocks elsewhere
Johnny Rocket's   7507 Melrose Ave., Hollywood ☎(213) 651-3361, map **4**C5, funky '50s-style, simple fast food, excellent people-watching from sidewalk tables
Pink's   711 N La Brea Ave., Hollywood ☎(213) 931-4223, map **4**C5, lousy location, great dogs
Russell's   5656 E 2nd St., Naples ☎(310) 434-0226, map **1**E3, an off-the-beaten-track, neighborhood café serving what may be the best burgers in LA
Tail O'the Pup   329 N San Vicente Blvd., West Hollywood ☎(310) 652-4517, map **4**C4, landmark Pop Art kiosk with not bad burgers and dogs
The Wiener Factory   14917 Ventura Blvd., Sherman Oaks ☎(818) 789-2676, map **1**B2, unprepossessing, but probably the best hotdogs in LA to stay or to go

INEXPENSIVE CHINATOWN
ABC Seafood   708 New High St., LA ☎(213) 680-2887, map **6**D9, for noodles and *dim sum*
Grandview Gardens   944 N Hill St., LA ☎(213) 624-6084, map **6**D9, for *dim sum*
Hunan   980 N Broadway, LA ☎(213) 626-5050, map **6**D9, for truly spicy foods
Mandarette   8386 Beverly Blvd., Beverly Hills ☎(213) 655-6115, map **4**C4, Chinese equivalent of a *tapas* bar, with tasty titbits galore
Mandarin Deli   Chinese Food Center, 727 N Broadway, LA ☎(213) 623-6054, map **6**D9, and 356 E 2nd St., Little Tokyo, LA, map **6**D9, for noodles and dumplings

KOREAN
Dong Il Jang   3455 W 8th St., Mid-Wilshire ☎(213) 383-5757, map **5**D7, Korean and Japanese specialties in classy surroundings

Hanil   989 Dewey Ave., Mid-Wilshire ☎(213) 480-8141, map **5**D7,
kimchi heaven: fermented cabbage, garlic and chili … delicious!
Korea Gardens   950 S Vermont Ave., Mid-Wilshire ☎(213) 388-
3042, map **5**D7, table-top BBQ Korean-style

OMELETS, SANDWICHES, SALADS
Alice's Restaurant   1043 Westwood Blvd., Westwood ☎(310) 478-
0941, map **3**D1, California cuisine, excellent views
Café Rodeo   360 N Rodeo Dr., Beverly Hills ☎(310) 273-0300,
map **3**C3, super-value snacks in glitter gulch
The Egg and the Eye   5814 Wilshire Blvd., LA, in the Craft and Folk
Art Museum ☎(213) 933-5596, map **4**D5, salads and omelets
TGI Friday   13470 Maxella St., Marina del Rey ☎(310) 822-9052,
map **1**C1, swinging singles and a very long menu

PIZZA
California Pizza Kitchen   Beverly Center, LA ☎(310) 854-6555,
map **4**C4, affordable designer pizzas; also at 207 S Beverly Dr., Beverly
Hills, map **3**C3
Il Fornaio   301 N. Beverly Dr. Beverly Hills ☎(310) 550-8330, map
3C3, authentic Italian pizza and pasta done very well, plus marvelous
bakery
Little Toni's   4745 Lankershim Blvd., North Hollywood ☎(818)
763-0131, map **1**B2, friendly neighborhood pizza with outstanding
pizza
Mario's   1001 Broxton St., Westwood ☎(310) 208-7077, map **3**D1,
fine pizza, clichéd decor
Palermo   1858 N Vermont Ave., Los Feliz ☎(213) 663-1430, map
5B7, Sicilian style for big appetites
La Strega   400 S Western Ave. ☎(213) 385-1546, map **5**D7, not the
cheapest, but good, with a stunning wine list
Wildflour Boston Pizza   2807 Main St., Santa Monica ☎(310) 399-
9990, map **1**C1, tiny restaurant, geared mostly toward superb design-
your-own takeouts

Entertainments

The performing arts

Like the movies, the performing arts in LA are a 20thC phenomenon. History here is counted in decades rather than centuries. But, as in most aspects of life, the city has raced to catch up. Like it needs Downtown skyscrapers, a city that wants to be taken seriously at home and abroad seems to need a vigorous performing arts scene. Money and growing numbers of people aspiring to cultural vitality and sophistication have made possible the remarkable transformation of LA from a near desert artistically to a blossoming oasis that young cities elsewhere can only dream of.

Probably the most characteristic and exciting feature of this buoyant scene is that it is determinedly multicultural. With a mind to the city's vivid cocktail of races, languages, traditions and cultural echoes, arts impresarios offer much more than a predictable mix of European classics. For sure, Mozart is frequently on offer. But so are a *gamelan* orchestra, Brazilian samba dancers, Peruvian flautists and Flamenco. Recent hits have included the American Indian Dance Theater, the Peking Acrobats and the Moscow Circus.

THE MOVIES

Still, LA's favorite performing art continues to be homegrown cinema. Motion pictures in LA are fresh from the cutting rooms, and Angelenos are watching movies today that the rest of the world won't see for months. There are excellent cinemas all over Greater LA, usually multi-screen and often to be found inside the better shopping malls — although it is likely that many will be showing the same choice of a dozen new movies.

And the popcorn is *wonderful*. A jumbo-sized helping is the best value for money, and surprisingly easy to munch your way through.

THE STAGE

Less expected, and contrary to preconceptions widely held outside the city, theater here is alive and flourishing. There are a staggering 150 legitimate theaters. There are fewer of the blockbuster musicals or classic revivals than habitués of Manhattan or London's West End are used to. But *Les Misérables, Phantom of the Opera* or something like it is usually playing somewhere. And Shakespeare and Molière appear from time to time.

But the real strength is in contemporary and experimental drama. Classical music and dance are equally well represented. Among noteworthy resident companies are the **LA Philharmonic**, the **Music Center Opera**, the **LA Chamber Orchestra**, the **LA Contemporary Dance Company** and the **Lewitzky Dance Company**. At the same time, LA attracts top names from elsewhere. In 1992 LA's major venues played host to Isaac Stern, Yo-Yo Ma, the Soviet Philharmonic, and the Royal Danish Ballet, plus many more.

The following list notes a selection of the major venues for the performing arts. The "Sunday Calendar" section of the *Los Angeles Times* runs complete listings of current cinema, theater, music and dance, and *California Magazine* can also be very useful.

Buy tickets in advance from agencies such as **Ticketron** (☎ *(310) 670-2311)* and **Mutual** (☎ *(213) 627-1248)*.

BALLET AND CLASSICAL MUSIC

The **Ambassador Auditorium** *(300 W Green St., Pasadena* ☎ *(818) 304-6161)* is part of a religious college campus. The luxuriously appointed, architecturally splendid auditorium annually books as many as 100 concerts. Nearly all of the performers and performing groups are of international stature.

The **Dorothy Chandler Pavilion** *(Los Angeles Music Center, 135 N Grand Ave.* ☎ *(213) 972-7211, map 6D9)* is a splendid 3,197-seat Downtown concert hall, home of the Los Angeles Philharmonic and the Joffrey Ballet. Other orchestras and recitalists also guest here.

A huge, recently renovated hall in Downtown, the **Shrine Auditorium** *(665 Jefferson Blvd.* ☎ *(213)(213) 748-5116, map 6E8)* is used primarily for touring dance troupes, and the American Ballet Company regularly performs here. And in the Mid-Wilshire district, the **Wilshire Ebell Theater** *(4401 W 8th St.* ☎ *(213) 939-1128, map 5D6)* is a wonderful 1924 Renaissance-style theater used by the Los Angeles Ballet.

Outdoor theaters used for classical music and ballet include the **Greek Theater** *(2700 N Vermont Ave.* ☎ *(213) 410-1062, map 5A7)* in Griffith Park, an outdoor amphitheater that books a broad range of entertainment from classical ballet to light opera and rock concerts. The **Hollywood Bowl** *(2301 N Highland Ave.* ☎ *(213) 850-2000, map 5B5)*, a natural amphitheater in the hills N of Hollywood, hosts scores of concerts as well as the summer season by the Philharmonic. It also presents pop concerts.

CINEMA

Predictably, Los Angeles has movie theaters in hundreds. Both **Hollywood** and **Universal City** have state-of-the-art theaters with the most technically advanced projection and sound systems. **Downtown** has the greatest architectural wonders, though most of the movies are in Spanish. But **Westwood Village** is the focal point for first-run movies.

Of special interest to cineasts with a sense of history are El Capitan Theater (see page 64) and MANN'S CHINESE THEATER (see pages 65 and 96). These movie industry shrines are both on Hollywood Blvd., and recently both have been restored to their original glory.

THEATER

The major theaters are located Downtown, in Hollywood and in Beverly Hills.

The **Ahmanson Theater** *(Los Angeles Music Center, 135 N Grand Ave.* ☎ *(310) 410-1062, map 6 D9)* is a major Downtown theater with 2,100 seats, used for major dramas and by the Center Theater Group, and occasionally by the Los Angeles Civic Light Orchestra. It presents touring troupes mostly doing musicals and musical comedy.

The **Mark Taper Forum** *(Los Angeles Music Center, 135 Grand Ave.* ☎ *(310) 410-1062, map 6 D9)*, a 750-seat house, is used primarily by the local Center Theater Group and Mark Taper Forum/Laboratory, who offer a consistent diet of new, often experimental works. A festival of new plays is held every spring.

The **Pantages Theater** *(6233 Hollywood Blvd.* ☎ *(800) 852-9772, map 5 B6)*, LA's largest theater, with 2,288 seats, is used for touring Broadway and other companies.

The **Pasadena Playhouse** *(37 S El Molino Ave.* ☎ *(818) 356-7529)* was founded in 1917 and restored and relaunched in 1986 following a 20-year closure. The 700-seat auditorium stages major drama with some of the best actors in town.

The **Shubert Theater** *(2020 Ave. of the Stars, ABC Entertainment Center* ☎ *(800) 233-3123, map 3 D3)* is a 1,828-seat palace for Broadway-produced, long-running plays and musicals.

Many smaller theaters present contemporary or experimental plays. Ticket prices are modest. Up-to-the-minute listings of venues and performances are to be found in *LA Weekly*.

LA by night

Set aside the cliched laid-back image. LA is a high-energy town; to paraphrase Warren Zevon — I'll sleep when I'm dead. Meanwhile, I aim to party. To prioritize it exactly is difficult, but along with working out, eating out, hanging out and the beach, nightlife is a hugely important leisure activity.

Angelenos are social animals. And, as inhabitants of the entertainment capital of the world, they require that the choice be rich and varied. Their taste is eclectic, fickle even. Moods and fashions change, and it can be difficult for the visitor to get an up-to-the-minute fix on which are the most popular or fashionable places of the moment.

The local press tries to keep pace. But a better solution is not to chase ephemera. Rather, go for places that have stood the test of time. Don't expect to club hop between Bel Air and Burbank. Like everything else in the greater city, its nightlife is spread out; distances are frequently measured in hour-long freeway rides, not the width of streets. Parking can be difficult and expensive. Sometimes, especially for comedy clubs, pre-paid reservations are essential. So, plan ahead and focus on a specific geographic area.

WHERE TO HEAD

This shouldn't be too difficult. Much of the best of LA after dark is to be found in just three areas: **Hollywood**, **West Hollywood** and **Santa Monica**.

Of these, only Hollywood ranks relatively high on sleaze. Many of those cruising Sunset and Hollywood Blvds. seem to be auditioning for bit parts in a movie by Federico Fellini. But the clamp-down on hookers and sex shows that began prior to the 1984 LA Olympic Games continues, and efforts to re-create the pre-World War II glamor of Hollywood Blvd. are bearing fruit. Such tawdriness as persists will appeal to connoisseurs of that peculiarly LA style of seediness represented in the novels of James Ellroy and Robert Campbell. But move on to Melrose Ave. and parts of La Cienega Blvd., and the scene becomes much trendier and altogether less menacing.

COMEDY

So what's special? Comedy, certainly. LA's comedy clubs are a showcase for both rising and established talent. Robin Williams, Eddie Murphy and scores of others will testify that, if you want to grab the attention of a Hollywood agent or producer, this is the place to do it. Moreover, many of those who have made it already still return to play the clubs from time to time. Apparently, it keeps them in touch and on their toes. Stand-up routines are usually sharp, fast, sophisticated and adult — and most comedy clubs have a bar and restaurant frequented by customers to match. The best such clubs are in Hollywood.

MUSIC

Clubs with live music, rock, disco, jazz, folk, Country & Western and elevator music piano are even more numerous. Some may find the rock somewhat dated. However, if Guns 'n Roses are to your taste, there are plenty of clones at work.

The recording industry draws a great many up-and-coming bands to LA. At the same time, there are always plenty of visiting acts in town. Either way, the paying customers are an equally important, and often more provocative, part of the show.

Jazz may be a richer musical vein. Los Angeles always has a number of well-known players in residence, and their numbers are augmented by film and studio players who sometimes put the stars in the shade.

Disco is disco is disco. Only big-name balladeers and cabaret singers are under-represented in LA. Most are more easily found in Las Vegas.

NIGHT CUSTOMS

At most places, door policy is pretty relaxed. You don't have to be famous, beautiful or skimpily dressed by Armani to get in, though it always helps. What may be essential is a preparedness to spend a long time in line on the sidewalk. And if you're looking to star-gaze at joints such as **On the Rocks** on Sunset Blvd., it's best to be all four.

Bars usually don't filter people at the door, and tend to be less intimidating to first-time visitors. In them, the enthusiasm is more for human contact, people-watching and conversation than the consumption of large quantities of alcohol. Nowadays, the politically correct term for a drunk is *chemically inconvenienced.* Whatever the language, it is decidedly unfashionable to over-indulge.

USEFUL TO KNOW

The following list notes only a handful of the best-known clubs. In addition to checking magazines and daily newspapers for information on what, where and who's hot, look for copies of the free tabloid *LA Weekly,* distributed in a variety of public places and at some hotels. It offers exhaustive surveys and listings of available entertainment.

The bigger the name on the marquee, the more advisable it is to reserve in advance. Most clubs sell advance tickets at the door. Check with **Ticketron** (☎ *(213) 670-2311)* and **Mutual** (☎ *(213) 627-1248).*

BARS

Meeting people, seeing and being seen is the thing. By no means everyone sticks to designer water. But the majority are guided by LA's draconian drink-driving laws.

BARNEY'S BEANERY
8447 Santa Monica Blvd., West Hollywood
☎*(213) 654-2287. Map* **4***C4* ▥ *to* ▥
▤ *Open 6am-2am.*
A small neighborhood bar immortalized by sculptor Ed Kienholz and boasting more than 200 different beers. Friendly no-nonsense atmosphere refined over 70 years.

CARLOS 'N CHARLIE'S
8240 Sunset Blvd., West Hollywood ☎*(213) 656-8830. Map* **4***B4* ▥ ▤ ◑ ◫ ♪ ⬤
by valet ▣ ▣ ▨ *Open 11.30am-2am.*
Carlos 'N Charlie's is much more than a bar. It has a goodish Mexican restaurant attached, and the upstairs space functions as disco, cabaret and comedy workshop. The regular singles crowd is smart but more relaxed than the preening fashion victims that inhabit some LA nightspots.

CARLOS & PEPE'S
2020 Wilshire Blvd., Santa Monica ☎*(213) 828-8903* ▥ *to* ▥ ▤ ⬤ ▣ ▣ ▨
Open 11am-2am.
Stylish Mexican-style decor, central bar and a young Westside clientele who crowd the place around happy hour. Good bar snacks.

GRAND AVENUE BAR
506 S Grand Ave., LA (Biltmore Hotel)
☎*(213) 624-1001* ▥ ▤ ↴ ▣ ▣ ▣
▨ *Open Mon-Fri 11.30am-1.30am; Sat 6.30pm-1.30am.*
This is an interior-designed bar with Italian marble tables, Mies van der Rohe chairs, artworks changed seasonally, and live jazz in the evening. The bar attracts an upscale business crowd, but most of the action is around the lunchtime buffet and early evening.

NICKY BLAIR'S
8730 Sunset Blvd., West Hollywood
☎*(213) 659-0929. Map* **4***B4* ▥ ▤
⬤ *by valet* ▣ ▣ ▣ ▨ *Open 6pm-2am.*
A glossy, high-energy, designer-clad clientele makes this a popular watering hole with entertainment industry highfliers and hangers-on. It can all be a bit intimidating, but it's ideal for beautiful people or beautiful people-watching.

POLO LOUNGE
9641 Sunset Blvd., Beverly Hills (Beverly Hills Hotel) ☎*(213) 276-2251. Map* **3***C3*
▥ ▤ ☺ ⬤ *by valet* ▣ ▣ ▣ ▨ *Open 7.30am-1.30am.*
Once *the* place to see, be seen, do deals

and generally feel good about the good life in Los Angeles, this is nowadays essentially an exercise in nostalgia.

RAINBOW

9015 Sunset Blvd., West Hollywood
☎(213) 278-4232. Map 3C3 ▢ ▨ ⇌ ○
⬗ ⊠ *AE* ⊙ ⊡ *VISA* *Open nightly 6pm-2am.*

Marilyn Monroe and Joe Di Maggio were engaged here (before its current incarnation, of course), and the restaurant still claims to serve the best chicken soup in California. Less than elegant, but it has evolved into something of a local institution since it converted to the Rainbow in 1972. The dark and atmospheric bar, restaurant and new wave music disco are popular with young ultra-hip singles on the prowl.

RANGOON RACKET CLUB

9474 Santa Monica Blvd., Beverly Hills
☎(213) 274-8926. Map 3C3 ▨ ⇌ ⬗
by valet *AE* ⊙ ⊡ *VISA*

Hollywood colonial, with ceiling fans, rattan and waiters dressed for the Raj. Sleek Beverly Hills clientele.

REBECCA'S

2025 Pacific Ave., Venice *☎(213)*
306-6266. Map 1C1 ▨ ⇎ ⇌ ⬗ *by valet* *AE* ⊙ ⊡ *VISA* *Open Sun-Thurs 6pm-midnight; Fri-Sat 6pm-2am.*

Desperately fashionable bar/restaurant designed by architect Frank Gehry and frequented by over-achieving singles who tend to drive European cars and wear expensive European clothes. The atmosphere, however, is pure conspicuous-consumption LA. Inexplicably, alligator- and octopus-shaped objects hang from the ceiling; the tables are of black marble. Not for those lacking in self-esteem. The Mexican food is good but expensive.

YE OLDE KING'S HEAD

116 Santa Monica Blvd., Santa Monica
☎(213) 451-1402. Map 1C1 ▢ ⇌ *Open 11am-2am.*

The name says it all. A "British" pub complete with darts, fish & chips and warm draft beer. Popular with homesick expatriates and young Anglophile locals alike.

CABARET AND COMEDY

Fun, fun, fun, for grown-ups. Even the male strippers play it for laughs. Don't take your maiden aunt or your children. Most clubs have an over-18 rule.

CHIPPENDALES

3739 Overland Ave., West LA *☎(213)*
202-8850. Map 3F3 ▨ ⊠ *AE* ⊙ *VISA*
Open Sun-Thurs 6.30pm-2am; Fri-Sat 6.30pm-4am. Shows continuous. Variable cover charge.

Good-natured cabaret with male exotic dancers strutting their well-muscled stuff for an all-female audience. Male customers are admitted after 10pm.

COMEDY STORE

8433 W Sunset Blvd., West Hollywood
☎(213) 656-6225. Map 4B4 ▨ ⊠
Shows nightly from about 8.30pm. Variable cover charge plus two-drink minimum.

The fare is comedy and occasional magic acts. The store has three rooms: **The Main Room** (the best local comedians mixed with big names trying out new acts for Las Vegas); the **Original Comedy Store** (a smaller room given over mostly to rising young acts); and **The Belly Room** (intimate, for female performers only). Weekends draw the sharpest talent; Monday is the night when anyone can get up on stage.

A branch, **Comedy Store West** (*1621 Westwood Blvd., Westwood ☎(213) 477-4751, map 3 D2*), books some of the same acts, but has only a beer and wine license, and admits minors.

GROUNDLINGS THEATER

7307 Melrose Ave., West Hollywood
☎(213) 934-9700. Map 4C5 ▨ *Shows nightly from about 8pm. Variable cover charge.*

Among the best laughs in town. Resident talented cast with polished sketches, routines and improvisation. Alumni include Pee-wee Herman.

IMPROVISATION

8162 Melrose Ave., West Hollywood
☎*(213) 651-2583. Map 4C4* 📷 ⊨ ⍴
Shows nightly from about 8.30pm. Variable cover charge plus two-drink minimum.

There is a weekly cycle, which includes Off the Wall improvisational theater (Monday), new comic faces and singers (Tuesday, Wednesday), stand-up comics (Thursday), and booked acts plus drop-ins, the latter sometimes including big names (Friday, Saturday). Sunday is for auditions.

LA CAGE LOS ANGELES

643 N La Cienega Blvd., West Hollywood
☎*(213) 657-1091. Map 4C4* 📷 ⊨ 🔀
Open Tues-Sat 7pm-2am. Closed Sun-Mon
☎ *for show times. Variable cover charge.*

Long-running female impersonator show spun off from the movie. Plenty of outrageousness and glitter. Not for the prudish.

ROSE TATTOO

665 N Robertson Blvd., West Hollywood
☎*(213) 854-4455. Map 4C4* 📷 ⊨ ⍴
🔀 *Open nightly 5.30pm-2am. Shows 9pm-1am. Variable cover charge.*

Fashionable club with a clientele that is predominantly gay but welcomes women. Entertainments include 1950s and '60s groups, singers, exotic revues and talent contests.

VERDI RISTORANTE DI MUSICA

1519 Wilshire Blvd., Santa Monica ☎*(213) 393-0706. Map 1C1* 📷 ⊨ *Open Tues-Sun 6pm-2am. Closed Mon.*

Theater/restaurant with a refined atmosphere and resident repertory group performing opera and Broadway hits.

DANCE CLUBS AND ROCK

Not really for wrinklies, but for the young, lithe and energetic. Try and dress the part.

CLUB LINGERIE

6507 W Sunset Blvd., Hollywood ☎*(213) 466-8557. Map 5B6* 📷 ⍴ 🔀 *Open Mon-Sat 9pm-2am. Closed Sun.*

Well-established venue for new wave, rock and reggae, known to regulars as Club Underwear. The fashion show staged by the chic clientele is sometimes better than the music. The DJs know their stuff.

LIGHTHOUSE

30 Pier Ave., Hermosa Beach
☎*(310) 376-9833* 📷 ⍴ *Open Mon-Fri 4pm-1.30am; Sat-Sun 10am-1.30am. Show times and cover charges vary, so check first.*

For years (since the 1950s, in fact) Lighthouse was advertised as a jazz club and waterfront dive. Now, after a facelift, the musical fare has changed to reggae, R&B and rock.

THE PALACE

1735 N Vine St., Hollywood ☎*(213)*

462-3000. Map 5B6 📷 ⊨ ⍴ *Open Sun-Thurs 9pm-2am; Fri-Sat 9pm-4am. Cover charge varies.*

This beautifully converted 1927 theater with three bars presents major rock names, jazz, R&B and dancing, all under the same roof.

THE PALOMINO

6907 Lankershim Blvd., North Hollywood
☎*(818) 764-4010* ⊨ ⍴ *Open Mon-Sat 10am-2am; Sun 4pm-2am. Cover varies.*

LA's major country music showcase looks rather shabby these days, but some would say it always did, and it still attracts major names and the crowds. Also rock, R&B, blues.

THE PROBE

836 N Highland Ave., Hollywood ☎*(213) 669-1000. Map 4C5* 📷 ⍴ ⊙ ⍴ ⍦ *Open usually 9pm-3am.*

Changes its persona nightly. Monday is **Club With No Name**, with Hollywood rock; Tuesday is **Cathouse**, a leather 'n' rock disco; Sunday is **1970**, all hot pants and Sex Pistols. Don't expect admission unless you look the part.

ROXBURY

8225 Sunset Blvd., West Hollywood
☎*(213) 656-1750. Map 4B4* 💺 ⇒ ☿ ⊙
◨ ♪ *Open Tues-Sat. Closed Sun-Mon.*
According to the glitterati, this is still the hottest place in town. Live blues bar and dance club are liveliest on Tuesday and Friday.

ROXY

9009 Sunset Blvd., West Hollywood
☎*(310) 276-2222. Map 3C3* 💺 ▣ ☿

Show times vary. Two-drink minimum.
Not the premier rock venue that it once was, but this is still a comfortable Art Deco spot featuring up-and-coming local bands. It is especially popular these days with the heavy metal crowd.

MADAME WONG'S WEST

2900 Wilshire Blvd., Santa Monica ☎*(310) 828-7361* 💺 ☿ ⊙ ◨ ♪ ✺ *Open nightly. Variable cover charge.*
Three bars, video games, two floors, live bands, DJs, dancing. Small wonder this mainstream club boasts more bands with recording contracts than any other in LA.

JAZZ

Not to be missed. As American as angel hair pasta with clam sauce.

AT MY PLACE

1026 Wilshire Blvd., Santa Monica ☎*(213) 451-8596. Map 1C1* 💺 ☿ *Open Mon-Sat 7pm-2am, Sun 3pm-1am. Shows nightly* ☎ *for times. Variable cover charge.*
The hangout for many of LA's best studio musicians leans toward jazz, but also offers rock, R&B, comedy.

THE BAKED POTATO

3787 Cahuenga Blvd., N Hollywood
☎*(818) 980-1615* 💺 ☿ *Open 7pm-2am. Show times vary* ☎ *for times. Variable cover charge.*
Contemporary jazz in intimate surroundings is the main point. But as the name suggests, baked potatoes are a specialty for those who arrive hungry.

CONCERTS BY THE SEA

100 Fisherman's Wharf, Redondo Beach
☎*(213) 379-4998* 💺 ⇒ ☿ ⊠ *Open Thurs-Sun 8.30-2am. Closed Mon-Wed. Show times and cover charge variable.*
Not exactly luxurious surroundings, but there are big-name mainstream performers and a musically sophisticated clientele.

DONTE'S

4269 Lankershim Blvd., N Hollywood
☎*(818) 769-1566* 💺 ⇒ ☿ *Variable cover charge. Open nightly 7.30pm-2am.*

Established jazz supper club serving Italian food to the sound of fusion, mainstream and big band sounds. Chuck Mangione debuted here.

LINDA'S

6715 Melrose Ave., Hollywood ☎*(213) 934-6199. Map 4C5* 💺 ⇒ ☿ *No cover. Open nightly 6pm-midnight.*
Very hip Hollywood club/restaurant with off-the-wall decor and nightly cabaret from owner Linda Keegan and guests.

NUCLEUS NUANCE

7267 Melrose Ave., Hollywood ☎*(213) 939-8666. Map 4C5* 💺 ⇒ ☿ ✺ *Open nightly 6pm-2am. Two-drink minimum. Shows from 9.30pm.*
Top-name artists play jazz and blues in a relaxed setting favored by young professionals.

VINE ST. BAR & GRILL

1610 N Vine St., Hollywood ☎*(213) 463-4050. Map 5B6* 💺 ⇒ ◨ ☿ ♪ *Open nightly 5pm-midnight. Two-drink minimum.*
Small, elegant supper club serving good Northern Italian food and featuring established artists. Expensive, but worth it with performers such as Nina Simone and Dizzy Gillespie making appearances.

147

Shopping

Where to go

Want to shop till you drop? Los Angeles is the place. Its wealth and huge population, for whom consumerism is not a dirty word, and cheerful shop assistants, for whom service is more a pleasure than a chore, ensure great shopping. Choice and quality are outstanding. Sales are frequent and offer significant savings, especially in the current economic climate. Most stores are also very cooperative when it comes to returning goods for exchange or refund. And, if you buy in the sale and return to discover that the price has been dropped even further, they'll usually refund the difference.

However, outside the malls, districts with tight clusters of attractive stores are rare, so for the full range visitors will need to drive.

Apart from well-known streets such as **Rodeo Dr.** and **Melrose Ave.**, some of the best shopping is in the huge shopping malls, which are generally well designed, user-friendly and anchored by one or more major department stores. Major malls include **ARCO Plaza**, **The Beverly Center**, **Century City**, **Glendale Galleria**, **Santa Monica Place**, **Sherman Oaks Galleria**, **Westside Pavilion** and **Woodland Hills Promenade**. And well-stocked chain stores include **The Broadway**, **Bullock's**, **I. Magnin**, **May Company**, **Neiman-Marcus**, **Nordstrom**, **Robinson's** and **Saks Fifth Avenue**.

Parking beneath the malls is easier than on fashionable streets, and many stores will validate parking. Sales are frequent and well publicized in the local press. Specialty stores will probably require a longer haul; it's prudent to telephone before setting out.

In the following pages we explore the main shopping areas of Greater Los Angeles.

COASTAL (map 10|5-6)

SANTA MONICA has the best shopping of the coastal cities, in its range of stores, their easy accessibility and civilized atmosphere. Cooling sea breezes add to the pleasures of strolling and browsing.

Main St. (*s of the end of Santa Monica Freeway*) was horribly run down until the mid-1970s; now it rivals Melrose Ave. for trendiness. The mix is familiar enough: fashion, antiques, art galleries, gifts, home accessories, sportswear and goods, including surfer's heaven at **Horizons West** (*2011 Main St.*). But in all there are about 100 stores along nine manageable blocks, and peppered between them are pleasant restaurants, cafés and pubs, making for a very relaxed morning's or afternoon's meander.

Montana Ave. *(10 blocks N of Santa Monica Freeway)* in turn rivals Main St. in its range of stores. The best of them are on the ten blocks between 7th St. and 16th St. and include good clothing stores, especially for children, as well as a variety of stores selling gifts, jewelry, stationery, rugs etc.

Santa Monica Place *(Broadway, between 2nd St. and 4th St.)*, designed by the ubiquitous Frank Gehry, and recently refurbished to include live palm trees, is a bright, skylit 3-story mall with ocean views and about 160 small shops, plus branches of **The Broadway** and **Robinson's** department stores. The fast-food outlets in EATZ **Cafe Court** are well placed for people-watching.

Nearby is **Santa Monica Mall** *(3rd St., between Broadway and Wilshire Blvd.)*, a recently remodeled pedestrian mall with a range of shops that are cheaper, on the whole, than those in the other main shopping areas.

VENICE (just s of Santa Monica) is best known for the nonstop carnival that enlivens its **Boardwalk**. Also on the Boardwalk is an open-air market selling sportswear, posters, sunglasses etc. The quality isn't Rodeo Dr., but neither are the prices. Elsewhere in Venice, notably on **Market St.**, there are some interesting galleries.

DOWNTOWN (map **6**)

Nowadays Downtown is best known for several diverse, indoor plazas in business and hotel towers. It also has fine stores on the street, notably around Chinatown, Olvera St. and Little Tokyo. The only drawback is that Downtown parking can be expensive, so be sure to ask stores for validation.

Among the plazas, ARCO **Plaza** *(Flower St., between 5th St. and 6th St., map 6 D9)* has two large underground levels of 60 restaurants and stores, though of late the economic slow-down has taken its toll.

Bonaventure Shopping Gallery *(Figueroa St., between 4th St. and 5th St., map 6 D9)* has six circular levels of restaurants, services and shops.

Broadway Plaza *(W 7th St. and Figueroa St., map 6 D8)* has a multilevel 30-shop gallery anchored by the department store **The Broadway**, where good clothes, cosmetics and kitchenware are moderately priced.

Finally, **Seventh Market Place** *(Figueroa St. and 7th St., map 6 D8)* is the newest and most attractive of the Downtown malls, with 60 shops and specialty stores in an airy, open environment. In the daytime, food and drinks purchased from adjacent outlets may be consumed at open-air tables — ideal for people-watching.

A very different shopping environment exists elsewhere in Downtown. For example, **CHINATOWN** *(bounded by Ord St., Alameda St., Barnard St. and Yale St., map 6 D9)* has scores of small shops selling foodstuffs, imported silks, objets d'art, traditional medicines and household goods. Noteworthy is the **New China Emporium** *(727 N Broad-*

way, map 6 D9), is a small department store selling inexpensive goods from the People's Republic of China.

LITTLE TOKYO *(bounded by 3rd St., Alameda St., 1st St. and Los Angeles St., map 6 D9)* has two major shopping areas: **Japanese Village Plaza** *(327 E 2nd St.)* and **Little Tokyo Sq.** *(333 S Alameda St.).* In both, scores of boutiques and small shops sell Japanese goods, books and magazines. And for Mexican handicrafts, go to **OLVERA ST.**

The **GARMENT DISTRICT** *(Los Angeles St., from 7th St. to Washington Blvd., map 6 E8)* has excellent clothing bargains, available both from shops along the street and at outlets in the **Cooper Building** *(near 9th St., map 6 E8)* and **The California Mart** *(Olympic Blvd., map 6 E9).* Many are designer-label seconds, so check carefully.

Other Downtown services and shops include:

• **Brooks Bros.**   604 S Figueroa St., map **6**D8. Traditional clothing for men and women.

• **Henry's Camera Hi-Fi and Video**   516 W 8th St., map **6**E8. A wide selection, with discounts and a multilingual staff.

• **Western World Apparel**   615 W 7th St., map **6**D8. Leatherwear, Levis and Stetsons.

• **Thomas Bros. Maps and Books**   603 W 7th St., map **6**D8. Absolutely the best maps to Los Angeles and California, plus travel books and accouterments.

HOLLYWOOD (maps **4** and **5**)

Stylish West Hollywood is altogether more interesting to shoppers than Hollywood proper. The latter is best for bookstores, cameras and a few novelty stores, including the fantasy lingerie of Frederick's of Hollywood. The former has The Beverly Center, one of LA's best shopping malls, varied and fashionable shops including some of the best galleries and antique stores on and around Melrose Ave., plus the rather touristy delights of Farmers Market.

The Beverly Center *(at Beverly Blvd. and La Cienega Blvd., map 4 C4),* with its dour concrete facade, is not much to look at from the outside. However, inside it is an attractive, spotlessly clean, galleried mall of 900,000 square feet with some 200 quality shops and restaurants, 14 movie theaters and, at ground level, **Irvine Ranch Market**, probably the best-stocked supermarket in Los Angeles. At one end of the mall is **The Broadway** department store; at the other is the slightly more upscale store **Bullock's.** Beneath are four levels of parking.

Farmers Market *(W 3rd St. and Fairfax Ave., map 4 C5)* is best known for its produce and food stalls. In all, the open-air complex has 150 shops selling fresh fruits, vegetables, meats, seafood, breads and pastries, souvenirs and gifts. It's pricier than the neighborhood supermarket, but more fun. (See also page 84.)

LA CIENEGA BLVD. *(N from the Beverly Center to Melrose Ave., map 4 C4)* ought to be renamed "Carpet Canyon"; stores selling Eastern and native American rugs and carpets occupy almost every inch. Farther up La Cienega *(between Melrose Ave. and Willoughby Ave.)* are more than a score of art galleries. The other major attraction is the frankly-named

Trashy Lingerie *(402 La Cienega Blvd.)*. A small membership fee dissuades passing voyeurs from ogling the corseted saleswomen, but the erotic merchandise is displayed in the windows.

HOLLYWOOD BLVD. *(w of intersection with Vine St., map 5 B5-6)* is not nearly as sleazy as it used to be, at least not in daytime. However, there is not much to interest shoppers, save a few discount clothing stores, vendors of over-priced Hollywood memorabilia, some decent bookstores clustered near the intersection with Cherokee Ave., including the movie buffs' favorite **Larry Edmunds** *(6658 Hollywood Blvd.)*, and the original **Frederick's of Hollywood** *(6608 Hollywood Blvd.)* for extravagantly styled, moderately priced lingerie. Newspapers and magazines from across the world are available at **World Book and News** *(1652 N Cahuenga Blvd., map 5 B6)*.

MELROSE AVE. *(between Doheny Dr. and Highland Ave., map 4 C4-5)* is not quite as exclusive or as expensive as Rodeo Dr., but it is probably the snazziest and most interesting shopping strip in LA. And, with a concentrated 40-blocks-worth before the glamor peters out after Highland Ave., it is also the longest. (Valley enthusiasts might claim this for Ventura Blvd., but that admirable street lacks the density of stores; walking the 3-mile length of Melrose at one go would be a chore, but walking Ventura would be an Olympian task.)

The western stretch is the more expensive, featuring scores of antique stores (with the fanciest on **Melrose Pl.**), galleries, and stores selling specialist books, furniture and home accessories (especially Art Deco) and designer fashions. Going E from Fairfax Ave., privilege gives way to punk, the stores are progressively less pricey, the California-style fashions younger, the artwork not originals but numbered prints, the jewelry paste rather than precious stones. The gift stores are full of amusing gadgets and knickknacks, and **Vinyl Fetish** *(7350 Melrose Ave.)* is one of LA's best record stores for imports.

SUNSET BLVD. *(going w from intersection with Crescent Heights, map 4 B4)* is notable primarily for the high-fashion outlets at **Sunset Plaza** *(on Sunset Strip)* and for **Tower Records** *(8801 Sunset Blvd.)*, billed as the largest record store in the world, which reputedly has in stock, or is able to find, just about any recording. Across the street is **Tower Video**: overseas visitors should remember that tapes are in the US "NTSC" system and may not work in their home country.

VALLEYS (map 10l6)

Like everything else in the Valleys, the shopping is very spread out. Each community has its own concentration, some better than others. Traveling from E to w, the following are the most noteworthy.

The best shopping in **PASADENA** is on **Lake St.** *(between Colorado Blvd. and California Blvd., map 1 B3)* and at **Pasadena Plaza** *(opposite Pasadena Hilton on Los Robles Ave. and Colorado Blvd.)*. In addition to the usual range of clothing and other stores, the former has branches of **I. Magnin** and **Bullock's** and some elegant arcades. The recently opened **Plaza** has 120 shops. Less predictable is the **Rose Bowl Flea Market** *(Rose Bowl Dr.)*, held on the second Sunday of each month.

In **GLENDALE**, the **Glendale Galleria** *(Central Ave. and Colorado Blvd., map 1 B3)* is vast, with some 250 shops. Although not the swankiest mall in town, it's getting better and has plenty to offer, including outposts of department stores **Nordstrom** and budget-conscious **J.C. Penny**. Weekends are very crowded, so it's better to shop on a weekday.

VENTURA BLVD. *(from Studio City to Woodland Hills, map 1 B2)* runs through half a dozen communities, with clumps of excellent shops along its length. Of the malls, **Sherman Oaks Galleria** *(Ventura Blvd. and Sepulveda Blvd.)* and the adjacent open-air **Sherman Oaks Fashion Square** are popular with Valley residents; **Woodland Hills Promenade** *(Topanga Canyon Blvd. and Oxnard St.),* anchored by **Robinsons** and **Bullock's Wilshire**, is generally regarded as being among the poshest in town; and **Topanga Plaza** *(Topanga Canyon Blvd. and Vanowen St.),* although less upscale, is bigger (160 shops and restaurants) and its choices more varied. (Unless you have a specific chore on Ventura Blvd., Topanga Plaza is more easily accessed via the Ventura Freeway.)

WESTSIDE

BEVERLY HILLS has much of the best, and perhaps inevitably the most expensive, shopping in Los Angeles. It is to be found within the so-called "Golden Triangle" bordered by **Wilshire Blvd.** on the s, **Little Santa Monica Blvd.** on the N and **Crescent Dr.** on the E *(map 3 C3)*. Slicing across the triangle is **N Rodeo Dr.**, $2\frac{1}{2}$ blocks of ritzy stores where consumption is about as conspicuous as it gets, even in LA.

Most of the big international names in fashion, jewelry, accessories and cosmetics are represented along the tree-lined, flower-bedecked street. Forget the parking meters, which will eat up your change; there is public parking, free for 2 hours, opposite the Beverly Rodeo Hotel. Other free parking lots are located throughout Beverly Hills.

Among the establishments on **RODEO DR.** are:

- **ADULT TOYS**: **Hammacher Schlemmer** *(#309),* gadgets for people who have almost everything.
- **BEAUTY PARLORS**: **Elizabeth Arden** *(#434);* **Vidal Sassoon** *(#405).*
- **HOME ACCESSORIES**: **La Provence of Pierre Deux** *(#428).*
- **JEWELERS**: **Cartier** *(#370);* **Fred Joaillier** *(#401);* **Van Cleef & Arpels** *(#300).*
- **MEN'S AND WOMEN'S FASHIONS**: **Fred Hayman**, previously Giorgio *(#273),* American and European clothes; cocktails and coffee from an antique Gaggia. Buyers for TV soap *Dallas* shopped here.
- **MEN'S FASHION**: **Battaglia** *(#306),* Italian designer labels; **Bijan** *(#420),* by appointment, the most expensive menswear in town; **Jerry Magnin/Polo** *(#323),* both conservative and trendy attire.
- **WOMEN'S FASHION**: **Celine** *(#460),* natural fabrics, classic clothes and leather; **Collections A** *(#458),* top Japanese designers; **Courrèges** *(#447),* French fashions; **Rodeo Collection** *(between Little Santa Monica Blvd. and Brighton Way),* a Post-Modern five-level mall hosting 35 big-name retailers including **Fogal**, **Gianni Versace** and **Louis Vuitton.**
- **LEATHER AND SILKS**: **Gucci** *(#347);* **Hermès** *(#343):* two landmark

names for handmade leather accessories and wonderful classic silks.

Adjacent streets too have much to interest the serious shopper. On Wilshire Blvd. near the intersection with Rodeo Dr. are:

- **Abercrombie & Fitch** *(#9424)*, sporting goods
- **Brentano's** *(#9528)*, for a wide range of books
- **I. Magnin** *(#9634)*, California-based specialist in fine clothes and sportswear
- **Neiman-Marcus** *(#9700)*, Dallas-based, famous for imported accessories and fashions
- **Robinson's** *(#9900)*, department store strong in clothes and gifts
- **Saks Fifth Avenue** *(#9600)*, designer collections, distinctive accessories
- **Tiffany & Co.** *(#9502)*, distinguished New York jewelers/silversmiths

Other stores worthy of special note are:

- **Advance Coin & Stamp Co.** *(9857 Little Santa Monica Blvd., map 3 D3)*, antique coins, stamps, and paper money
- **Banana Republic** *(9669 Little Santa Monica Blvd., map 3 C3)*, LA flagship of the San Francisco-based retailer of safari chic
- **Church's English Shoes** *(9633 Brighton Way, map 3 C3)*, bench-made men's footwear
- **Francis-Orr** *(320 N Camden Dr., map 3 C3)*, luxury stationery
- **Galatee** *(419 N Bedford Dr., map 3 C3)*, imported lingerie
- **Hunter's Books** *(420 N Beverly Dr., map 3 C3)*, an excellent bookstore specializing in showbiz and the arts
- **Kron Chocolatier** *(9529 Little Santa Monica Blvd., map 3 C3)*, handmade chocolates
- **The Scriptorium** *(427 N Cañon Dr., map 3 C3)*, historical manuscripts, letters
- **The Sharper Image** *(Little Santa Monica Blvd. at Camden Dr., map 3 C3)*, gadget heaven
- **Williams-Sonoma** *(317 N Beverly Dr., map 3 C3)*, designer kitchen goods

Farther down Wilshire Blvd. toward Downtown stands **Bullock's Wilshire** *(#3050, map 5 D7)*, a superb 1920s Art Deco department store (illustrated on page 37), with a chandeliered tearoom by Herman Sach.

Century City Shopping Center *(Ave. of the Stars and Little Santa Monica Blvd., map 3 D2)*, an 80-shop open-air complex diagonally opposite the ABC ENTERTAINMENT CENTER, is one of LA's earliest malls. It has the usual designer clothing, gift and accessory stores, plus a lively food hall, **Century City Magazines** for a wide range of newspapers and magazines, **Nickelodian** for CDs, records, tapes and video discs, and a number of good restaurants. A score of reasonably priced fast-food outlets can be found in its lively **Marketplace.**.

Westside Pavilion *(Pico Blvd. and Westwood Blvd., map 3 E2)* is a newer mall in Post-Modern style. The overall effect is less elegant than Century City, but there is a wider range of shops and prices.

Westwood Village *(N of Wilshire Blvd. at Westwood Blvd., map 3 D1)*, adjacent to the UCLA campus, is excellent for discount bookstores, stationers, art materials, casual preppie clothing, sportswear, handicrafts.

What to look for

In the following pages, we survey various categories of shopping experience that are distinctively LA. Map references will help you locate all streets within the area covered by our maps.

ART GALLERIES AND ANTIQUES
In by far the largest art market in the Western US, **West Hollywood** (especially **La Cienega Blvd.** and **Melrose Ave.**) has the greatest concentration of galleries. **Downtown** is the new boom area. Artists are named only to indicate a gallery's style, not its whole roster. Hours are mostly Tuesday to Saturday 10am-5pm — and by appointment.

- **Ankaum Gallery** *(657 N La Cienega Blvd., map 4 C4)*, Bob Kane, David Remfry, Jan Sawka, Morris Boderson, plus other well-known contemporary artists
- **Antiquarius LA Antique Market** *(8840 Beverly Blvd., map 4 C4)*, some 70 stalls with a wide range of antiques and objets d'art
- **Antique Amusements** *(14502 Ventura Blvd.)*, vintage pinball machines, jukeboxes and vending machines, all lovingly restored
- **Fantasies Come True** *(7408 Melrose Ave., map 4 C5)*, Disney artwork from Mickey Mouse onward
- **Dorothy Goldeen Gallery** *(1547 9th St., Santa Monica)*, contemporary paintings and sculpture, with emphasis on new artists
- **Harry A. Franklin** *(9601 Wilshire Blvd., map 3 D3)*, traditional tribal sculpture from sub-Saharan Black Africa plus pre-Columbian artifacts
- **Galerie Marumo** *(8424 Melrose Ave., map 4 C4)*, Los Angeles branch of Paris firm specializing in Impressionists and 19th and 20thC French masters
- **Gallery of Eskimo Art** *(2665C Main St., map 6 E8)*, Eskimo art from Alaska and Canada
- **Gemini G.E.L.** *(8365 Melrose Ave., map 4 C4)*, art publishers with gallery showing works by Sam Francis, David Hockney, Jasper Johns, Robert Rauschenberg, plus sculpture by Noguchi, di Suvero, Serra
- **Gideon** *(8748 Melrose Ave., map 4 C4)*, 17th-19thC maps and wildlife and botanical prints
- **Goldfield** *(8400 Melrose Ave., map 4 C4)*, Remington, Russell, Bierstadt, Payne and other 19th-20thC painters of the American West
- **Kirk de Gooyer** *(1308 Factory Pl.)*, abstract paintings, drawings and sculptures by Tom Lieber, Robert Hernandez, Karla Klarin and others
- **G. Ray Hawkins** *(7224 Melrose Ave., map 7 C5)*, art photography by Ansel Adams, Max Yavno and many others
- **Margo Leavin** *(812 N Robertson Blvd., map 4 C4)*, paintings, drawings and graphics by Johns, Hockney, Rauschenberg, Jim Dine, Charles Gaines, Robert Motherwell, Edward Ruscha and Andy Warhol

- **B. Lewin** (*266 N Beverly Dr., map 3 C3*), Mexican masters
- **Main St. Gallery** (*2803 Main St., map 6 F8*), Japanese antiques and folk art
- **Many Horses Gallery** (*740 La Cienega Blvd., map 4 C4*), American Indian art
- **Neil G. Ovsey Gallery** (*705 E 3rd St., map 6 D9*), Woods Davy, Vivian Kerstein, Constance Mallinson, Claes Oldenburg, Rauschenberg, Ruscha plus a range of other contemporary Californians and New Yorkers
- **Peterson Galleries** (*270 N Rodeo Dr., map 3 C3*), Californian, Western, Impressionists and Masters
- **M. M. Shinno** (*5820 Wilshire Blvd., map 4 D5*), contemporary Japanese prints plus work in many media by local artists of Asian descent
- **Tortue Gallery** (*2917 Santa Monica Blvd.*), broad range from young Californians to European masters
- **Stephen White** (*752 N La Cienega Blvd., map* 4C4), 19th and 20thC photographers.

BOOKSTORES

Bibliophiles should note that Booksellers Row on **Westwood Blvd.** is not what it was; high rents have pushed out some, and closed down others altogether. Many out of print and specialty booksellers are now to be found on **Santa Monica's Third St. Promenade**. Others worth a visit include the following:

Melrose Avenue
Map 4C4-5.

- **Art & Architecture Books of the Twentieth Century** (*#8375*)
- **Bennett & Marshall** (*#8214*), antiquarian specializing in early science, medicine and travel
- **Bodhi Tree** (*#8585*), occult and religion
- **Canterbury** (*#8344*), out-of-print history, literature and philosophy
- **Cosmopolitan** (*#7007*), secondhand and out-of-print titles
- **William & Victoria Daily** (*#8216$\frac{1}{2}$*), art and rare books, and fine prints
- **Golden Apple** (*#7753*), comics, science fiction, fantasy
- **Elliot M. Katt** (*#8568*), performing arts, new, used, old
- **Michael R. Thompson** (*#8320*), fine printing, rare and scholarly books, manuscripts

Specialists elsewhere

- **Amerasia Bookstore** (*129 Japanese Village Plaza, map 6 D9*), specializing in books on Asia from history to cooking
- **Book Soup** (*8818 Sunset Blvd., map 4 C4*), selection of general-interest books
- **A Change of Hobbit** (*1433 2nd St., Santa Monica*), science fiction, fantasy, horror

- **Cherokee Book Store** *(6607 Hollywood Blvd., map 5 B6)*, first editions and rare Americana
- **Collectors Book Store** *(1708 N. Vine St., map 5 B6)*, movie memorabilia, books, scripts, magazines, costumes, props, posters
- **Houle Rare Books & Autographs** *(7260 Beverly Blvd., map 4C5)*, first editions, Western Americana, Press books
- **Larry Edmund's Cinema & Theater Books** *(6658 Hollywood Blvd., map 5 B5)*, new and secondhand books, current and back-issue magazines on all the performing arts, and studio photos of stars (some autographed)
- **Phoenix Bookstore** *(514 Santa Monica Blvd.)*, metaphysics, philosophy, psychology

Chain and general bookstores

- **Children's Book & Music Center** *(2500 Santa Monica Blvd.)*, books for children of all ages
- **Crown Books** *(throughout Los Angeles)*, current titles in hardback and paperbacks at attractive discount prices
- **Dutton's** *(11975 San Vicente Blvd., 5146 Laurel Canyon Blvd.)*, new and used titles
- **B. Dalton** *(throughout Los Angeles)*, full range of current titles

CAMERAS AND PHOTOGRAPHY

Prices are very competitive, for new and used equipment, and photographic gear from all the major manufacturers can be found.

- Professionals favor **Pan Pacific Camera** *(825 N La Brea Ave., Hollywood, map 4 C5)*. They offer the whole range, from an entire system of bodies and lenses to a replacement for the small widget that's gone missing.
- Discount-minded snappers head for **Frank's Highland Park Camera** *(5715 N Figueroa St., Highland Pk.)*, which offers a full range of gear at bargain-basement prices.
- For film processing of color and black & white, plus enlargements, mounting, lamination or passport photos, go to **Attila Photo/One Hour Lab** *(5750 Wilshire Blvd., Hollywood, map 4 D5)*.

DEPARTMENT STORES

Almost invariably at least one department store anchors each of the major shopping malls to be found across Greater LA. In descending order of glitziness, the major chains to look out for are **Saks Fifth Avenue**, **Neiman-Marcus**, **I. Magnin**, **Nordstrom**, **The Broadway**, **Bullock's**, **Robinson's** and the **May Company**.

The upscale stores such as Saks are strong on designer fashion at glitzy prices. The less expensive offer most things from clothes to cosmetics to cookware.

Some stores are sights in their own right. **Bullock's Wilshire** is an Art Deco classic, as is **I. Magnin** at 3050 Wilshire Blvd.

FASHION AND ACCESSORIES

There is the full range of big-name designers, to be found in signature shops and within the pricier department stores. **Rodeo Dr.** (see page 152) has a hard-to-match concentration of high-fashion boutiques. A platinum charge card is a useful accessory. More noteworthy and typically LA are the large number of shops selling casual clothes and leisurewear throughout the city.

Much of the merchandise is manufactured locally, is of high quality, and competitively priced. Natural materials, such as cotton, linen and silk, are prevalent. They suit the climate. The best places for casual attire for men and women frequently have more than one location, usually in one or more of the major malls.

- For **SAFARI CHIC** in comfortable and practical designs and fabrics, do not miss **Banana Republic** *(9669 Little Santa Monica Blvd., Beverly Hills, map 3 C3).*
- **Eddie Bauer** *(Beverly Center, La Cienega and Beverly Blvds., West Hollywood, map 4 C4)* also specializes in **OUTDOOR CLOTHING**, plus travel accessories and luggage.
- Equally comfortable but less macho **LEISUREWEAR** at affordable prices is available from **CP Shades** *(2937 Main St., Santa Monica).*
- **CASUAL COTTON** is the specialty of **The Gap** *(1931 Wilshire Blvd., Santa Monica),* which carries all the basics.
- Families can shop for what's called **ACTIVEWEAR** at the **Esprit Superstore** *(8491 Santa Monica Blvd., West Hollywood, map 4 C4).*
- An astounding range of **WOMEN'S SWIMWEAR** is available from **Everything But Water** *(Marina Marketplace, 13455 Maxella Ave., Marina del Rey),* which carries sizes from 4 to 24 plus maternity and mastectomy outfits.
- Women and men heading for the **BEACH** should check out **Sweats & Surf** *(South Bay Galleria, 1815 Hawthorne Blvd., Redondo Beach).* There's everything you could possibly need for a day in, on or by the nearby Pacific Ocean.
- **Val Surf** *(4810 Whitsett Ave., North Hollywood)* stocks everything the fashion-conscious **SURFER** could ever want.
- If Hollywood **GLAMOR** is a must, **A Star is Worn** *(7303 Melrose Ave., West Hollywood, map 4 C5)* probably has it on the racks. The store specializes in almost-new used clothing. The attraction for its customers is who's done the using. This is the place to shop for Cher's old gowns. But it is definitely not a thrift shop; prices are high.
- For genuine **OUTLET BARGAINS**, try the **Citadel Outlet Collection** *(5675 E Telegraph Rd., Downtown)* with its 40 stores, or **The Cooper Building** *(860 S. Los Angeles St., Downtown, map 6 E8),* which has 60 family discount stores.

Jewelry

This is big business in such a flamboyant and style-conscious city, with designs to match the milieu. There are plenty of first-rate craftsmen at work with the finest raw materials. Splendid costume jewelry is also widely available at affordable prices.

- **Laykin et Cie** *(at I. Magnin, 9634 Wilshire Blvd, Beverly Hills, map 3D3)* are a firm of long-established family-owned jewelers renowned for classic pieces rather than anything frivolous.
- Wackier things are offered by the **M Gallery** *(8649 W. Sunset Blvd, West Hollywood, map 4B4)*, and by the nearby **Butler & Wilson** *(8644 W. Sunset Blvd., West Hollywood, map 4B4)*. The former features top modern designers; the latter specializes in what are called faux gems. Both are popular with the smart set.

Leather goods

- For classic American bags and briefcases it's hard to better **The Coach Store** *(Century City Shopping Center, 10250 Santa Monica Blvd., map 3D2)*.
- North Beach Leather *(8500 Sunset Blvd., West Hollywood, map 4B4)* has a huge collection of leather and suede apparel for men and women.
- **The Leather Club** *(9555 Santa Monica Blvd., Beverly Hills, map 3C3)* has designer leatherwear and a tailoring service.
- **Falconhead** *(11911 San Vicente Blvd., Brentwood)* has a wide range of handmade boots, belts and buckles.

RECORDS/TAPES/CDs/VIDEOS

Tower Records *(8801 Sunset Blvd., West Hollywood, map 4C4)* basks in the reputation of being the best record store on earth. The range of recorded music to suit all tastes is stunning, both for current and older material. Vast though it is, the place gets crowded, and staff can appear harassed. But this really is one-stop shopping, and a journey to Sunset Strip can save the time, effort and heartache involved in shopping at lesser stores. Video is across the street.

TOYS

- **California Toys & Costumes** *(752 S Broadway, Downtown, map 6E9)* has a huge range of toys for all ages. Not for the child who already has everything, but affordable fun.
- **Imaginarium** *(Century City Shopping Center, 10250 Santa Monica Blvd., Century City, map 3D2)* is best described as kid-friendly. Hundreds of toys and games for children of all ages.
- **Toys & Joys** *(7375 Melrose Ave., West Hollywood, map 4C5)* appeals to adults as much as children, with its quirky range of toys, games, gizmos and more.

WINE

A selection of reliable outlets scattered across the greater city:
- **Greenblatt's** *(8017 Sunset Blvd., Hollywood, map 4B4)*
- **Vendome** *(327 N Beverly Dr., Beverly Hills, map 3C3)*
- **Lawry's California Center** *(570 W Ave. 26, Los Angeles, map 6C10)*
- **Trade Joe's** *(610 S Arroyo Pkwy, Pasadena)*
- **Wally's Liquor & Gourmet Foods** *(2107 Westwood Blvd., map 3E2)*
- **The Wine Merchant** *(9701 Santa Monica Blvd., map 3D3)*

Recreation

Outdoor activities

In Los Angeles, recreation means beaches before anything else. There are hundreds of public tennis courts and scores of public golf courses, but local pressure on these is intense enough to limit their use by visitors. However, the situation is somewhat easier on weekdays and during school term.

BEACHES

Beaches readily accessible from LA start at **Zuma Beach County Park**, on the Pacific Coast Highway, 8 miles N of Malibu. Zuma is good for bodysurfing, surfing and fishing. Moving E and S, **Westward Beach** is popular with swimmers, surfers and divers, **Surfriders Beach** is good for surfing and windsurfing, and the area around **Malibu Pier** attracts swimmers, surfers, divers and fishermen. With a few short interruptions, the whole sandy arc of **Santa Monica Bay** is a public beach, from **Topanga State Beach** in the N to **Redondo State Beach** in the S. Sections of particular interest, from N-S, are:

- **Will Rogers State Beach**, named after the cowboy-humorist, is good for swimming, surfing and windsurfing. It is also one of the better beaches for families with children. There is a children's playground, plus volleyball courts and picnic areas.
- **Santa Monica Beach** is also good for swimming, and is one of the best for location, cleanliness and amenities. Draws huge crowds.
- **Muscle Beach**, close to Santa Monica Pier, is the place for body builders.
- **Venice Beach**, directly S, has a particular charm, mainly because the walkway behind it is a meeting place for roller-skaters, skateboard fans and practitioners of other arcane styles of locomotion. The beach is great for swimming and surfing and has good amenities. A good way to take in both is by bicycle, available for rent from booths on the beachside cycle path. Be sure to take some valid ID.
- **Marina del Rey**, adjoining Venice, has excellent ocean beaches and a sheltered sandy beach, suitable for small children, inside the huge yacht harbor. Among the facilities are boat rental, volleyball courts, picnic areas and wheelchair access to shops and cafés. However, parking can be a problem.
- To the S of LAX, **Manhattan Beach** finds favor with volleyball and

Frisbee enthusiasts. The Strand, an elevated walkway, has delightful views.

- **Hermosa Beach** is a toned-down version of Venice popular with surfers, and **Redondo Beach** is similar to Manhattan Beach, only less glossy.

BICYCLING AND ROLLER-SKATING

The two most attractive routes for cycling are along the coast and in Griffith Park.

The coast route, known as the **South Bay Bicycle Trail**, starts at Santa Monica and runs some 20 miles s to Torrance. There is a network of cycle paths running inland. Bicycles are available for rent from booths along the route, notably from **Sea Mist Rental** (*1619 Ocean Front Blvd., Santa Monica*) and the **Venice Pier Bike Shop** (*21 Washington Blvd., Venice*).

Griffith Park also has a network of bicycle trails, though they are more strenuous than the beachside route. Rent bicycles from **Woody's Bicycle World** (*3157 Los Feliz Blvd., Los Feliz*).

Roller-skaters tend to head toward **Santa Monica** and **Venice**. Skates can be rented along the beach and the boardwalk.

FISHING

Pier fishing is available at **Santa Monica Pier**, **Venice Pier** and **Redondo Beach Municipal Pier**. Party boats for offshore trips berth at Santa Monica Pier, **Marina del Rey**, and **King Harbor** at Redondo Beach. See Yellow Pages under "Fishing Parties" for a complete list of boat operators.

FITNESS FACILITIES

Few cities are as devoted to the body beautiful as Los Angeles. Gymnasiums and fitness centers abound. Joggers often head for the beaches. Alternatively, there are some attractive running paths, notably **Beverly Gardens**, between Doheny Drive and Wilshire Blvd. (*map 3 D3*), through the heart of Beverly Hills, and **Pacific Palisades**, along Ocean Ave., between San Vicente Blvd. and Colorado Ave.

The bigger hotels have responded to the demand among visitors by installing their own facilities, and others often have close relationships with nearby clubs. Look for the ♉ symbol in our hotel listings. In addition, YMCAs will sell daily memberships at reasonable prices.

For information on temporary use of outside fitness centers, gymnasiums, aerobics classes etc., consult the ads in *LA Weekly, Los Angeles Magazine* and the Yellow Pages.

GOLF

Los Angeles has more public greens than any other city in the United States. Most central of the public courses are **Harding**, 6,945 yards, par 72, rated 70, and **Wilson**, 6,945 yards, par 72, rated 71.5 (*both are in GRIFFITH PARK, map 1 B2*). Local registered players may reserve starting times; visitors must wait for openings.

For information on LA's seven 18-hole courses ☎(213) 485-5555, and on LA County's 16 courses (mostly in the San Fernando Valley) ☎(213) 738-2961.

HORSEBACK RIDING

Once again, GRIFFITH PARK is the place, with 250 miles of trails. Four stables rent out horses (see Yellow Pages under "Stables"). Or contact **Griffith Park Equestrian Center** (☎ *(818) 840-9063).*

TENNIS

Visitors who are intent on playing tennis in LA should stay at a hotel with its own courts, or one that has arrangements with a nearby club. Look for the ✂ symbol in our hotel listings.

City residents may reserve court time at the 12-court **Vermont Canyon Center** *(Griffith Park on Vista del Valle Dr., map 1 B2);* visitors must wait for an opening. Nearby, the four-court **Peppertree Lane** is first-come first-serve. There is an hourly charge for play at both places. For information on the city's 60 tennis facilities ☎(213) 485-5566.

SAILING AND WINDSURFING

Marina Beach at Marina del Rey is excellent for both, and boats of all sizes, and boards, can be rented by the half-day. Lessons are also available (see Yellow Pages).

Los Angeles for children

Los Angeles and the neighboring areas offer visiting children innumerable opportunities to exhaust their pent-up energies in instructive play. Some of the more extraordinary possibilities are listed on this and the following two pages.

Where no page reference is given, look for the heading (printed in SMALL CAPITALS) in the alphabetical LA'S SIGHTS A TO Z. See also SAN DIEGO FOR CHILDREN, page 246.

ANIMAL PARKS, ZOOS AND WILDLIFE REFUGES
In California, as in much of the rest of the world, increasing emphasis is placed on designing zoos that put animals into the best possible reconstructions of their native habitats. Real-life encounters with wild animals lie within comparatively easy reach.
- Living Desert (see PALM SPRINGS, page 176)
- Los Angeles Zoo (see GRIFFITH PARK)

BEACHES
California's open ocean beaches seldom allow parents with small children to relax, primarily because of heavy surf. However, some ocean and many bay beaches are ideal for tots and youngsters, although the best of these are some way to the N and S of LA itself. Those listed below are popular with families. See also OUTDOOR ACTIVITIES on page 159-60, and for our selection of California's best sandy beaches, see the map on pages 18-19.
- Dana Harbor (see ORANGE COUNTY, page 175)
- Doheny State Beach (see ORANGE COUNTY, page 175)
- Marina del Rey (see OUTDOOR ACTIVITIES, page 159)
- Mission Bay (see SAN DIEGO/BEACHES, page 243)
- Santa Barbara beach (see SANTA BARBARA, page 181)
- Silver Strand State Park (see SAN DIEGO/BEACHES, page 243)
- Will Rogers State Beach (see OUTDOOR ACTIVITIES, page 159)

"EXPERIENCES"
Variety is the spice of life, and there's lots of *that* in LA.
- DONUT HOLE — the ultimate donut experience?
- Griffith Observatory (see GRIFFITH OBSERVATORY) — planetarium, laserium, telescope viewing
- Mitsubishi IMAX Theater (see EXPOSITION PARK) — spectacular 3-D travel simulation
- VENICE — street performers, exhibitionists and extroverts: definitely for older children only

THE OLD WEST
California grew up with Indian wars, the Gold Rush and other such Hollywood myths. One lively souvenir of the real thing in LA is:
- GENE AUTRY WESTERN HERITAGE MUSEUM (found under A for AUTRY) — dazzling special effects, Imagineering by Walt Disney

PARKS, PLAY AREAS, SPACES FOR RAMBLING

The city has copious open spaces to refresh children with high-octane energy to run off. For those of very tender years, you have to look more carefully.

- ECHO PARK — lake with paddle boats
- ELYSIAN PARK — nature trails across chaparral-covered hills
- GRIFFITH PARK — unrivaled hiking, horseback riding and picnic opportunities
- SANTA MONICA PIER — bumper rides, park, play area
- Will Rogers State Beach (see OUTDOOR ACTIVITIES, page 159) — playground, picnic area, beach suitable for children

SCIENCE MUSEUMS

In California's high-technology society, touchable science exhibits for children rank near the top of approved playgrounds with parents and youngsters alike.

- California State Museum of Science and Industry (see EXPOSITION PARK) — talking computers, aircraft, IMAX films
- George C. Page Museum of La Brea Discoveries (see HANCOCK PARK) — fossils, reconstructed Pleistocene animals, views of fossil pits
- Los Angeles County Museum of Natural History (see EXPOSITION PARK) — dioramas, dinosaurs

SHOPS

- Children's Book and Music Center (see SHOPPING, page 156)
- Toy stores: see SHOPPING, page 158

THEME AND AMUSEMENT PARKS

Since Walt Disney first blended thrill rides into more appealing and instructive environments than the carnival or fairground, theme parks have blossomed, notably in California. These are the major ones.

- DISNEYLAND (see page 166)
- Knott's Berry Farm (see ORANGE COUNTY, page 172)
- SIX FLAGS MAGIC MOUNTAIN

TOURS OF THE ENTERTAINMENT INDUSTRIES

What with the movies and TV, California has its fair share of industries requiring unusual equipment and skills. Many of these offer tours of their operations. A few are noisy and active enough enterprises to engross children. Three examples:

- BURBANK STUDIOS (children aged 10 and over)
- NATIONAL BROADCASTING COMPANY TELEVISION STUDIO
- UNIVERSAL STUDIOS

TRANSPORT MUSEUMS

Although contemporary California lives by automobile and airplane, it has museums in celebration of railroads and ships as well as its current favorites. In or near LA are the following:

- Aerospace Building (see EXPOSITION PARK) — airplanes, space craft

- *Queen Mary* and *Spruce Goose* (see LONG BEACH, page 169) — the largest ocean liner and wooden aircraft afloat (it's a seaplane)
- Travel Town (see GRIFFITH PARK) — antique airplanes and trains, opportunities for clambering, and rides

OTHER MUSEUMS
There are some that don't quite fit any particular bag but are all the same loved by children.

- HEBREW UNION COLLEGE AND SKIRBALL MUSEUM — enjoyable Old Testament tableaux
- Hobby City Doll and Toy Museum (see ORANGE COUNTY, page 172) — 3,000 dolls and toys in a half-sized replica of the White House
- The Living Sea (see LONG BEACH, page 169) — Jacques Cousteau's sea-exploration museum
- LOS ANGELES CHILDREN'S MUSEUM — exploring the senses, workshops, kids' TV studio

VIEWPOINTS
Always popular with older children are those breathtaking views from the tops of high buildings, or from LA's encircling hills.

- CITY HALL
- ELYSIAN PARK
- Griffith Observatory (see GRIFFITH PARK)
- Westin Bonaventure hotel (see WHERE TO STAY)

Excursions

Environs of Los Angeles

As ever with LA and Southern California, mobility is the key. All the areas and specific destinations listed below are easily accessible by one or other means of transportation — car, bus, plane, boat or train. And some of them are closer in time and effort than crossing Greater LA in rush hour. Angelenos do it, so why not visitors?

CATALINA ISLAND

Map 10J6. 27 miles offshore from Los Angeles. Served daily by a fleet of tour boats from San Pedro and Long Beach (reservations usually required summer and weekends) i **Catalina Chamber of Commerce**, *PO Box 217, Avalon 90704* ☎*(310) 510-1520;* **Visitors' Information and Service Center** ☎*(310) 510-2500;* **Catalina Cruises** ☎*(213) 775-6111/832-4521.*

Movie stars escape to Catalina on their yachts or in their airplanes, followed by crowds of tourists who make the two-hour crossing on a fleet of comfortable passenger ferries and hydrofoils. Standard day-trip crossings allow passengers four hours ashore. Special cruises allow a full day trip. Spring and fall are the best times to visit.

For all the summer crowds, the 28-mile-long island (officially called **Santa Catalina Island**) remains a fine place for escapists. Its only town, **Avalon**, is a quiet hillside beach resort with the air and architecture of a Mediterranean village and a resident population of only some 2,500. A particular charm is the near absence of cars, which are replaced by a sort of zoo-train, and bicycles that can be rented inexpensively. Avalon has overnight accommodations; the Chamber of Commerce *(for ☎ see above)* makes reservations.

The rest of the island, no less than 86 percent of it in fact, is untamed natural beauty protected by the Santa Catalina Conservancy: mountains, canyons, cliffs, coves, sandy beaches and free-roaming wildlife.

SIGHTS AND PLACES OF INTEREST

Catalina Casino

On its rocky promontory, the 12-story building, Art Deco with overlays of Spanish Colonial, houses a movie theater *(☎ (213) 510-0179),* a museum *(▨ open Easter-end Oct 1-4pm, 8-10pm; remainder of year Sat 1-4pm, 8-10pm, Sun and holidays 1-4pm ; entrance fee includes tour of building)* and, far from least, the **Avalon Ballroom**, which once drew 6,200 to a single dance. Crowds today are not quite that large, but big bands do book here, mostly on weekends.

RECREATION

Avalon has two sand beaches lapped by warm ocean waters ideal for swimming. **Crescent Beach** is in front of the town. **Pebble Beach** is E of the arrival pier. **Catalina Island Golf Course** *(PO Box 1564, Avalon 90704* ☎*(310) 510-0530)* has a 9-hole layout. It also has hourly-fee tennis courts.

EXCURSIONS

Catalina offers a number of tours. The most unusual are an after-dark flying fish boat trip (spotlights excite the fish to soar alongside and even over the boat), and a glass-bottom boat trip across Avalon's undersea gardens.

Bus tours of the unspoiled interior leave from the **Island Plaza** at the center of town, or from the nearby **pier**.

DISNEYLAND ★

PO Box 3232, Anaheim 92803, Santa Ana Freeway/I-5 to Harbor Blvd. exit in Anaheim; entrance on Harbor Blvd. between Ball Rd. and Katella Ave. ☎(714) 999-4565 ▨ ✗ ▬ ═ ✸ ♿ ➡ AE *Open daily 9am-midnight May-Sept; remainder of year daily 10am-6pm, Sat-Sun 9am-midnight, but schedule expands for some holidays (check with above address).*

Walt Disney's inspired marriage of the amusement park and the Hollywood set opened on July 17, 1955 to rave reviews. The park has never lost that original luster in spite of gaining at least a score of imitators and outposts in Florida, Japan and Europe. One of its secrets is constant renewal of the major attractions. As important, the management pays great attention to such things as putting a little fun into standing in lines, and getting to and from the parking lots, no small matter when attendance runs at some 13 million a year.

Disney prides itself on crowd management, but if there's one constant complaint it must be the long lines. So expect to line up for popular attractions. This can be a major trial with very young children and can upset well-thought-out itineraries. Budget an hour or more at popular attractions, except during the slow winter months or late in the day.

On the plus side, there's a baby-care center (facilities, but no sitters), a day kennel, lockers and plentiful rest rooms.

Disneyland **"Passports"** include admission and unlimited use of all attractions, except arcades; there are seasonal discounts for people aged over 60, and 2- or 3-day "passports." Food and gift stores will inevitably run costs higher.

Tackling the densely packed park within a single day is nigh on impossible. The **Disneyland Railroad** provides previews of each section. The train departs on its $1\frac{1}{2}$-mile loop from Main Street USA.

Each section of the park has a share of Disneyland's 25 restaurants ranging in style from fast food to fairly elaborate dinner houses.

No description of Disneyland will produce willing suspension of disbelief, but the place itself does with margin to spare. An outline can only give hints. Many have taken the hint already; Disneyland is the second most popular attraction in the world, with more than 13 million visitors. Only the Magic Kingdom's Florida outpost attracts more.

ON WITH THE SHOW . . .

Disneyland consists of seven "theme" lands. Main Street USA is the gateway, and the plaza extending from it leads to the gates of other sections, in clockwise order: Adventureland, Frontierland, New Orleans Square, Bear Country, Fantasyland and Tomorrowland. All sections have strolling musicians, street performers and living, breathing hosts dressed as Disney cartoon characters, including Mickey Mouse, 60 years old in 1988. ("I hope we never lose sight of one thing," said Walt Disney, "that it all started with a mouse.")

The sections are also populated by remarkably lifelike human and animal characters animated by a Disney invention called Audio-Animatronics. The audio part explains itself; the figures are wired for sound. The animatronics that make them move are an ingenious combination of electronic signals and pneumatic joints hidden under uncannily flesh-like hides. The technique is also applied to animals, birds and flower figures.

Adventureland has flat-bottom boats that tour re-creations of Asia, Africa and the South Pacific. Each stream has an animated adventure to go with it. Hippos charge, elephants bathe, crocodiles stand sulky guard over temple ruins, and the Swiss Family Robinson makes an appearance.

Critter Country is a re-creation of America's Northwest wilderness, the vehicle a Davy Crockett canoe, the entertainment by animated bears. It also features Splash Mountain, which begins as a relatively sedate water ride aboard a hollowed out "log," and climaxes in a thrilling fall of five stories in under two seconds.

Fantasyland features characters from Disney Studio movies, who gather inside the gates of Sleeping Beauty's castle to conduct dressed-up carnival rides. An anachronistic flivver re-creates Mr Toad's Wild Ride through 19thC England. There is a wilder ride to be had in whirling cups from the Mad Hatter's Tea Party. But the real white-knuckle trip is the 14-story drop from the top of the Matterhorn in a bobsled. More sedately, a circus train visits Cinderella, Pinocchio and the Three Little Pigs, and a carousel has knightly horses from King Arthur's court.

Frontierland is where the whole of the pioneering Old West is represented one way or another. On the rivers of America are a Mississippi stern-wheeler, the *Mark Twain,* and a square-rigger, *Columbia.* Visitors can pole out to Tom Sawyer's island on the raft and, in a nifty piece of navigation, go for a voyage on the *Columbia.* Big Thunder Mountain Railroad goes through a mine at juddering speed in spite of rock-slides, floods and bats.

Main Street USA is idealized turn-of-the-century Americana; horse-drawn wagons and buggies are the only vehicles in a town of nickelodeons, ice cream parlors, and other shops perfectly scaled for children. Inside the Opera House, in a show called *Great Moments With Mr*

Lincoln, an animated figure of Abraham Lincoln gives a lecture on American history.

New Orleans Square has Mardi Gras parades and Dixieland jazz (by real players, not mechanical animations this time) and some eerie sides of the Old South, including boat trips through a pirate-infested Caribbean, and a journey through a house haunted by hologram ghosts.

Tomorrowland changes constantly, trying to keep up with its subjects: space and science. Among the innovations are Star Tours (inspired by the *Star Wars* movies), a stunning journey through outer space re-created on a 40-passenger flight simulator, and Captain Eo, a 3-D space adventure starring Michael Jackson (directed by Francis Ford Coppola and produced by George Lucas). The rides — Submarine Voyage, Star Tours and Space Mountain — still thrill.

In addition to these more or less permanent attractions, the park schedules rock, pop and folk concerts, and big-band concerts with dancing. The fullest schedules are on summer evenings and at Christmas. A fine fireworks display goes up at 9pm.

LONG BEACH

Map 10I6. On San Pedro Bay, 21 miles s of Los Angeles via the Long Beach Freeway/SR-7, or via the San Diego Freeway/I-405. Long Beach Airport served daily by PSA; bus connections from Los Angeles International by Airport Service Inc. (☎(714) 776-9210). City served daily by Greyhound Lines and Trailways, Inc. i Long Beach Visitors and Convention Bureau, 180 E Ocean Blvd., Long Beach 90802 ☎(310) 436-3645.

Long Beach is one of a number of cities lost, in many ways, in the giant sandwich of Greater Los Angeles. Searching for identity beyond being a center of oil production, a US Navy base and a deepwater freight harbor, the city has made a bid for the tourist trade with the *Queen Mary,* and a large convention center used almost as much for concerts as for business meetings. And yet it keeps mostly to itself one of the finest family beaches in all of Southern California. Coves with even gentler shores, marinas and a fishing pier add luster.

EVENT   Long Beach Grand Prix, a Formula 1 auto race through downtown, in mid-March.

SIGHTS AND PLACES OF INTEREST

Long Beach Museum of Art

2300 E Ocean Blvd., Long Beach, adjoining the beach 1.4 miles E of Long Beach Convention Center ☎(310) 439-2119 ▦ Open Wed-Sun 1-5pm. Closed Mon, Tues, major holidays.

A permanent collection of works by contemporary Southern Californians, in a 1912 Craftsman-style building on an attractively landscaped site dotted with sculptures.

Port Adventure Harbor Cruise

Pier J, Long Beach ☎(310) 547-0802 ▬ Cruises daily.

A comfortable boat takes 90-minute trips through the busy maze of Long Beach and San Pedro Harbors, visiting areas inaccessible by land.

RMS Queen Mary and the Spruce Goose ★

Pier J, Long Beach. At end of Long Beach Freeway/SR-7 ☎ *both sights (310) 435-3511,* **Queen Mary** *(310) 435-4747,* **Spruce Goose** *(800) 421-3732* ☎ ✱ *Open 10am-6pm, June 22-Labor Day 9am-9pm.*

Assuming it survives its current crisis, there are three ways to go aboard this great old ship: as a hotel guest (see HOTELS A TO Z), as a visitor to the restaurants and shops, or on a self-guided tour.

The 50,000-ton *Queen Mary*, launched in 1934 and bought by Long Beach after its retirement in 1964, is the largest, most luxurious ocean liner still afloat. Elegant furnishings and fittings and painstaking craftsmanship reflect 1930s Art Deco styles. The period menus on display are not to be missed; prewar appetites appear to have been prodigious. There is also a sound-and-light show and a lifeboat demonstration. Children will enjoy **The Living Sea** (✱), a museum devised by Jacques Cousteau.

The astonishing dome — the world's largest clear-span geodesic dome — alongside RMS *Queen Mary* houses Howard Hughes' *Spruce Goose*. The 320-foot wingspan made it at one time the largest wooden airplane ever to fly, though it did so just once, and barely, for one mile on November 2, 1947.

One ticket buys both giants, plus exciting audiovisual displays.

ORANGE COUNTY

Map 11I6. Straddles both San Diego Freeway/I-405 and Santa Ana Freeway/I-5 and adjoins Los Angeles County to the N i **Anaheim Area Visitors and Convention Bureau**, *800 W Katella Ave., Anaheim 92802* ☎*(714) 999-8999; also, visitor center at the Anaheim Convention Center across Katella from Disneyland.* **American Express Travel Service Office**, *3200 Bristol St., Costa Mesa 92626* ☎*(714) 540-3611.*

Orange County is served daily by the following services:

- **AirCal** and **Western Airlines** (John Wayne-Orange County Airport at Costa Mesa)
- **Airport Service Inc.** bus from John Wayne-Orange County and Los Angeles International to Disneyland and Grand hotels
- **Amtrak** stops at Fullerton, Santa Ana, San Juan Capistrano and San Clemente
- **Greyhound Lines** and **Trailways, Inc.** (no local service within county or from Los Angeles)
- **RTD** *(* ☎*(213) 626-4455)* has a bus service between Los Angeles Downtown and Disneyland and Knott's Berry Farm.
- Local transportation: **Orange County Transit District** *(* ☎*(714) 636-7533),* a countywide public transit system; **Fun Bus** *(* ☎*(714) 635-1390),* a loop run encompassing many hotels, Disneyland and Knott's Berry Farm

Orange County, which is known from afar for **Disneyland** and **Newport Beach** and for returning arch-conservatives to Congress, is the most famous playground in a state full of famous playgrounds.

Disneyland and the kindred **Knott's Berry Farm** anchor a series of parks and entertainments in the Anaheim-Buena Park area. Except for

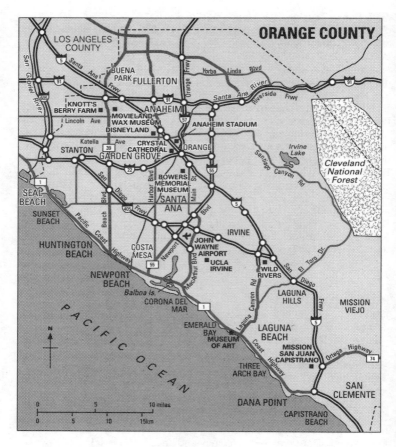

these, the industrial-residential towns in flat northern Orange County are of limited interest to visitors. (Between 1955 and 1965 the orange groves that gave the county its name were torn out, and the area became what Los Angeles has often been accused of being: 49 suburbs in search of a city.) The beach towns in the hilly s, on the other hand, uphold the paradisaical view of Southern California.

Newport Beach is the home of the most affluent society of boat people on the whole Pacific Coast. Marinas, shops and restaurants, as well as many beach homes, are crowded onto a long, low-lying peninsula, the islands inside the bay, and the mainland shore opposite. Adjoining **Corona del Mar** forms a tennis and golf suburb. This area is within easy reach of Disneyland and John Wayne-Orange County Airport.

More remote **Laguna Beach**, farther s, began as an art colony and still retains some of that flavor. Its gallery-lined shopping streets have a small-town atmosphere. The **Laguna Museum of Art** *(307 Cliff Dr.,*

Laguna Beach ☎ *(714) 494-6531, open Tues-Sun 11am-5pm)* has changing exhibits that focus on the work of California artists, both historic and contemporary. The museum has a satellite gallery at **South Coast Plaza** *(3333 Bristol St., Suite 1000, Costa Mesa, open Mon-Fri 11am-9pm, Sat 10am-6pm, Sun 11am-5pm)*. Lacking a harbor, Laguna Beach is much more beach-oriented than Newport Beach.

Other shoreside towns N and S beg not to be overlooked: **Huntington Beach** for surfing; **Capistrano Beach** for beaches and its mission; nearby **Dana Point** for beaches and boating; and **San Clemente** too for its beach.

If Orange County lacks a center, at least its web of freeways makes travel simple. To get around reasonably well, visitors need only know freeways I-405, I-5 and SR-55, plus the Pacific Coast Highway/SR-1, Beach Blvd./SR-39, Harbor Blvd. and MacArthur Blvd.

Although the county is compact enough to be explored as a whole, visitor attractions listed below are divided into those inland in the general area of Anaheim/Buena Park and those along the shore. DISNEYLAND has its own separate entry: see page 166.

EVENTS • **Dana Point Harbor Festival of Whales**. First three weekends in February. Celebrates the migration of gray whales with offshore tours plus lectures and other programs on sea life *(i Dana Point Harbor Association, 25102 Del Prado, Dana Point 92629)*.

• **Festival of the Arts and Pageant of the Masters**. Irvine Bowl, Laguna Beach. Early July-late August. Most celebrated aspect is locals portraying figures in living tableaux of famous paintings *(i Festival of Arts of Laguna Beach* ☎ *(714) 494-2685)*.

INLAND

Anaheim Stadium
2000 State College Blvd., Anaheim, adjacent to Orange Freeway/SR-57 at Katella Ave. exit.

The 70,000-seat stadium is the shared home of the California Angels baseball team *(☎ (714) 634-2000)* and the Los Angeles Rams football team *(☎ (213) 277-4748)*.

Bowers Memorial Museum
2002 N Main St., Santa Ana, near Main St. exit from Santa Ana Freeway/I-5 ☎*(714) 972-1900* 🖭 ➥ *Open Tues-Sat 9am-5pm; Sun noon-5pm. Closed Mon; major holidays.*

Orange County does have a past, much of it locked up in this museum. Displays include some fine Indian and early Californian relics, important documents of the Mexican and Spanish eras, and early California art. Exhibitions change periodically.

Disneyland ★
The Magic Kingdom has a separate entry on page 166.

Garden Grove Community Churches 血
12141 Lewis St., Garden Grove, SE of Disneyland near Chapman Ave. exit from Santa Ana Freeway/I-5 ☎*(714) 971-4000.*

Southern California has a long history of attempts to fit religion to local climate and society. None has produced a more remarkable set of buildings than the **Crystal Cathedral** and two earlier structures.

The Crystal Cathedral, 128 feet high and 410 feet long, towers above the flat landscape, an abstract geometric form of white steel trusses cloaked in silver tempered glass. Designed by architects Philip Johnson and John Burgee and opened in 1980, the church seats 2,862. Pastor Dr Robert Schuller had earlier (in 1955) commissioned a steel and glass building by International Style architect Richard Neutra with the novel intent of making his church services visible (and audible through speakers) to drive-in worshipers in a 1,400-capacity parking lot.

In this most automobile-oriented region of the world, the idea worked well enough to require not only the Crystal Cathedral, but also a 15-story administration building called **Tower of Hope**, designed by Dion Neutra, Richard's son.

Hobby City Doll and Toy Museum

1238 S Beach Blvd., Anaheim ☎(714) 527-2323. Open daily 10am-6pm.
A half-sized replica of the White House housing 3,000 dolls and toys from around the world, in one of the largest museums of its kind in the world.

Knott's Berry Farm

8039 Beach Blvd., Buena Park, Beach Blvd. exit from Riverside Freeway/SR-91; main entrance on Beach Blvd. between La Palma Ave. and Crescent Ave.; auxiliary entrances on La Palma Ave. and Western Ave. ☎(714) 827-1776 ☎
▣ ☴♣✈ AE ⊙ VISA Open May-Sept, Sun-Thurs 9am-midnight, Fri-Sat 9am-1am; remainder of year Mon-Tues 10am-6pm, Fri-Sun 10am-9pm, but schedule expands for some holidays (check first). Closed Dec 25.
This is the other major theme park in Orange County. With 150 acres, Knott's Berry Farm is bigger than Disneyland and older. The first restaurant dates back to 1934, the first amusement rides to the 1940s, when the Knott family still had a working berry farm. But the main distinction between it and its near neighbor is that the themes in Knott's focus entirely on nostalgia rather than fantasy. Also, there is greater emphasis on thrill rides in the theme sections called Fiesta Village, Old West Ghost Town and Roaring Twenties. With four million visitors a year, it ranks seventh in the world's top ten attractions.

There are age and height restrictions on some rides including Boomerang, the newest, which reaches speeds of 50mph and turns riders upside down six times in under a minute. In all there are 165 rides.

In **Fiesta Village**, a loop roller coaster called Montezooma's Revenge is a white-knuckle trip. The theme of Mexico and early California is carried into shops, demonstrations of crafts and a Mexican restaurant. El Cinema Grande shows movies on a 180° screen, and well-known rock bands play live music.

Bandits in the **Old West Ghost Town** hold up every trip of the Butterfield Stage and every run of the Denver Rio Grande narrow-gauge railroad. The thrill ride is in hollowed-out logs on an old-fashioned, Paul Bunyanesque logging flume. Visitors looking for quieter thrills can pan for gold. The saloon serves sarsaparilla or boysenberry punch, and has can can dancers. Fried chicken is the specialty of the restaurant, a much enlarged successor to the original.

Newly opened is **Indian Trails**, a two-acre, $2-million tribute to the

American Indian heritage, where visitors can try their hand at sand painting or beading.

The big thrill ride in the **Roaring Twenties** is a corkscrew roller coaster. Amid considerable attention to pioneer flying, there is a 20-story parachute tower (the chutes drop on guy wires with riders securely perched on small platforms). Well-known entertainers and/or ice shows play at the Good Time Theater. A dance hall, Cloud 9, helps keep the Charleston alive and kicking.

Movieland Wax Museum
7711 Beach Blvd., Buena Park ☎(714) 521-4740 ▄▄ *Open Mon-Sat 9am-8pm.*
Some 240 motion picture and TV stars, from John Wayne to Mr Spock, replicated in wax, with convincing movie-set backdrops. Scary scenes from *Halloween, Aliens* and their ilk in the **Black Box**.

Museum of World Wars and Military History
7884 La Palma Ave., Buena Park ☎(714) 952-1776 ▄▄
Weapons, vehicles, uniforms, flags and posters from the 18thC to World War II. The collection is said to be the largest in the US.

Oak Canyon Nature Center
200 S Anaheim Blvd., Anaheim; from Riverside Freeway/SR-91, s on Imperial Highway to Nohl Ranch Rd.; e to Walnut Canyon Rd., then follow it to its end ☎(714) 998-8380 ▄▄ *but donation welcome. Open 9am-5pm except major hols.*
Within 58 compact acres, a hands-on interpretive center, six miles of hiking trails and staff naturalists teach useful lessons about everything from roadrunners to rattlesnakes to anyone wishing to explore regional wilderness safely and intelligently in any season.

Orange County Performing Arts Center
600 Town Center Dr., in South Coast Plaza Town Center, Costa Mesa. For information and tickets ☎(714) 556-2787.
Symphony orchestras, opera and ballet companies and Broadway shows perform in the 3,000-seat Segerstrom Hall. Outside is Isamu Noguchi's sculpture garden.

San Juan Capistrano Library
31495 El Camino Real ☎(714) 493-1752. Open Mon-Thurs 10am-9pm, Fri-Sat 10am-5pm.
Architect Michael Graves has produced what some consider a Post-Modern masterpiece, echoing and contradicting its more famous neighbor, the Mission.

NEWPORT BEACH AND THE COAST

Huntington Beach Pier
Pacific Coast Highway/SR-1 at the foot of Main St., Huntington Beach.
If there is one perfect place to watch surfers at peak form, this is it. Wave action around the pier makes top-drawer riders in this area use its pilings as a sort of slalom course. Waves just alongside are reliable for long rides.

Lovell Beach House ☷
1242 West Ocean Front, Balboa Peninsula, Newport Beach (NE corner of 13th St. and Beach Walk). Private residence: no public access, but can be viewed from outside.

Regarded as a masterpiece of modern architecture, Rudolph Schindler's 1926, Bauhaus-influenced beach house, an exercise in space and structure, is an ingenious Constructivist design raised on five concrete cradles. It is considered to be one of the few 1920s buildings in the US to match the best-known European modern-movement buildings of that period, its clean geometry and thoughtful details making it well worth a visit.

Mission San Juan Capistrano

31882 Camino Capistrano, one block w of SR-74 junction with I-5 ☎(714) *493-1111* 🖸 *Open 7am-5pm.*

Founded by Father Junipero Serra in 1776, San Juan Capistrano, seventh of the missions, is one of the most moving to visit. Its ornately decorated church is the only known remaining site at which Serra said Mass. Its wider fame is as the home to which the swallows return every year, in romantic tales, on St Joseph's Day, March 19. The birds migrate south around October 23, the date on which the patron saint of the mission died.

Newport Harbor Art Museum

850 San Clemente Dr. 🖸 *but donation requested. During exhibitions, open Tues-Sun 11am-5pm; also Fri 6-9pm; closed Mon. Museum is closed between exhibitions: call beforehand* ☎(714) 759-1122.

Permanent and rotating exhibitions are devoted almost entirely to contemporary Southern California artists.

Richard Nixon Library and Birthplace

18001 Yorba Linda Blvd, s on I-5 then e on SR-91, n on SR-57 to Yorba Linda exit ☎(714) 993-3393 🖸 ⬤ *Open Mon-Sat 10am-5pm, Sun 11am-5pm.*

Orange County's latest, and arguably most bizarre, new attraction. The disgraced former President's rehabilitation continues in this shameless $21-million 9-acre one-theme park. On offer are audiovisual recollections of the Nixon-Kennedy debates, the Watergate scandal, Nixon's final days in the Whitehouse, a video "conversation" with Nixon, plus memorabilia and the restored farmhouse where "Tricky" Dick was born in 1913.

Wild Rivers

8800 Irvine Center Dr., Irvine, adjacent to San Diego Freeway/I-5 at Irvine Center Dr. exit ☎(714) 768-9453 🖸 ▣ *Open 10am-8pm mid-June to mid-Sept: 11am-5pm weekends and hols mid-May to mid-June and mid-Sept to end Sept. Closed remainder of year.*

The theme is water, most of it wild, but some of it tame. There are 40 water rides and attractions in the 20-acre park, and some plummet from five-story-high **Wild River Mountain**. On the **Bombay Blaster**, you drop the full five stories in five seconds inside a soft foam tube . . .

A more sedate section called **Explorers Island** has gentle, drifting rides, and three huge swimming pools.

RECREATION

Beaches and recreation are almost synonymous in Orange County, but fishing, boating, tennis and golf count for almost as much with locals and visitors alike. For visitors, beaches and fishing are accessible everywhere. Tennis and golf are associated primarily with hotels because of heavy local pressure on public courts and courses.

From the Los Angeles County line at Seal Beach s to Newport Beach, the Orange County coast is low-lying, virtually one continuous sandy beach. From Newport Beach s the coast grows more rugged, and sandy beaches are more apt to be short, at the back of coves. Much of the shore is State beach property. Most of the vacation and resort beaches range s from Huntington Beach.

Beaches of particular interest, N to s, include:

- **Santa Ana River County Beach**, Newport Beach's share of the long sandy strand.
- Surfing is good at the mouth of the **Santa Ana River** and at **Newport Pier**; the latter is also a favored place for pier fishermen.
- At the tip of the Balboa peninsula, a spot called **The Wedge** is legendary among body surfers.
- **Laguna Beach** has a length of white sand for swimmers and sunbathers extending s from a small developed park area at Laguna Canyon Rd./Broadway. The park has picnic tables, volleyball nets and other amusements.
- Some miles s, **Aliso Beach County Park** has picnic tables and lawns, and a fishing pier. The beach is good for swimming, and surfing is reliably excellent here.
- **Doheny State Beach**, adjoining Dana Harbor to the s and forming the shore of Capistrano Beach, is one of the most popular in the system. Surfing is good at the mouth of a lagoon.
- Inside **Dana Harbor**, a sheltered beach is excellent for families with small children.

PALM SPRINGS

*On SR-111, 103 miles E of Los Angeles via I-10. Palm Springs Airport served daily by Alaska Airlines, American Airlines, TWA, Western Airlines, and commuter lines from Los Angeles and San Diego. City served daily by Greyhound Lines. Local transportation: most hotels provide van or limousine service to and from the airport. Sunline (☎(619) 323-8157) provides useful intercity service in the Coachella Valley. Downtown Palm Springs has a London double-decker called the 'Sun Special' i **Palm Springs Convention & Visitors Bureau**, 255 N El Cielo Rd., Suite 315, Palm Springs 92262 ☎(619) 770-9000. Useful publications: 'Key' and 'Palm Springs Life's Desert Guide.'*

Palm Springs is to deserts what *Carmen* is to operas. What other opera has such tunes in such a straightforward story? What other desert has 70 lush golf courses, 600 tennis courts and 7,500 swimming pools?

In strictest truth, Palm Springs has only a fraction of either total. The rest are in the connected communities of **Cathedral City**, **Rancho Mirage**, **Palm Desert** and **La Quinta**, all farther down the Coachella Valley. However, Palm Springs is good shorthand for the lot because it was the first link in the chain and gave rise to the rest.

Built on alluvium at the foot of the steep, barren San Jacinto Mountains, Palm Springs started as a winter retreat for the stars in the early days of

Hollywood. Today, the stars still come to the resort, but it has also become a retirement town for the wealthy. For vacations, rich or not so rich, spring and fall have become popular seasons as well as winter, but only confirmed desert rats spend much time in this town in the heat of summer.

SIGHTS AND PLACES OF INTEREST

Desert Museum ⚏

At 101 Museum Dr., two blocks w of North Palm Canyon Dr., via Tahquitz-McCallum Way ☎*(619) 325-7186* ▣ ▬ *Open Tues-Sat 10am-5pm; Sun 1-5pm. Closed Mon.*

In the fine natural history section, permanent dioramas explain the basics of the local desert ecosystem. There are also changing displays of art relating to the desert. The pure art sections include attractive sculpture gardens and several galleries. A small permanent collection of paintings is continuously augmented by traveling exhibitions.

Living Desert ☆

At 47-900 Portola Ave., $1\frac{1}{2}$ miles s of SR-111 ☎*(619) 346-5694* ▣ ⚹ ▬ *Open Sept-May daily 9am-5pm. Closed (except to Grayline tours) June-Aug.*

On 350 acres of ridge and wash there are living specimens of most of the plants and animals native to the area. The plants and some of the animals are easy to see on either of two walks, one a stroll in the 20 acres nearest the parking lot, the other a stiff 5-mile hike covering the whole reserve. The highlight is a building where a special lighting system turns day into night so that the desert's nocturnal creatures can be seen going about their business.

Palm Springs Aerial Tramway

Lower station is $3\frac{1}{2}$ miles off SR-111 on Tramway Rd. at Palm Springs N city limit ☎*(619) 325-1391* ▣ ▬ *Open Mon-Fri 10am-9.15pm; Sat-Sun 8am-9.15pm. Closed Sept.*

Two 80-passenger streetcars give riders dramatic views of Palm Springs and the desert between **Chino Canyon** (at an elevation of 2,643 feet) and **Mountain Station** (at 8,516 feet). Evening passengers can eat dinner at a steak house at the top. Indeed, the dinner package is more attractive that the overpriced ride. Mountain Station is the gateway to 13,000-acre **Mt. San Jacinto State Park**, a well-used hiking area from spring to fall, and a modest snow-sports area in winter.

NEARBY SIGHTS

Cabot's Old Indian Pueblo Museum ⚏

Map 11I7. 67624 Desert View Ave., Desert Hot Springs ☎*(619) 329-7610* ▣ ▬ *Open Wed-Mon 9.30am-4.30pm. Closed Tues; major holidays.*

Cabot Yerxa belonged to the legion of desert eccentrics. His 35-room Pueblo-style house, built mostly with homemade adobe and salvage, is testimony not only in itself, but through its random collections of Indian and Inuit memorabilia and general souvenirs of Yerxa's life.

Joshua Tree National Monument

Map 12I8. From Los Angeles, 124 miles E via I-10 and SR-62 to Twentynine Palms.

In 870 square miles of rolling to mountainous desert, the national monument preserves the greatest natural stands of the spiky tree after which it is named. Joshuas *(Yucca brevifolia)* grow at relatively cool elevations above 3,000 feet; the stubbier Mojave Yucca *(Yucca schidigera)* grows lower down. The great desert preserve also supports fine herds of desert bighorn sheep, although few visitors catch glimpses of these shy animals. Only lightly touched by man, the park still has as one of its most intriguing aspects the abandoned **ranch of William Keys**, the ghostly subject of daily free tours from park headquarters at Twentynine Palms.

Joshua Tree NM lies within easy reach of Palm Springs. Although the park has campgrounds, most have no water or fuel, and campers must bring their own. Also, day trippers from nearby desert communities must bring water for themselves and their car radiators.

Salton Sea

Map 12J8. 45 miles SE of Palm Springs on SR-111.

This accidentally man-made inland desert sea, 38 miles long, 228 feet below sea level and stocked with salt-tolerant corvina, is one of Southern California's most popular fishing lakes in summer, although it is more pleasant to visit in winter. Along the eastern shore, the extensive **Salton Sea State Recreation Area** caters to campers, swimmers and boatmen, and has a natural history interpretive center. At the s tip of the lake, a **national wildlife refuge** is a stopover for 250 species of migrating shore birds. Nearby are several mineral hot springs.

RECREATION

Golf and tennis   Greater Palm Springs has numerous courses and courts open to the public, others described as "semi-private" where visitors are sometimes welcome, and still more that are strictly private. For a comprehensive list, see the monthly *Palm Springs Life's Desert Guide* from the Convention and Visitors Bureau (☎ *(619) 770-9000)*.

SAN SIMEON

Map 9H4. On SR-1, 248 miles NW of Los Angeles.

San Simeon is essentially synonymous with the opulent, grotesque castle of newspaper baron William Randolph Hearst (1863-1951). Yet a whole village surrounds the main house, and a state beach and a cluster of motels and shops flank the hilltop monument.

Architect Julia Morgan and the master craftsmen who built San Simeon, the castle, high above the sea, began in the 1920s using walls, furnishings, and sometimes entire rooms taken from historic buildings in Europe. The main purpose was to give Hearst a fit place in which to keep company with movie queen Marion Davies and many other Hollywood VIPs. The result is an astonishingly eclectic building; here a Roman pool, there a Gothic dining room, and everywhere fine pieces of art. The mix-and-match extravagance is overwhelmingly vulgar, but San Simeon is none the less fascinating as a result.

After Hearst's death, his family gave this residential core of their 275,000-acre estate to be used as a State Historical Monument open to the public. The castle, now known as the **Hearst San Simeon State Historical Monument** (🏛 ★ ☎ *(805) 927-2020* 🅿 ✗ *open 8.30am-3.30pm, closed Thanksgiving, Dec 25, Jan 1*), offers three separate tours, each beginning with a five-mile bus ride up what Hearst called "Enchanted Hill."

Tour One is of the main floor of the mansion plus gardens and guesthouse. Tour Two takes in several upper-story bedrooms, Hearst's libraries and the kitchen. Tour Three includes still more bedrooms, but focuses on art. The tours may be taken consecutively or on separate days, but each must be reserved and paid for separately. Each lasts about two hours and involves a substantial amount of walking and climbing. Some tickets are available at the Visitor Center (which also houses a permanent exhibit detailing Hearst's career), but advanced reservations are advised (☎ *(800) 444-7275 or (619) 452-1950)*.

W.A. Swanberg's *Citizen Hearst* is recommended reading before visiting San Simeon.

SANTA BARBARA

Map 10I5. Straddles US-101, 96 miles N of Los Angeles. Served daily by American, United and commuter airlines, Amtrak and Greyhound Lines
*i **Conference and Visitors Bureau**, P.O. Box 299, Santa Barbara 93102*
*☎(805) 965-3021; **Santa Barbara Chamber of Commerce**, 1 Santa Barbara St. ☎(805) 965-3021. For driving routes, see page 191.*

Santa Barbara comes close to living up to the myth of California as earthly paradise. No climate is more benign in a state famous for benign climates. Even the sea is tempered here by a shield of offshore islands. In addition to these natural advantages, the small city has a rare civility owing in part to long-standing wealth, in part to one of the nine campuses of the University of California, and in part to well-remembered Spanish beginnings.

Santa Barbara started out as a Spanish presidio and mission in the 1780s. In every quarter, it still looks as if it has been transported lock, stock and barrel from some Spanish hillside. Subtropical gardens half hide villas with white walls and red-tiled roofs. Even the public buildings appear to have been designed in Seville or Jerez. And the local feeling for a Mediterranean way of life goes beyond architecture: Santa Barbara awakens slowly, and does not hurry to bed at night.

Santa Barbara's particular charm as a resort city is that it has made no effort to be a resort city. The major hotels hide away from downtown traffic routes. Local public transportation is excellent. Downtown stores and shopping centers serve local needs first, and visitors' needs only incidentally. The shops and restaurants are nevertheless excellent, partly owing to high standards, partly because of Santa Barbara's role as a principal escape for Los Angelenos. It is largely they who keep resorts and hotels sold out weeks in advance all summer long, and on weekends year round. But it is a different, slower-paced LA crowd than the one found at Palm Springs.

Many newcomers to Santa Barbara are bewildered by the orientation

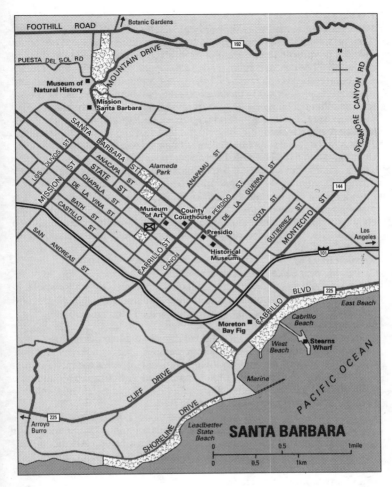

of the coast, which causes the sun to rise over the Pacific and set over the hills behind the town.

SIGHTS AND PLACES OF INTEREST

County Courthouse of Santa Barbara ⅏

1100 Anacapa St., at Figueroa St. ☎ ◀€ Open Mon-Fri 8am-5pm; Sat-Sun and holidays 9am-5pm ✗ on Wed and Fri at 10.30am.

Spanish Colonial-style flourishes here in architect William Mooser's 1926 monumental collection of plain and fancy tiles, decorated beams, columns and arches. A clock tower, open weekdays only, gives fine views across the city. Pleasant gardens much used for pageantry fill a block-square site.

The harbor

Santa Barbara's small boat harbor begins at the foot of State St., and has three main elements. **Stearns Wharf** is a refurbished collection of restaurants, tourist shops and bait stores for pier fishermen. Around to the w, the breakwater holds offices for operators of offshore cruises and charter boats, as well as boat sales agencies, tackle stores and marina offices. Between these extremities a smaller pier is the home base of a fleet of party fishing boats, which sail on half-day and full-day trips, mostly for calico and sand bass, rock cod and halibut.

Mission Santa Bárbara

E Olivos St., at Laguna St., 4 blocks toward the mountain from State St., via Los Olivos St. ☎ *(805) 682-4713* 🔲 *Open 9am-5pm.*

This is called the "Queen of the Missions" because of its comparatively refined Romanesque design and construction. Santa Barbara was founded in 1786, but the present buildings date from 1812-20, having replaced earlier structures damaged in an earthquake. Tenth in the chain, the mission has a small museum of its founding era. Its church remains in active use, the only mission continuously in the hands of its founding order.

Moreton Bay Fig

Chapala St., near Santa Barbara's main beach.

Specimens of this gigantic New Zealand native tree exist elsewhere in Southern California, but no other thrives quite as this one, which was planted in 1877. The canopy measures some 160 feet in diameter.

Museum of Art

1130 State St. ☎ *(805) 963-4364* 🔲 *but donation expected. Open Tues-Sat 11am-5pm; Sun noon-5pm. Closed Mon; holidays.*

A small museum, but well endowed by local patrons with an impressive collection of Classical sculpture, Asian art and American paintings. It also has an excellent doll collection.

Presidio of Santa Barbara State Historic Park

123 E Cañon Perdido St. 🔲 *Open Mon-Fri 9am-noon, 1-4pm. Closed Sat-Sun.*

Today, only two of the original buildings of the 1782 Spanish fort survive, **El Cuartel**, the guards' house, and **La Caneda Adobe**, a military residence, but they serve as a reminder of the plain, dusty lives lived by most early Californians. The **Presidio Chapel** is a re-creation of an early Spanish church.

Santa Barbara Botanic Gardens

1212 Mission Canyon Rd., 1½ miles N of Mission ☎ *(805) 682-4726* 🔲 *✗ $!S on Thurs at 10.30am. Open 8am to sunset.*

The gardens occupy 75 acres laced by paths. Native plants cluster in groups defined by ecological zones from Santa Barbara Channel Island to desert. There is also a display showing how local Indians used plants. A lovely place in the spring.

Santa Barbara Historical Museum

136 E de la Guerra St. ☎ *(805) 966-1601* 🔲 *✗ on Wed at 1.30pm. Open Tues-Fri noon-5pm; Sat-Sun 1-5pm. Closed Mon.*

In a modern adobe built in the style of early structures, handsomely mounted displays of the city's Spanish and Mexican origins dominate, but Chinese and Anglo history receive equally attractive attention. Action-filled engravings and lithographs by Edward Borein give life to historic objects on display. Scholars may use the **Gladhill Library**.

Santa Barbara Museum of Natural History
2559 Puesta del Sol Rd., two blocks N of Mission ☎*(805) 682-4711* ▣ *✗ on Sun at 2pm. Open Mon-Sat 9am-5pm; Sun 10am-5pm. Closed Thanksgiving; Christmas; New Year.*

Thoughtful displays in the Spanish-style museum building explain how a wide variety of life forms can thrive in the region. Two acres of gardens amplify the lessons.

RECREATION
Beaches
For all practical purposes, Santa Barbara has preserved all its white-sand beaches for public use. The city beach bears several names along its $3\frac{1}{2}$-mile length:

- Running E from the city harbor they are **West, Cabrillo** and **East.**
- Equally sandy **Leadbetter State Beach** lies W of the harbor via an extension of Cabrillo Blvd.
- Families with small children will find the calmest waters in the harbor between the breakwater and **Stearns Wharf**, but all of these warm-water beaches are safe for swimming.
- Volleyball nets are at the E end of the city beaches where Cabrillo Blvd. bends inland.
- Although there are public buildings, including a competition swimming pool adjacent to the harbor, the beaches have few amenities; dressing is best done at the hotel, picnics best prepared beforehand.
- Secluded **Arroyo Burro** lies 2 miles W of town via Cliff Dr.

Golf
Santa Barbara and its suburbs have two public 18-hole courses and a third open to guests staying at many of the city's hotels. The public ones are **Sandpiper** *(7925 Hollister Ave., Goleta* ☎*(805) 968-1541)*, 7,066 yards, par 72, rated 73.4, and **Santa Barbara Community** *(3500 McCaw Ave.* ☎*(805) 687-7087)*, 5,964 yards, par 70, rated 65.5. The private course open to hotel guests is **Montecito Country Club** *(920 Summit Rd.* ☎*(805) 969-3216)*, 6,145 yards, par 71, rated 68.6.

Tennis
The city of Santa Barbara maintains two fine complexes: **Municipal Courts** *(Salinas St., via Old Coast Highway)*, with 12 lighted courts, and **Las Positas** *(1002 Las Positas Rd.)*, with six lighted courts.

Wineries
In Bob Thompson's chapter on WINES AND WINERIES, there is a section listing the wineries of northern Santa Barbara County. Tastings, and sometimes tours, are possible. See page 198.

Farther afield

There are engaging and easily accessible places to visit beyond Los Angeles, San Diego and adjacent areas. That the two pre-eminent destinations are **Las Vegas** and **Tijuana**, the first in another state (Nevada), the second in another country (Mexico), ought not to discourage travelers. The Interstates make for easy driving.

Strangely, the two cities have much in common. Both have the feel of a honky-tonk. They share a kind of get rich quick (or in the case of Vegas casinos, get poor quick) nervous energy. Both depend heavily on money spent by visitors and devote much of their energy to entertaining out-of-towners. Neither pretends to be other than it is — in the case of Las Vegas, America at its showiest, in a self-indulgent, neon-lit, adult theme park that never closes; in the case of Tijuana, Mexico at its most exuberant, garish, and with third-world plumbing.

On balance, Las Vegas is the more attractive and easier to manage. Well-bred, sophisticated, steeped in history it isn't. But neither does it have the slums or the beggars that rather take the gloss off any romance that still attaches to Tijuana. Nor are there long lines and Customs/Immigration interrogations when you seek to re-enter California from Nevada. Exiting Mexico, on the other hand, can be a trial. Don't go to either if excess and raucous good fun offends. Do if you want to join in.

LAS VEGAS

266 miles NE of Los Angeles. Map 12G8. McCarran Airport served by most major US airlines. Services also by Amtrak, Greyhound and Trailways i Las Vegas Chamber of Commerce, Convention Center ☎(702) 735-3611 ⒻⓍ(702) 735-6200.
Bright, brash, cheerful and energetic, Las Vegas is the big time, the 24-hours-a-day, seven-days-a-week magnet for gamblers. The Strip has the biggest hotels and casinos in Nevada, and the surest supply of big-name entertainers. But in recent years Las Vegas has subtly and consciously changed. Nowadays it is rather more than a sometimes X-rated Disneyland for adults, and the showgirls go topless only for the late shows.

To be sure, the newest hotels still offer wall-to-wall gambling, but they also seek to cater to families with children. Their fantasies are themed with families in mind. The sprawling **Excalibur**, complete with fairy-tale turrets, jousting knights and white-knuckle rides courtesy of Dynamic Motion Simulators, is a sort of King Arthur goes to Hollywood and gets lost in the desert. The more deluxe **Mirage** nods toward Polynesia and has an extraordinary erupting volcano, a lavish and spectacular magic show to amaze and delight all ages, a collection of rare Siberian white tigers, and a 20,000-gallon tropical saltwater aquarium. The latter, bubbling away behind the hotel's check-in desk, relaxes guests at what is said to be their most anxious moment: wondering if their reservation is in order. In 1993 the newest of all will be the **MGM Grand**, complete with Disney-style amusement park drawing on MGM legends, most notably *The Wizard of Oz*.

Las Vegas 50 years ago was a desert railroad junction with a population of 8,000 people. Imagination, and the zero rate of income tax for State residents, works wonders. Today the population is 800,000 and growing, making it the largest US city founded in the 20thC. Yet the city is viewed almost as another suburb by Los Angelenos used to driving such distances regularly. Last year, 21 million people visited. The enormity of it all is breathtaking.

The only slow period is mid-December to New Year. The busiest is early January. Don't arrive without a confirmed room reservation.

VISITOR ATTRACTIONS

For most visitors, Las Vegas is **The Strip**, formally Las Vegas Blvd., otherwise known as Glitter Gulch, which roughly parallels I-15 for most of its path through town. On this sleepless street of dreams, and occasional nightmares, are nearly all of the gaming city's casinos and hotels, its major shopping malls and department stores.

What with the gambling, the world-class entertainment, the eating, drinking and hotel-centered amusements, it is easy to attempt nothing else. But there are a number of exciting alternatives. The bell captain at any major hotel will arrange tours, plus nightclub reservations etc. etc.

Within the city, and very much of it, is the **Liberace Museum** (*1775 E Tropicana Ave.* ☎ *(702) 798-5595),* filled with schmaltzy memorabilia of the late crown prince of glitz. On display are pianos said to have belonged to Chopin and George Gershwin, as well as the costumes, cars and knickknacks of the bejeweled, bouffant-haired entertainer.

A major annual occasion is the **National Finals Rodeo** at the Cowboy Superbowl, in December.

The most popular attraction within striking distance is the **Hoover Dam** (*i* ☎ *(702) 293-8367),* which with an admission fee of just $1 is a bargain. The 727-foot-high dam straddles the Nevada-Arizona border 30 miles E of Las Vegas along Highway 93. Behind the dam is **Lake Mead** (*i* ☎ *(702) 293-8096),* 115 miles long and popular for boating, swimming, waterskiing and fishing.

The **Grand Canyon** is farther, 300 miles E of Las Vegas. **Scenic Airlines** (☎ *(702) 739-1900)* and **Air Nevada** (☎ *(702) 736-8900)* do brisk business in flights through the mile-deep, 280-mile-long Canyon.

HOTEL-CASINOS

The major hotel-casinos with big-name entertainment are:

- **Aladdin Hotel**   3667 Las Vegas Blvd., Box 14217, Las Vegas, NV 89114 ☎(702) 736-0111 ▥ 1,000 rooms
- **Bally's–Las Vegas**   3645 Las Vegas Blvd. S, Las Vegas, NV 89109 ☎(702) 739-4111 ▥ 2,832 rooms
- **Caesar's Palace**   3570 Las Vegas Blvd. S, Las Vegas, NV 89109 ☎(702) 731-7110 ▥ 1,608 rooms
- **Circus Circus**   2880 Las Vegas Blvd. S, Las Vegas, NV 89109 ☎(702) 734-0410 ▥ 2,793 rooms
- **Dunes**   3650 Las Vegas Blvd. S, Las Vegas, NV 89109 ☎(702) 737-4110 ▥ 1,282 rooms

The **Excalibur Hotel & Casino** is the world's largest resort/hotel, with 4,032 rooms and more than 500,000 square feet of entertainment area.

- **Excalibur Hotel & Casino**   3850 Las Vegas Blvd. S., Las Vegas, NV 89193 ☎(702) 597-7777 ▥ 4,032 rooms
- **Frontier**   3120 Las Vegas Blvd. S, Box 14397, Las Vegas, NV 89114 ☎(702) 794-8200 ▥ to ▥ 592 rooms
- **Las Vegas Hilton**   3000 Paradise Rd. (adjoining convention center), Box 15087, Las Vegas, NV 89114 ☎(702) 732-5111 ▥ 3,174 rooms
- **The Mirage**   3400 Las Vegas Blvd. S., Las Vegas, NV 89109 ☎(702) 791-7111 ▥ to ▥ 3,049 rooms
- **MGM Desert Inn**   3145 Las Vegas Blvd. S, Box 14607, Las Vegas, NV 89114 ☎(702) 733-4444 ▥ 820 rooms
- **Riviera**   2901 Las Vegas Blvd. S, Las Vegas, NV 89114 ☎(702) 734-5301 ▥ 2,200 rooms
- **Sahara**   2535 Las Vegas Blvd. S, Box 14337, Las Vegas, NV 89114 ☎(702) 737-2111 ▥ to ▥ 1,000 rooms

EATING OUT

Las Vegas is not really at the cutting edge of American cuisine. Although some hotels, such as **The Mirage** and **Bally's**, boast fine restaurants, what the city does best is cheap and cheerful. Very cheap, in fact. Major hotels run round-the-clock restaurants, usually including one or more all-you-can-eat cafeteria-style buffets. The food at these is straightforward Americana, and the standard is remarkable given the ravenous hordes they feed. The buffet at the **Circus Circus** hotel reckons to feed 12,000 people per day. The only drawback is the lines. Eating this well this cheaply can involve a great deal of patient shuffling.

SHOPPING

For one-stop shopping the best place is **Fashion Show Mall** (*Spring Mountain and The Strip, just E of the I-15*), which houses 140 boutiques, along with department stores **Neiman Marcus**, **Saks Fifth Avenue**, the **May Company**, **Bullock's** and **Dillards**. All the major chain stores are here, plus plenty more.

TIJUANA

Map 11K7. For BORDER FORMALITIES, PUBLIC TRANSPORT AND TOURS *see below*
i Av. Revolución and Calle 1 ☎ *(66) 858-472.*

Once a very shabby town, Tijuana is now merely shabby, with a style not purely Mexican, but sufficiently different from neighboring San Diego to attract crowds of visitors from the north.

PUBLIC TRANSPORT AND TOURS

Tijuana is best reached from San Diego. From there, **Greyhound** *(120 Broadway, map 7C3)* and **Mexicoach** *(Santa Fe Depot, on Broadway at Kettner, map 7C2)* operate daily bus trips into Tijuana. **Gray Line** and other companies offer package tours.

The **San Diego Trolley**, part of **San Diego Metropolitan Transit**, runs from San Diego's Santa Fe Depot, the Amtrak station, to the Tijuana border crossing. Pick up the trolley at the station or anywhere along its Downtown route. From the border it is a shortish walk or a cab ride into the Mexican city. SDMT buses also serve the city and adjacent areas as far as San Ysidro, on the Mexican border opposite Tijuana.

BORDER FORMALITIES

For visits of less than 72 hours reaching not more than 75 miles beyond the border, US citizens need neither passport nor visa to enter Mexico. For longer stays or trips deeper into the country, the Mexican government requires tourist cards, which can be obtained free from Mexican consulates *(225 Broadway, Suite 225, San Diego 92101* ☎ *(619) 231-8414, map 7C2, and 125 Paseo de la Plaza, Los Angeles 90012* ☎ *(213) 624-3261)* or from Mexican government tourist offices *(600 B St., Suite 1220, San Diego 92101* ☎ *(619) 236-9314, map 7C3, and 9701 Wilshire Blvd., Beverly Hills 90212* ☎ *(213) 274-6315, map 3D3).* Naturalized citizens of the US must carry naturalization papers or US passports.

For citizens of other countries, regulations can be slightly more complicated. All visitors must have tourist cards, and there are some additional visa requirements for citizens of certain nations. All non-US citizens intending to visit Mexico from the US should inquire at a Mexican consulate before crossing the border.

The US does not regulate entry into Mexico, but does control return traffic. To re-enter the US, all non-US citizens except Canadians must have a valid multiple-entry visa and a passport. Canadians may re-enter the US with any proof of citizenship.

Leaving Mexico by car can be tedious and time-consuming. There are often long lines, particularly on Sunday evening.

AUTOMOBILE INSURANCE

No foreign insurance is valid in Mexico, and no foreign insurance company may act for a client in Mexico. Several companies with San Diego offices specialize in short-term policies for foreign drivers in Mexico. Check with a tourist office or travel agent for a list. Arrange insurance before crossing the border.

VISITOR ATTRACTIONS

Tourist-oriented shops are concentrated on the main street, **Av. Revolución**, between Calle 2 and Calle 9. Apart from shopping and too many margaritas, Tijuana has various other attractions that are worthy of attention.

Jai-alai, a scintillatingly quick wall-and-ball game (the ball travels at up to 180mph), is played at the **Palacio de Jai-Alai** *(on Revolución)* every evening except Thursday. The betting is as fast and furious as the game, though it helps to understand the latter before risking the former.

Bullfighting, not for animal rights sympathizers or even the mildly squeamish, is usually on Sundays. The largest bullrings are **El Toreo de Tijuana** *(on Agua Caliente, s of town)* and the **Plaza Monumental** *(by the port)*. The **Hipódromo de Agua Caliente** racetrack *(SE of town toward the Country Club)* features dog-racing on weekday evenings and horse-racing on weekends *(for information ☎ (66) 862-002, or in San Diego ☎ (619) 260-00)*.

The **Cultural Center** *(Independencia and Paseo de los Héroes ☎ (66) 841-111, open 11am-7pm)* is a good introduction to Mexican culture, with a panoramic OMNIMAX movie theater housed in a modernistic structure.

The beach isn't bad either. **Playa Rosarito** *(20 miles s down the Ensenada toll road Mexico-1)* is an improving resort area with a long beach, bars, *taco* stands, hotels and restaurants, especially along Blvd. Benito Juárez. Farther along the toll road, the resort town of **Ensenada**, about 70 miles s of Tijuana and only an hour's drive from the US border, is a major sport-fishing center, handsomely set on the fine white-sand bay of Todos Santos. There is a duty-free shopping district on and near Av. Lopez-Mateos, and of particular interest is a store offering folk art at bargain prices.

California touring

Those parts of California that are easily accessible from Los Angeles divide naturally into three separate touring areas. Any of these areas can be enjoyed alone, but even better perhaps is to move from one area to another, sampling different routes in each. The maps in this section show the main roads. For more detail, refer to maps **9-12**.

AREA: COAST SOUTH OF LOS ANGELES

Los Angeles does not quite fill up all of California s of the Tehachapi Mountains; it leaves room for several richly attractive seashore resorts along the Orange and San Diego County coasts, some equally attractive golf and tennis resorts inland, plus Disneyland and all its competitors. The bonus, just 18 miles s of downtown San Diego, is Mexico.

These disparate places can be woven into an astonishingly diverse but persistently urban vacation at any time of year. Winter may be the finest season for cooler, cleaner but still sun-warmed air, and smaller crowds.

Distances pose no problems. The 127-mile drive from Los Angeles to San Diego requires little more than two hours at favorable times. Adding the major attractions of Orange County to an itinerary adds little to the total mileage since they fall on or near to I-5, the direct freeway between Los Angeles and San Diego.

San Diego is an underrated but not uncrowded subtropical seaside resort nearly perfect for family vacations. History suffuses the city. It has one of the world's great zoos. Its range of recreations encompasses deep-sea fishing, open-ocean or bay boating, surfing, golf, tennis, and the acquisition of theatrical tans on bay or ocean beaches or beside elegant resort pools. San Diego is California's second most populous city after Los Angeles, although it is smaller than **Tijuana**, its Mexican next-door neighbor.

Orange County's grove of small cities offers not just **Disneyland**, but a whole galaxy of amusement parks and motion-picture-related museums satisfying to adults and children alike. The county also has excellent beaches and small-boat harbors.

Only experience can teach proper appreciation of the Friday afternoon exodus of urban-weary Los Angelenos to their favorite weekend retreats. But not even experience can unearth reliably uncrowded hotels, restaurants or parks. Ordinary motels sometimes book solid for weeks in advance in summer. Weekends and holidays tend to be sold out far in advance all year long.

A car is essential for getting about in Orange County. San Diego has relatively efficient local transport, although the sprawling nature of the city means long, slow bus rides between some of the prime attractions.

Los Angeles to San Diego

The point to keep in mind is that it is mostly a matter of getting there. The most sensible method may be Amtrak, pursuing a slow but scenic route close to the shore for much of the train journey. Flying is not a

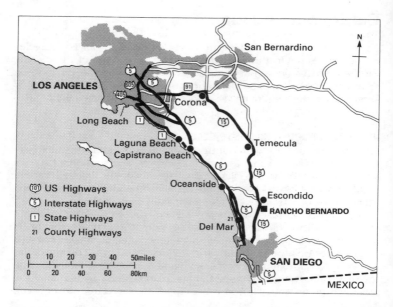

bad idea either, because it is quick. As a means of passage, driving comes rather far down the list . . . . Even making the trip by boat would be preferable if this were possible.

The fast way

See map above. From LA, use I-5.

The virtue is speed.

The coast route

See map above. From LA, use I-405 or I-605 s to SR-22; then w on SR-22 to SR-1; then SR-1 s to its intersection with I-5; then I-5 s to Oceanside; then s on county route S-21.

In part of Orange County, and again in part of San Diego County, slower roads run closer to the shore than does I-5. In Orange County, SR-1 passes through several attractive beach towns, notably **Laguna Beach** and **Capistrano Beach**. In San Diego County, S-21 touches **Oceanside** and **Del Mar**. The attractions include **Mission San Juan Capistrano** and several pleasant beach parks.

But these roads should not be oversold as scenic routes. Frequently they burrow along through commercial strip developments, or behind rows of apartments. Only occasionally do they give views out to sea, or chances to stop and explore the shore.

The inland route

See map above. From Los Angeles, head s on I-5 to freeway SR-91, then E on the latter to Corona. From there, travel SE on I-15 through Escondido to San Diego.

On this inland route, which is nearly all freeway, are **Rancho Bernardo** and other golf resorts, a small wine district at **Temecula**, and San Diego Zoo's famous **Wild Animal Park** near Escondido. The drive itself is unlikely to enchant except for a few miles near **Escondido** where avocado orchards nestle into strangely shaped, rocky hills.

AREA: COAST BETWEEN SAN FRANCISCO AND LOS ANGELES

This is the most diverse of all California's regions in its nature and in its human development, the one that most calls for thoughtful appraisal of the parts as well as the whole.

For at least half of the 400 miles between San Francisco and Los Angeles, steep hills press hard against the Pacific Ocean shoreline, keeping wild beauty intact, most famously in **Big Sur**, but in other districts as well.

Where the hills do not come so close to the shore, **Santa Barbara** and the **Monterey Peninsula** have grown into two dissimilar but equally urbane oases of civilization. Santa Barbara lies back beneath its reliable sun in conscientious tribute to its Spanish beginnings, while Monterey affects a certain Yankee bustle. Santa Barbara *allows* tourists, while Monterey courts them. In some mysterious way they are mileposts in the psychological shift that differentiates Southern and Northern California.

Between the extremes of Big Sur wilderness and small city urbanity come all the other shadings of human activity. Within this region, ocean water temperatures change sharply from warm to cold, changing the onshore climate from warm and sunny to cool and foggy, and changing small seaside towns slowly and inconsistently from sleepy resorts to hardworking fishing and/or farming villages. Somewhere among **Avila Beach**, **Cambria**, **Morro Bay**, **Santa Cruz** and **Half Moon Bay** is a town to please any coast watcher looking for an alternative to Santa Barbara or Carmel and the rest of the Monterey Peninsula.

In the chain of coastal valleys, farming is the mainstay all along. Horses and cattle browse the dry, grassy slopes. Down in the bottomlands, crops change in direct cooperation with the weather, from citrus near Santa Barbara to artichokes near San Francisco, with vineyards scattered all along the way. Inland towns most likely to attract a visitor's eye are **Ojai**, **Solvang**, **San Luis Obispo** and **San Juan Bautista**.

Tucked here and there into the landscape are some of the best bits of California history, including William Randolph Hearst's legendary **San Simeon**, and several **Franciscan missions** less touched by time than those closer to the great urban centers. The most notable missions are **La Purísima Concepción** near Lompoc, and **San Antonio de Padua**, to the w of US-101 near King City.

Spring and fall bring the most pleasant weather to the northern end of the territory. Winter offers nothing more fierce than occasional lingering rain. Summer is the season of fogs all along the coast, but inland it is also a season of heat. Toward Santa Barbara the climate stays benign all year round.

Santa Barbara and the Monterey Peninsula both have dozens of hostelries running the gamut from costly resort hotel to plain motel. In the territory between the two cities, both range and numbers dwindle. Most resorts and some hotels are booked solid for a week in advance

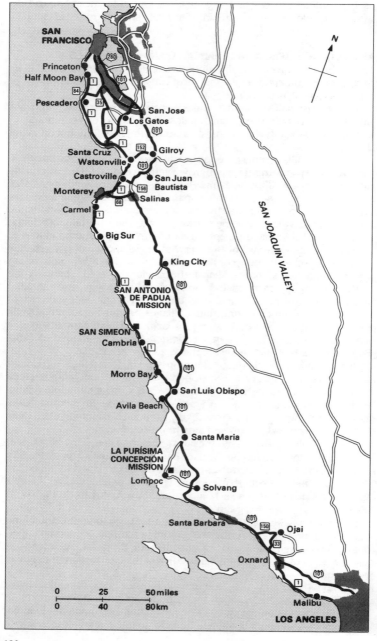

through the summer; weekend vacancies can be hard to find as much as a month ahead.

Unquestionably, a car is more than merely useful. Santa Barbara has a fine transit system; compact Carmel can be explored satisfactorily on foot. Otherwise, a lack of independent transport may be a substantial handicap.

Los Angeles to Monterey and back

See map opposite. From LA, N via US-101 to intersection with SR-1 near San Luis Obispo, then N on SR-1 to Monterey. Return on SR-68 to Salinas, then US-101 to Los Angeles.

The drive in either direction takes a long day, especially the leg of the journey on high, winding SR-1, so the best plan is to allow two days for driving in addition to however many are budgeted for Monterey-Carmel. So many en-route attractions — **Santa Barbara**, **San Simeon**, **Big Sur**, the **Santa Ynez Valley** and **Mission San Antonio de Padua** — demand attention that it is advisable to allow more travel time. It is also sensible to make the loop in the order suggested, with SR-1 as the northbound leg. The road follows sheer cliffs, for a time at elevations nearing 1,000 feet, and having the other traffic lane as a margin can lower the anxiety level a great deal. However, even if it means driving S, on no account should anyone who has a chance to make the coastal journey pass it by.

Mission San Antonio is reached via Jolon Rd., which turns W from US-101 just N of King City in Monterey County, then rejoins the highway 33 miles farther S. The **Santa Ynez Valley** requires somewhat more complicated navigating if the plan is to drive from end to end. From a point just S of **Santa Maria**, Betteravia Rd. leads E to Sisquoc; from there Foxen Canyon Rd. runs S to Los Olivos. From Los Olivos several local roads continue S to **Solvang** or Santa Ynez, and SR-246. Confirmed backroads drivers will continue SE on SR-246/SR-154 to **Santa Barbara**. Alternatively, SR-246 leads quickly W to US-101.

For collectors of missions, one of the most beautiful, **La Purísima Concepción**, can be reached via a loop on the opposite side of US-101 from the Santa Ynez Valley. To reach La Purísima, exit from US-101 on SR-1 at Santa Maria. From the mission, it is possible to return to US-101 directly via SR-246 through Buellton, or to progress more slowly on the extension of SR-1.

Los Angeles-Santa Barbara day trip

See map opposite. From LA, head N on SR-1 through Oxnard to intersection with US-101; then follow the latter to its intersection with SR-33. Take SR-33 N to Ojai. From there, return to US-101 via SR-150 for the last few miles into Santa Barbara. Return to LA via US-101.

Santa Barbara provides a remarkable change of pace from Los Angeles. The small city, rich in Californian history, rich in resorts, and rich in per-capita income, strolls while Los Angeles runs, and sunbathes while LA talks business.

On US-101, getting there is not half the fun. The main highway follows a plodding route through built-up countryside for all but the last few miles. Meanwhile, the stretch of SR-1 from **Malibu** to Oxnard stays close to a remarkably unspoiled shore, and the detour into **Ojai** passes through pleasing farm country.

AREA: PALM SPRINGS, DEATH VALLEY, THE DESERTS

In California the word "desert" immediately evokes thoughts of **Palm Springs**, **Death Valley**, or both. This response is somewhat narrow, for there are thousands of square miles of desert in the state, but it is, in the main, correct. Little of the rest matters much to visitors, with the possible exception of **Anza-Borrego Desert State Park**, the formidably salty **Salton Sea**, and the banks of the **Colorado River** where it has been dammed to form **Lake Havasu**.

In fact, California has a **High Desert** and a **Low Desert**. Death Valley, in spite of ranging down to 272 feet below sea level, is part of the High Desert, a small area more formally known in California as the "**Mojave**," and contained entirely within the state. Palm Springs, at an elevation of 475 feet, is part of the Low Desert, which extends upward and eastward across Arizona under the general name of **Colorado Desert**.

No two areas of desert could be less like each other than Palm Springs and Death Valley. Palm Springs is all oasis, a veritable exposition of swimming pools, golf courses and tennis clubs. Death Valley, meanwhile, is pure stark desert, except for one small oasis supporting two hostelries and one golf course.

Palm Springs is less than two hours from downtown Los Angeles, just off freeway I-10. **Death Valley**, however, is not quite on the way to anywhere, being a considerable detour from freeway I-15 between Los Angeles and Las Vegas. In both places, November to March is the high season; April to May and September to October are the next most popular periods; and June to August is when places close down — or go half-price for serious desert rats.

Like Palm Springs, **Lake Havasu** is a sort of refutation of deserts: its principal attraction is its water. **Anza-Borrego State Park**, like Death Valley, preserves a pure patch of desert, although not in such dramatic terrain. The **Salton Sea**, believe it or not, is an attraction for fishermen, having been stocked with a salt-tolerant fish called corvina.

Most of the other places to stay in the desert are freeway towns such as **Barstow**, **Blythe** and **Needles**, all of them pleasant enough, but refuges rather than destinations for vacationers. A few towns just outside the Palm Springs zone cater to genuine desert rats, prime among them being **Yucca Valley** and **Indio**.

Los Angeles to Palm Springs
See map opposite.

Palm Springs, like San Diego, is an attractive place to visit from LA. Again, as in the case of San Diego, getting there is principally a means to an end. Surface transport, by car or by bus, is the most probable means. Amtrak does not serve the town, and only feeder airlines fly between LA and the desert resort.

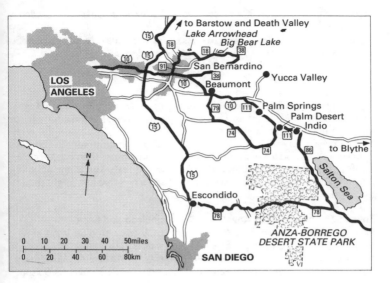

The quick way
See map above. I-10 courses swiftly from Downtown LA to the outskirts of Palm Springs, where SR-111 turns to the resorts.

Few attractions interrupt the journey, which is very nearly flat, and consistently in populous country.

The slow way
See map above. At the town of Beaumont, SR-79 turns s from I-10.

Following SR-79 to its junction with SR-74, then going E on the latter, adds both miles and time to the journey, but repays the cost with some of Southern California's finest mountain scenery, and the most dramatic entry into Palm Springs/Palm Desert.

A Low Desert loop
See map above. From LA, take I-15 to Escondido, then head E on SR-78 to its intersection with SR-86; then N on the latter to Indio; then w on SR-111 to the Palm Springs area. From Palm Springs, head N on SR-111 to I-10, then w to LA.

Although the drive can be made in one long day, more time is needed to savor this countryside.

The journey is most comfortable in the winter months, but most beautiful in March to April, the time when desert wildflowers bloom. In addition to miles of fine desert scenery in **Anza-Borrego Desert State Park**, the route touches the intensely saline **Salton Sea**.

A mountain escape
See map above. From the intersection of I-10 and SR-91 at San Bernardino, travel N on SR-91 to SR-18. SR-18 and SR-38 form a scenic loop through the San

Bernardino mountains. SR-38 connects with I-10 a few miles ε of its intersection with SR-91.

This route reaches **Lake Arrowhead** and **Big Bear Lake**, greatly favored as low-key retreats by Los Angeles residents.

GRAND TOURS

There is something endlessly beguiling about the idea of Grand Tours. Exhausting to both mind and body, they still appeal because they force so many reactions in so short a time.

The classic Grand Tours spanned the European continent in the days of luxury ships and luxury trains, and took in little more than capital cities. California is short on both luxury trains and capitals, but the state is big enough and diverse enough to permit several tours that just might qualify as grand.

Tour 1: The coast — Los Angeles to San Francisco and back

Maps 9 and 10, and map on page 190. From Los Angeles, N on SR-1 and/or US-101 to Santa Barbara. From Santa Barbara, N on US-101 to Avila Beach or Cambria. From that area, N on SR-1 to the Monterey Peninsula. From Monterey, N on SR-1 to San Francisco. From San Francisco, S on US-101 to San Luis Obispo. From San Luis Obispo, S on US-101 to Los Angeles.

The itinerary anticipates overnight stops in Santa Barbara, Avila or Cambria, and Monterey on the northward leg, and in San Luis Obispo on the southward run. This tour might just as well start in San Francisco as Los Angeles but, either way, when going N, use SR-1, which clings to sheer cliffs high above the sea for much of the distance between **San Simeon** and the **Big Sur** country, and travel s on US-101.

The basic program allows equally for luxury or budget travel all along. In either case, there are many attractions to choose from. In particular, the long haul from San Francisco to San Luis Obispo can be lightened with visits to **San Juan Bautista** and the **Mission San Antonio de Padua**. Serious eaters should attempt to arrive at mealtimes in **Half Moon Bay/Pescadero** and perhaps **Salinas** and **Solvang**, as well as the stopover towns.

This is an all-year route. Since so many of the attractions are man-made and indoors, winter rains do little to spoil the trip. The emphasis on human contributions does not mean there is no scenery; the shore and several inland valleys have moments of surpassing beauty, but scenery watchers may do best in spring or fall, when coastal fogs are less frequent.

Tour 2: Los Angeles to San Francisco through the Sierra

Maps 9 and 10. From Los Angeles N on I-5 and SR-99, then w on SR-198 to Hanford. From Hanford, ε on SR-198 into Sequoia National Park. From Sequoia National Park, w and N via SR-180, SR-41 and SR-49 into the Gold Country. From the Gold Country, SR-49 to its intersection with SR-89, then double back on SR-89 to Lake Tahoe. From Lake Tahoe, s on Nevada's SR-207-206 to SR-4, w on SR-4, then s on SR-49 and SR-120 to Yosemite National Park. From Yosemite, w on SR-120, I-205 and I-580 to San Francisco.

The itinerary assumes overnight stops at **Hanford**, **Sequoia National Park**, one of the **Gold Country** towns, **Lake Tahoe** and **Yosemite**. Because much of the attraction is scenery, the plan calls for some days of heavy driving. To give variety, the trip loops back on itself, rather than following the straightest possible line. The buttonhook route, having saved the high points for last, does not lend itself to a start from San Francisco.

A certain variation in the excellence of food and accommodations is to be expected along this route. Hanford and Tahoe contain the brightest opportunities for eaters, with the Gold Country coming not too far behind. Except for Tahoe, where a broad range exists, accommodations are quaint and comfortable rather than luxurious.

Fall weather tends to be sunny but temperate. In summer, much of the route can be very hot indeed. Spring weather puts these mountains in their best light, but chill rains are a possibility.

Tour 3. From Los Angeles to Las Vegas; the deserts

*Map **11** and **12**, and map on page 193. From Los Angeles, SE via I-15 and SR-78 to SR-86, then N on SR-86 and SR-111 to Palm Springs. From Palm Springs, N on SR-62 and SR-247 to Barstow. From Barstow, NW on SR-58, then N on US-395, and SR-178 into Death Valley. From Death Valley, SE on SR-190, SR-127 and SR-178 into Nevada.*

The itinerary assumes overnight stops in **Palm Springs**, **Barstow** and **Death Valley**. True desert rats may opt for **Indio**, **Yucca Valley**, or one of the other properly dry towns around Palm Springs. In the main, though, the route is designed to keep more than a modicum of comfort in the stops between Los Angeles and Las Vegas. Excellent accommodations and restaurants can be found at Palm Springs and Death Valley, and there are sound opportunities for both at Barstow.

As with all desert routes, the view tends to be depressingly familiar for miles on end. Scenic high spots come only now and again. In this case, **Anza-Borrego Desert State Park**, the **Salton Sea** and the mountains around Palm Springs provide a rich diet on the first day's drive. The road out of Death Valley has superb rocky formations for at least half of the journey to Las Vegas. Only on the third leg, from Barstow as far as Trona, does the pace slow to normal.

Winter, from November through February, is the most comfortable season for the tour. The following month, the chance of heat grows from possible to probable, but as this is the time when the wildflowers bloom in the desert, the price is not too great.

Vacationers planning to make this jaunt in late spring, summer or fall face a much reduced choice of accommodations, and truly great heat. Indeed, only experienced desert hands with reliable cars should consider attempting it. In any season, first-time visitors to the desert should study the basic rules of desert survival before setting out.

Wines and wineries

by Bob Thompson

Touring the vineyards

California is now considered to be among the best wine-producing countries of the world, but this status is relatively new. Although the state has been producing wine for 150 years, her modern wine industry has grown almost from scratch since the 1960s and is still expanding rapidly.

Nearly all the fine wines come from the coastal valleys close to San Francisco. However, California offers other regions that produce excellent wines and whose vineyards are a pleasure to visit. Within easy traveling distance of Los Angeles are the regions of **San Luis Obispo**, **Santa Barbara** and **Temecula**.

Every season has its charms, but April to May and September to November are the great months for photographers and picnickers, and harvest time in September and October is the most instructive. Veteran visitors recommend planning to visit no more than three cellars in a single day to avoid sensory overload.

It can be assumed that wineries welcoming visitors are open from 10am-4pm. Large wineries with guided tours tend to be open daily. Smaller ones usually close one or two days a week, so a telephone call first to check on opening times is recommended.

For road directions and visiting hours, request a free copy of *California is Wine Country* from the **Wine Institute** (*165 Post St., San Francisco, CA 94108* ☎ *(415) 986-0878*).

The wine regions

SAN LUIS OBISPO
Map **9H4**.

The county of San Luis Obispo has two vineyard districts, a warm one with a long history of growing fine Zinfandel, and a cool one with a quickly earned reputation for Chardonnay. The old-time area centers on the town of Paso Robles; the recently developed Edna Valley area lies just s of the city of San Luis Obispo.

Readily visited (tasting, sometimes tours)

CORBETT CANYON
2195 Corbett Canyon Rd., Arroyo Grande
☎*(805) 544-5800.*
Sizeable firm draws grapes from a wide area to make reliably attractive table wines. Shadow Creek sparkling wines come from the same cellars.

COTTONWOOD CANYON
4330 Santa Fe Rd., San Louis Obispo
☎*(805) 546-WINE.*
Newcomers to the region who specialize in Chardonnay and Pinot Noir.

EBERLE WINERY
Highway 46 East, Paso Robles ☎*(805) 238-9607.*
Winery with excellent record for Cabernet Sauvignon and Muscat Canelli.

EDNA VALLEY VINEYARD
2585 Biddle Ranch Rd., San Louis Obispo
☎*(805) 544-9594.*
Excellent barrel-fermented Chardonnay; good Pinot Noir, including rosé.

JUSTIN VINEYARDS AND WINERY
11680 Chimney Rock Rd., Paso Robles
☎*(805) 238-6932.*
Known for their Estate Chardonnay.

MAISON DEUTZ
453 Deutz Dr., Arroyo Grande
☎*(805) 481-1763.*
A Franco-American sparkling wine cellar, using traditional champagne-method techniques. Excellent cellar to tour.

MARTIN BROTHERS
2610 Buena Vista Rd., Paso Robles
☎*(805) 238-2520.*
Family winery making superb Chenin Blanc, Sauvignon Blanc and Chardonnay. Also a pioneer with Nebbiolo.

PESENTI WINERY
2900 Vineyard Dr., Templeton ☎*(805) 434-1030.*
A family-owned winery that makes a broad range of wines for the local market from its own 65 acres of vineyards.

ROSS KELLER WINERY
985 Orchard Avenue, Nipomo ☎*(805) 929-3627.*
Another newcomer producing a range of wines including Gewürztraminer, rosé and Johannisberg Riesling.

TALLEY VINEYARDS
3031 Lopez Dr., Arroyo Grande ☎*(805) 489-0446.*
All the wines are estate except for White Zinfandel from a neighbor's grapes.

WILD HORSE WINERY
2484 Templeton Rd., Templeton ☎*(805) 434-2541.*
Owner/winemaker Ken Volk is gaining a name for his Pinot Noirs. He also makes Cabernet Sauvignon, Merlot and Chardonnay.

YORK MOUNTAIN WINERY
York Mountain Rd. West, Templeton
☎*(805) 238-3925.*
Established in the 1880s, this winery is in the steep hills w of Paso Robles. A wide range of wines, including champagne, port and sherry.

SANTA BARBARA

Map 10/5.

Vineyards planted from 1970 onward have begun to earn this part of northern Santa Barbara County a considerable reputation, especially for white wines from Chardonnay, Sauvignon Blanc and White Riesling grapes. It is easy and pleasing to tour as a backroad alternative to freeway US-101 between Solvang and Santa Maria.

Readily visited (tasting, sometimes tours)

AU BON CLIMAT
PO Box 113, Los Olivos ☎*(806) 688-8630.*
Specialist in ultra-toasty single vineyard Chardonnays and firmly oaked Pinot Noirs.

THE BRANDER VINEYARD
2401 Refugio Rd., Los Olivos ☎*(805) 688-2455.*
Small cellar designed after *petit château* of Bordeaux specializes — fittingly — in estimable Sauvignon Blanc.

BYRON VINEYARD AND WINERY
5230 Tepusquet Rd., Santa Maria ☎*(805) 937-7288.*
Small, family-owned cellar is beautifully set in a remote canyon. The wines are worth the trip.

J. CAREY CELLARS
1711 Alamo Pintado Rd., Solvang ☎*(805) 688-8554.*
Winery in quaint old barn is a reliable source of a range of varietals; whites stand out.

FIRESTONE VINEYARDS
5017 Zaca Station Rd., Los Olivos ☎*(805) 688-3940.*
Broad list of appealing wines, especially Johannisberg (white) Riesling and Gewürztraminer. Cabernet Sauvignon sets standard for region. Excellent tours of modern cellar, the Santa Ynez Valley's largest.

FOXEN VINEYARD
Foxen Canyon Rd., Santa Maria ☎*(805) 937-4251.*
The aim of this vineyard is to make old-fashioned, hand-crafted French-style wines. They make Cabernet Sauvignon, Chardonnay, Pinot Noir and Chenin Blanc.

THE GAINEY VINEYARD
3950 Highway 246 East, Santa Ynez ☎*(805) 688-0558.*
A very broad range of wines, but the focus is on Cabernet and Chardonnay.

MOSBY WINERY AT VEGA VINEYARDS
9496 Santa Rosa Rd., Buellton ☎*(805) 688-2415.*
One of the newer wineries in Santa Barbara. They make Chardonnay, Gewürztraminer, Johannisberg Riesling and Pinot Noir.

OLD CREEK RANCH AND WINERY
10024 Old Creek Rd., Oakview ☎*(805) 649-4132 .*
A small winery with mostly local sales. It grows Chenin Blanc and Sauvignon Blanc on its own 10 acres, but makes other wines from bought-in grapes.

RANCHO SISQUOC WINERY
Foxen Canyon Rd., Santa Maria ☎*(805) 934-4332.*
Tiny, hidden-away cellar is appealing for all of its wines, all the more so for their rarity.

SANFORD WINERY
7250 Santa Rosa Rd., Buellton ☎*(805) 688-3300.*
Small cellar dedicated particularly to excellence in Pinot Noir, but also making fine Chardonnay, Sauvignon Blanc.

SANTA YNEZ VALLEY WINERY
343 North Refugio Rd., Santa Ynez ☎*(805) 688-8381.*
Sound wines across a ranging list.

ZACA MESA WINERY
6905 Foxen Canyon Rd., Los Olivos
☎*(805) 688-3310.*

Well-established firm offers a range of appealing, often stylish wines. Tours of well-equipped cellars are instructive.

TEMECULA
Map 11J7.

In relentlessly rolling hills just E of 1-15, between Riverside and San Diego, a plethora of small wineries has recently joined a pair of larger-scale pioneers who can be visited at the expense of a brief detour from the highway. New to winemaking, the district is still sorting out which are its most suitable grapes.

Readily visited (tours)

CALLAWAY VINEYARDS AND WINERY
32720 Rancho California Rd., Temecula
☎*(714) 676-4001.*
The pioneer and by far the largest of Temecula wineries. Excellent tours.

MAURICE CARRIE WINERY
34255 Rancho California Rd., Temecula
☎*(714) 676-1711.*
A family-owned winery which makes a broad range of wines plus a generic red named Cody's Crush and a generic white called Heather's Mist.

CULBERTSON WINERY
32575 Rancho California Rd., Temecula
☎*(714) 699-0099.*
Specialists in Champagne-method sparklers.

GALLEANO WINERY
4231 Wineville Rd., Mira Loma ☎*(714) 685-5376.*
The Galleanos offer a broad range of wines at their winery, including a Chianti, pink Chablis and Muscat.

MOUNT PALOMAR WINERY
33820 Rancho California Rd., Temecula
☎*(714) 676-5047.*
Small, with almost a countrified sense of style.

SAN ANTONIO WINERY/MADDALENA VINEYARDS
737 Lamar St., Los Angeles ☎*(213) 223-1401.*
A large concern with a broad range of consistently agreeable wines.

San Diego

Life's a beach

California began at San Diego in 1542 when Juan Rodriguez Cabrillo made the first landfall by a European at Point Loma. In 1769, Gaspar de Portola founded a presidio and Padre Junipero Serra planted a cross near the mouth of the San Diego River, establishing the first European settlement within the state.

Traces of Spanish history linger, but are scattered in this strikingly American city, the second largest in California. Perhaps the Middle America impression is exaggerated because the US-Mexican border and the city of Tijuana are just 18 miles south, but San Diego is still surprising after the Mediterranean flavors of other coastal cities all the way north to San Francisco.

The city doesn't really resemble either of its more celebrated neighbors to the north. It has neither the radical refinement of San Francisco, nor the glitz and excitement of Los Angeles. Perhaps what it really lacks is a mythology, something to capture the imagination. San Diego isn't really famous for anything; no gold rush, no love revolution, no Hollywood, no earthquakes, few celebrity residents to mention.

CONTEMPORARY SAN DIEGO

That said, it is pure California and deserves in some respects to be compared with both its neighbors. Some would say it has the best of each of them. There is an increasingly vibrant downtown, ritzy suburbs, a splendid urban park, history to spare, a lively performing arts scene, some excellent restaurants, and beach culture to rival anything to the north. The weather is certainly California's best; average daytime temperature is 70°F (21°C), humidity is low, smog is swept away by sea breezes, and annual rainfall is about 10 inches. And the city is neither as congested nor as frantic as one would expect of either the second biggest in California or the sixth biggest in the United States. The population of the city is roughly 1.1 million, and of the County 2.5 million.

Contemporary San Diego is a huge military port, major tuna-fishing harbor and commercial center, with literally hundreds of square miles of suburbs sprawling across a series of hills and mesas separated from each other by steep-sided arroyos (streams). Inevitably some parts are more attractive and interesting than others.

Nowadays, Downtown, officially dubbed "Central City," is one of them. Its resurgence is dated from 1985 and the opening of the wonderfully imaginative al fresco shopping complex Horton Plaza, which covers six-and-a-half city blocks, and is named, like much else in Downtown, after Alonzo Horton, the man who first developed the district in the 19th century. Since then much of the Victorian heart of the city, dubbed the Gaslamp Quarter, has been rescued from near dereliction, its lovingly restored buildings enlivened with restaurants, clubs, shops and hotels, and protected as a National Historic District.

Not that the Downtown area is simply an outpost of the heritage industry: if there's a second anchor to its renewed life and prosperity, it must be the new Convention Center, a striking waterfront artwork with roofs, quite literally, like sails. This development, along with other modernistic new buildings and many more painstaking restorations, speaks of a renewed confidence and vitality in the city. True, it lacks the charisma of California's two other great cities. But as an attractive destination for visitors it isn't only a match for them, it is nosing ahead.

THE GREATER CITY

The zoo, in Balboa Park near the city center, is one of the most famous in the world. The beaches at La Jolla, Pacific Beach, Mission Bay and Coronado have four entirely different characters. La Jolla smells even more of money than it does of salt water; it has the chic touches. Tom Wolfe found The Pump House Gang of surfers at Windansea at La Jolla in the early 1960s; today surfers still reign from Windansea south through Pacific and Mission Beaches to the San Diego River mouth, although nonsurfers also will be charmed by the affluent resort. The great recreation area of Mission Bay has no permanent population to speak of, only hotel guests, while Coronado is a peaceful, quiet, low-key community of people who delight in their isolation on the sandy peninsula that forms the outer side of San Diego Bay.

If San Diego's long history is not a magnet of quite the same power, it does lend some interesting fillips. Cabrillo National Monument, Old Town and Balboa Park's museums hold the highlights. Moreover, those parts of San Diego likely to interest visitors are relatively easy to reach, and there is less likelihood of getting totally lost, either geographically or otherwise, than in altogether huger Los Angeles. And, though an automobile is essential for moving around the greater city, there are many relatively compact areas — among them Downtown, Mission Beach, La Jolla, Coronado, Del Mar — where walking can be a delight.

San Diego's architecture

San Diego's most celebrated architect is Irving Gill (1870-1936), who started his own practice in the city in 1896. His inspiration was the Spanish Mission style with a dash of Cubism, and the results were straightforward reinforced concrete buildings employing simple geometric elements: straight lines, arcs, cubes and circles. Much of Gill's best work is to be found in La Jolla, notably the **La Jolla Women's Club** (1914) *(715 Silverado St.)*, the **San Diego Museum of Contemporary Art** (1916) *(700 Prospect St.)* and the **La Jolla Recreation Center** *(615 Prospect St.)*. Not by Gill, but also in the Spanish Colonial mold, is Downtown's **Santa Fe Depot** (1915, John Bakewell).

Equally noteworthy is the pioneering work of Bertram Goodhue (1869-1924). His interests were different. They included Ancient Egyptian, Persian, Byzantine and, most important, Spanish Baroque. Indeed, his work for the landmark Panama-California Exposition (1915-16) in Balboa Park, including the **California Quadrangle**, with its soaring **California Tower**, is credited with sparking a revival in Spanish Renaissance architecture throughout the state.

Surprisingly for change-mad Southern California, San Diego can also boast a marvelous concentration of fine Victorian buildings. Most are to be found in the lovingly preserved Gaslamp Quarter, and they include the **William Heath Davis House** (1850), a Cape Cod prefabricated saltbox on Island Ave. *(#410)* and now a museum, the one-time **Louis Bank of Commerce** (1887), the city's first granite building on 5th Ave. *(#835)*, now a restaurant, and the grandiose **Villa Montezuma** (1887) on K St *(#1925)*. Other precious Victorians have been relocated to Heritage Park in Old Town.

Of more recent construction, but warranting international attention, are La Jolla's **Salks Institute** (1963-65, Louis I. Kahn) *(10010 N Torrey Pines Rd.)*, a severe cluster of concrete buildings reminiscent of Le Corbusier, the harborside **Convention Center** (1990, Arthur Erickson), which suggests a modernistic sailing ship topped with teflon-coated sails, and the magnificently welcoming **Horton Plaza** shopping mall (1985, Jon Jerde), which achieves a mood somewhere between shoppers' theme park and 21stC urban piazza.

Visitors should watch out for all these and much more when touring San Diego. But most will probably want to make a social journey to the city's most visited attraction, the Cabrillo National Monument. Apart from the views, the highlight is the old **Point Loma Lighthouse** (1854). It was one of the first on the US Pacific coast and is probably the city's most beloved link with its past.

Basic information

Travel and transport

ABOUT THIS CHAPTER
Much general practical information of importance to visitors to San Diego applies equally to those visiting Los Angeles. See pages 42-58, and in particular **pages 42-46**.
What follows in this chapter is specific to San Diego.

GETTING THERE
By road   San Diego is located on the Pacific Coast, 127 miles s of Los Angeles. There are two major N-S routes:
- The I-5 coming down through LA and then skirting the coast, passing La Jolla, Mission Bay Park and Old Town before entering the city center.
- The I-15 coming from the NE, passing through Las Vegas and the Mojave desert before changing to the SR-15 and joining the I-5 just s of the city.
- Entry into the city is via the SR-163.

By air   San Diego is served daily by a handful of international carriers, all the major domestic airlines and various commuter airlines. The city's international airport, **Lindbergh Field** (☎ *(619) 231-5220),* is located on the shores of San Diego Bay, just $1\frac{1}{2}$ miles from Downtown. This is a supremely convenient arrangement for travelers, though less welcome to those beneath the flight path. There are taxis, shuttle buses and Avis, Hertz and National car rental agencies at the airport.

By rail and road   The city is also served by **Amtrak** (☎ *(800) 872-7245),* and the bus lines **Greyhound Lines** (☎ *(619) 239-9171)* and **Trailways** (☎ *(619) 239-9171),* with connections through Los Angeles. For anyone who enjoys railroads, the ride to or from LA, much of it along the Pacific coastline, is very pleasant.

DRIVING
Love it or loathe it, the automobile is far and away the best way to get around San Diego. The city and surrounding areas have an excellent network of freeways and main streets, allowing easy access to major attractions. Traffic flows freely most of the time, save for morning and evening rush hours, when Downtown and the Coronado Bridge are best avoided, and during the summertime weekend rush to the beaches. Parking is seldom a problem, except at busy beaches. But

expect to pay for it, either at on-street meters, which are closely policed, or in garages. Some stores and restaurants will validate parking for customers if asked.

Speed limits on freeways are 55mph, on streets usually 35mph. Drivers are ticketed for driving dangerously slowly as well as dangerously fast. Pedestrians have right of way at intersections and crosswalks.

Walking is recommended and enjoyable only at the beach towns and through the major shopping and entertainment streets of Downtown and the Gaslamp Quarter.

PUBLIC TRANSPORT

Not really a practical option for moving around the city: the best to be said for the **San Diego Metropolitan Transit** (**SDMT**) is that it is inexpensive to use. However, for anyone with curiosity and the time to ramble, the **Special Day Tripper Pass**, with unlimited access to city buses, the San Diego Trolley and the **San Diego-Coronado Ferry**, is a bargain. Tickets are available from the **Transit Store** (*Broadway and 5th Ave.* ☎ *(619) 233-3004, map 8 C4*).

The bright red **San Diego Trolley** (☎ *(619) 231-8549*) is a notable exception to the grim realities of public transport in Southern California. Riding it is a clean, reliable, fast and enjoyable experience. There are two lines: the East Line running from Downtown to El Cajon, and the South Line, which skirts Downtown's Bayside and Chula Vista before terminating at San Ysidro on the Mexican border. The trolley runs from Columbia and C Sts., two blocks E of Amtrak's Santa Fe Depot, between 5am and midnight. Other lines are planned.

Moving between the many attractions scattered widely throughout Balboa Park is easiest on the free **Balboa Park Tram**. It starts at the Inspiration Point Parking Lot and runs every day from 9.30am-5.30pm.

TAXIS

They are easy to find at airports, major hotels, attractions and Downtown, but not so easy elsewhere. Useful for short rides, they are otherwise expensive.

- **Coronado Cab** ☎ (619) 435-6211
- **La Jolla Cab** ☎ (619) 453-4222
- **Yellow Cab** ☎ (619) 234-6161

On-the-spot information

TELEPHONE AREA CODES AND 800 NUMBERS

Telephone numbers in San Diego (City and County) are prefixed by the **619** area code, followed by a 7-digit number. When dialing within San Diego, dial only the final seven digits. Omit the 619 area code. When dialing into San Diego from outside, say from Los Angeles, dial **1**, then **619**, then the 7-digit number. When dialing out of San Diego to none-619 areas, dial **1**, then the area code, then the number.

For toll-free numbers prefixed by **800**, inside or out of San Diego, dial **1**, then **800**, then the 7-digit numbers.

USEFUL ADDRESSES AND TELEPHONE NUMBERS
American Express Travel Service   1020 Prospect St., La Jolla ☎(619) 459-4161; Mission Valley Center, Ste 1424, 1640 Camino del Rio N ☎(619) 297-8101
Dentist referral   ☎(619) 223-5391
Doctor referral   ☎(619) 565-8161
Fire/Police/Medical emergencies   ☎911
Mexican Consulate   225 Broadway, Suite 225, San Diego 92101 ☎(619) 231-8414, map **7**C3
Mexican Government Tourist Office   600 B St., Suite 1220, San Diego 92101 ☎(619) 236-9314, map **7**C3
Recorded calendar of events   ☎(619) 239-9696
San Diego Convention & Visitors Bureau   1200 Third Ave., Suite 824, San Diego 92101 ☎(619) 232-3101, map **7**B3
San Diego Police Department (non-emergency)   ☎(619) 531-2000
Ticketron   Information ☎(619) 565-9949; sales ☎(619) 268-9686
Travelers' Aid   ☎(619) 232-7991
Weather and Beach Report   ☎(619) 225-9492

POST OFFICE
The main post office is located at 2535 Midway Drive ☎(619) 293-5410.

PHARMACIES
Harbor View Hospital Pharmacy   120 Elm St. ☎(619) 232-6341
Juniper Pharmacy   2272 1st Ave. ☎(619) 232-7353
Longs Drug Stores   71 Horton Plaza ☎(619) 231-9361, map **7**C3

TOURS
Gray Line Tours   ☎(619) 231-9922 for city tours
Harbor Excursions   ☎(619) 234-4111
San Diego Mini Tours   ☎(619) 234-9044

USEFUL PUBLICATIONS
The *San Diego Tribune* and the *San Diego Union* are the city's newspapers, especially useful to visitors in their Friday and Sunday editions. The *San Diego Magazine* is an upscale monthly glossy. The *San Diego Reader* is a free weekly, offering perhaps the best and most wide-ranging information on entertainment and nightlife.

The San Diego calendar of events

See also PUBLIC HOLIDAYS on page 51, WHALE-WATCHING on page 245, and the CALENDAR OF EVENTS for Los Angeles on pages 60-62.

JANUARY

Opera on the Concourse. Series of free lunchtime concerts. Opera, operetta and musical comedy outside Civic Theater ☎(619) 232-7636.
• **Martin Luther King Day Parade** ☎(619) 230-2050. • **San Diego Opera Season**. Through May, five grand operas at the Civic Theater.

FEBRUARY

Wildflowers Bloom in the Desert. Flowers bloom briefly in Anza-Borrego Desert State Park ☎(619) 767-5311.

MARCH

• **Ocean Beach Kite Festival**. Kite-building, decorating and flying contests for all ages ☎(619) 531-1527. • **St. Patrick's Day Parade**. Irish march and festival, with traditional music and dance ☎(619) 299-7812.

APRIL

Coronado Flower & Garden Show. Spring blossoms in Spreckels Park and Coronado's private gardens ☎(619) 437-8788. • **Del Mar National Horse Show**. Pacificside Fairgrounds host thousands of horses and riders in two weeks of competition ranging from show-jumping to Western ☎(619) 296-1441, 755-1161.

MAY

Pacific Beach Block Party. Free beach party with live music, arts & crafts, entertainment, food stalls ☎(619) 483-6666. • **Tijuana Bull-fighting Season**. Most Sundays, through mid-September, but not June ☎(619) 232-5049. • **Cinco de Mayo Festival**. Old Town San Diego State Park hosts Hispanic revels ☎(619) 296-3161.

JUNE

Indian Fair. Native Americans from throughout the southwest gather in Balboa Park. Tribal dancing, arts & crafts, ethnic food ☎(619) 239-2001. • **Del Mar Fair**. San Diego's annual County Fair. Carnival, entertainments, livestock shows, for three weeks ☎(619) 755-1161.
• **National Shakespeare Festival**. Old Globe Theatre, San Diego ☎(619) 239-2255.

JULY

Coronado Promenade Concerts. Eclectic musical mix of Sunday evening concerts in Spreckels Park. Concerts start 6pm, through September ☎(619) 437-8788. • **Twilight in the Park Summer Concerts**. Family entertainment in Balboa Park, Tuesdays, Wednesdays, Thursdays from 6.30pm, through Labor Day ☎(619) 699-4205.

• **Summer Organ Festival**. Mondays at 8pm at the Spreckels Organ Pavilion in Balboa Park, through September ☎(619) 226-0819. • **Coronado Independence Day Celebration**. Parade, rough water swim, Navy air/sea demonstrations and fireworks over Glorietta Bay ☎(619) 437-8788. • **La Jolla Independence Day Celebration**. Concerts in Scripps Park and spectacular fireworks display at La Jolla Cove ☎(619) 454-1444. • **San Diego Comic Convention**. Comics crowd San Diego Convention Center. Open to the public ☎(619) 525-5000. • **Starlight Musicals**. San Diego Civic Lights Opera in outdoor musicals at Starlight Bowl, Balboa Park ☎(619) 544-7827. • **Festival of Bells**. Marks the founding of California's first mission. Bells and animals are blessed at Mission San Diego de Alcalá ☎(619) 281-8449. • **World Championship Over-the-Line Tournament**. Beach softball elimination contest attracting thousands of competitors to Fiesta Island, Mission Bay ☎(619) 688-0817. • **Trek to the Cross**. Marks the founding of Mission San Diego de Alcalá in 1769 ☎(619) 298-7038. • **Mission San Luis Rey Fiesta**. Birthday celebrations of the "King of Missions," with carnival, flea market, Fiesta Queen Pageant and nonstop entertainment ☎(619) 757-3651, 757-7380. • **Free Summer Jazz Festival**. Saturdays from 5.30pm at the Old Ferry Landing ☎(619) 435-8895. • **Del Mar Racing**. Daily (except Tuesday) thoroughbred racing, through September at Del Mar Fairgrounds. • **Annual Sand-Castle Days**. Imperial Beach sand-castle/sculpture extravaganza ☎(619) 424-6663.

AUGUST
Latin American Festival. Arts, crafts, entertainment, food at Bazaar del Mundo, Old Town ☎(619) 296-3161. • **World Body Surfing Championships**. International competition starts at 6.30am at Oceanside Municipal Pier. Competitors and spectators welcome ☎(619) 966-4535. • **Annual Summerfest**. La Jolla Chamber Music Society hosts 12 concerts featuring top musicians ☎(619) 459-3728. • *Mariachi* **Festival**. *Mariachi* bands, food and entertainment at San Diego Concourse ☎(619) 299-2190. • **California Ballet Season**. Through March at different locations around the city ☎(619) 560-6741. • **Annual Greek Festival**. Live Dance (including lessons), entertainment, crafts, food at Saints Constantine and Helen Greek Orthodox Church in Cardiff-by-the-Sea ☎(619) 942-0920. • **Miramar Naval Air Station Show**. Military and civilian displays, including Blue Angels ☎(619) 537-NAVY.

SEPTEMBER
Annual American Indian Day. Arts & crafts, singers, dancers, food and entertainment in Balboa Park ☎(619) 281-5964.

OCTOBER
La Jolla Chamber Music Society Season. Through April, at the San

Diego Museum of Contemporary Art ☎(619) 459-3724. • **San Diego Symphony Season**. Through May, at the Copley Symphony Hall ☎(619) 699-4205. • **Annual Columbus Day Parade**. Through Downtown ☎(619) 698-0545. • **Annual Underwater Pumpkin Carving Contest**. Scuba divers in Halloween mood off La Jolla Shores ☎(619) 565-6054. • **San Diego Chamber Orchestra Season**. Through May, with guest artists ☎(619) 753-6402.

NOVEMBER

San Diego International Boat Show. America's best, with 500 exhibitors and 250,000 visitors at the Convention Center ☎(619) 274-9924.

DECEMBER

Annual Oceanside Children's Christmas Parade. High school bands, floats, Santa Claus from 10am ☎(619) 966-4530. • **San Diego Marathon**. Including 14 miles of "scenic coast line" ☎(619) 268-5882. • **Mission Bay Christmas Boat Parade of Lights**. Best views from Crown Point, E side of Vacation Island and W side of Fiesta Island ☎(619) 488-0501.

Sightseeing

San Diego's neighborhoods

Once upon a time San Diego County encompassed an astonishing 37,000 square miles, taking in much of Riverside, San Bernadino and Imperial Counties. Today it's smaller, covering 4,261 square miles, with the city proper spreading out from the harbor more than 20 miles to the N, S, and E. The population of the County is 2.5 million, that of the city over 1 million and rising, the whole spread through the collection of communities along the 76 miles of coastline down to the Mexican border and inland through the hills, canyons and valleys.

But for all that San Diego remains a major commercial port and a home to the US military, while having successfully transformed itself into a bustling metropolis, the place still feels like a resort. You can well imagine it being the sort of place where England's King Edward VIII would meet Mrs Wallace Simpson. Legend has it that they first met at the legendary HOTEL DEL CORONADO (see page 226). Today they'd probably be surfing or throwing frisbees on the beach.

Still, now as then, the city and adjacent parts of the County naturally break down into nine reasonably distinct areas. Those points of interest printed in SMALL CAPITALS in the following pages are discussed at much greater length in SAN DIEGO'S SIGHTS A TO Z, which follow on pages 216-223, and in NEARBY SIGHTS, on page 224.

DOWNTOWN *(see detailed maps 7-8)*

Downtown is most clearly identified as the area between San Diego Bay to the W, the I-5 (San Diego Freeway) to the N and E, and the Coronado Bridge to the S. It is laid out, more or less, in a grid system bounded on the Bay by Harbor Dr., with E-W streets numbered alphabetically and N-S streets numbered numerically.

The major E-W thoroughfare is Broadway. At the **HARBOR** end is the **Broadway Pier**, a renovated World War II pier that houses the **San Diego Maritime Museum**. To the E along Broadway is the **Santa Fe Depot** railroad terminus, a marvelous Spanish Colonial-style building dating from the 1915 Panama-California Exposition.

Between here and **HORTON PLAZA**, and the massive, pastel-hued shopping mall of the same name, there isn't much of interest, though most locals regard the mirrored skyscrapers built in recent years as a marked improvement on the sleazy bars, porn parlors and cheap hotels that they displaced. And most are also glad to see that the Neo-Baroque **Spreckels**

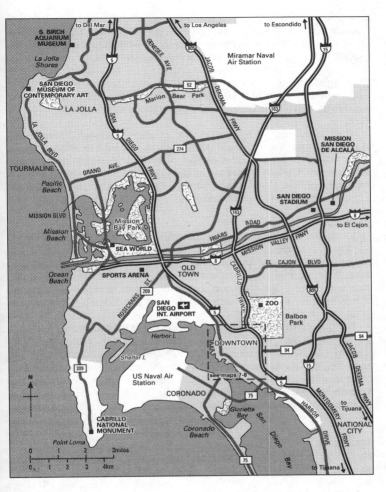

Theater *(121 W Broadway),* another legacy of the 1915 Exposition, has survived the re-development.

To the s of Broadway and Horton Plaza, in a long rectangle defined by 4th and 6th Aves. and W Harbor Dr., is the **GASLAMP QUARTER**, 16 blocks of Victoriana that far-sighted San Diegans have saved from demolition. The one-time red light district isn't yet fully restored to 19thC elegance, but already much has been done to repair and revitalize the area. There are red-brick sidewalks and Gaslamp-style street lamps. Many of the buildings have been restored to house hotels, shops, restaurants, cafés, theaters, nightclubs, offices, galleries and artists' studios.

The **William Heath Davis House** *(410 Island Ave.),* which dates from 1850 and is the Quarter's oldest surviving building, is now a museum. Other buildings worthy of special note are the **Louis Bank of Commerce** (1887), on 5th Ave. *(#835),* between E and F Sts, a Romanesque Revival Building that is probably the most beautiful in the Quarter. Legend has it that Wyatt Earp used to eat there in the days when the first floor housed an oyster bar. At the corner of F St. and 5th Ave is the **Keating Building** (1890) *(nowadays, Croche's restaurant, at 802 5th Ave.),* a fine example of Romanesque Revival that in its day was the final word in modern office buildings, boasting steam heating and a wire cage elevator.

There is much more to the Gaslamp Quarter than some distinguished buildings. Mostly, there's the chance to walk and explore. And, at night, the restaurant and nightclub scene is probably the most vivid and exciting in San Diego. Certainly there are long lines outside the hottest spots. It is a measure of Downtown's comeback that increasing numbers of people are choosing to live there as well as to work there.

OLD TOWN

This is where San Diego began. OLD TOWN is the compact area between the I-5 San Diego Freeway to the s and w, the I-8 Mission Valley Freeway to the N, and the altogether less engaging **Uptown** district to the E. It is said to attract more visitors than any other San Diego attraction, and that includes the Zoo and Balboa Park. Mostly it is a triumph of preservation and restoration and the slick, well-managed marketing of history.

The biggest draw is its three parks: **Presidio Park**, around the site of the first Spanish fort on **Presidio Hill**, the adjacent OLD TOWN **State Historic Park**, the one-time center of San Diego in an earlier incarnation, and **Heritage Park**, a sort of old homes' home for noteworthy buildings otherwise threatened with demolition. Also of note is the **Bazaar del Mundo**, an ersatz Spanish shopping plaza.

Shops, galleries and restaurants in the area are mostly to be found on San Diego Ave.

SOUTH BAY

This is the area between Downtown and the Mexican border, which takes in **National City**, **Chula Vista**, **Imperial Beach** and **San Ysidro**. Much of the South Bay area is served by the San Diego Trolley, which runs from Downtown's Santa Fe Depot to the Mexican border opposite Tijuana.

National City is primarily a concentration of shipbuilding yards, industry and commerce, though it does boast some beautifully restored Victorian homes. **Chula Vista** is the second largest city in San Diego County. Of most interest to visitors are its **Wildlife Refuge** *(at foot of E St.)* and an impressive range of sporting and boating facilities. Farther s, **Imperial Beach** is most famous for its annual sand-castle-building competition. End of the trolley bus line is **San Ysidro**, a good base for short trips into Mexico, though probably best known for its **Factory Outlet Center** *(4498 Camino de la Plaza),* which sells cut-price goods from more than 30 major retailers.

CORONADO

To the E of Downtown across a narrow stretch of San Diego Bay lies Coronado. Sometimes mistaken for an island, it is in fact a bulbous peninsula at the end of a long, narrow spit of sand.

There are three ways to get there: by road, either crossing the two-mile-long **Coronado Bay Bridge**, from which there are magnificent views over the harbor, or the long way around via the **Silver Strand Highway**, or by the **San Diego Bay Ferry** from Downtown's Embarcadero to Coronado's **Old Ferry Landing**.

The northern half of Coronado is a US Naval Air Station (from where Charles Lindbergh began his record-breaking flight in the *Spirit of St Louis*) and is off-limits to the public. The remainder of its 5.3 square miles refers to itself as **The Village**, and it is small enough, well-established enough, peaceful enough, and possesses sufficient sense of community to justify the appellation. Mostly the area is residential; the permanent population is around 25,000, not a few of them retired Navy personnel.

But 30 miles of sandy beaches (see BEACHES, page 243), several boating marinas, and the historic HOTEL DEL CORONADO (see page 226) are magnets for visitors. There is a **Trackless Trolley** to ferry non-drivers around the peninsula.

POINT LOMA

Commanding the other side of the entrance to San Diego Bay, to the N and W of Coronado, Point Loma is a 7-mile-long peninsula with water on three sides. Parts of it house US military installations; others are given over to the expensive homes of old-money residents, Hispanic architectural styles being the most popular.

Toward the southern tip of Point Loma is the CABRILLO NATIONAL MONUMENT, marking the first European landfall in California by Juan Rodriguez Cabrillo in 1542. The surrounding park has some rugged unspoiled scenery, an old lighthouse, spectacular views and lookout points for whale-watching. To the NW are **Sunset Cliffs**, sheer rock faces carved into bizarre jagged shapes by the surf. Point Loma, or more exactly the Shelter Island Yacht Harbor, is also home to the **San Diego Yacht Club**, more often than not the holder of the America's Cup. Sports fishermen and scuba divers depart from here on weekends.

MISSION BAY

To the N of Point Loma, this is San Diego's 4,600-acre aquatic playground. Mission Bay has only a small residential population, living in a assorted mix of condos, luxury houses and beach cottages along Mission Blvd., the main N-S artery. For the rest, it is almost all public parks, 27 miles of sandy beaches, the waters of the dredged-out bay itself, pleasure-boat moorings, hotels and restaurants.

And, of course, there is SEA WORLD, the aquatic theme park that is one of the city's most popular attractions. Every kind of water and beach sport is on offer, from jet-skiing and wind-surfing to roller-skating and kite-flying. The oceanside N-S **Boardwalk** offers a colorful moving tableau of Southern California beach bacchanalia at its most outrageous — and, on summer weekends and holidays, at its most congested. Among the latest attractions is **Belmont Park**, an 18-acre shopping and recreation complex complete with traditional roller coaster and fast food.

PACIFIC BEACH

To the N of Mission Bay lies Pacific Beach, in recent years transformed from sleepy suburb into one of the hippest of San Diego's beach communities. Much of the area is residential, wide streets lined with tall palm trees. But along **Ocean Blvd.** and **Garnet Ave.** are scores of fashionable bars, nightclubs, discos, restaurants and shops that attract young, boisterous crowds. **Ocean Boulevard Park** is designed for walking, bicycling or sunset-watching from the bluff top. And the centerpiece of all this, at the foot of Garnet Ave., is the 700-foot **Crystal Pier**, built in the 1920s and popular with fishermen and surfers.

LA JOLLA

La Jolla lies to the N of Pacific Beach, between the I-5 San Diego Freeway to the E and the Pacific Ocean to the W. The name translates from Spanish as *The Jewel*, and that is how its mostly well-off residents tend to regard it — as a kind of Monte Carlo West. More than anything, this suggests that few of them have visited the Mediterranean enclave. Pleasant and attractive as La Jolla undoubtedly is, it doesn't even begin to match up to the original.

At the same time, locals refer to its dinky commercial center as *The Village*, and they do this with justice. There is a strong sense of community, albeit a glossy, manicured, privileged community intent on keeping the grimmer aspects of reality at bay. Still, who can blame them? The atmosphere is relaxed and civilized. The streets, impeccably clean and lovingly planted with eucalyptus or palm, are small, human-scale and pedestrian-friendly. Along and around the axis formed by **Prospect St.** and **Girard Ave.** they are lined with discreet hotels, boutiques, galleries and restaurants. And the million-dollar-plus residential homes, clinging along the coastline or scattered across the inland hills, are testaments to good taste — provided your taste begins and ends with Mediterranean-style pastel stucco and red-tiled roofs.

The natural setting helps a lot: the sky is almost invariably a flawless azure blue, gentle breezes waft in off the ocean, and the seven miles of coastline provide a delightfully unpredictable mix of small sheltered beaches, coves, steep cliffs and tidal caves.

But La Jolla isn't only about genteel self-indulgence; just mostly. The SAN DIEGO MUSEUM OF CONTEMPORARY ART is sited here. And to the N of The Village is the splendid **La Jolla Shores** beach, the 1,000-foot **Scripps Pier**, the world-famous **Scripps Institute of Oceanography** and the STEPHEN BIRCH AQUARIUM MUSEUM. Still farther N is the TORRES PINES STATE RESERVE, a wild 1,700-acre preserve for the rare and ancient *Pinus Torreyana* trees.

To the E is the 1,200-acre campus of the **University of California at San Diego**, widely regarded as one of the country's intellectual powerhouses, and much of San Diego's reputation as a hi-tech trailblazer rests on work done here or at one of the nearby research institutes. A large academic community lives nearby. Overlooking all this is **Mt. Soledad**, an 800-foot hill with good views toward the sea.

SAN DIEGO COUNTY

By no means everywhere in the county area is worth a visit. So the remainder of this section covers only those places in the country that are especially interesting or engaging destinations worth the extra effort to get there. Among the worthiest are the coastal communities N of La Jolla, best explored via the too often neglected US-101, which parallels the ocean and runs gently through the seaside towns, changing its name as it goes.

Traveling N, the first stop is **Del Mar**, a well-groomed enclave of affluence that seeks, and probably succeeds, in outdoing La Jolla in good taste, real-estate prices and exclusivity. Its most famous attraction, founded in 1937 by the late Bing Crosby, is the oceanside **Del Mar Racetrack and Fairgrounds**, with a thoroughbred racing season running from July to September. At other times the town is a chic alternative to San Diego and its suburbs for dining, shopping, strolling and beautiful-people-watching. **Camino Del Mar**, particularly around the toney **Del Mar Plaza**, is the best place to do this.

Farther N, **Cardiff-by-the-Sea** is different again from Del Mar, and indeed Cardiff, Wales. It is a small, subdued beachside town, neither chic nor ostentatiously affluent, but unceremonious and congenial.

Even farther N, and altogether more zany, is **Encinitas**, home of the **Self-Realization Fellowship Retreat and Hermitage** for disciples of Yogi Paramanhansa Yogananda. The Yogi certainly chose a marvelous spot when he set up his retreat in the 1940s. The views and adjacent surfing beach, **Swami's**, are something special. So too are Encinitas' flowers. The town is famous for them, and they cover the inland hills.

Much of northern San Diego County is taken up by the 125,000-acre **Camp Pendleton Marine Corps Base**, but civilians are welcome to tour the base seven days a week. Inland San Diego County has less to offer than the coast. Much of it is arid and featureless, or dotted with nondescript new developments. The exceptions are **Mission San Luis Rey**, the MOUNT PALOMAR OBSERVATORY (see page 224) and the **San Pasqual Valley**.

San Diego's sights A to Z

In this section we explore the city's highlights in greater detail. Many of these are concentrated under single headings. Here is a list of places of interest covered under those headings, with their page numbers.

BALBOA PARK *(see pages 216-219)*
- Aerospace Museum
- Botanical Building
- California Tower
- Centro Cultural de la Raza
- International Aerospace Hall of Fame
- Museum of Man
- Museum of Photographic Arts
- Natural History Museum
- Old Globe Theatre
- Reuben H. Fleet Space Theater and Science Center
- San Diego Automotive Museum
- San Diego Model Railroad Museum
- San Diego Museum of Art
- San Diego Zoo
- Spreckels Organ Pavilion
- Starlight Bowl
- Timken Art Gallery

THE HARBOR *(see page 220)*
- Convention Center
- Maritime Museum

OLD TOWN *(see pages 221-222)*
- Bazaar del Mundo
- Casa de Bandini
- Historical Museum
- Junipero Serra Museum
- San Diego Union Building
- Seeley Stables
- State Historic Park
- Whaley House Museum

BALBOA PARK

Map 8A4-B6 ▣ to park itself, but ▩ to most exhibits within the park ✱ The new Balboa Park Tram is a convenient way to explore. It originates at the Inspiration Point Parking Lot and passes through the heart of the Park, stopping 11 times. The tram is free i at corner of El Prado and Plaza de Panama.

The oldest and one of the largest of the great municipal parks on the Pacific Coast, Balboa contains not only San Diego's famous zoo but many of the city's museums, and still has room to spare for outdoor theaters, a municipal golf course, picnic lawns and playgrounds. Near

Downtown, the park's main features are on or near El Prado, between the 6th Ave. and Laurel St. entrance and any of several entrances off Park Blvd.

Aerospace Museum and International Aerospace Hall of Fame

s of El Prado at 2001 Pan American Plaza ☎*(619) 234-8291* ▨ ✱ *Open 10am-4.30pm. Closed holidays.*

The **Aerospace Museum** is an extraordinary circular building commissioned by the Ford Motor Company for the 1935 California Pacific International Exposition. It contains a replica of Charles Lindbergh's *Spirit of St Louis,* built in San Diego, as was the original, by craftsmen from the Ryan company. But the most striking flying machine in the hall is Leonardo da Vinci's uncanny anticipation of the hang-glider. Other original and reproduction small aircraft span the age of flight from the Wright brothers to US Navy carrier jets. Under the same roof, the **International Aerospace Hall of Fame** honors great fliers with displays of memorabilia. At night, the outline of the museum is picked out spectacularly in blue neon.

Botanical Building

E half of El Prado ▨ *Open Sat-Thurs 10am-4.30pm. Closed Mon-Wed; holidays.*

The Botanical Building, in a former railroad depot, now houses lush collections of tropical and subtropical plants. Long lawns frame the large **Lily Pond** in front, which has giant koi fish and water lilies.

California Tower and Museum of Man

w end of El Prado ☎*(619) 239-2001. Museum* ▨ *open 10am-4.30pm, closed Jan 1, Thanksgiving, Dec 25.*

The original entrance to the park was the California Quadrangle, a group of Baroque buildings constructed as part of the 1915 Panama-California Exposition. The most striking feature, the **California Tower**, is a 200-foot-tall bell tower designed by Bertram Goodhue and Carleton Winslow (architects of the Los Angeles Central Library). Many consider it to be the finest example of Spanish Renaissance architecture in California, or indeed anywhere. The iron weather vane atop the blue-tiled tower is in the shape of a Spanish galleon like that sailed by Juan Rodriguez Cabrillo, the first European to explore San Diego Bay.

The **Museum of Man** *(under the California Tower)* has major sections dealing with prehistoric man and North American Indians. But by far the most intriguing permanent displays are Mayan. Lucid translations of religious symbols and the Mayan arithmetic system accompany massive original carved stones. Artisans sometimes demonstrate old crafts in the main foyer.

Natural History Museum

E end of El Prado ☎*(619) 232-3821* ▨ *Open 10am-5pm mid-June to Sept; 10am-4.30pm remainder of year. Closed Jan 1; Dec 25.*

The Natural History Museum contains paleontologic and contemporary displays of animals, plants and minerals. An especially contemporary note is struck in *On The Edge: Threatened, Endangered, Extinct,* an exhibit that looks at wildlife in peril and efforts to save it.

Performances

The **Old Globe Theatre** *(next to California Tower* ☎ *(619) 239-*

2255) is a reconstruction of the Bard's original theater in London and the site of San Diego's National Shakespeare Festival in June. Other performance spaces in the park include the **Spreckels Organ Pavilion** *(center of park* ☎ *(619) 226-0819)*, where frequent free concerts are given on the massive 5,000-pipe organ, thought to be the largest in the world located outdoors, and the **Starlight Bowl** *(next to Aerospace Museum* ☎ *(619) 544-7800)*, which presents popular musicals mid-June to early September.

Reuben H. Fleet Space Theater and Science Center
E end of El Prado ☎*(619) 238-1233* ✱ *Open 10am-9pm.*

This single building houses three attractions. The multimedia **Space Theater** (★ ▓▓) creates eerie illusions of travel in space via movies shown on a hemispheric screen, known as **OMNIMAX**, which is also used for conventional planetarium shows. The adjoining **Science Center** (★ ▓▓ ✱) teaches a broad range of scientific lessons both basic and complex through interactive displays that entertain children and adults alike. The **Laserium** has laser shows all day. Weekend crowds often overwhelm all three facilities.

San Diego Museum of Art
Midway along El Prado ☎*(619) 232-7931* ▓▓ *Open Tues-Sun 10am-5pm. Closed Mon; Jan 1; Thanksgiving; Dec 25.*

One of the most important museums in California, this has permanent collections of European masters from the early Renaissance to the early 20thC, as well as early American decorative arts and Mexican paintings. The Italian Renaissance, Dutch and Spanish Baroque collections are especially noteworthy. The Permanent Collection includes works by Bosch, Bronzino, Giorgione and Veronese. Also on display are Braque's *Still Life,* Rembrandt's *Young Man with a Cock's Feather in his Cap* and Reuben's *Allegory of Eternity.*

The **Sculpture Garden** features work by Moore, Hepworth, Rodin, Zuniga and Rickey. There is also a wing devoted to Asian art, featuring Indian and Persian paintings, Japanese prints and Buddhist sculptures and bronzes. A rental gallery has contemporary local works.

San Diego Zoo ★
Park Blvd. at Village Pl. ☎*(619) 231-1515* ▓▓ ⚹ ▣ ✱ *Open July 1-Labor Day 9am-6pm; Mar 1-June 30 and Labor Day-Oct 31 9am-5pm; Nov 1-Feb 28 9am-4pm.*

One of the most important and famous zoos in the world, this is home to some 800 animal species, including one of two koala groups in the US. Other collections of particular interest include primates and reptiles, and plants valued at $1 million.

Of course, ideas about zoos have changed since San Diego's was built in 1922, and it is possible that animal-loving visitors will be offended by some of its cages and sunken concrete enclosures. Not a few of the animals appear unhappy — scarcely surprising perhaps in the case of, say, the polar bears. Nevertheless, earnest efforts have been and continue to be made to create environments in which captive animals might lead lives that are both bearable to them and visible to the public.

Among the first to benefit from the bigger, more animal-friendly enclosures have been the African gorillas and the Sumatran tigers. The gorillas now have five times the space they had before. Work continues on creating approximations of natural environments for other animals, but there is still a long way to go.

Among the zoo's better aspects is its enthusiasm for real life conservation. Of particularly concern is the future of the earth's severely threatened tropical rain forests — a subject on which tour bus guides are both knowledgeable and outspoken. And children are well catered to at the **Children's Zoo**, where they are able to meet and pet a wide variety of creatures. The tour buses and an overhead tramway help visitors to get around the often steep 128 acres, but even with these aids this is a place for walking shoes.

If possible, avoid weekends, when the zoo is usually too crowded for comfort. The animals are most active early, before the heat of the day makes them drowsy. (See also SAN DIEGO WILD ANIMAL PARK on page 224.)

Timken Art Gallery

Near the middle of El Prado ☎*(619) 239-5548* ▣ *Open Tues-Sat 10am-4.30pm; Sun 1.30-4.30pm. Closed Mon; Jan 1; Sept; Thanksgiving; Dec 25.*

The privately endowed small museum contains a collection of Russian icons. There are, in addition, oil paintings by old masters, including Rembrandt, Rubens, El Greco and Brueghel.

And also . . .

Balboa Park has several smaller museums and cultural centers, as well as outdoor recreation grounds. Among them are the **Centro Cultural de la Raza**, which is dedicated to creating, promoting and preserving Mexican, Indian and Chicano art and culture; the **Museum of Photographic Arts**; the **San Diego Automotive Museum** (✵); and the **San Diego Model Railroad Museum** (✵). Also worth exploring are the park's several delightful gardens. A visitor center near the corner of El Prado and Plaza de Panama has maps and informative leaflets.

CABRILLO NATIONAL MONUMENT

At the end of SR-209 ☎*(619) 557-5450* ▣ ✵ ➤ *Open 9am-7.45pm mid-June to Labor Day; 9am-5.15pm rest of year.*

At the tip of Point Loma, this is among the most visited of all American national monuments or parks, preserving within 144 acres a micro-section of coastline said to be little changed from the day Cabrillo landed. Also within the monument are a lighthouse built in 1854; a lookout point for watching migrating gray whales from November through March; an

Old **Point Loma Lighthouse**

interpretive center; a statue of Cabrillo donated by Portugal; and some fine tidepools. Not least, the high ground affords magnificent views back to the city: the old lighthouse stands 420 feet above sea level.

GASLAMP QUARTER

Between 4th Ave., Broadway, 6th Ave., and Harbor Dr. ☎ *(619) 233-5227. Map 8C4-D4* ✗ *(see below)* **i** *Gaslamp Quarter Foundation, 401 Island Ave.*

Creeping restoration of the Victorian Quarter is one of the most welcome and exciting developments in San Diego in recent years. A walking tour of the 16-block district begins at 11am on Saturdays. But most people will be happy just to wander, admiring the renovated buildings and exploring the many shops, galleries, restaurants and clubs that are enlivening the previously seedy district.

The Foundation is headquartered in the **William Heath Davis House** *(see address above)*, a mid-19thC, two-story, Cape Cod wooden prefab moved to its present location from New Town and restored as a museum in 1984. However, gentrification of the area is far from complete, and panhandlers and derelicts appear still to find it irresistibly attractive. So have your wits about you, especially after dark.

THE HARBOR

Map 7A2-8E4.

San Diego crowds the most interesting parts of its great harbor into a stretch reaching from Grape St. on the N side to the B St. Pier, encompassing within eight blocks its Maritime Museum and working piers for the tuna fleet. The Embarcadero runs right along the seawall. Seaport Village lies just s; the small boat harbors and marinas of **Harbor Island** and **Shelter Island** (see FISHING on page 244) are not far N, but are out of easy walking distance.

Three vessels form the heart of the **San Diego Maritime Museum** *(1306 N Harbor Dr., at foot of Broadway* ☎ *(619) 234-9153* 🗺 🚗 ✻ *open 9am-8pm)*. The centerpiece is the square-rigged *Star of India*, built in Great Britain in 1863 as the *Euterpe* and now the oldest merchant ship afloat and seaworthy. Berthed with her are the old San Francisco Bay ferryboat *Berkeley* and the British-built luxury steam yacht *Medea*. The vessels contain displays of local maritime history; women are requested to wear low heels for below-deck touring.

At Grape Street Pier the docks are built so that passers-by can watch tuna fishermen mending their nets. Also on the Harbor, at the foot of 5th Ave., is an eye-catching addition to the waterfront scene, the $165-million **Convention Center**. Since it opened in November 1989, the building has become a city landmark. As well as its convention facilities, there are public amenities, notably a bayside amphitheater and an outdoor plaza for bay-watching.

HORTON PLAZA �🏛

In Downtown, on 1st and 4th Aves., between Broadway and G St. ☎ *(619) 239-8180. Map 7C3. Stores open Mon-Fri 10am-9pm; Sat 10am-6pm; Sun 11am-6pm. Restaurants and theaters have extended hours.*

Even if Horton Plaza didn't offer the best concentration and selection of shopping in San Diego, it would be a major attraction. Even in Southern California, where a great deal of thought and money goes into creating shopping malls, there has really been nothing to match it since it opened in 1985. Above all, it is a celebration of the city's al fresco lifestyle, managing at the same time to be a kind of urban theme park, wittily and extravagantly echoing the Southland's architectural heritage.

The Plaza is big: five floors high and ranged across six city blocks. Though there are 140 of them in all, for the most part the department stores, shops, restaurants and 7-screen cinema are familiar enough to mall enthusiasts. It is the arrangement that is different and fun: around a series of wide open-air galleries overlooking a central first-floor palazzo, all connected with a zany crisscrossing of stairways and escalators, the whole vividly colored, and provided with 2,300 parking spaces to accommodate the daily crowds.

Doubtless what architect Jon Jerde and the developers had in mind was to encourage upscale shoppers to explore ever farther into the complex and to linger — in which case they succeeded with a vengeance. Expect to spend at least one hour and probably a lot longer, even if you only stopped by for a toothbrush. The top deck especially offers great views of Downtown and the waterfront.

Elsewhere there are usually mime artists, jugglers, jazz bands and street musicians adding to the carnival atmosphere. If that isn't enough, the Plaza also houses the **San Diego Repertory Theater** *(79 Horton Plaza)*. If any single development can take credit for the Downtown revival, this is it.

MISSION SAN DIEGO DE ALCALÁ ▥

10818 San Diego Mission Rd. Take I-8 E to I-15/Murphy Canyon Rd., then N
☎*(619) 283-7319* ▨ ▬ *Open daily 9am-5pm. Closed Dec 25.*
The first of the 21-mission chain, now on a sharp knoll looking across to ultramodern **San Diego Stadium**, the mission chapel, a small museum and garden create a serene atmosphere, although not quite a sense of earlier times, owing to overwhelming development around and about. Father Junipero Serra founded the mission in 1769, then moved it from its original location near Old Town to this site in 1774.

OLD TOWN

Close to the intersection of I-5 and I-8. For State Historic Park ☎*(619)*
237-6770 ✗ *daily at 2pm. Cars are banned from the park, so all tours are on foot* ℹ *Visitor's Center, 4002 Wallace St.*
Near the site of Gaspar de Portola's original presidio, Old Town preserves some of the earliest buildings in San Diego's first civil community. A **State Historic Park** encompasses about half of a 12-square-block area rescued from decay as part of the city's observance of the US bicentennial.

The park and its surrounding area contain examples of adobes from the Spanish population and brick or frame buildings from the early Anglo settlers. Construction dates range from 1810-70. These buildings house an engaging mixture of museums, shops and restaurants. The main area is bounded by Juan St. and Congress St. and by the Pacific Highway and Twiggs St. Limited parking and some large open spaces mean a good deal of walking across fairly level ground.

Inside the park there are several small museums. One, simply called **The Historical Museum**, has a model of Old Town in 1870, plus displays of artifacts. The **San Diego Union Building** *(2626 San Diego Ave. ☎ (619) 297-2119* 📷 *open 10am-6pm, closed Jan 1, Thanksgiving, Dec 25)* is a reconstruction of the original offices and production plant of the city's major newspaper. **Seeley Stables** *(2648 Calhoun St.* 📷 𝙆 ✳ *open 10am-6pm summer, 10am-5pm rest of year, closed Jan 1, Thanksgiving, Dec 25)* houses a collection of horse-drawn vehicles including some stagecoaches. Other buildings include an early schoolhouse and several residences and small businesses.

One of the most impressive structures, **Casa de Bandini** *(2660 Calhoun St.)*, is occupied by an elegantly furnished Mexican restaurant of the same name. The hacienda was originally built in 1829 for Juan Bandini, a Peruvian who at that time was the town's richest man. Of more doubtful provenance is the **Bazaar del Mundo** *(2754 Calhoun St.)*. A tiny part of it dates back to the early 19thC; the rest is an imaginative 1970s addition. In some ways it is like Los Angeles' Olvera St., writ large. Still, the colorful bazaar, with its shops and restaurants, is very popular with visitors who incline to the view that this is what early San Diego *should* have been like.

Outside the park are two more historic museums. To the E, **Whaley House Museum** *(2482 San Diego Ave. ☎ (619) 298-2482* 📷 *open Wed-Sun 10am-4.30pm)*, San Diego's first brick house, is a restoration of a prestigious family's residence built in 1857. To the N, the San Diego Historical Society's **Junipero Serra Museum** *(2727 Presidio Dr., Presidio Park ☎ (619) 297-3258* 📷 *(but donation requested), open Mon-Sat 9am-5pm, Sun noon-5pm, closed Jan 1, Thanksgiving, Dec 25)* houses important early documents and artifacts and a scholarly library.

SAN DIEGO MUSEUM OF CONTEMPORARY ART 🏛

700 Prospect St. and Eads Ave., La Jolla ☎ (619) 454-3541 📷 *Open Tues-Fri 10am-5pm; Sat-Sun 12.30-5pm. Closed Mon; hols.*

The only art museum in the region focusing exclusively on modern art and design has both a permanent collection and traveling exhibitions. The best of the permanent 20thC collection are post-1950s, Minimalist, Pop and Post-Modern works. These include Warhol's *Flowers,* Oldenburg's *Alphabet, Good Humor,* and Kelly's *Red, Blue, Green.* The museum also takes a lively interest in film, and there is an annual festival of animation.

The building itself is of interest. Built by architect Irving Gill in 1916, and reflecting his devotion to the plain white walls, sweeping arches and boxy shapes of both Mission and International styles, it was originally the oceanside home of Ellen Browning Scripps. In 1941 local art lovers bought it, for $10,000, and turned it into a museum.

For some 18 months from late 1992 the museum will be closed for wholesale renovation. Architect Robert Venturi, responsible for the Sainsbury Wing of the National Gallery in London, will be paying homage to Gill, while adding new spaces, an enclosed sculpture garden, more library and education space, and a café. Meanwhile, **SDMoCA Downtown**, a brand-new 10,000-square-foot triangular building at Kettner and Broadway opposite the Santa Fe Depot *(map 7 C2)*, will take over. When the La Jolla restoration is finished, probably in 1994, the museum will continue in both locations.

SEA WORLD ☆

1720 South Shores Rd., San Diego; exit w off I-5 onto Sea World Dr. ☎*(619) 226-3901* ▪ *✗* ▪ *✱* ▬ *Open daily 9am-dusk.*

At the s shore of Mission Bay, this first-rate 150-acre marine zoological theme park is built around sensational shows by killer whales, porpoises and other sea mammals, but is hardly limited to them. No less than 16,000 creatures live here: marine mammals, penguins, fishes, reptiles and invertebrates. The spacious grounds have educational exhibits, a petting pool, and a recreation area for children called **Cap'n Kids World**. Some of the aquariums, notably the **Shark Exhibit**, are spectacular. But the cutest creatures on show have to be the Alaska sea otters rescued from the calamitous *Exxon Valdez* oil spill in 1989.

STEPHEN BIRCH AQUARIUM MUSEUM ☆

8602 La Jolla Shores Dr. ☎*(619) 534-6933* ▣ ▬ *✱ Open daily 9am-5pm.*

A new $9-million complex of 36 aquariums. It replaces the Scripps Aquarium, which opened in 1950 and won a worldwide reputation. The new facility promises to be even better. Displays include tanks of rare fish from around the world, models of tidepools, and depictions of oceanographic research work. Main feeding times for the animals are Sunday and Wednesday at 1.30pm. A shuttle bus takes visitors from parking lot to aquarium.

TORRES PINES STATE RESERVE ◁€

12000 N Torres Pines Rd., between La Jolla and Del Mar, one mile s of Carmel Valley Rd., via I-5 freeway. For **i** ☎*(619) 755-2063* ▣ *✱* ▬ *Open 9am-sunset.*

This is a place that almost always features when native San Diegans are asked to identify their favorite haunts. The wild 1,700-acre reserve was established in 1921, primarily to protect the extremely rare and picturesque *Pinus Torreyana,* trees that are found only in two parts of California. (The other is Santa Rosa Island, off Santa Barbara.) The gnarled and wind-bent trees, atop 300-foot-high cliffs, are said to date from the Ice Age. There are several hiking trails winding through the groves of pines. Views over the ocean, especially at sunset, can be magnificent. The wide, sandy beach too is a treasure.

Nearby sights

Two of San Diego's intriguing contributions to science lie to the E and NE of the city in desert hills. Farther N lie the nearest vineyards.

MOUNT PALOMAR OBSERVATORY

Palomar, N of Escondido, 20 miles E of I-15 via SR-76 ☎*(619) 742-3476* 💷
➤ *Open daily 9am-5pm. Closed Dec 25.*

One of the world's great optical observatories, Palomar has the 200-inch (5-meter) **Hale Telescope**, among others. In the same building, the **Greenway Museum** displays photos of the observatory's sightings.

SAN DIEGO WILD ANIMAL PARK

15500 San Pasqual Valley Rd., Escondido ☎*(619) 234-6541 or (619) 231-1515* 🃏 🖵 ⚥ ➤ *Open mid-June to Labor Day 9am-9pm; Labor Day-Oct 31 and Mar 1 to mid-June 9am-5pm; Oct 31-Apr 30 9am-4pm.*

This 1,800-acre property belonging to the San Diego Zoological Society is a beautifully natural home for more than 2,200 free-roaming African and Asian animals. It is also both a reverse zoo (human visitors get around in monorail cars or other cages) and a pseudo-safari theme park complete with restaurants, live music shows and other diversions.

TEMECULA VALLEY VINEYARDS

60 miles N of San Diego, just E of the I-15 freeway: exit onto Rancho California Rd. 𝒳 𝒾 *SO Coast Vintners Association, PO Box 1601, Temecula, CA 92390* ☎*(714) 699-3626.*

These Southern California vineyards, actually in Riverside County, are not as celebrated as the well-established names from the wine country in the N of the state, and they probably don't deserve to be. Not yet anyway. But they are easily accessible from San Diego, and are well worth a visit, for wine lovers at least.

Temecula's first shot at cultivating grapes for wine was in the 1840s. The soil, and the climate, with a gap in the coastal mountain range channeling cooling breezes into the valley, create growing conditions said to be similar to those in the South of France. The business didn't really take off until the 1960s and '70s. But now there are 11 wineries scattered across the foothills of the valley, all of them offering tastings and tours. Some make a small charge, others do not. Most have picnic areas and shops selling their wines at prices slightly below normal retail, as well as specialty foods.

Temecula vintages include Cabernet Sauvignons, Chardonnays, a variety of *méthode champenoise* whites, blushes, Muscat Canelli dessert wines, and even a cream sherry.

See also WINES AND WINERIES, page 199.

Where to stay

Making your choice

San Diego County has an ample range of accommodations from luxury to budget, and everything in-between. As you'd expect in a city where the slogan of many is "Life's a beach," there is an exceptional choice of hotels on or near the ocean, often with contiguous sandy beach. Particularly enchanting areas are **La Jolla**, **Del Mar** and **Coronado**, all of which are well provided for.

The principal alternatives for visitors are either these resort-style properties or hotels in **Downtown**. The relative ease of moving around San Diego means that either option will work equally well for business and/or pleasure. The more appealing of the Downtown hotels are to be found around the **harbor**, near **Horton Plaza** or in the **Gaslamp Quarter**. Among them are several thoughtful restorations of older buildings. The breadth of choice and convenience is more limited in other areas.

SHOP AROUND
Frequently room rates are lower during the winter months. What's more, thousands of new hotel rooms are coming on stream as San Diego blossoms. So it could pay to shop around. The accommodations detailed below are, in our view, the best. But the listing is limited by space.

Particulars of the full range of hotels and motels in the San Diego area are available from the **San Diego Convention & Visitors Bureau** *(1200 Third Ave., Suite 824, San Diego, CA 92101* ☎ *(619) 232-3101* ☒ *(619) 696-9371, map 7B3).*

HOW TO USE THIS CHAPTER
The following alphabetical list of hotels is selective, covering a broad spectrum of size, price, area and character. Addresses, telephone and fax numbers are given, and other symbols denote many categories of information, from ◀€ (good view) to 👥 (conference facilities). The luxury hotel (🏨) and good-value (♣) symbols are awarded in only a small number of cases.

See HOW TO USE THIS BOOK on page 7 for a full list of symbols.

Price categories for hotels listed on the following pages are intended only as guidelines to average prices. There are four bands: inexpensive (▥), moderate (▥), expensive (▥) and very expensive (▥). They are based on the approximate cost, in fall 1992, of a double room with bathroom, including the cost of breakfast. Single rooms are not much cheaper. Even with cost inflation, hotels will normally remain in the same price category.

Symbol	Category	Current price
▥	very expensive	over $210
▥	expensive	$160–210
▥	moderate	$100–160
▥	inexpensive	$50–100

San Diego's hotels A to Z

DEL CORONADO ▥ ★
1500 Orange Ave., Coronado, CA 92118
☎(619) 435-6611 ▥ to ▥ 691 rms ⚓
≋ AE ⊕ ⊙ VISA ⚲ ≪ ≋ ⚲ ≋ ≋
‡ □ ⌂ ⚲ Y ♫ ♩ ☂ ▣

Location: Fronting the beach on the w side of Coronado peninsula. The Hotel Del, as the locals call it, has been a San Diego institution since 1888, and whether you stay there or not it demands to be visited. After all, it is designated an Historic National Landmark. The location is as splendid as ever, the external aspect as majestic, and the views and Pacific sunsets, seen through swaying palm trees from the balcony of oceanside rooms, are romantic and memorable. The wooden red and white Victorian gingerbread buildings, especially the main dining room, with its 30-foot-high sugar pine ceiling, the quaint antique elevators and peaceful courtyard are rich in historical echoes: from Edward VIII and Mrs Wallace Simpson, who are said to have met here, to Marilyn Monroe, who filmed *Some Like It Hot* here with Jack Lemmon and Tony Curtis, to a dozen US Presidents who have stayed here.

That said, the Del seems to be trading somewhat on its vivid history. To be honest, it has seen better days. A century on, the hotel is neither intimate and friendly nor grand and luxurious. Some imaginative refurbishment would work wonders, as would a concerted attempt to speed-up the service. Be warned also that the evening brings squadrons of noisy, low-flying US Navy aircraft heading home to the N of the Coronado peninsula. Still, families with children and a feel for history will probably enjoy it and remember their stay forever.

THE EMPRESS HOTEL OF LA JOLLA ✿
7766 Fay Ave., La Jolla, CA 92037
☎(619) 454-3001 Fax(619) 454-6387 ▥
72 rms ⊟ ≋ AE ⊕ ⊙ VISA ⚲ ⚲ ♫ ⚲
‡ □ ⌂ ⚲ ☂ ▣

Location: Four blocks from the beach in the heart of La Jolla. For more than a decade this was a residential hotel for well-heeled, long-stay guests. The intimacy and friendliness of that era have survived a change of ownership and extensive modernization and remodeling. The rooms are bright and spacious, particularly the suites, which are equipped with a huge free-standing Jacuzzi bathtub in a corner of the bedroom, and a useful kitchenette. As well as offering a complimentary Continental breakfast, the Empress has an award-winning Italian restaurant, **Manhattan** — with *singing* waiters. Though not as close to the beach as some La Jolla hotels, it is within gentle walking distance of pretty much everything the Village has to offer.

OTHER LA JOLLA INNS OF AMERICA

Among other members of this generally excellent chain in the San Diego area are: **Pacific Terrace Inn** (☎ *(619) 581-3500 ▥ to ▥*), a deluxe Motor Inn with large, modern rooms and balconies overlooking Pacific Beach, and **Stratford Inn** (☎ *(619) 755-1501 ▥*), a comfortable motor inn close to both Del Mar beach and the race track. For central reservations ☎(800) 367-6467.

HORTON GRAND ▥

311 Island Ave., San Diego, CA 92101
☎*(619) 544.1886* ▣*(619) 239-3823.*
Map 8D4 ▥ *110 rms* ⬛ ➡ ▣ ▣ ▣
▣ ⬛ ⬥ ☐ ▣ ⬥ ▼ ▤

Location: Downtown, in the Gaslamp District, 3 blocks N of the Convention Center. Another charming Gaslamp District renovation, although strictly speaking the Victorian-era component parts of this building began life elsewhere. The resulting amalgam still has an authentic period feel to it, not least because of the small wrought-iron balconies, net curtains and fireplaces. The historical ragbag, which includes a small Chinese museum, a restaurant named after a once infamous brothel-keeper, and an incongruously bright and spacious lobby, have nevertheless made for a winning combination for those eager to get a taste of the District's vivid past. Certainly, the Horton Grand is loaded with historical echoes and continues to play a part in bringing the Gaslamp back to life. It is slightly less convenient for the area's nightlife than other hotels a few blocks N, but is perfectly located for the convention center and the harbor. The rooms are cozy, and the bar serves high tea.

HORTON PARK PLAZA ▥

520 E St., San Diego, CA 92101 ☎*(619) 232-9500* ▣*(619) 238-9945. Map 8C4*
▥ *65 rms* ⬛ ➡ ▣ ▣ ▣ ⬥ ◁ ⬛
⬥ ☐ ▣ ⬥ ▼ ▤ ⬛ ⬥ ▼ ♪ ⬥

Location: Downtown, in the Gaslamp District, one block E of Horton Plaza. Before extensive renovation and conversion in 1988, this 1913-vintage building was the San Diego Savings Bank and then the city's Jewelry Exchange. The new owners did not skimp on the job, and the work of skilled craftsmen is much in evidence. Nowadays it is a small, stylish, European-style hotel, well located for Downtown business and recreation. There are marvelous cityscape views from the rooftop terrace of the **Gaslamp Club**, where complimentary Continental breakfast is offered, and some of San Diego's liveliest nightlife, and its best shopping, is just minutes away. Rooms are large and tastefully furnished. One warning — the street life can become boisterous after midnight, so light sleepers should request a high floor. These also, as it happens, have the best views, particularly the W-facing rooms, which look across the city to San Diego Bay.

HYATT REGENCY LA JOLLA

3777 La Jolla Village Dr., La Jolla, CA 92037 ☎*(619) 552-1234* ▣*(619) 552-6066 ▥ to ▥ 400 rms* ⬛ ➡ ▣
▣ ▣ ▣ ⬥ ⬥ ⬥ ▼ ⬛ ⬥ ☐ ▣ ⬥
▼ ♪ ⬥ ▤

Location: One block E of the I-5. This is part of **The Aventine**, an ambitious and controversial 1989 development of hotel, offices and restaurants, in the hills to the NE of La Jolla Village. Some locals love it, others hate it. The hotel demands a response. Architecturally it is a medley of borrowings, from ancient Rome to Post-Modern and much else in-between. Interior design is equally audacious and makes a refreshing change from the ersatz Victoriana that so often seeks to pass itself off as luxury in four-star hotels. There is a fabulous health club right next door.

LE MERIDIEN ▥

2000 2nd St., Coronado, CA 92118
☎*(619) 435-3000* ▣*(619) 435-3032*
▥ *to* ▥ *300 rms* ⬛ ➡ ▣ ▣ ▣ ▣
⬥ ⬥ ⬥ ⬥ ⬥ ▼ ⬛ ⬥ ☐ ▣ ⬥
▼ ♪ ⬥ ▤

Location: On the Bay, N of Coronado Bridge. In the early 1980s Coronado residents thought long and hard about the kind of development that should be approved for this 16-acre site overlooking San Diego Bay. They seem to have chosen well. The understated luxury of Le Meridien, with low pastel buildings set amid tropical gardens, waterfalls and lagoons, could scarcely be bettered. The decor is French Provincial, and rooms, bathrooms and terraces are all extra large. And for those who demand additional privacy and pampering, there is a small complex of one- and two-bedroom villas with private swimming pool. As befits such a ritzy resort hotel, the recreational facilities are first-class: in addition to all the facilities you'd expect, there are a few you wouldn't, including a dock for pleasure craft, waterskiing, cycling, and a championship golf course next door. There is also a water taxi running between the hotel and Downtown. Le Meridien's restaurants, **L'Escale** and especially MARIUS (SEE WHERE TO EAT), are outstanding.

SAN DIEGO HILTON BEACH AND TENNIS RESORT

1775 E Mission Bay Dr., San Diego, CA 92109 ☎*(619) 276-4010* Ⓕ*(619) 275-7991* ▥ *to* ▥ *354 rms* ➤ ➾ ▣
▣ ▣ ▥ ⅋ ⅋ ⟪ ➤ ➤ ▣ ⅋ ⅏
▢ ▨ ⅋ ♈ ⅋ ⟫ ▣

Location: In Mission Bay Park, just n of Sea World Dr. When development of the Mission Bay area began 30 years ago, Hilton were quickest to spot the recreational potential, and here is the result: a delightful tropical parkland setting, spectacular views, a beach on the doorstep, and just about every aquatic diversion you can think of. Obviously, the hotel isn't as up-to-the-minute as the newer resort properties. But rooms in the main building are spacious, with patio or balcony. And there are more exclusive bungalows in the grounds. For those who want to mix business with pleasure, Downtown is just a short ride down the nearby I-5.

ANOTHER HILTON

Also in the Greater San Diego area is **Del Mar Hilton** (*15575 Jimmy Durante Blvd., Del Mar, CA 92014* ☎ *(619) 792-*

5200 Ⓕ*(619) 792-9538* ▥ *to* ▥*),* adjacent to Del Mar Race Track, $\frac{1}{2}$ mile from the beach and shopping, with lots of sporting amenities within the hotel.

SHERATON GRAND TORREY PINES 🏨

10950 N Torrey Pines Rd., La Jolla, CA 92037 ☎*(619) 558-1500* Ⓕ*(619) 450.4584* ▥ *to* ▥ *400 rms* ▣ ➾ ▣
▣ ▣ ▥ ⅋ ⅋ ⟪ ➤ ➤ ➤ ⅋ ⅏ ⅏
▢ ▨ ⅋ ♈ ⅋ ⟫ ▣

Location: n of La Jolla Village, to the w of the I-5. Rooms in this 1989-vintage Sheraton are arranged to take full advantage of the glorious location. All have balconies or patios, many with ocean views, others overlooking the beautifully tended gardens. The Torrey Pines is at the gilt-edged end of the Sheraton spectrum; rooms are spacious, and the decor takes inspiration from the natural surroundings — plenty of daylight, wood and stone. Service too is emphasized, with a butler on every floor. **Torrey Pines Golf Course** is right next door, and **Black's Beach**, La Jolla's strictly illegal but nonetheless popular nude beach, is nearby.

OTHER SHERATONS

. . . in the San Diego area include **Sheraton Grand on Harbor Island** (*1590 Harbor Dr., San Diego, CA 92101* ☎ *(619) 291-6400* Ⓕ *(619) 294-9627* ▥ *to* ▥*),* close to the airport and Downtown, with great harbor views, and **Sheraton Harbor Island Hotel** (*1380, Harbor Island Dr., San Diego, CA 92101* ☎ *(619) 291-2900* Ⓕ *(619) 294-3279* ▥*),* a more modest motor inn with the same convenient location and captivating views.

US GRANT 🏨

326 Broadway, San Diego, CA 92101 ☎*(619) 232-3420* Ⓕ*(619) 232-3626. Map 7C3* ▥ *to* ▥ *280 rms* ▣ ➾ ▣
▣ ▣ ▥ ⅋ ♈ ⅋ ⅏ ▢ ▨ ⅋ ♈ ⅋ ▣

Location: Downtown, across the street from the Horton Plaza. Like much else in Downtown San Diego, the Grant languished in the 1960s and '70s. And, like much of Downtown, it recovered both its prestige and respectability in the '80s. Indeed, after a 3-year, $80-million restoration of the original, opened in 1910 by the son of the President it was named after, the Grant is an altogether more deluxe place than ever before. The chandeliered lobby is popular with monied locals, and the **GRANT GRILL** (see page 234) is a San Diego institution, though like many such the reputation rests more on familiarity than any culinary genius. Rooms are very comfortable, and a few of the suites verge on the magnificent. Some visitors might find the atmosphere and the decor rather too formal and stuffy. And it's easy to believe that women were barred from the lunchtime Grill until 1972. Still, the Downtown location is convenient for business travelers, the address remains celebrated, and the service is attentive.

LA VALENCIA

1132 Prospect St., La Jolla, CA 92037
☎*(619) 454-0771* ☒*(619) 552-6066* ▥
100 rms ⬤ ⇶ ᴀᴇ ⊕ ⊙ ᴠɪsᴀ ⌂ ⚓ ⟨⟨
⩫ ⬥ ♆ ✦ ⬜ ⬖ ⁒ ⟁ ⬥ ▣
Location: La Jolla Village, two blocks from the ocean. Soon after it opened in 1926, La Valencia became a firm favorite with vacationing Hollywood stars. La Jolla has grown since then, and today's Hollywood stars tend to jet-set farther afield, although celebrity sightings in La Valencia's serene lobby are still reported. It remains quiet and exclusive. Many of the rooms have delectable views over La Jolla Cove and the ocean, and the beach is just a short walk away. True, the decor looks somewhat dated, most of the rooms are not very big, and the ambience is a bit snooty. But that could be counted as part of the charm. La Valencia has plenty of regulars, service is impeccable, and the hotel's **Whaling Bar** is a must for the socially aspiring.

WESTGATE

1055 2nd Ave., San Diego, CA 92101
☎*(619) 238-1818* ☒*(619) 232-4526.*
Map 7C3 ▥ *to* ▥ *223 rms* ⬤ ⇶ ᴀᴇ
⊕ ⊙ ᴠɪsᴀ ⚓ ⬥ ✦ ⬜ ⟁ ⁒ ⬥ ▣
Location: In the Downtown financial district, one block N of Horton Plaza. It is a matter of taste whether you find the Westgate a temple of European-style elegance or an overdose of baroque self-indulgence, horribly misplaced in Southern California. Either way, the hotel offers affordable luxury, with lavishly appointed public areas and comfortable rooms. Not the place for beach bums, but very fine for city types.

Where to eat

Innovation and excitement

A decade ago it would have been difficult to sing the praises of many of the city's restaurants. Food and service were generally second-rate. Things have changed, and how! Nowadays locals spend an average of $2,000-plus a year on eating out. In San Diego these days it can be a glorious experience, especially for lovers of seafood and Cal-Mex cuisine.

Both of these passions make sense. San Diego has long been, and remains, a major fishing port with fresh fish and shellfish landed daily. As for the Mexican connection, the border is just 15 miles to the s. No major US city is closer.

Not too long ago the cooking tended toward what could be called the traditional: a mostly European tradition of somewhat overcooked seafood, endless lobster thermidor and heavy fish stews, and a South of the Border tradition with Mexican dishes, groaning platefulls of *tamales, burritos* and re-fried beans. Both traditions still have their exponents.

But ideas travel fast in California and, as is the case farther N, what's in vogue is lighter, healthier food. Fish is flash-grilled or broiled. Delight is found in novel combinations and natural flavors, rather than bulk and an overwhelming embellishment of fresh ingredients. The new wave of young chefs draw up their menus on the basis of which ingredients are best and freshest, so what's on offer can change frequently.

San Diego continues to have its fair share of what are known, dismissively and unfairly, as "meat and potato restaurants," serving unimaginative and reliable American grills. But they are no longer the benchmark of good eating. California's cuisine is still evolving, and cosmopolitanism is at work here just as it is in Los Angeles and San Francisco. There are fine Italian, Japanese, Thai, French and Greek restaurants. The exchange of ideas and techniques, especially the trans-Pacific marriage dubbed "Cal-Asian," promises more innovation and excitement to come.

Save for a handful of places that take themselves far too seriously, informality is the norm, and, wherever humanly possible, a wonderful ocean view, or at very least an imaginative decor, comes on the house. Just as remarkable, prices tend to be very reasonable, even at the posh end of the market.

HOW TO USE THIS CHAPTER
The following alphabetical list of restaurants is selective, covering a broad spectrum of cuisine, price, area and character. Addresses and

telephone numbers are given, and symbols denote other useful points of information, from ▆ (good wines) to 🍴 (open-air dining). The luxury restaurant (⬡) and good-value (♣) symbols are awarded in only a small number of cases.

See HOW TO USE THIS BOOK on page 7 for a full list of symbols.

Price categories for restaurants listed on the following pages are intended only as guidelines to average prices. There are four bands: inexpensive (▥), moderate (▥), expensive (▥) and very expensive (▥). They are based on the approximate cost, in fall 1992, of a meal for one with service, tax and house wine. Even with cost inflation, restaurants will normally remain in the same price category.

Symbol	Category	Current price
▥	very expensive	over $65
▥	expensive	$45–65
▥	moderate	$30–45
▥	inexpensive	under $30

San Diego's restaurants A to Z

ANTHONY'S STAR OF THE SEA ⬡
1360 N Harbor Dr., San Diego ☎(619) 232-7408. Map **7B2** ▥ 🍴 ◀€ ▆ ▼ AE ● VISA Open nightly 5.30-10.30pm.

Anthony's isn't likely to appeal to anyone wanting to be at the cutting edge of San Diego style and culinary innovation. But if tradition, pampering and predictability attract, then this is the place. One of the few San Diego restaurants to require male diners to wear jacket and tie, it is a formal, expertly choreographed experience. Your waiter will be wearing a tuxedo, will know everything about the dishes on offer, and will do a creditable tableside performance with crepes suzette. Plenty of crystal and silverware, elegant furnishings and an enviable waterfront location add up to an undeniably exclusive experience. Seafood predominates, although, by current mores, it is overdone and old-fashioned. The hors d'oeuvres, particularly the simple shellfish dishes, can be very good. Entrées are reliable European standards that thumb a nose at faddish innovation. Puddings are rich and uncompromising. Reservations are essential. *Special-*

ties: Littleneck clams; sole stuffed with lobster; crabmeat and shrimp; lobster thermidor.

ATHENS MARKET TAVERNA 🍴
109 West F St., San Diego ☎(619) 234-1955. Map **7C3** ▥ to ▥ ▼ 🎵 ♣ AE ● ● VISA Open Mon-Thurs 11.30am-11pm; Fri-Sat 11.30am-midnight; Sun 4-11pm.

This cozy Greek taverna is atmospheric any time of the week. But it really lets down its hair on weekend nights when belly dancers take to the floor, between bouts of traditional Greek dancing. The food is unfussy and authentic, the portions generous. *Specialties: Greek salad; lokaniko; roast lamb; baklava.*

CAFE JAPENGO
8960 University Center Lane, La Jolla ☎(619) 450-3355 ▥ to ▥ 🍴 ▼ AE ● ● VISA Open Mon-Fri 11.30am-2.30pm, 5.30-10.30pm; Sat-Sun 5.30-10.30pm.

Very popular with trendy 20-somethings, Cafe Japengo is not so much Cal-Asian as Asian-Cal. The menu draws freely on known Oriental dishes, then gives them a California twist. The hi-tech decor and the slick waiters are as voguish as the food and the clientele. There are booths for those who want a degree of privacy, and a *sushi* bar. *Specialties: Roasted red snapper; Thai pork with basil and eggplant; fried rice.*

FAT CITY

2137 Pacific Coast Highway, San Diego. **Tropical Patio** ☎*(619) 232-2334,* **China Camp** ☎*(619) 232-1367,* **Top's Grill** ☎*(619) 232-2334* ▥ to ▥ ➳ 🚗 ⚏ ▰ ♈ ♒ ⚱ AE CD VISA *Open Mon-Thurs 11am-midnight; Fri-Sat 5pm-2am; Sun 5pm-midnight.*

Seen from the outside, especially at night, Fat City appears to be a wonderfully vulgar confection: a flight of Art Deco fantasy lit with garish neons of pink and electric blue. In fact, it houses three distinct restaurants with just one thing in common, a magnificent 30-foot-long Art Nouveau rosewood and teak bar allegedly dating from the turn of the century. The bar itself is popular for drinks, snacks, coffee and desserts. The **Tropical Patio** is for casual open-air snacking amid palms and flowers, with live entertainment and dancing at the weekend, and champagne brunch in the warmer months. Award-winning **China Camp** aims to re-create the mood of a 19thC California mining camp. One suspects that the food now, Cantonese, Mandarin and Szechuan-style favorites, is better than the food then. **Top's Grill** is another example of California meets Pacific Rim Asia. Out of the wood-burning brick oven come consequences like Peking duck pizza. Not the finest dining in town, perhaps, but lively, enjoyable and, rare in Southern California, open till late. The Fat in Fat City, by the way, isn't a comment on the customers or the food; it's named after the owner, Tom Fat.

FIO'S ▥

801 5th Ave., San Diego ☎*(619) 234-3467. Map* **8***C4* ▥ to ▥ ♈ AE CD CD VISA *Open Mon-Thurs 11.30am-3pm, 5-11pm; Fri-Sat 11.30am-3pm, 5pm-midnight; Sun 5-11pm.*

Fio's is one of the most chic and popular restaurants in the Downtown area. The Gaslamp District location certainly helps. Fio's is at the heart of what is probably the hottest concentration of nightlife in San Diego. The restaurant is housed in a fine Victorian building, and a great deal of effort has gone into its stylish, award-winning decor. There are Etruscan columns, a granite bar, open kitchen, well-spaced tables and booths, crisp white tablecloths, impeccable service and, on the other side of large picture windows, a lively street scene. A large part of Fio's attraction is the chance to see and be seen. It's seems like a bonus that the California-Italian food is of the highest order. *Specialties: Designer pizzas; linguine with smoked scallops; spit-roasted duck.*

THE FISH MARKET/TOP OF THE MARKET

750 N Harbor Dr., San Diego ☎*(619) 232-3474. Map* **7***C2* ▥ to ▥ ➳ ◁≪ ♈ AE CD CD VISA *Open daily 11am-10pm.*

A big harborside complex is home to these two seafood restaurants. They are part of a wider Southern California enterprise that has six restaurants, two fishing boats, a fishery, an oyster farm and its own smokehouse. Both are good fun, good value, and serve a staggering variety of fish, shellfish and crustaceans from local and more distant waters. **The Fish Market**, on the first floor, is the cheaper, more informal of the two. The emphasis is on fresh ingredients simply prepared and presented. The **Oyster Bar** and the **Sushi Bar** exemplify this, while fish is more often than not mesquite charbroiled. There is a retail seafood market near the entrance. Upstairs, **Top of the Market** is also mostly about seafood, and many of the dishes on offer are the same as those downstairs. At least the basic ingredients are. Preparations are still simple, but the sauces and garnishes are more innovative and exciting. There's also the added choices of veal, steak, lamb chops and a wider selection of pasta combinations and salads. The upstairs wine list too is longer and more impressive. Still, the main pluses of upstairs over downstairs are a more elegant decor, a less raucous atmosphere, and fabulous views across the harbor to the Coronado Bay Bridge. The drawback, of course, is higher prices. *Specialties: Steamed shellfish combination; Oysters Rockefeller; warm spinach salad with baby scallops; charbroiled Hawaiian Albacore; zabaglione.*

IL FORNAIO

301 Del Mar Plaza, 1555 Camino Del Mar, Del Mar ☎*(619) 755-8876* ▥ *to* ▥ ↝ ◈ ➡ ⌂ ⴲ ᴀᴇ ◉ ᴠɪsᴀ *Open Mon-Thurs 7am-11pm; Fri 7am-midnight; Sat 8am-midnight; Sun 8am-11pm.*

Located atop Del Mar's new, elegant, upscale mall, this outpost of the Italian-based Il Fornaio chain justifies on its own the drive N from San Diego. The cuisine is Northern Italian, with its deepest roots in Tuscany, although fresh local produce is used wherever possible. The main strengths are the pizza, mesquite-grilled seafood, and spit-roasted game and poultry. That said, the antipasti, pasta, breads and puddings are also very good indeed.

Really spectacular are the interior design and setting. The main dining area is rich in marble, polished woods and hand-painted murals, with a non-stop floorshow provided by chefs at work in an open kitchen along one side of the room. There is also a pleasant bar and a bakery counter. Outside is a large terrace, with blissful views across the ocean. The smart but relaxed, sometimes boisterous, utterly contemporary mix is proving very successful. Il Fornaio is usually overflowing with stylish people having a good time. Even those with reservations can expect a wait to be seated. Opposite is **Enoteca**, a wine bar under the same ownership, with a wider selection of wines than the restaurant itself. There is a nominal corkage charge on bottles bought from Enoteca for drinking in Il Fornaio. *Specialties: Calzone; spinach and egg linguine with shrimps, garlic and parsley; Italian sausages with stewed peppers and grilled polenta; bistecca alla fiorentina; warm bread pudding.*

FRENCH SIDE OF THE WEST

2202 4th Ave., San Diego ☎*(619) 234-5540* ▥ ■ ⴲ ᴀᴇ ◉ ᴠɪsᴀ *Open Mon-Thurs 5.30-9.30pm; Fri-Sat 5.30-10.30pm; Sun 5.30-9.30pm.*

The specialty at this rustic, authentically French restaurant is the fixed-price menus, including daily specials. Four- and five-course dinners include *charcuterie,* soup, salad, a choice of entrée, and pudding, and are exceptionally good value. Since opening in 1988, The French Side has regularly been voted into the top handful of Continental restaurants by customers and critics alike. The ambience is best described as candle-lit intimate, and there is an almost reverential respect for good food. Reservations are essential. *Specialties: Charcuterie; steak with white peppercorn sauce; chicken in mushroom and tomato sauce.*

GEORGE'S AT THE COVE ⌂

1250 Prospect St., La Jolla ☎*(619) 454-4244* ▥ *to* ▥ ↝ *by valet* ◈ ➡ ⌷ ■ ⌂ ⴲ ᴀᴇ ◉ ◉ ᴠɪsᴀ *Open Mon-Thurs 11.30am-2.30pm, 5.30-10pm; Fri-Sat 11.30am-2.30pm, 5-11pm; Sun 10am-3pm, 5-10pm.*

When George Hauer opened his namesake restaurant in 1984, its *nouvelle* style seemed a tad trendy for monied La Jolla. Nowadays it ranks with the best and most fashionable places not just in La Jolla but in greater San Diego, and has become almost a regular hangout for high-achieving baby boomers with educated palates. It deserves to be; George's gets everything right. The oceanside location with views of the Pacific is superb, booths and tables are well spaced across the main dining room, the welcome and the service are friendly, the atmosphere toney but relaxed, the mood romantic and convivial, the clientele smart but unstuffy, and the food manages to be wonderfully innovative and consistent at the same time. The staple here is seafood fresh from the quay, the preferred style *nouvelle* California, with a menu that changes according to the best that's available. A few entrées cater to unreconstructed meat-eaters, but even these benefit from imaginative flourishes; the New York Strip, for example, comes with caramelized garlic *demi-glacé*. There is also an impressive and sensibly priced list of mostly California wines. Sunday's champagne brunch adds whole new meanings to eggs benedict.

Upstairs is **George's Ocean Terrace and Cafe**, with a bar and large open-air terrace offering views even better than those in the main restaurant. The food here is less expensive but every bit as exciting, especially the rôtisserie specialties and Cal-Mex dishes. The crowd is younger and more rakish than down below (see GEORGE'S CAFE, page 239). *Specialties: Salmon and shrimp sausage with sweet and sour cabbage; abi flash-grilled rare with wasabi and poppyseed sauce; linguine tossed with grilled scallops in garlic herb broth; blueberry cobbler.*

THE GRANT GRILL ⌂

326 Broadway, San Diego, in the US Grant Hotel. ☎*(619) 239-6806. Map 7C3*
▥ to ▥ ▬ ☎ ⌑ ▤ ▾ AE ⊕ VISA
Open Mon-Fri 7am-2pm, 5.30-11pm; Sat 5.30-11pm. Closed Sun.

Like the hotel that houses it (the US GRANT), the Grill underwent a costly renovation in the early 1960s. The opulent dining room looks better than ever, but the cooking hasn't quite recovered the authority of earlier years, when women were banned at lunchtime and this was San Diego's last word in power dining. Tradition and simplicity of preparation remain the keynotes, with heavy-duty roasts, grilled meats and seafoods. The burgers and the cheeseboard are exceptional, and the lunchtime buffet is good value for hearty eaters. *Specialties: Mock turtle soup; daily roast; cheeses.*

MARIUS ⌂

2000 2nd St., Coronado, in the Le Meridien Hotel ☎*(619) 435-3000* ▥ to ▥ ▬
▬ ⌑ ▤ ▾ AE ⊕ ▢ VISA *Open Tues-Sun 6-10.30pm. Closed Mon.*

Well-heeled foodies usually rate this award winner the best restaurant in town, though it is too formal for some tastes. Still, the country-French decor and the Provençal cuisine, with some uniquely Californian spins, make for a delightful dining experience. It is difficult to fault anything. From tableware, to flowers, to service, to exquisitely presented dishes, everything is as it should be. Of course, there are prices to match, although the daily menu degustation can be considered a bargain under the circumstances. *Specialties: Lobster broth; breast of duckling with honey and lemon; roasted pineapple with ginger.*

PACIFICA GRILL

McClintock Plaza, 1202 Kettner Blvd., San Diego ☎*(619) 696-9226. Map 7B2* ▥
▬ ⌑ ▤ ▾ AE ⊕ ▢ VISA *Open Mon-Fri 11.30am-2.30pm, 5.30-10pm; Sat 5.30-10.30pm; Sun 5-10pm.*

This is one of the restaurants we must applaud for helping transform eating out in San Diego from humdrum to fun, as well as for rescuing and remodeling a turn of the century warehouse. Pacifica is sometimes accused of copycatting current San Francisco restaurant styles, and the high ceilings, stark decor, generous spaces, floorshow kitchen layout and breezy manner do seem to echo the northern city. And why not? Everyone, including the staff, appears to be enjoying themselves hugely.

The food is quintessentially contemporary southwestern: a kind of Cal-Mex-Asian hybrid, grounded in seafoods and mesquite grilling, but with plenty of inventiveness alongside. Service is attentive and well informed, while the California wine list is thoughtful and reasonably priced. Indeed, the entire Pacifica experience is excellent value for money, not least the daily *Cinco Platos* menu fixed price. The custom, like the food, is eclectic. *Specialties: Warm spinach salad with grilled lamb and oyster mushrooms; takoshimi of peppered Hawaiian ahi with Chinese salsa; cornflour fettucini with chile-spiced shrimp, crab and scallops; crème brulée.*

PANDA INN

506 Horton Plaza, San Diego ☎*(619)*
233-7800. Map 7C3 ▥ ☐ ➡ 🚗 ☐ ■ ☿
🆎 ⊙ 🆅 *Open daily 11am-10pm.*
Nowadays San Diego is a match for Los
Angeles and San Francisco when it
comes to California cuisine and its
numerous mutations. Authentic
Chinese restaurants still have some way
to go before they impress as much.
That's not to say that Panda Inn isn't
good, just that it doesn't begin to rival
similar establishments in, for example,
LA's Monterey Park or San Francisco's
Chinatown. Probably the simple reason
is that there isn't a comparably large and
discriminating Chinese community to
push its standards along. Still, the restaurant, on the top deck of the marvelous Horton Plaza shopping mall, is in a
pleasant spot and serves piquant Szechuan and Hunan dishes. The locals love
it. *Specialties: Hunan-style lamb;
chicken in garlic sauce; sweet and pun-
gent shrimp.*

PEOHE'S

1201 1st St., Old Ferry Landing, Coronado
☎*(619) 437-4474* ▥ ◀€ 🚗 ■ ☿ 🆎
⊙ ⊙ 🆅
The overwhelming attraction of
Peohe's is the prime Coronado location,
with a spectacular view of San Diego
Harbor and Downtown. The decor too
is striking: a tropical whimsy of waterfalls, lush vegetation, bridges, and even
slips for diners arriving by private boat.
There is a patio dining area to make the
most of all this. The emphasis is on fresh
seafood, and the options include an
oyster bar. *Specialties: Oysters; lobster
club sandwich; paella.*

TOP O' THE COVE ⌂

1216 Prospect St., La Jolla ☎*(619)*
454-7779 ▥ *to* ▥ ➡ *by valet* ◀€ ▬
☐ ■ ☿ 🐦 🍴 🆎 ⊙ 🆅 *Open Mon-Sat*
11.30am-2pm, 5.30-10.30pm; Sun
10.30am-3pm, 5.30-10.30pm.
The core of this cliff-top building overlooking La Jolla Cove dates back to
1884, when a wealthy San Diegan built
it is as a beach bungalow, and it ceased
to be a private house only in 1955. Since
then it has developed into a venerable
La Jolla institution, easily identified by a
towering Morton fig tree, usually lit up
with fairy lights, in its streetside courtyard. The Pacific ocean views and sunsets are spectacular and these, along
with impeccable service, candlelight,
English-quaint decor, and an almost
ethereal atmosphere have won it a reputation for romantic dining. The much
sought-after tables by the windows are
essential for the full effect. The menu is
Continental, and while the food is much
better than reliable, it is not cutting-
edge California. But those exhausted by
the drive for ever wackier marriages of
diverse flavors and techniques will probably applaud this. Certainly, Top o' the
Cove has plenty of monied regulars returning time and again for the certain-
ties of its salads, seafood, veal and lamb
specialties. The chef talks regularly with
local fishermen, and daily fish dishes
change with market availability. There
are some interesting fixed-price menus,
and the wine list, with more than 900
selections, is extraordinary, with prices
to match for the most distinguished vintages. *Specialties: Fettucine del mar; esca-
lope de veau aux champignon; côte
d'agneau; poisson du jour.*

Affordable eats

One of the many appealing things about San Diego is that it is possible to eat well, inexpensively, and in pleasant surroundings. The following is a selection of the wide range of available cuisines.

BBQ
Clay's Texas Pit Bar-B-Q   5752 La Jolla Blvd., La Jolla ☎(619) 454-2388
Kansas City Barbecue   610 W Market St. ☎(619) 231-9680, map 8D4

BREAKFAST
Cafe Broken Yolk   3350 Sports Arena Blvd. ☎(619) 226-0442, and 1851 Garnet Ave., Pacific Beach ☎(619) 270-0045
The Eggery   4130 Mission Blvd., Pacific Beach ☎(619) 274-3122
Hob Nob Hill   2271 1st Ave. ☎(619) 239-8127

HAMBURGER
Corvette Diner   3946 5th Ave. ☎(619) 542-1001
Johnny Rockets   7863 Girard Ave., La Jolla ☎(619) 456-4001, and 15550 Camino del Mar, del Mar ☎(619) 775-1954

LATE-NIGHT DINING
Croce's   802 5th Ave. ☎(619) 233-4355, map 8C4
Dobson's   956 Broadway Circle ☎(619) 231-6771, map 7C3
Saska's   3768 Mission Blvd. ☎(619) 488-7311

MEXICAN
Alfonso's   1251 Prospect Ave., La Jolla ☎(619) 454-2232
Old Town Mexican Cafe y Cantina   2489 San Diego Ave.
☎(619) 297-4330

PIZZA
Filippi's Pizza Grotto   1747 India St. ☎(619) 232-5095, map 7B3
Sammy's Woodfired Pizza   702 Pearl St., La Jolla ☎(619) 456-5222

SUSHI
Mr Sushi   1535 Garnet Ave., Pacific Beach ☎(619) 581-2664
Yakitori II   3740 Sports Arena Blvd. ☎(619) 223-2641

THAI
Five Star Thai Cuisine   816 Broadway ☎(619) 231-4408, map 8C4
Karinya   4475 Mission Blvd. ☎(619) 270-5050
Thai Chada   142 University Ave. ☎(619) 297-9548

Entertainments

Performing arts

Among major US cities, San Diego gets a high ranking for its theater, music and dance. Theater is probably best served, with more than 60 companies performing a wide range of material from tried and tested classics to off-the-wall avant-garde. Surprisingly often, work originated here makes it to Broadway and off-Broadway. The city also has resident symphony and opera companies. And the benign weather allows for several open-air auditoria.

Ticket outlets include **Ticketmaster** (☎ *(619) 298-5070)*, **Ticketron** (☎ *(619) 565-9947)* and **Arts Trix** (☎ *(619) 238-3810)*, which sells half-price tickets on the day of the event. Below are some of the city's major venues and companies. Consult the *San Diego Reader* newspaper and *San Diego Magazine* for detailed what's on listings.

THEATER, CLASSICAL MUSIC AND DANCE

- The **California Ballet** (☎ *(619) 560-5676)* presents modern and classical ballet at different city venues.
- The 3,000-seat **San Diego Community Concourse** *(202 C St., Downtown* ☎ *(619) 236-6510, map 7C3)* hosts the San Diego Opera, musicals, ballet etc.
- Founded in 1976, the **San Diego Repertory Theater** *(79 Horton Plaza* ☎ *(619) 235-8025, map 7C3)* is among San Diego's liveliest companies. The Rep routinely stages eight plays a year, including Charles Dickens' *A Christmas Carol,* which shows up every Christmas, along with original, experimental and often mischevious works. It also features a workshop for Latin American playwrights.
- The six-month winter season of the **San Diego Symphony Orchestra** *(Copley Symphony Hall, 1247 7th Ave., Downtown* ☎ *(619) 699-4205, map 8B4)* runs from October to May. Between June and September they move outdoors to Embarcadero Marina Park South to play Summer Pops *(for info* ☎ *(619) 534-3960).*
- The **Simon Edison Center for the Performing Arts** *(Balboa Park* ☎ *(619) 239-2255)* comprises several venues: the **Old Globe Theatre** (the oldest professional theater in California), the outdoor **Lowell Davies Festival Theatre** and **Cassius Carter Centre Stage**. A program of classic and contemporary drama, and the National Shakespeare Festival in June.
- Also in Balboa Park are other outdoor arenas: the **Spreckels Organ**

Pavilion *(☎(619) 226-0819)*, with frequent free concerts July through September on (probably) the world's largest outdoor organ, and the **Starlight Bowl** *(☎(619) 544-7800)*, which specializes in popular musicals mid-June to early September.

• **Spreckels Theater** *(121 Broadway, Downtown ☎(619) 235-0494, map 7 C3)*, dating from 1915, is still going strong with popular drama, musicals and special events.

San Diego by night

Nightspots are to be found across Greater San Diego, but the heaviest concentrations of desirable clubs and bars are to be found Downtown and at Pacific Beach and La Jolla. Many of the better bars feature live music, ranging from jazz to rock'n'roll to R&B to folk. In line with current fashion, the music, mood and clientele often varies on different nights of the week.

The latest information on who's playing what, when and where is in the *San Diego Reader,* a free weekly paper. The monthly *San Diego Magazine* also carries comprehensive listings.

The following eclectic selection includes bars, cafés, comedy, dancing and live music venues.

AVANTI'S
875 Prospect St., La Jolla ☎(619) 454-4288 ☿ ♪ Nightly 5pm-1.30am.
Piano player until about 9pm, when samba music and romantic ballads take over. Mellow La Jolla crowd.

B STREET CALIFORNIA GRILL & JAZZ BAR
425 W. B St., Downtown ☎(619) 236-1707. Map 7C3 ═ ☿ ♫ ♪ Nightly 8pm-midnight.
Jazz, mostly latin and fusion, plus rhythm & blues in neon light and amid yuppie clientele.

BELLY UP TAVERN
143 S. Cedros Ave. Solano Beach ☎(619) 481-9022 ☿ ♫ ♪ ♥ Nightly 6pm-midnight.
One of San Diego County's premier live music venues for blues, rock, reggae, jazz and country music by big-name performers. Well worth the drive.

BLIND MELONS
710 Garnet Ave., Pacific Beach ☎(619) 483-7844 ♪ ♥ Nightly 9pm-2am.
Classic beach bar with live blues, R&B

and reggae, with local and out-of-town performers.

BULA'S PUB
170 Orange Ave., Coronado ☎(619) 435-4466 ☿ Daily 11am-2.30pm, 5-10pm.
Friendly and easy-going Californian bar popular with the sailing community.

CITY COLORS
Omni San Diego Hotel, 910 Broadway Circle, Downtown ☎(619) 239-2200. Map 7C3 ☿ ● Mon-Sat 8pm-2am. Closed Sun.
Disco dancing to Top 40 hits.

CLUB RED ONION
3125 Ocean Front Walk, Mission Beach ☎(619) 488-9040 ═ ☿ ● ♪ Daily 11am-11pm.
Raunchy dancing and drinking fronting the busy beach boardwalk, with so-so Mexican restaurant next door.

THE COMEDY STORE
916 Pearl St., La Jolla ☎(619) 454-9176 ▨ ═ ☿ ♫ Nightly: call for showtimes and reservations.
Another outpost of the well-established

comedy chain, featuring stand-up from top professionals and aspiring amateurs.

CONFETTI

5373 Mission Center Rd., Mission Valley
☎*(619) 291-8635* ♈ ◉ *Nightly 8pm-2am.*
Yuppie singles and college kids dance to mixture of Top 40 hits and progressive music.

CROCE'S

802 5th St., Downtown ☎*(619) 233-4355.*
Map 8C4 ⇛ ♈ ♪ *Daily 8am-2pm,*
5pm-midnight.
So much is going on under the Croce name that it is hard to know where to list them. The **Restaurant & Jazz Bar** serves up better than average California cuisine, and some of the city's best live jazz. Next door's **Top Hat Bar & Grill** features live rhythm & blues and a non-smoking comedy showcase. There is also a late-night coffee shop. The crowd is mostly young and hip. The location is at the crossroads of the Gaslamp District's voguish after-dark action. Ingrid Croce owns all three establishments, named in memory of her late husband, singer/songwriter Jim Croce.

CLUB DIEGO'S

860 Garnet Ave., Pacific Beach ☎*(619)*
272-1241 ⇛ ♈ ◉ *Daily 11am-midnight.*
By day a Mexican Cantina. By night a lively bar and dance club.

GELATO VERO CAFFE

3753 India St., San Diego ☎*(619)*
295-9269 ⚑ *Daily 7.30am-1am.*
The attractions here are Italian coffee, rich gelato ice cream and delicious pastries.

GEORGE'S CAFE

1250 Prospect St., La Jolla ☎*(619)*
453-4244 ⇚ ⇛ ♈ *Daily 11.30am-*
2.30pm, 5.30-11pm.
Upstairs from the top-notch GEORGE'S AT THE COVE restaurant, the Cafe has great but less expensive California cuisine, a pleasant bar, magnificent ocean views from the terrace, and beautiful people too.

HARD ROCK CAFE

909 Prospect St., La Jolla ☎*(619)*
454-5101 ⇛ ♈ *Daily 11am-midnight.*
A recent addition to the global chain trafficking in burgers and rock nostalgia. Bits and pieces from Eric Clapton, Chuck Berry and other rock'n'roll icons are on display.

HUMPHREY'S

2241 Shelter Island Dr., Shelter Island
☎*(619) 224-3577* ⇛ ♈ ♪ *Daily*
7am-3pm, 5.30-10.30pm.
Mostly a goodish seafood restaurant, this is also a noted jazz venue. Outdoor summer concerts are especially recommended.

IMPROVISATION

832 Garnet Ave., Pacific Beach ☎*(619)*
483-4520 ⇛ ♈ ▣ *Nightly: call for show*
times and reservations.
Reliable stand-up from national and local comedians in 1930s vaudeville setting.

JAVA COFFEEHOUSE-GALLERY

837 G St., Downtown ☎*(619) 235-4012.*
Map 8C4 ⚑ *Daily 7am-2am.*
More than 30 specialty coffees, tasty snacks, plus owner Doug Simay's impressive private collection of Southern California art on display, and a wonderfully diverse clientele.

KARL STRAUSS' OLD COLUMBIA
BREWERY & GRILL

1157 Columbia St., Downtown ☎*(619)*
234-2739. Map 7C3 ⇛ ♈ *Daily*
11.30am-10pm.
Delicious customized beer brewed on the premises by the owner.

LA JOLLA BREWING CO.

7536 Fay Ave., La Jolla ☎*(619) 456-2739*
⇛ ♈ *Daily 11am-midnight.*
Another home-brew pub. The gimmick here is historic La Jolla and surfing.

MCP'S IRISH PUB

1107 Orange Ave., Coronado ☎*(619)*
435-5280 ⇛ ♈ ♪ *Daily 10am-2am.*
Draft Guinness, Irish-American food, plus Irish and contemporary music.

MISTER A'S

2550 5th Ave., Downtown ☎(619) *239-1377* ═ ☖ ♪ *Daily 11am-2.30pm, 6-10.30pm.*

The restaurant is upscale, traditional and pricey. The penthouse bar, atop the Financial Center, has the best panoramic views in town. Jackets required.

PANNIKIN

7467 Girard Ave., La Jolla ☎ (619) *454-5453* ☖ *Daily 6.30am-9pm.*

Good coffee and people-watching.

PATRICK'S II

428 F St., Downtown ☎(619) 233-3077. *Map 8C4* ☖ ♪ *Nightly 8pm-midnight.*

Popular Downtown venue for R&B, Blues, jazz and karaoke.

PRINCESS OF WALES

1665 India St., San Diego ☎(619) *238-1266. Map 7B3* ☖ *Daily 11am-1am.*

San Diego's version of the Princess Diana cult, complete with British beers, British pub food, darts and predictable Di iconography. Fun for terminally homesick Brits and unreconstructed royalists.

QUEL FROMAGE

523 University Ave., Hillcrest ☎(619) *295-1600* ☖ *Daily 7.30am-11pm.*

Cozy café with a wide choice of coffees, teas and cakes. Most interesting is the changing display of works by local artists.

ST JAMES BAR

4370 La Jolla Village Dr., La Jolla ☎(619) *453-6650* ═ ☖ *Mon-Sat 5.30-11pm. Closed Sun.*

Trendy bar/restaurant favored by well-heeled La Jollans.

Shopping

Where to look

The retail mall has reached its apotheosis in Southern California, and two of the most outstanding examples are to be found in Greater San Diego. Downtown's massive **Horton Plaza** and the much smaller **Del Mar Plaza** are imaginative triumphs of user-friendly design, and they are part of the authentic urban experience of West Coast America in the 1990s.

Social scientists argue that malls serve automobile-centered Californians in ways in which piazzas served Renaissance Italians: places in which not only to shop, eat and drink but also to see and be seen, to meet people, to hang out. Good parking facilities make all the difference. And if further proof were needed that malls are here to stay, fashionable restaurateurs are opening up in them too.

At the same time, San Diego shoppers are not obliged exclusively to haunt the malls. There are plenty of street-level shops, particularly in coastal communities such as **La Jolla** and **Ocean**, **Mission** and **Pacific Beaches**.

Except on Sunday, shops in malls keep longer hours than individual shops. Opening times vary, but Monday to Saturday 10am to 9pm is the norm.

MALLS

- **Horton Plaza** *(1st and 4th Aves., Downtown, map 7 C3),* 140 shops, including **Nordstrom**, **Robinson's** and **The Broadway** department stores, and **Farmers Market** for top-notch groceries. Just about everything is available in this marvelous mall, from fine art to swimwear, aspirin to diamonds.
- **Fashion Valley** *(Friar's Rd. at Highway 163, Mission Valley),* 145 shops, with the emphasis on clothing and specialty stores.
- **La Jolla Village Sq.** *(8657 Villa La Jolla Dr., La Jolla),* 50 upscale shops here anchored by **I. Magnin** and **May Co.**
- **Del Mar Plaza** *(1555 Camino del Mar, Del Mar),* 35 elegant specialty stores overlooking the Pacific Ocean.
- **Daniel's Market** *(Market Level, Del Mar Plaza, 1555 Camino Del Mar* ☎ *(619) 481-8191* Fx *(619) 481-8136, open daily from 6am-10pm),* an upscale grocery and deli for gourmets, has many fans. They also deliver: telephone or fax your grocery list.
- **San Diego Factory Outlet Center** *(4498 Camino de la Plaza, San*

241

Ysidro), genuine bargains here from more than 30 factory stores that include **Levi's**, **Eddie Bauer** and **Nike**.

- Also of interest is the discount book warehouse, **Kobley's Swap Meet** *(Sports Arena Blvd., San Diego)*, a mall with a difference. From 7am-3pm Thursday-Sunday this becomes a giant open-air garage sale. Plenty of bargains, and 2 million visitors last year.
- **Seaport Village** *(849 W Harbor Dr., Downtown, map 7D2)*, 65 specialty stores arranged like an olde-worlde shopping village in 14 landscaped acres.

GALLERIES

The biggest concentration of galleries is Downtown, especially in the Gaslamp Quarter and Horton Plaza. **Swahn Fine Arts** *(861 5th Ave., map 8C4)* is probably the leading gallery for contemporary fine art. Among artists represented are Mark Kotabi and Peter Max.

Other Downtown galleries of note include **Dyassen Gallery** *(178 Horton Plaza, map 7C3)*, **Lane Gallery** *(173 Horton Plaza, map 7C3)*, **Circle Gallery** *(2501 San Diego Ave.)*, **Pratt Gallery** *(2161 India St.)*, which specializes in Southern California artists, and **Village Gallery** *(219 Horton Plaza, map 7C3)*, which is good for lithographs and etchings.

Among La Jolla galleries are **Galleria 56** *(5630 La Jolla Blvd.)*, specializing in 20thC masters, **Gateway Gallery** *(1025 Prospect St.)* for Impressionists, **Jones Gallery** *(1264 Prospect St.)* for American painting and sculpture, and **Riggs Gallery** *(875 Prospect St.)* for contemporary paintings.

BOOKS

The major chain booksellers, such as **Brentano's**, **Doubleday**, **Waldenbrooks** and **B. Dalton**, are represented throughout the city, usually in one or other of the major malls mentioned above. For more specialized bookstores, consult the comprehensive list produced by the **San Diego Booksellers Association** *(write to P.O. Box 1908, San Diego 92112)*.

Recreation

Outdoor activities

BEACHES

For sensible reasons of safety, San Diego's 33 ocean beaches are divided into swimming and surfing zones. Mission Bay and southern San Diego Bay have sheltered waters for swimming.

SWIMMING: Fine ocean swimming beaches include **Coronado Municipal Beach** (the whole shore of the town), **La Jolla Shores**, w of La Jolla Shores Dr., via Vallecitos, and parts of **Pacific** and **Mission** beaches. **Silver Strand State Park**, s of Coronado, has a well-developed bayside beach. Several sections of shorelines in Mission Bay also have sandy beaches.

SURFING: Surfers have an extraordinary choice of beaches all along the ocean shore. Favored among them are **Windansea**, off La Jolla Blvd. at Del Norte, **Tourmaline**, off Mission Blvd. at Loring, in La Jolla, and **Ocean Beach**, just s of the San Diego River mouth via Sunset Cliffs Blvd. to Niagara. Prime times for surfers are early morning and just before sunset.

WINDSURFING: The best places are **Santa Clara Point** and **Chula Vista Harbor**.

NUDITY: Between La Jolla Shores Beach and Torres Pines State Beach is **Black's Beach**. This was once the area's only legal nude beach. Although nudity is now outlawed, the practice continues. The beach, beneath steep cliffs, is hard to reach; the best route is a 15-minute hike from Torres Pines.

DOGS: Near to Ocean Beach is **Dog Beach**, where family pets are free to roam.

BOATING

Both **sailboats** and **powerboats** can be rented on San Diego and Mission Bays, and some marinas offer short courses in sailing. **Jet skis** are also available for rent. At the other extreme, every sort of **paddle-boat** can be rented at Mission Bay. See telephone book Yellow Pages under "Marinas." Note also that all of the major hotels on Mission Bay have boats for rent.

The E end of the South Pacific Passage section of Mission Bay is reserved for **jet skis** and high-speed **water-skiers**. The navy restricts skiing in some areas of San Diego Bay, but it is permitted in Glorietta Bay and in sheltered waters behind Harbor and Shelter Islands.

FISHING

San Diego claims to have the largest sportfishing fleet in the world. In California "the world" tends to mean, well, California. Nevertheless, there is an extraordinary choice on offer.

Traditionally the saltwater fishing season opens in April, and the best fishing is in summer and fall. Likely catches on short, half-day trips include bass, bonito, barracuda, halibut and rock cod. On longer trips down around Mexico's Coronado Islands, some 14 miles from San Diego, anglers can hope for yellowtail, yellowfin and big-eyed tuna. Tackle is usually available for those who do not have their own, and first-timers are welcomed.

Party boat companies operate from **Quivira Basin** on Mission Bay, **San Diego Sportfishing Landings** on San Diego Bay near Shelter Island, and from the northern suburb of **Oceanside**. All offer half-day trips. More information can be obtained from the **Sportfishing Council** (☎ *(619) 297-0787).*

Public pier fishing can be productive in San Diego. Bonito and halibut are the commonest catches from deep water; yellowfin and spotfin croaker feed at the breaker line. Piers in the area include **Ocean Beach Pier** and **Shelter Island Pier** in San Diego, and **Harbor Fishing Pier** and **Oceanside Pier** upcoast at Oceanside. No fishing license is required. Tackle may not be available for rent at all of these piers, but may be obtained from nearby. See Yellow Pages under "Fishing Bait."

GOLF

San Diego County has some 70 courses. About a third are open to the public; resort courses open to guests at affiliated hotels increase that number almost to half.

Public courses of particular interest include:

- **Coronado Golf Course** *(2000 Visalia Row, Coronado* ☎ *(619) 435-3121),* 6,306 yards, par 72, rated 70
- **Cottonwood Country Club** *(3121 Willow Glen Rd., El Cajon* ☎ *(619) 442-9891),* Ivanhoe Course 6,719 yards, par 73, rated 72.1, Monte Vista Course 6,100 yards, par 72, rated 66
- **Torrey Pines Municipal** *(11480 N Torrey Pines Rd., La Jolla* ☎ *(619) 453-0380),* South Course 6,649 yards, par 72, rated 71.5, North Course 6,317 yards, par 72, rated 69.8

Torrey Pines and Coronado are impossibly crowded on weekends. The best time at both is weekdays from noon onward. The long drive E helps keep Cottonwood more available.

There are two grand golf and tennis resorts in the region:

- **La Costa Country Club**, 2 miles E of the beach town of Carlsbad via La Costa Ave., has 36 holes of fine golf available only to guests at the **La Costa Hotel and Spa** *(Costa del Mar Rd., Carlsbad* ☎ *(619) 438-9111)*
- **Rancho Bernardo Inn and Country Club** *(17550 Bernardo Oaks Dr., San Diego, 2 miles NE of I-15 on the N side of Escondido* ☎ *(619) 487-0700)* is open to fee play, with guests at the Inn having priority for starting times

Two less costly golf and tennis resorts:

- **Singing Hills Lodge** (*3007 Dahesa Rd., El Cajon* ☎ *(619) 442-3425*) has 54 holes of golf
- **Whispering Palms Country Club** (*Rancho Santa Fe* ☎ *(619) 756-2471*) also has 54 holes

TENNIS

San Diego has scores of public courts. Nonresidents must pay a daily court fee, and all players must make reservations. The most likely centers for players looking for an opponent are:

- **Morley Field** (*Balboa Park*), 25 courts
- **Mission Bay Youth Field** (*at NE tip of Mission Bay*), 8 courts
- **Robb Field** (*just off Sunset Cliffs Dr., across the San Diego River from Mission Bay*), 12 courts
- **Coronado Tennis Center** (*near the Hotel del Coronado*), 8 courts
- **La Jolla Recreation Center** (*615 Prospect at S side of town*), 9 courts

All the golf and tennis resorts noted under GOLF have tennis facilities. **La Costa** has 25 courts, **Rancho Bernardo** 16, **Singing Hills** 12 and **Whispering Palms** 11.

WHALE-WATCHING

This is probably one of the "must do's," especially for families visiting San Diego at the right time of year. Every winter, from December to March, thousands of California gray whales migrate 5,000 miles from Alaskan waters to the breeding grounds off Baja California. The busiest time is mid-January, when up to 200 whales a day have been sighted.

Official Whale Watch weekend is in the third week of January. Stay on dry land and watch from Cabrillo National Monument, or take a narrated harbor tour with **Harbor Excursion** (*1050 N. Harbor Dr.* ☎ *(619) 234-4111, map 7C2*). The boat voyage takes about three hours and, though sightings cannot be guaranteed, most people manage to glimpse some whales, if only a vanishing tail fin or two.

San Diego for children

San Diego and the neighboring areas offer visiting children innumerable opportunities to exhaust their pent-up energies in instructive play. Some of the more extraordinary possibilities are listed below.

Where no page reference is given, look for the heading (printed in SMALL CAPITALS) in the alphabetical SAN DIEGO'S SIGHTS A TO Z. See also LOS ANGELES FOR CHILDREN, page 162-164.

ANIMAL PARKS AND ZOOS
In California, as in much of the rest of the world, increasing emphasis is placed on designing zoos that put animals into the best possible reconstructions of their native habitats. San Diego is far ahead of the rest in this effort. Real-life encounters with wild animals and marine creatures lie within comparatively easy reach. They include one of the world's greatest marine mammal shows, which has lifted much from the old-fashioned circus and put it into permanent surroundings of great style.
- Living Desert (see PALM SPRINGS, page 176)
- SAN DIEGO WILD ANIMAL PARK (see NEARBY SIGHTS, page 224)
- San Diego Zoo (see BALBOA PARK)
- SEA WORLD
- STEPHEN BIRCH AQUARIUM MUSUEM

BEACHES
California's open ocean beaches seldom allow parents with small children to relax, primarily because of heavy surf. However, some ocean and many bay beaches are ideal for tots and youngsters. Those listed below are popular with families. See also OUTDOOR ACTIVITIES on page 243, and for our selection of California's best sandy beaches, see the map on pages 18-19.
- Dana Harbor (see ORANGE COUNTY, page 175)
- Doheny State Beach (see ORANGE COUNTY, page 175)
- Mission Bay (see BEACHES, page 243)
- Silver Strand State Park (see BEACHES, page 243)

PARKS AND SPACES FOR RAMBLING
The city and environs has some fine open spaces to refresh children with high-octane energy to run off.
- BALBOA PARK — as well as all the famous attractions, there are plenty of playgrounds and picnic grounds
- CABRILLO NATIONAL MONUMENT — spectacular coastal scenery, whale-watching (November through March), lighthouse
- TORRES PINE STATE RESERVE — rare trees, hiking trails, magnificent views over the ocean

SCIENCE MUSEUMS
In California's high-technology society, touchable science exhibits for children rank near the top of approved playgrounds with parents and youngsters alike.

- Reuben H. Fleet Space Theater and Science Center (see BALBOA PARK) — interactive science, space travel, laser shows

THEME AND AMUSEMENT PARKS

Since Walt Disney first blended thrill rides into more appealing and instructive environments than the carnival or fairground, theme parks have blossomed, notably in California. These are the major ones within striking distance of San Diego.

- DISNEYLAND (see page 166)
- Knott's Berry Farm (see ORANGE COUNTY, page 172)

TRANSPORT MUSEUMS

Although contemporary California lives by automobile and airplane, it has museums in celebration of sailing ships and railroads as well as its current favorites. In San Diego:

- Aerospace Museum (see BALBOA PARK)
- San Diego Automotive Museum (in BALBOA PARK)
- San Diego Maritime Museum (see THE HARBOR)
- San Diego Model Railroad Museum (in BALBOA PARK)
- Seeley Stables (see OLD TOWN)

VIEWPOINTS

Always popular with older children are those breathtaking views from the tops of high buildings, or from natural viewpoints.

- CABRILLO NATIONAL MONUMENT
- Coronado Bay Bridge (see CORONADO, page 213)
- HORTON PLAZA
- Mt. Soledad (see LA JOLLA, page 215)
- TORRES PINE STATE RESERVE

Index

Bold page numbers indicate main entries.
Italic page numbers indicate illustrations and maps.

Index of place names

Aliso Beach County Park, 175
Anaheim, 27
Antelope Valley, 70
Arcadia, 69
Arizona, 44
Arroyo Burro, 181
Avalon, Catalina Island, 165
Avila, 194
Avila Beach, 71, 72, 189

Barstow, 192, 195
Bel Air, 15, 30, 65
Berkeley, 29
Beverly Hills, 21, 29, 51, 53, 62, 63, 64, 65, 100, 103
  hotels, 110
  restaurants, 123, 125
  shops, 152
  theaters, 142
Big Sur, 189, 191, 194
Black's Beach, 243
Blythe, 192
Brentwood, 65, 88, 125
Burbank, 61, 64, 69, 110

Cabrillo Beach, 181
Calico, 71
Cambria, 189, 194

Camino Del Mar, 215
Capistrano Beach, 73, 171, 175, 188
Cardiff-by-the-Sea, 215
Carmel, 191
Catalina Island, 25, 61, 68, **165-6**
Cathedral City, 175
Central Coast, 63, **71-2**
Central Los Angeles, 63, **69-70**, 82
  hotels, 111
  sights and places of interest, 74
Central Valley, 23, 24, 25, 28, 29
Century City, 21, 39, **65-6**
Chinatown, 61, 63, 64
  restaurants, 125, 138
  shops, 149-50
Chino Canyon, 176
Chula Vista, 212, 243
Coastal Los Angeles, 63, **66-7**, 109-10, 111, 125
  map, *67*
  shops, **148-9**
  sights and places of interest, 74
Coastal ranges, 24

Coloma, 29
Colorado Desert, 24, 70, 192
Corona del Mar, 61, 72, 170
Coronado, 202, **213**, 225
Coronado Municipal Beach, 243
Crescent Beach, 166

Dana Harbor, 162, 175
Dana Point, 73, 171
Death Valley, 24, 34, 59, 70, 71, 192, 195
Del Mar, 188, 202, 215, 225
Dog Beach, 243
Doheny State Beach, 162, 175
Dolores Mission, 26
Downtown Los Angeles, 21, 22, 36, 38, 48, 51, 53, **63-4**
  buses, 76
  hotels, 109, 111
  movie theaters, 141
  restaurants, 123, 125
  shops, **149-50**
  sights and places of interest, 74
  theaters, 142

Los Angeles index

San Diego index

List of street names

A substantial selection of streets mentioned in the text and labeled on the maps is listed below, with map references.

Los Angeles

Numbered streets

1st St., **6**D9-10
3rd St., **3**C3-**6**D9
5th St., **6**D9-E9
6th St., **4**D4-**6**E10
7th St., **5**D7-**6**E10
8th St., **5**D6-**6**E9
11th St., **6**E8-9
20th St., **6**E8

Named streets

Academy Dr., **6**C9
Adams Blvd., **4**E4-**6**F9
Alameda St., **6**F9-D9
Alta Loma Rd., **4**B4
Alvarado St., **6**D8-B9
Amar Rd., **2**C4-5
Atlantic Blvd., **1**C3
Ave. of the Stars, **3**D2-3

Barnard St., **6**D9
Beachwood Dr., **5**B6-A6
Bedford Dr., **3**C3
Beverly Blvd., **3**C3-**6**D9
Beverly Dr., **3**A3-D3
Brighton Way, **3**C3
Broadway, **6**F8-C10
Bronson Ave., **5**F6-A6
Broxton St., **3**D1
Burton Way, **3**C3-**4**C4

Cahuenga Blvd., **5**C6-A5
Camden Dr., **3**C3
Cañon Dr., **3**C3
Central Ave., **6**F9-D9

Colorado Blvd., **1**B3-2B4
Crescent Dr., **3**C3
Crescent Heights Blvd., **4**E4-B4
Crystal Springs Dr., **1**B2
Crystal Springs Rd., **6**A8
Curson Ave., **4**E4-B5

Dewey Ave., **5**D7
Doheny Dr., **3**D3-A3
Durand Dr., **5**A6

Elden Way, **3**C2
Elliot Ave., **2**C4
Elysian Park Ave., **6**C9
Exposition Blvd., **5**F6-7

Fairfax Ave., **4**E4-B5
Figueroa St., **6**F8-D9
Flower St., **6**F8-D9
Foothill Freeway, **1**A2-B3

Gayley Ave., **3**D1
Glendale Ave., **1**B3
Glendale Blvd., **6**C8-D9
Glendale Freeway, **1**B3
Golden State Freeway, **6**A8-C10
Gower St., **5**C6-B6
Grand Ave., **6**F8-D9

Hacienda Blvd., **2**C4
Harbor Freeway, **6**F8-D9
Highland Ave., **5**D5-B5
Hilgard Ave., **3**D1-C2
Hill St., **6**D9
Hillhurst Ave., **5**B7
Holloway Dr., **4**C4

Hollywood Blvd., **5**B5-7
Hollywood Freeway, **5**A5-**6**D9
Hollywood Way, **1**B2
Hoover Blvd., **5**F7-B7
Hope St., **6**F8-D9
Hudson Ave., **5**B6

Iowa St., **3**E1

Japanese Village Plaza, **6**D9
Jefferson Blvd., **3**G3-**6**F8

La Brea Ave., **4**G5-B5
La Cienega Blvd., **4**G4-A4
Larchmont Blvd., **5**C6
Le Conte Ave., **3**D1-2
Lincoln Blvd., **1**C1-D2
Little Santa Monica Blvd., **3**D2-C3
Long Beach Freeway, **1**E3-C3
Los Angeles St., **6**E8-D9

Main St., **6**F8-D10
Manchester Ave., **1**C2
Marathon St., **5**C6-7
Melrose Ave., **4**C4-**5**C7
Melrose Pl., **4**C4
Menlo St., **5**F7
Mission Blvd., **2**C5-6

New High St., **6**D9

Observatory Rd., **5**A7
Olive St., **6**E8-D9
Olvera St., **6**D9

Olympic Blvd., **3**E1-
   6E10
Ord St., **6**D9
Overland Ave., **3**E2-G3

Pacific Ave., **1**C1
Pacific Coast Highway,
   1C1-**2**F5
Palos Verdes Dr.,
   1E2
Park Ave., **6**C8-B9
Park View, **6**D8
Pasadena Freeway,
   6D9-C10
Pershing Sq., **6**D9
Pico Blvd., **3**E1-**6**E8
Pomona Freeway,
   1C3-**2**C6
Prospect Ave., **6**B8

Robertson Blvd.,
   3E3-**4**C4
Rodeo Dr., **3**C3-D3

San Bernadino Freeway,
   1C3-**2**B6
San Diego Freeway,
   1A1-**2**E5
San Pedro St., **6**F8-D9
San Vicente Blvd., **4**C4-D5
Santa Ana Freeway,
   1C3-**2**F6
Santa Barbara Ave.,
   5F7
Santa Monica Blvd.,
   3D1-**5**B7
Sepulveda Blvd., **3**D1-G3
Spring St., **6**D9-C10
Stadium Way, **6**B9-C9
State Dr., **5**F7
Stone Canyon Rd., **3**C1
Sunset Blvd., **3**C1-**6**D9
Sycamore Ave., **4**D5-B5

Temple St., **5**C7-**6**D9

University Ave., **6**E8

Van Ness Ave., **5**C6-B6
Ventura Blvd., **1**B1-2
Ventura Freeway, **1**B1-2
Vermont Ave., **5**F7-A7
Via Rodeo, **3**C3
Victory Blvd., **1**B1-2
Vine St., **5**C6-B6

W Ave., **6**C10
Washington Blvd.,
   3G1-**6**F10
Western Ave., **5**F7-B7
Westmoreland Ave.,
   5E7-B7
Westmount Dr., **4**C4
Westwood Blvd., **3**D1-E2
Whittier Blvd., **1**C3-**2**C4
Willoughby Ave., **4**C4-
   5C6
Wilshire Blvd., **3**D1-**6**D8

Yale St., **6**D9
Yucca St., **5**B5-6

San Diego

Numbered streets

1st-3rd Ave., **7**D3-A3
1st St., Coronado,
   7E1-F3
2nd St., Coronado,
   7E1-F2
4th-11th Ave., **8**D4-A4
12th-18th Ave., **8**D5-B5
19th-20th Ave., **8**D6-B6

Other streets

B St., **7**C1-**8**C6
Broadway, **7**C2-**8**C6

Broadway Circle,
   7C3

C St., **7**C2-**8**C6
Columbia St., **7**C3-A3

E St., **7**C2-**8**C6

F St., **7**C2-**8**C6

G St., **7**C2-**8**C6
Grape St., **7**A2-**8**A4

Harbor Dr., **7**A2-
   8F6
Horton Plaza, **7**C3

Imperial Ave., **8**D4-6
India St., **7**C3-A2
Island Ave., **7**D3-**8**D6

Kettner Blvd., **7**C2-A2

Market St., **7**C2-**8**C6

Orange Ave., **7**F2-E2

Pacific Highway, **7**C2-A2
Park Blvd., **8**B5-A5

San Diego Freeway,
   7A2-**8**B6
State St., **7**C3-A3

CONVERSION FORMULAE

To convert	Multiply by
Inches to Centimeters	2.540
Centimeters to Inches	0.39370
Feet to Meters	0.3048
Meters to feet	3.2808
Yards to Meters	0.9144
Meters to Yards	1.09361
Miles to Kilometers	1.60934
Kilometers to Miles	0.621371
Sq Meters to Sq Feet	10.7638
Sq Feet to Sq Meters	0.092903
Sq Yards to Sq Meters	0.83612
Sq Meters to Sq Yards	1.19599
Sq Miles to Sq Kilometers	2.5899
Sq Kilometers to Sq Miles	0.386103
Acres to Hectares	0.40468
Hectares to Acres	2.47105
Gallons to Liters	4.545
Liters to Gallons	0.22
Ounces to Grams	28.3495
Grams to Ounces	0.03528
Pounds to Grams	453.592
Grams to Pounds	0.00220
Pounds to Kilograms	0.4536
Kilograms to Pounds	2.2046
Tons (UK) to Kilograms	1016.05
Kilograms to Tons (UK)	0.0009842
Tons (US) to Kilograms	746.483
Kilograms to Tons (US)	0.0013396

Quick conversions

Kilometers to Miles	Divide by 8, multiply by 5
Miles to Kilometers	Divide by 5, multiply by 8
1 meter =	Approximately 3 feet 3 inches
2 centimeters =	Approximately 1 inch
1 pound (weight) =	475 grams (nearly $\frac{1}{2}$ kilogram)
Celsius to Fahrenheit	Divide by 5, multiply by 9, add 32
Fahrenheit to Celsius	Subtract 32, divide by 9, multiply by 5

Clothing sizes chart

LADIES
Suits and dresses

Australia	8	10	12	14	16	18	
France	34	36	38	40	42	44	
Germany	32	34	36	38	40	42	
Italy	38	40	42	44	46		
Japan	7	9	11	13			
UK	6	8	10	12	14	16	18
USA	4	6	8	10	12	14	16

Shoes

USA	6	$6\frac{1}{2}$	7	$7\frac{1}{2}$	8	$8\frac{1}{2}$
UK	$4\frac{1}{2}$	5	$5\frac{1}{2}$	6	$6\frac{1}{2}$	7
Europe	38	38	39	39	40	41

MEN
Shirts

USA, UK	14	$14\frac{1}{2}$	15	$15\frac{1}{2}$	16	$16\frac{1}{2}$	17
Europe, Japan Australia	36	37	38	39.5	41	42	43

Sweaters/T-shirts

Australia, USA, Germany	S		M		L		XL
UK	34		36-38		40		42-44
Italy	44		46-48		50		52
France	1		2-3		4		5
Japan			S-M		L		XL

Suits/Coats

UK, USA	36	38	40	42	44
Australia, Italy, France, Germany	46	48	50	52	54
Japan	S	M	L	XL	

Shoes

UK	7	$7\frac{1}{2}$	$8\frac{1}{2}$	$9\frac{1}{2}$	$10\frac{1}{2}$	11
USA	8	$8\frac{1}{2}$	$9\frac{1}{2}$	$10\frac{1}{2}$	$11\frac{1}{2}$	12
Europe	41	42	43	44	45	46

CHILDREN
Clothing

UK

Height (ins)	43	48	55	60	62	
Age	4-5	6-7	9-10	11	12	13

USA

Age	4	6	8	10	12	14

Europe

Height (cms)	125	135	150	155	160	165
Age	7	9	12	13	14	15

KEY TO MAP PAGES

KEY TO MAP SYMBOLS

Area Maps

=O= Superhighway (with access point)

Main Road / Four-lane Highway

Other Main Road

Secondary Road

Minor Road

🛡 Interstate Highway

🛡 US Highway

㉗ State Highway

_ _ _ Ferry

Railroad

✈ Airport

✦ Airfield

_ _ _ State Boundary

_ _ _ _ National Park Boundary

■ Place of Interest

⚲ Good Beach

Forested Area

11 Adjoining Page No.

City Maps

Place of Interest or Important Building

Built-up Area

Park

|↑ ↑| Cemetery

Railroad

ℹ Tourist Information

🚗 Parking / Garage

⊞ Hospital

✉ Post Office

→ One-way Street

```
0   10   20   30   40   50miles
├───┼────┼────┼────┼────┤
0       20   40   60   80km
```

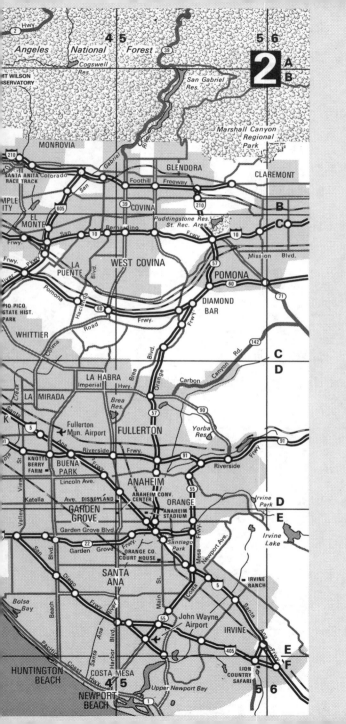

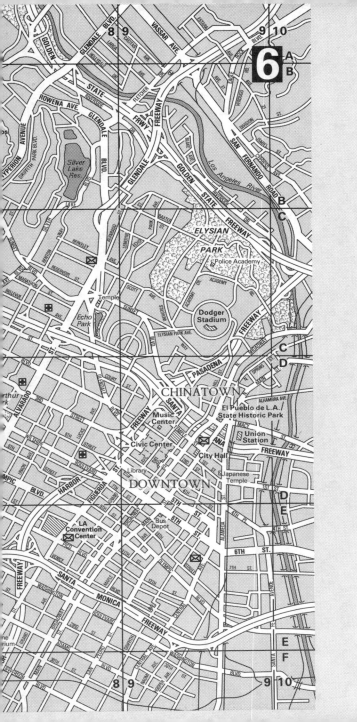

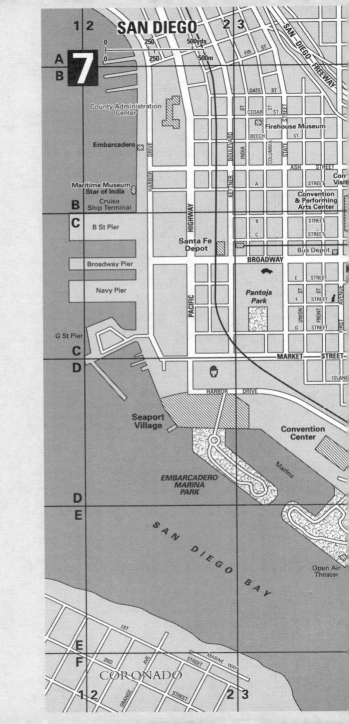

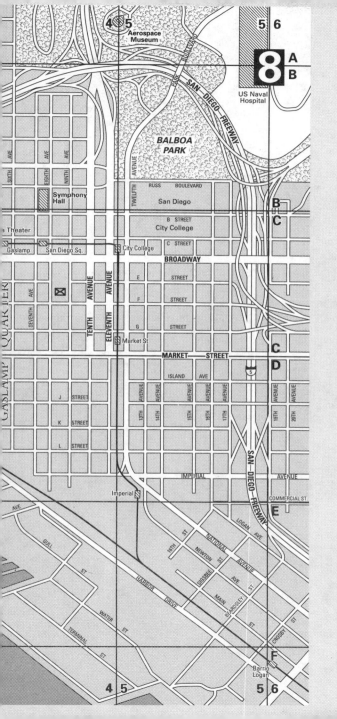

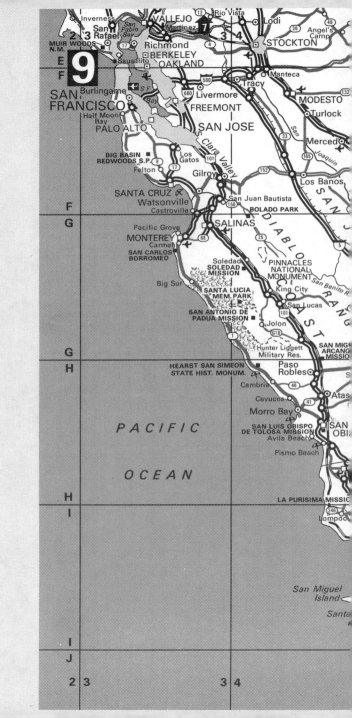

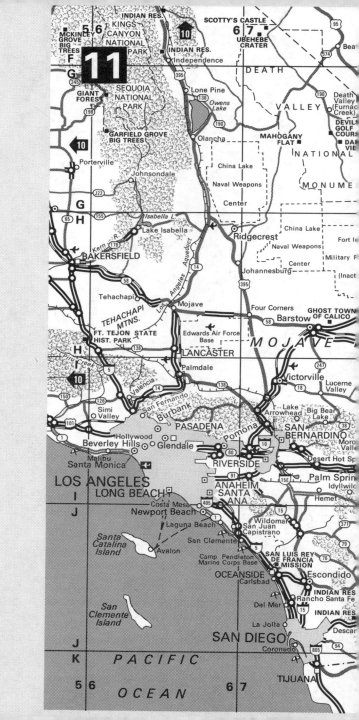

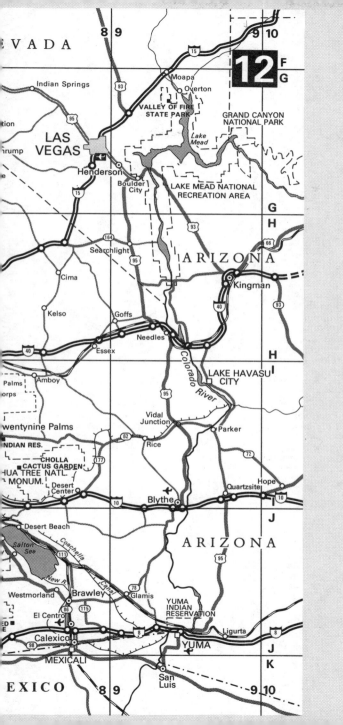

What the papers said:

- "The expertly edited American Express series has the knack of pin-pointing precisely the details you need to know, and doing it concisely and intelligently." (*The Washington Post*)

- "*(Venice)* ... the best guide book I have ever used." (*The Standard* — London)

- "Amid the welter of guides to individual countries, American Express stands out...." (*Time*)

- "Possibly the best ... guides on the market, they come close to the oft-claimed 'all you need to know' comprehensiveness, with much original experience, research and opinions." (*Sunday Telegraph* — London)

- "The most useful general guide was *American Express New York* by Herbert Bailey Livesey. It also has the best street and subway maps." (*Daily Telegraph* — London)

- "...in the flood of travel guides, the *American Express* guides come closest to the needs of traveling managers with little time." (*Die Zeit* — Germany)

What the experts said:

- "We only used one guide book, Sheila Hale's *Amex Venice*, for which she and the editors deserve a Nobel Prize." (Eric Newby, London)

- "Congratulations to you and your staff for putting out the best guide book of *any* size *(Barcelona & Madrid)*. I'm recommending it to everyone." (Barnaby Conrad, Santa Barbara, California)

- "If you're only buying one guide book, we recommend American Express...." (*Which?* — Britain's leading consumer magazine)

What readers from all over the world have said:

• "The book *(Hong Kong, Singapore & Bangkok)* was written in such a personal way that I feel as if you were actually writing this book for me." (L.Z., Orange, Conn., USA)

• "Your book *(Florence and Tuscany)* proved a wonderful companion for us in the past fortnight. It went with us everywhere...." (E.H., Kingston-on-Thames, Surrey, England)

• "I feel as if you have been a silent friend shadowing my time in Tuscany." (T.G., Washington, DC, USA)

• "We followed your book *(Los Angeles & San Francisco)* to the letter. It proved to be wonderful, indispensable, a joy...." (C.C., London, England)

• "We could never have had the wonderful time that we did without your guide to *Paris*. The compactness was very convenient, your maps were all we needed, but it was your restaurant guide that truly made our stay special.... We have learned first-hand: *American Express — don't leave home without it.*" (A. R., Virginia Beach, Va., USA)

• "Much of our enjoyment came from the way your book *(Venice)* sent us off scurrying around the interesting streets and off to the right places at the right times". (Lord H., London, England)

• "It *(Paris)* was my constant companion and totally dependable...." (V. N., Johannesburg, South Africa)

• "I could go on and on about how useful the book *(Amsterdam)* was — the trouble was that it was almost getting to be a case of not venturing out without it...." (J.C.W., Manchester, England)

• "We have heartily recommended these books to all our friends who have plans to travel abroad." (A.S. and J.C., New York, USA)

• "Despite many previous visits to Italy, I wish I had had your guide *(Florence and Tuscany)* ages ago. I love the author's crisp, literate writing and her devotion to her subject." (M. B-K., Denver, Colorado, USA)

• "We never made a restaurant reservation without checking your book *(Venice)*. The recommendations were excellent, and the historical and artistic text got us through the sights beautifully." (L.S., Boston, Ma., USA)

• "We became almost a club as we found people sitting at tables all around, consulting their little blue books!" (F.C., Glasgow, Scotland)

• "This guide *(Paris)* we warmly recommend to all the many international visitors we work with." (M.L., Paris, France)

• "It's not often I would write such a letter, but it's one of the best guide books we have ever used *(Rome)* — we can't fault it!" (S.H., Berkhamsted, Herts, England)

American Express Travel Guides

spanning the globe....

EUROPE
Amsterdam, Rotterdam
  & The Hague
Athens and the
  Classical Sites * ‡
Barcelona, Madrid &
  Seville #
Berlin, Potsdam &
  Dresden * (‡ as Berlin)
Brussels
Dublin
Florence and Tuscany
London
Moscow & St Petersburg *
Paris
Prague #
Provence and the
  Côte d'Azur *
Rome
Venice #
Vienna & Budapest

NORTH AMERICA
Boston and New
  England *
Los Angeles & San
  Diego
Mexico #
New York
San Francisco and
  the Wine Regions
Toronto, Montréal and
  Québec City #
Washington, DC

THE PACIFIC
Cities of
  Australia
Hong Kong
  & Taiwan
Singapore &
  Bangkok * ‡
Tokyo

*   Paperbacks in preparation   #   Paperbacks appearing August 1993
‡   Currently available as hardback pocket guides

Clarity and quality of information, combined with outstanding maps — the ultimate in travelers' guides

Buying an AmEx guide has never been easier....

The *American Express Travel Guides* are now available by mail order direct from the publisher, for customers resident in the UK and Eire. Payment can be made by credit card or cheque/P.O. Simply complete the form below, and send it, together with your remittance.

New paperback series (£6.99)   # Available from August 1993

☐ Amsterdam, Rotterdam & The Hague
1 85732 918 X

☐ Barcelona, Madrid & Seville #
1 85732 160 X

☐ Brussels
1 85732 966 X

☐ Cities of Australia
1 85732 921 X

☐ Dublin
1 85732 967 8

☐ Florence and Tuscany
1 85732 922 8

☐ Hong Kong & Taiwan
0 85533 955 1

☐ London
1 85732 968 6

☐ Los Angeles & San Diego
1 85732 919 8

☐ Mexico #
1 85732 159 6

☐ New York
1 85732 971 6

☐ Paris
1 85732 969 4

☐ Prague #
1 85732 156 1

☐ Rome
1 85732 923 6

☐ San Francisco and the Wine Regions
1 85732 920 1

☐ Tokyo
1 85732 970 8

☐ Toronto, Montréal & Québec City #
1 85732 157 X

☐ Venice #
1 85732 158 8

☐ Vienna & Budapest
1 85732 962 7

☐ Washington, DC
1 85732 924 4

Hardback pocket guides (£7.99)

☐ Athens and the Classical Sites
0 85533 954 3

☐ Berlin
0 85533 952 7

☐ Singapore & Bangkok
0 85533 956 X

While every effort is made to keep prices low, it is sometimes necessary to increase them at short notice. American Express Travel Guides reserves the right to amend prices from those previously advertised.

Please send the titles ticked above.   **LASD**

Number of titles @ £6.99 ☐   Value: £

Number of titles @ £7.99 ☐   Value: £
Add £1.50 for postage and packing   £   1 . 50

Total value of order: £
I enclose a cheque or postal order ☐ payable to Reed Book Services Ltd, or please charge my credit card account:

☐ Barclaycard/Visa   ☐ Access/MasterCard   ☐ American Express

Card number ☐☐☐☐☐☐☐☐☐☐☐☐☐☐☐☐☐☐☐☐☐

Signature _____   Expiry date _____

Name _____

Address _____

_____ Postcode _____

Send this order to American Express Travel Guides, Cash Sales Dept, Reed Book Services Ltd, PO Box 5, Rushden, Northants NN10 9YX ☎(0933) 410511.